IT HAPPENED IN EGYPT

By
C.N. & A.M. WILLIAMSON

It Happened In Egypt

by **C.N. & A.M. Williamson**

Copyright © 2023

All Rights reserved.
No part of this publication may be reproduced, stored in a retrieval system, or transmitted in any form or by any means, electronic, mechanical, photocopying or Otherwise, without the written permission of the publisher.

The author/editor asserts the moral right to be identified as the author/editor of this work.

ISBN: 978-93-57278-29-4

Published by

DOUBLE 9 BOOKS

2/13-B, Ansari Road, Daryaganj
New Delhi – 110002
info@double9books.com
www.double9books.com
Tel. 011-40042856

This book is under public domain

ABOUT THE AUTHOR

"***C. N. Williamson*** The Black & White magazine was started by British author and motorsport journalist Charles Norris Williamson (1859–1920). He is most well-known for his work on several books and travelogs alongside his wife, Alice Muriel Williamson. Williamson, who was raised at University College, London, and was born in Exeter, studied engineering there. Before becoming the founding editor of the Black and White in 1891, he worked as a writer for the Graphic for eight years. In 1881, he released a Life of Carlyle. Several of the Williamsons' novels and short tales went on to become movies.

A. M. Williamson American-English novelist Alice Muriel Williamson (8 October 1858 – 24 September 1933), also known as the ""C. N. and A. M. Williamson"" and ""Mrs. C. N. Williamson,"" wrote mostly under these aliases. Her father co-founded the Ohio State and Union Law Colleges, and she was born there in 1858. She took her maternal great grandfather's last name, ""Livingston,"" as her own in 1890. Forget-Me-Not published her debut serial, ""Confessions of a Stage-Struck Girl."" Her sense of humor would eventually emerge as one of her most distinctive writing traits."

CONTENTS

CHAPTER I 7

CHAPTER II 18

CHAPTER III 30

CHAPTER IV 36

CHAPTER V 47

CHAPTER VI 56

CHAPTER VII 63

CHAPTER VIII 71

CHAPTER IX 82

CHAPTER X 92

CHAPTER XI 102

CHAPTER XII 113

CHAPTER XIII 125

CHAPTER XIV 129

CHAPTER XV 145

CHAPTER XVI 161

CHAPTER XVII 168

CHAPTER XVIII 177

CHAPTER XIX 186

CHAPTER XX	201
CHAPTER XXI	209
CHAPTER XXII	217
CHAPTER XXIII	226
CHAPTER XXIV	237
CHAPTER XXV	248
CHAPTER XXVI	262
CHAPTER XXVII	272
CHAPTER XXVIII	282
CHAPTER XXIX	294
CHAPTER XXX	302
CHAPTER XXXI	309
CHAPTER XXXII	318

CHAPTER I

THE SECRET AND THE GIRL

The exciting part began in Cairo; but perhaps I ought to go back to what happened on the *Laconia*, between Naples and Alexandria. Luckily no one can expect a man who actually rejoices in his nickname of "Duffer" to know how or where a true story should begin.

The huge ship was passing swiftly out of the Bay of Naples, and already we were in the strait between Capri and the mainland. I had come on deck from the smoking-room for a last look at poor Vesuvius, who lost her lovely head in the last eruption. I paced up and down, acutely conscious of my great secret, the secret inspiring my voyage to Egypt. For months it had been the hidden romance of life; now it began to seem real. This is not the moment to tell how I got the papers that revealed the secret, before I passed them on to Anthony Fenton at Khartum, for him to say whether or not the notes were of real importance. But the papers had been left in Rome by Ferlini, the Italian Egyptologist, seventy years ago, when he gave to the museum at Berlin the treasures he had unearthed. It was Ferlini who ransacked the pyramids all about Meroë, that so-called island in the desert, where in its days of splendour reigned the queens Candace. Fenton, stationed at Khartum, an eager dabbler in the old lore of Egypt, sent me an enthusiastic telegram the moment he read the documents. They confirmed legends of the Sudan in which he had been interested. Putting two and two together—the legends and Ferlini's notes—Anthony was convinced that we had the clue to fortune. At once he applied for permission to excavate under the little outlying mountain named by the desert folk "the Mountain of the Golden Pyramid." At first the spot was thought to fall within the province given up to Garstang, digging for Liverpool University. Later, however, the *Service des Antiquités* pronounced the place to be outside Garstang's borders, and it seemed that luck was coming our way. No one but we two—Fenton and I—had any inkling of what might lie hidden in the Mountain of the Golden Pyramid. That was the great secret! Then Fenton had gone to the Balkans, on a flying trip in every sense of the word. It was only a fortnight ago—I being then in Rome—that I had had a wire from him in Salonica saying, "Friends at work to promote our scheme. Meet me on my return to Egypt." After that, several telegrams had been exchanged; and here I was on the *Laconia* bound for the land of my birth, full of hope and dreams.

For some moments distant Vesuvius had beguiled my thoughts from the still more distant mountain of the secret, when suddenly a white girl in a white hood and a long white cloak passed me on the white deck: whereupon I forgot mountains of reality and dreams. She was one of those tall, slim, long-limbed, dryad-sort of girls they are running up nowadays in England and America with much success; and besides all that, she was an amazing symphony in white and gold against an azure Italian sea and sky, the two last being breezily jumbled together at the moment for us on shipboard. She walked well in spite of the blue turmoil; and if a fair girl with golden-brown hair gets herself up in satiny white fur from head to foot she is evidently meant to be looked at. Others were looking: also they were whispering after she went by: and her serene air of being alone in a world made entirely for her caused me to wonder if she were not Some One in Particular.

Just then a sweet, soft voice said, close to my ear:

"Why, Duffer, dear, it can't possibly be you!"

I gave a jump, for I hadn't heard that voice for many a year, and between the ages of four and fourteen I had been in love with it.

"Brigit O'Brien!" said I. Then I grabbed her two hands and shook them as if her arms had been branches of a young cherry tree, dropping fruit.

"Why not Biddy?" she asked. "Or are ye wanting me to call ye Lord Ernest?"

"Good heavens, no! Once a Duffer, always a Duffer," I assured her. "And I've been thinking of you as Biddy from then till now. Only—"

"'Twas as clever a thing as a boy ever did," she broke in, with one of her smiles that no man ever forgets, "to begin duffing at an early age, in order to escape all the professions and businesses your pastors and masters proposed, and go your own way. Are ye at it still?"

"Rather! But you? I want to talk to you."

"Then don't do it in a loud voice, if you please, because, as you must have realized, if you've taken time to think, I'm Mrs. Jones at present."

"Why Jones?"

"Because Smith is engaged beforehand by too many people. Honestly, without joking, I'm in danger here and everywhere, and it's a wicked, selfish thing for me to come the way I have; but Rosamond Gilder is the hardest girl to resist you ever saw, so I'm with her; and it's a long history."

"Rosamond Gilder? What—the Cannon Princess, the Bertha Krupp of America?"

"Yes, the 'Gilded Babe' that used to be wheeled about in a caged perambulator guarded by detectives: the 'Gilded Bud' whose coming out in society was called the Million Dollar Début: now she's just had her twenty-first birthday, and the Sunday Supplements have promoted her to be the Golden Girl, alternating with the Gilded Rose, although she's the simplest creature, really, with a tremendous sense of the responsibility of her riches. Poor child! There she is, walking toward us now, with those two young men. Of course, young men! Droves of young men! She can't get away from them any more than she can from her money. No, she's stopped to talk to Cleopatra."

"That tall, white girl Rosamond Gilder! Just before you came, I was wondering who she was; and when you smiled at each other across the deck it sprang into my mind that—that—"

"That what?"

"Oh, it seems stupid now."

"Give me a chance to judge, dear Duffer."

"Well, seeing you, and knowing—that is, it occurred to me you might be travelling with—the daughter of—your late—"

"Good heavens, don't say any more! I've been frightened to death somebody would get that brilliant notion in his head, especially as Monny and her aunt came on board the *Laconia* only at Monaco. Esmé O'Brien is in a convent school not thirty miles from there. But that's the *deepest* secret. Poor Peter Gilder's fears for his millionaire girl would be child's play to what might happen, before such a mistake was found out if once it was made. That's just one of the hundred reasons why it would be as safe for Monny Gilder to travel with a bomb in her dressing-bag as to have me in her train of dependants. She telegraphed to New York for me, because of a stupid thing I said in a letter, about being lonely: though she pretends it would be too dull journeying to such a romantic country alone with a mere aunt. And she thinks I 'attract adventures.' It's only too true. But I couldn't resist her. Nobody can. Why, the first time I ever saw Monny she'd cast herself down in a mud-puddle, and was screaming and kicking because she wanted to walk while one adoring father, one sycophantic governess and two trained nurses wanted her to get into an automobile. That was on my honeymoon—heaven save the mark—! and Monny was nine. She has other ways now of getting what she wants, but they're even more effective. I laughed at her that first time, and she was so surprised at my impudence she took a violent fancy to me. But I don't always laugh at her now. Oh, she's a perfect terror, I assure you—and a still more perfect darling! Such an angel of charity to the poor, such a demon of obstinacy with the rich! I worship her. So does Cleopatra. So does everybody who doesn't hate her. So will you the minute you've been introduced. And by the way, why not? Why shouldn't I make myself useful for once by arranging a match between Rosamond Gilder, the prettiest heiress in America, and Lord Ernest Borrow, of the oldest family in Ireland?"

"And the poorest."

"All the more reason why. Don't you *see?*"

"She mightn't."

"Well, what's the good of her having all that money if she doesn't get hold of a really grand title to hang it on? I shall tell her that Borrow comes down from Boru, Brian Boru the rightful King of Ireland: and when your brother dies you'll be Marquis of Killeena."

"He'll not die for thirty or forty years, let's hope."

"Why hope it, when he likes nobody and nobody likes him, and everybody likes you? He can't be happy. And anyhow, isn't it worth a few millions to be Lady Ernest Borrow, and have the privilege of restoring the most beautiful old castle in Ireland? I'm sure Killeena would let her."

"He would, out of sheer, weak kindness of heart! But she's far too thickly gilded an heiress for me to aspire to. A few thousands a year is my most ambitious figure for a wife. Look at the men collecting around her and the wonderful lady you call Cleopatra. Why Cleopatra? Did sponsors in baptism—"

"No, they didn't. *Why* she's Cleopatra is as weird a history as why I'm Mrs. Jones. But she's Monny's aunt—at least, she's a half-sister of Peter Gilder, and as his only living relative his will makes her Monny's guardian till the girl marries or reaches twenty-five. A strange guardian! But he didn't know she was going to turn into Cleopatra. She wisely waited to do that until he was dead; so it came on only a year ago. It was a Bond Street crystal-gazer transplanted to Fifth Avenue told her who she really was: you know Sayda

Sabri, the woman who has the illuminated mummy? It's Cleopatra's idea that Monny's second mourning for Peter should be white, nothing but white."

"Her idea! But I thought Miss Monny, as you call her, adopted only her own ideas. How can a mere half-aunt, labouring under the name of Cleopatra, force her—"

"Well, you see, white's very becoming; and as for the Cleopatra part, it pleases our princess to tolerate that. It's part of the queer history that's mixing me up with the family. We've come to spend the season in Egypt because Cleopatra thinks she's Cleopatra; also because Monny (that's what she's chosen to call herself since she tried to lisp 'Resamond' and couldn't) because Monny has read 'The Garden of Allah,' and wants the 'desert to take her.' That book had nothing to do with Egyptian deserts; but any desert will do for Monny. What she expects it to do with her exactly when it has taken her, on the strength of a Cook ticket, I don't quite know; but I may later, because she vows she'll keep me at her side with hooks of steel all through the tour—unless something worse happens to me, or to some of us *because* of me." "Biddy, dear, don't be morbid. Nothing bad will happen," I tried to reassure her.

"Thank you for saying so. It cheers me up. We women folk are so in the habit of believing anything you men folk tell us. It's really quaint!"

"Stop rotting, and tell me about yourself; and a truce to heiresses and Cleopatras. You know I'm dying to hear."

"Not a syllable, until you've told me about *your*self. Where you're going, and what the dickens for!"

We laughed into each other's eyes. To do so, I had to look a long way down, and she a long way up. This in itself is a pleasantly Victorian thing for a man to do in these days of Jerrybuilt girls, on the same level or a story or two higher than himself. I'm not a tall man: just the dull average five foot ten or eleven that appears taller, while it keeps lean— so naturally I have a hopeless yearning for nymph-like creatures who pretend to be engaged when I ask them to dance. Still, there's consolation and homely comfort in talking with a little woman who makes you feel the next best thing to a giant. Biddy is an old-fashioned five foot four in her highest heels; and as she smiled up at me I saw that she hadn't changed a jot in the last ten years, despite the tragedy that had involved her. Not a silver thread in the black hair, not a line on the creamy round face.

"You're just yourself," I said.

"I oughtn't to be. I know that very well. I ought to be a Dido and Niobe and Cassandra rolled into one. I'm a brute not to be dead or look a hag. I've gone through horrors, and the secrets I know could put dozens of people in prison, if not electrocute them. But you see I'm not the right type of person for the kind of life I've had, as I should be if I were in a story book, and the author had created me to suit my background. I can't help flapping up out of my own ashes before they're cold. I can't help laughing in the face of fate."

"And looking a girl of twenty-three, at most, while you do it!"

"If I look a girl, I must be a phenomenon as well as a phoenix, for nobody knows better than you that my Bible age is thirty-one if it's a day. And I think Burke and Debrett have got the same tale to tell about you, eh?"

"They have. I was always delighted to share something with you."

"You can have the whole share of my age over twenty-six. There's one advantage 'Mrs. Jones' has. She can, if her looking-glass doesn't forbid, go back to that classic age dear to all sensible adventuresses. I'm afraid I come under the head of adventuress, with my alias, and travelling as companion to the rich Miss Gilder."

"You're the last person on earth for the part! Your fate was thrust on you. You've thrust yourself on no one. Miss Gilder 'achieved' you."

"Collected me, rather, as one of her 'specimens.' She has a noble weakness for lame ducks, and though she fails sometimes in trying to strengthen their game legs, she tries gloriously. She and her aunt have been travelling in France and Italy, guided by instinct and French maids, and already Monny has picked up two weird *protégées*, sure to bring her to grief. The most exciting and deadly specimen is a perfectly beautiful American girl just married to a Turkish Bey who met her in Paris, and is taking her home to Egypt. I haven't even seen the unfortunate houri, because the Turk has shut her up in their cabin and pretends she's seasick. Monny doesn't believe in the seasickness, and sends secret notes in presents of flowers and boxes of chocolate. But I have seen the Turk. He's pink and white and looks angelic, except for a gleam deep down in his eyes, if Monny inquires after his wife when any of her best young men are hanging about. Especially when there's Neill Sheridan, a young Egyptologist from Harvard, Monny met in Paris, or Willis Bailey, a fascinating sculptor who wants to study the crystal eyes of wooden statues in the Museum at Cairo. He is going to make them the fashion in America, next year. Yes, Madame Rechid Bey is a most explosive *protégée* for a girl to have, on her way to Egypt. I'm not sure even I am not innocuous by comparison;

though I do wish you hadn't reminded me of my poor little step-daughter Esmé, in her convent-school. If any one should get the idea that Monny—but I won't put it in words! Besides me, and the brand-new bride of Rechid Bey ('Wretched Bey' is our name for him), there's one more *protégée*, a Miss Rachel Guest from Salem, Massachusetts, a school-teacher taking her first holiday. That *sounds* harmless, and it looks harmless to an amateur; but wait till *you* meet her and see what instinct tells you about her eyes. Oh, we shall have ructions! But that reminds me. You haven't told me where you're bound—or anything."

"Thanks for putting me among the 'specimens.' But this sample hasn't yet been collected by Miss Gilder."

"You might be her salvation, and keep her out of mischief. She's quite wild now with sheer joy because she's going to Egypt. But do be serious, and tell me all I pine to know, if you want me to do the same by you."

"Well—though it's unimportant compared to what you have to tell! I'm an insignificant second secretary to Sir Raymond Ronalds, the British Ambassador at Rome. I've got four months' leave——"

"Ah, *that's* what comes of duffing so skilfully, and avoiding all the things you didn't want to do, till you got exactly what you did want! I remember when we were small boy and girl, and you used to walk down to the vicarage every day, to talk Greek or Latin or something with father——"

"No, to see you!"

"Well, you used to tell me, if you couldn't be the greatest prize-fighter or the greatest opera-singer in the world, you thought you'd like to be a diplomat.

"I haven't become a diplomat yet, in spite of Foreign Office grubbing. But I've been enjoying life pretty well, fagging up Arabic and modern Greek, and playing about with pleasant people, while pretending to do my duty. Now I've got leave on account of a mild fever which turned out a blessing in disguise. I could have found no other excuse for Egypt this winter."

"You speak as if you had some special reason for going to Egypt."

"I've been wishing to go, more or less, for years, because you know—if you haven't forgotten—I was accidentally born in Cairo while my father was fighting in Alexandria. My earliest recollections are of Egypt, for we lived there till I was four—about the time I met and fell in love with you. I've always thought I'd like to polish up old memories. But my special hurry is because I'm anxious to meet a friend, a chap I admire and love beyond all others. I want to see him for his own sake, and for the sake of a plan we have, which may make a lot of difference for our future."

"How exciting! Did I ever know him?"

"I think not."

"Well? Don't you mean to tell me who he is?"

I hesitated, sorry I had let myself go: because Anthony had written that he didn't want his movements discussed at present.

"I'll tell you another time," I said. "I want to talk about you. Anybody else is irrelevant."

"Clever Duffer! Your friend is a *secret*."

"Not he! But if there's a secret anywhere, it's only a dull, dusty sort of secret. You wouldn't be interested."

"Women never are, in secrets. Well, I'm glad somebody else besides myself has a mystery to hide."

"You're very quick."

"I'm Irish! But I'm merciful. No more questions—till you're off your guard. You're free to ask me all you like, if there's anything you care to know which horrid newspapers haven't told you these last few years."

"There are a thousand things. You didn't answer anybody's letters, after—after——"

"After Richard died. Oh, I can talk about it, now. It was the best thing that could happen for him, poor fellow. Life in hiding was purgatory. No, I couldn't answer letters, though my old friends (you among them) wanted to be kind. There wasn't anything I could let anybody do for me. Monny Gilder's different. You'll soon see why."

I smiled indulgently. But, though I was to be introduced to Miss Gilder for the purpose of being eventually gilded by her, at the instant my thoughts were for my childhood's sweetheart.

Brigit Burne made a terrible mess of things in marrying, when she was eighteen or so, Richard O'Brien, in the height of his celebrity as a socialist leader. People still believed in him then, at the time of his famous lecturing tour and visit to his birthplace on our green island; and though he was more than twice her age, the fascination he had for Biddy surprised few who knew him.

He was eloquent, in a fiery way. He had extraordinary eyes, and it was his pride to resemble portraits of Lord Byron. After an acquaintance of a month, Biddy married O'Brien (I had just gone up to Oxford at the time, or I should have tried not to let it happen), went to America with him, and voluntarily ceased to exist for her friends.

Poor girl, she must have had an awakening! He had posed as a bachelor; but after her marriage she found out (and the world with her) that he was a widower with one child, a little girl he had practically abandoned. Biddy adopted her, though the mother had been a rather undesirable Frenchwoman; and now when I saw her smiling at the tall white girl on the *Laconia*, I had thought for an instant that Biddy and her stepdaughter might be in flight together. O'Brien was a drunkard, as well as a demagogue; and not long after Brigit's flitting with him there was a scandal about the accepting of bribes from politicians on the opposing side, apparently his greatest enemies; but a minor scandal compared to what came some years afterward. O'Brien's name was implicated in the blowing up of the *World-Republican* Building in Washington, and the wrecking of Senator Marlowe's special train after his speech against socialist interests, but the coward turned informer against his friends and associates in the secret society of which he had been a leader, and saved himself by sending them to prison. From that day until his death he lived the life of a hunted animal flying from the hounds of vengeance. Brigit stood by him in spite of threats against her life as well as his, and the life of the child. Since then, though she answered none of our letters, we had heard rumours. The girl Esmé, whom the avengers had threatened to kidnap, was supposed to be hidden in some convent-school in Europe. As for Brigit, she was said to be training for a hospital nurse: reported to have become a missionary in India, China, and one or two other countries; seen on the music-hall stage, and traced to Johannesburg, where she had married a diamond-merchant; yet here she was on board the *Laconia*, unchanged in looks, or nature, and the guest of a much paragraphed, much proposed to American heiress *en route* to Egypt.

While Brigit was telling me the real story of her last two years, as governess, companion, teacher of music, and journalist, Miss Gilder regarded us sidewise from amid her bodyguard of young men. Evidently she was dying to know who was the acquaintance her darling Biddy had picked up in mid-Mediterranean the moment her back was turned; and at last, unable to restrain herself longer, she made use of some magic trick to attach the band of youths to her aunt. Then, separating herself with almost indecent haste from the group, she marched up to us, gazing—I might say, staring—with large unfriendly eyes at the intruder.

Brigit promptly accounted for me, however, rolling her "r's" patriotically because I reminded her of Ireland. "Do let me introduce Lord Ernest Borrow," she said. "I must have told you about him in my stories, when you were a child, for he was me first love."

"It was the other way round," I objected. "She wouldn't look at me. I adored her."

Biddy glared a warning. Her eyes said, "Silly fellow, don't you know every girl wants to be the one and only love of a man's life?"

I had supposed that this old craze had gone out of fashion. But perhaps there are a few primitive things which will never go out of fashion with women.

Now that I had Miss Gilder's proud young face opposite mine, I saw that it wasn't quite so perfect as I'd fancied when she flashed by in her tall whiteness. Her nose, pure Greek in profile, seen in full was —well, just neat American: a straight, determined little twentieth-century nose. The full red mouth, not small, struck me as being determined also, rather than classic, despite the daintily drawn cupid's bow of the short upper lip. I realized too that the long-lashed, wide-open, and wide-apart eyes were of the usual bluish-gray possessed by half the girls one knows. And as for the thick wavy hair pushed crisply forward by the white hood, now it was out of the sun's glamour, there was more brown than gold in it. I said to myself, that the face with the firm cleft chin was only just pretty enough to give a great heiress or a youthful princess the reputation of a beauty; a combination desired and generally produced by journalists. Then, as I was thinking this, while Brigit explained me, Miss Gilder suddenly smiled. I was dazzled. No wonder Biddy loved her. It would be a wonder if I didn't love her myself before I knew what was happening.

And so I should instantly have done, perhaps, if it hadn't been for Biddy's eyes seeming to come between mine and Miss Gilder's: and the fact that at the moment I was in quest of another treasure than a woman's heart. My thoughts were running ahead of the ship to Alexandria, to find out from Anthony Fenton ("Antoun Effendi" the biggest boys used to nickname him at school) more about the true history of that treasure than he dared trust to paper and ink and the post office.

So I put off falling in love with Rosamond Gilder till I should have seen Anthony, and tidied up my distracted mind. A little later would do, I told myself, because (owing to the fact that my ancestral castle had figured in Biddy's tales of long ago) I was annexed as one of the *protégés*; allowed to make a fifth at the small, flowery table under a desirable porthole in the green and white restaurant; also I was invited to go about with the ladies and show them Cairo. Just how much "going about," and falling in love, I should be able to do there, depended on "Antoun Effendi." But when Biddy congratulated me on my luck, and chance of success in the "scheme," I said nothing of Anthony.

CHAPTER II

CLEOPATRA AND THE SHIP'S MYSTERY

Now, at last, I can skip over the three days at sea, and get to our arrival at Alexandria, because, as I've said, the exciting part began soon after, at Cairo.

They were delightful days, for the *Laconia* is a Paris hotel disguised as a liner. And no man with blood in his veins could help enjoying the society of Brigit O'Brien and Rosamond Gilder. Cleopatra, too, was not to be despised as a charmer; and then there was the human interest of the *protégées*, the one with the eyes and the one who had reluctantly developed into the Ship's Mystery.

Still, in spite of Biddy and Monny and the others, and not for them, my heart beat fast when, on the afternoon of the third day out from Naples, the ship brought us suddenly in sight of something strange. We were moving through a calm sea, more like liquefied marble than water, for it was creamy white rather than blue, veined with azure, and streaked, as marble is, with pink and gold. Far away across this gleaming floor blossomed a long line of high-growing lotus flowers, white and yellow against a silver sky. The effect was magical, and the wonder grew when the big flower-bed turned into domes and cupolas and spires rising out of the sea. Unimaginative people remarked that the coast looked so flat and uninteresting they didn't see why Alexander had wanted to bother with it; but they were the sort of people who ought to stop at home in London or Birmingham or Chicago and not make innocent fellow-passengers burn with unchristian feelings.

Soon I should see Anthony and hear his news. I felt sure he would be at Alexandria to meet the ship. When "Antoun Effendi" makes up his mind to do a thing, he will crawl from under a falling sky to do it. As the *Laconia* swept on, I hardly saw the glittering city on its vast prayer-rug of green and gold, guarded by sea forts like sleepy crocodiles. My mind's eyes were picturing Anthony as he would look after his wild Balkan experiences: brown and lean, even haggard and bearded, perhaps, a different man from the smart young officer of everyday life, unless he'd contrived to refit in the short time since his return to Egypt—a day or two at most, according to my calculation. But all my imaginings fell short of the truth.

As I thought of Anthony, Mrs. East came and stood beside me. I knew she was there before I turned to look, because of the delicate tinkling of little Egyptian amulets, which is her accompaniment, her *leit motif*, and because of the scent of sandalwood with which, in obedience to the ancient custom of Egyptian queens, she perfumes her hair.

I don't think I have described Monny Gilder's aunt, according to my conception of her, though I may have hinted at Biddy's. Biddy having a habit of focussing her sense of humour on any female she doesn't wholly love, may not do Mrs. East justice. The fact is, Monny's aunt is a handsome creature, distinctly a charmer who may at most have reached the age when Cleopatra— Antony's and Caesar's Cleopatra—died in the prime of her beauty. If Mrs. East chooses to date herself at thirty-three, any man not a confirmed misanthrope must believe her. Biddy says that until Peter Gilder was safely dead, Clara East was just an ordinary, well-dressed, pleasure-loving, novel-reading, chocolate-eating, respectable widow of a New York stockbroker: superstitious perhaps; fond of consulting palmists, and possessing Billikens or other mascots: (how many women are free from superstition?) slightly oriental in her love of sumptuous colours and jewellery; but then her mother (Peter Gilder's step-mother) was a beautiful Jewish opera singer. After Peter's death, his half-sister gave up novels for Egyptian and Roman history, took to studying hieroglyphics, and learning translations of Greek poetry. She invited a clairvoyant and crystal-gazer, claiming Egyptian origin, to visit at her Madison Square flat. Sayda Sabri, banished from Bond Street years ago, took up her residence in New York, accompanied by her tame mummy. Of course, it is the mummy of a princess, and she keeps it illuminated with blue lights, in an inner sanctum, where the bored-looking thing stands upright in its brilliantly painted mummy case, facing the door. About the time of Sayda's visit, it was noticed by Mrs. East's friends (this, according to Biddy) that the colour of the lady's hair was slowly but surely changing from black to chestnut, then to auburn; she was heard to remark casually that Queen Cleopatra's hair had been red. She took to rich Eastern scents, to whitening her face as Eastern women of rank have whitened theirs since time immemorial. The shadows round her almond-shaped eyes were intensified: her full lips turned from healthful pink to carmine. The ends of her tapering fingers blushed rosily as sticks of coral. The style of her dress changed, at the moment of going into purple as "second mourning" for Peter, and became oriental, even to the turban-like shape of her hats, and the design of her jewellery. She did away with crests and monograms on handkerchiefs, stationery, luggage and so on, substituting a curious little oval containing strange devices, which Monny discovered to be the "cartouche" of Cleopatra. Then the whole truth burst forth. Sayda Sabri's crystal had shown that Clara East, née Gilder, was the reincarnation of Cleopatra the Great of Egypt. There had been another incarnation in between, but it was of no account, and, like a poor relation who has disgraced a family, the less said about it the better.

The lady did not proclaim her identity from the housetops. Rare souls possessing knowledge of Egyptian lore might draw their own conclusions from the cartouche on her note-paper and other things. Only Monny and a few intimates were told the truth at first; but afterward it leaked out, as secrets do; and Mrs. East seemed shyly pleased if discreet questions were asked concerning her amulets and the cartouche.

Now, I never feel inclined to laugh at a pretty woman. It is more agreeable, as well as gallant, to laugh with her; but the trouble is, Cleopatra doesn't go in for laughter. She takes life seriously. Not only has she no sense of humour, but she does not know the difference between it and a sense of fun, which she can understand if a joke (about somebody else) is explained. She is grateful to me because I look her straight in the eyes when the subject of Egypt is mentioned. Sheridan from Harvard has been in her bad books since he put Ptolemaic rulers outside of the pale of Egyptian history, called their art ornate and bad, mentioned that each of their queens was named Cleopatra and classified the lot as modern, almost suburban.

Mrs. East, leaning beside me on the rail, was burning with thoughts inspired by Alexandria. She had "Plutarch's Lives" under her arm, and "Hypatia" in her hand. Of course, she dropped them both, one after the other, and I picked them up.

"Do you know, Lord Ernest," she said, in the low, rich voice she is cultivating, "I don't mind telling you that I felt as if I were coming home, after a long absence. Monny wanted to see Egypt; I was dying to. That's the difference between us."

"It's natural," I answered, sympathetically.

"Yes—considering everything. Yet we're both afraid. She in one way, I in another. I haven't told her. She hasn't told me. But I know. She has the same impression I have, that something's going to *happen* —something very great, to change the whole of life—in Egypt: 'Khem,' it seems to me I can remember calling it. You know it was Khem, until the Arabs came and named it Misr. Do you believe in impressions like that?"

"I don't disbelieve," I said. "Some people are more sensitive than others."

"Yes. Or else they're older souls. But it may be the same thing. I can't fancy Monny an old soul, can you?—yet she may be, for she's very intelligent, although so self-willed. I think what she's afraid of is getting interested in some wonderful man with Turkish or Egyptian blood, a magnificent creature like you read of in books, you know; then you have to give them up in the last chapter, and send them away broken-hearted. I suppose there *are* such men in real life?"

"I doubt if there are such romantic figures as the books make out," I tried to reassure her. "There might be a prince or two, handsome and cultivated, educated in England, perhaps, for some of the 'swells' are sent from Egypt to Oxford and Cambridge, just as they are in India. But even if Miss Gilder should meet a man of that sort, I should say she was too sensible and clear-headed—"

"Oh, she is, almost too much so for a young girl, and she has a detestation for any one with a drop of dark blood, in America. She doesn't even like Jews; and that makes friction between us, if we ever happen to argue, for—maybe you don't know?—my mother was a Jewess. I'm proud of her memory. But that's just *why*, if you can understand, Monny's *afraid* in Egypt. Some girls would like to have a tiny flirtation with a gorgeous Eastern creature (of course, he must be a bey, or prince or something, otherwise it would be *infra dig*), but Monny would hate herself for being attracted. Yet I know she dreads it happening, because of the way I've heard her rave against the heroines of novels, saying she has no patience with them; they ought to have more strength of mind, even if it broke their hearts."

I wondered if Biddy, too, suspected some such fear in the mind of her adored girl, and if that were one reason why she had turned matchmaker for my benefit. Since the first day out she had used strategems to throw us together: and it seemed that, years ago, when she used to teach the little girl French, Monny's favourite stories had been of Castle Killeena, and my boyish exploits birds'-nesting on the crags. (Biddy said that this was a splendid beginning, if I had the sense to follow it up.)

"And you?" I went on to Mrs. East. "What do you feel is going to happen to you in the land of Khem?"

"Oh, I don't know," she sighed. "I wish I did! And 'afraid' isn't exactly the word. I just know that something will happen. I wonder if history does repeat itself? I should hate to be bitten by an asp——"

"Asps are out of fashion," I comforted her. "I doubt if you could find one in all of Egypt, though I remember my Egyptian nurse used to say there were cobras in the desert in summer. Anyhow, we'll be away before summer."

"I suppose so," she agreed. "Yet—who knows what will become of any of us? Madame Rechid Bey will be staying, of course. I don't know whether to be sorry for her or not. The Bey's good-looking. He has brown eyes, and is as white as you or I. Probably it's true that she's been too seasick to leave her room for the last ten days, though Monny and Mrs. O'Bri—I mean, Mrs. Jones—think she's shut up because men stared, and because Mr. Sheridan talked to her. As for me, there's always that question asking itself in my mind: '*What* is going to happen?' And I hear it twice as loud as before, in sight of Alexandria. Rakoti, we Lagidae used to call the city." As she spoke, the long, oriental eyes glanced at me sidewise, but my trustworthy Celtic features showed a grave, intelligent interest in her statements.

"It must be," she went on, encouraged, "that I'm the reincarnation of Cleopatra, otherwise how *could* I have the sensation of remembering everything? There's no other way to account for it! And you know my modern name, Clara, does begin with 'C.' Sayda must be right. She's told lots of women the most extraordinary things. You really ought to consult her, Lord Ernest, if you ever go to New York."

I did not say, as Neill Sheridan might, that a frothy course of Egyptian historical novels would account for anything. I simply looked as diplomatic training can teach any one to look.

Evidently it was the right look in the right place, for Cleopatra continued more courageously, recalling the great Pharos of white marble which used to be one of the world's wonders in her day; the Museum, and the marvellous Library which took fire while Julius Caesar burned the fleet, nearby in the harbour.

"Think of the philosophers who deserted the College of Heliopolis for Alexandria!" she said. "Antony was more of a soldier than a student, but even he grieved for the Library. You know he tried to console Cleopatra by making her a present of two hundred thousand MSS. from the library of the King of Pergamus. It was a generous thought—like Antony!"

"Does the harbour looked changed?" I hastened to inquire.

"Not from a distance, though landing may be a shock: they tell me it's all so Italian now. It was Greek in old days. I've read that there isn't a stone left of my—of the lovely place on Lochias Point, except the foundations they found in the seventies. But I must go to see what's left of the Baths, even though there's only a bit of mosaic and the remains of a room. Monny's anxious to get on to Cairo, but we shall come back to Alexandria later. Lord Ernest, when I shut my eyes, I really do seem to picture the Mareotic Lake, and the buildings that made Alexandria the glory of the world. Do you remember what Strabo said about Deinchares, the architect who laid out the plan of the city in the shape of a Macedonian mantle, to please Alexander?"

"I'm not as well up in history as you are," I said, "though I've studied a bit, because I was born in Egypt. Poor Alexander didn't live long in his fine city, did he? I wonder what he'd think of it now? And I wonder if his palace was handsomer than the Khedive's? That huge white building with the pillars and domes. I seem to remember——"

"What, you remember, too? You *ought* to consult Sayda!"

"I didn't mean exactly what you mean," I explained, humbly. "Still, why shouldn't I have lived in Egypt long ago? The learned ones say you're always drawn back where you've been in other states of existence——"

"That's true, I'm sure!"

"Well, then, why shouldn't I have the same sort of right to Egypt you have, if you were Cleopatra?—I believe you must have been, because you look as she ought to have looked, you know. Why shouldn't I have been a friend of Marc Antony, coming from Rome to give him good advice and trying to persuade——"

"Oh, *not* that he ought to give me up!"

"No, indeed: to urge him to leave the island where he hid even from you (didn't they call it Timonieum?). Why couldn't Antony play his cards so as to keep Cleopatra and the world, too? She'd have liked him better, wouldn't she? My friend Antoun Effendi—I mean Anthony Fenton,"—I stopped short: for the less said about Fenton the better, at present. But Cleopatra caught me up.

"What—have you really a friend Antony? Where does he live? and what's he like?"

I hesitated; and glancing round for inspiration (in other words for some harmless, necessary fib) I saw that Brigit and Monny had arrived on the scene. They had been pacing the deck, arm in arm; and now, arrested by Mrs. East's question, they hovered near, awaiting my answer with vague curiosity.

A twinkle in Biddy's eyes, which I caught, rattled me completely. I missed all the easiest fibs and could catch hold of nothing but the bare truth. There are moments like that, when, do what you will, you must be truthful or silent; and silence fires suspicion.

"What is he?" I echoed feebly. "Oh, Captain Fenton. He's in the Gyppy Army stationed up at Khartum, hundreds of miles beyond where Cook's boats go. You wouldn't be interested in Anthony, because he spells his name with an 'H', and he's dark and thin, not a bit like *your* Antony, who was a big, stout fellow, I've always heard, and fair." "Big, but *not* stout," Cleopatra corrected me. "And—and if he's incarnated again, he may be dark for a change. As for the 'H', that's not important. I wonder if we shall meet your Anthony? We think of going to Khartum, don't we, Monny?"

"Yes," said the girl, shortly. She was always rather short in her manner at that time when in her opinion her aunt was being "silly."

I gathered from a vexed flash in the gray eyes that there had never been any hint of an impending Antony.

"Is your friend in Khartum now?" Biddy ventured, in her creamiest voice. The twinkle was carefully turned off like the light of a dark lantern, but I knew well that "Mrs. Jones" was recalling a certain conversation, in which I had refused to satisfy her curiosity. Brigit's quick, Irish mind has a way of matching mental jigsaw puzzles, even when vital bits appear to be missing; and if she could make a cat's paw of Cleopatra, the witch would not be above doing it. I bore her no grudge—who could bear soft-eyed, laughing, yet tragic Biddy a grudge? —but I wished that she and Monny were at the other end of the deck.

"I—er—really, I don't know where my friend is just now," I answered, with more or less foundation of truth.

"I wonder if I didn't read in the papers about a Captain Fenton who took advantage of leave he'd got, to make a rush for the Balkans, and see the fighting from the lines of the Allies?" Biddy murmured with dreadful intelligence. "Can he be your Captain Fenton? I fancy he'd been stationed in the Sudan; and he was officially supposed to have gone home to spend his leave in England. Anyhow, there was a row of some sort after he and another man dropped down on to the Turks out of a Greek aeroplane. Or was it a Servian one? Anyhow, I know he oughtn't to have been in it; and 'Paterfamilias' and 'Patriot' wrote letters to the *Times* about British officers who didn't mind their own business. Why, I saw the papers on board this ship! They were old ones. Papers on ships always are. But I think they came on at Algiers or somewhere."

"Probably 'somewhere,'" I witheringly replied. "*I* didn't come on at Algiers, so I don't know anything about it."

"Diplomatists never do know anything official, do they, Duffer dear?" smiled Biddy. "I'll wager your friend is interesting, even if he does spell himself with an 'H', and weighs two stone less than his namesake from Rome. Mrs. East believes in reincarnation, and I'm not sure I don't, though Monny's so young she doesn't believe in anything. Just suppose your friend is a reincarnation of Antony without an 'H'? And suppose, too, by some strange trick of fate he should meet you in Alexandria or Cairo? You'd introduce him to us, wouldn't you?"

"It's the most unlikely thing in the world. And he'd be no good to you. He's a man's man. He thinks he doesn't like women."

"Doesn't like women!" echoed Monny Gilder. "He must be a curmudgeon. Or has he been jilted?"

"Rather not!" Too impulsively I defended the absent. "Girls go mad about him. He has to keep them off with a stick. He's got other things to think of than girls, things he believes are more important—though, of course, he's mistaken. He'll find that out some day, when he has more time. So far, he's been hunting other game, often in wild places. A book might be written on his adventures."

"What kind of adventures? Tell us about them," said Biddy, "up to the Balkan one, which you deny having heard of."

"You wouldn't care about his sort of adventures. There aren't any women in them," said I. "Women want love stories. It's only the heroines they care for, not the heroes, and I don't somehow see the right heroine for Fenton's story."

I noticed an expression dawning on Cleopatra's face, as I thus bereft her of a possible Antony (with an "H"). There was a softening of the long eyes, and the glimmer of a smile which said "Am I Cleopatra for nothing?"

Never had she looked handsomer. Never before had I thought of her as really dangerous. I'd been inclined to poke fun at the lady for her superstition and her cartouche, and Cleopatra-hood in general. But suddenly I realized that her make-up was no more exaggerated than that of many a beauty of the stage and of society: and that nowadays, women who are—well, forty-ish—can be formidable rivals for younger and simpler sisters. Not that I feared much for Anthony from Cleopatra or any other female thing, for I'd come to consider him practically woman-proof; still, I saw danger that the lady might make a dead set at him, if she got the chance, and all through my stupidity in giving away his name. "Antony" was a thrilling password to that mysterious "something" which she expected to happen in Egypt: and already she regarded my friend as a ram caught in the bushes, for a sacrifice on her altar. Instead of screening him I had dragged him in front of the footlights. But fortunately there was still time to jerk down the curtain.

I threw a glance at Brigit and Monny, and was relieved to find that their attention was distracted by a new arrival: Miss Rachel Guest from Salem, Massachusetts: a pale, thin, lanky copy of our Rose, with the beauty and bloom left out; but a pair of eyes to redeem the colourless face—oh, yes, a pair of eyes! Strange, hungry, waiting eyes.

When I am alone, I fear Monny's favourite *protégée*, who started out to "see the world" on a legacy of two thousand dollars, and won Miss Gilder's admiration (and hospitality) through her unassuming pluck. To my mind she is the ideal adventuress of a new, unknown, and therefore deadly type; but for once I rejoiced at sight of the pallid, fragile woman, so cheerful in spite of frail health, so frank about her twenty-eight years. She had news to tell of a nature so exciting that, after a whisper or two, Cleopatra forgot Anthony in her desire to know the latest development in the Ship's Mystery.

"My stewardess says he won't let his wife land till we're all off," murmured the ex-schoolmistress, in her colourless voice. "She heard the end of a conversation, when she carried the poor girl's lunch to the door—just a word or two. So we shan't see her again, I suppose."

"Oh, yes, we shall," said Monny. "If Wretched Bey can get a private boat, so can I. I'll not desert her, if I have to stay on board the *Laconia* the whole night."

All four began talking together eagerly, and blessing Miss Guest I sneaked away. Presently I saw that clever Neill Sheridan and handsome, actor-like Willis Bailey, the two *bêtes noires* of Wretched Bey, had joined the group.

By this time the roofs and domes and minarets of Alexandria sparkled in clearly sketched outlines between sunset-sky and sea; sunset of Egypt, which divided ruby-flame of cloud, emerald dhurra, gold of desert, and sapphire waters into separate bands of colour, vivid as the stripes of a rainbow.

There was a new buzz of excitement on the decks and in the ivy draped veranda café. Those who had been studying Baedeker gabbled history, ancient and modern, until the conquest of Alexander and the bombardment of '82 became a hopeless jumble in the ears of the ignorant. Bores who had travelled inflicted advice on victims who had not. People told each other pointless anecdotes of "the last time I was in Egypt," while those forced to listen did so with the air of panthers waiting to pounce. A pause for breath on the part of the enemy gave the wished-for opportunity to spring into the breach with an adventure of their own.

We took an Arab pilot on board—the first Arab ever seen by the ladies of my party—and before the red torch of sunset had burned down to dusky purple, tenders like big, black turtles were swimming out to the *Laconia*. We slaves of the Rose, however, had surrendered all personal interest in these objects. The word of Miss Gilder had gone forth, and, unless Rechid Bey changed his mind at the last minute, we were all to lurk in ambush until he appeared with his wife. Then, somehow, Monny was to snatch her chance for a word with the Ship's Mystery; and whatever happened, none of us were to stir until it had been snatched.

Arguments, even from Biddy, were of no avail, and mine were silenced by cold permission to go away by myself if I chose. It was terrible, it was wicked to talk of people making their own beds and then lying in them. It was nonsense to say that, even if the wife of Rechid Bey asked for help, we could do nothing. Of course, we would do something! If the girl wanted to be saved, she should be saved, if Monny had to act alone. Whatever happened, Mr. Sheridan and Mr. Bailey must remain in the background, as the very sight of them would drive "Wretched Bey" *wild!*

I was thinking of Anthony's surprise when one after the other, two tenders should reach the quay without me; and if the Gilded Rose had not been so sweet, her youthful cocksureness would have made me yearn to slap her. In spite of all, however, the girl's excitement became contagious as passengers crowded down the gangway and Rechid Bey did not appear.

"Allah—Allah!" cried the boatman and the Arab porters as they hauled huge trunks off the ship onto a float. Then one after the other the two tenders puffed away, packed from stem to stern. A few people for whom there was no room embarked in small boats manned by jabbering Arabs. Two of these cockle-shells still moved up and down under the black, mountainous side of the ship, and the officer whose duty it was to see the passengers off was visibly restless. He wanted to know if my lordship was ready; and my lordship's brain was straining after an excuse for further delay, when a man and woman arrived opportunely; Rechid Bey and a veiled, muffled form hooked to his arm; a slender, appealing little figure: and through the veil I fancied that I caught a gleam of large, wistful, anxious eyes.

The ladies were lying in wait out of sight, and I dodged behind the sturdy blue shoulders guarding the gangway. This was my first glimpse of the Ship's Mystery; and though I did not like my job (I had to surprise Rechid Bey and take his mind off his wife) my curiosity was pricked. The figure in sealskin looked very girlish; the veiled head was bowed. The mystery took on human personality for me, and Monny Gilder was no longer obstinate; she was a loyal friend. I did not see that we could be of use to the poor little fool who had married a Turk, yet I was suddenly ready to do what I could. As Rechid Bey brought his wife to the top of the gangway, I lounged out, and spoke. Disconcerted, the stout, good-looking man of thirty let drop the arm of the girl, putting her behind him. And this was what Monny wanted. They would have an instant for a few disjointed words: Monny might perhaps have time to promise help which the girl dared not ask, even behind her husband's back.

"Good evening," I said in French, taking advantage of a smoke-room acquaintance. "Is that smart boat down there for you? I was trying to secure it, in my best Arabic, but the fellow said it was engaged."

"Yes, it is mine," Rechid answered, civilly, trying to hide his annoyance. "I telegraphed from Naples to a friend in Alexandria to send me a private boat. I do not like crowds."

"Neither do I, so I waited, too," I explained. "They told me there were always boats, and my big luggage has gone. I suppose yours has, too?"

"No doubt," said Rechid Bey. "Good night, Milord Borrow."

He turned quickly to his wife, as if to catch her at something, but the slim veiled mystery stood meekly awaiting his will. To my intense relief Monny and her friends were invisible. I could hardly wait until the two figures had passed out of sight down the gangway, to know whether my skirmishing attack had been successful.

"Well?" I asked, as Miss Gilder, "Mrs. Jones," Cleopatra, Rachel Guest, and two maids filed out from concealment. "Did I give you time enough? Did you get the chance you wanted?"

"Yes, thank you ever so much," said Monny, with one of those dazzling smiles that would make her a beauty even if she were not the favourite Sunday supplement heiress. "I counted on you—and *she* had counted on me. She must have known I wouldn't fail her, for she had this bit of paper ready.

When I jumped out she slipped it into my hand. We didn't need to say a word, and Wretched Bey has no idea I came near her."

"A bit of paper?" I echoed, with interest. For it sounded the obvious secret thing; a bit of paper stealthily slid from hand to hand.

"Yes, with her address on it—nothing more in writing: but two other words, pricked with a pin. '*Save me.*' Don't you see, if her husband had pounced on it, no harm would have been done. He wouldn't have noticed the pin-pricks, as a woman would. I thought she was going to live in Cairo, and I believe she thought so too, at first. But she's written down the name of a house in a place called Asiut. Did you ever hear of such a town, Lord Ernest?"

"Oh, yes," said I. "The Nile boats stop there and people see tombs and mummied cats and buy silver shawls."

"Good!" said Monny. "*My* boat shall stop there, but not only for tombs or cats or silver shawls. I have an idea that the poor girl is frightened, and wants me to help her escape."

"Great heavens!" I exclaimed. "You mustn't on any account get mixed up in an adventure of that sort! Remember, this is Egypt——"

"I don't care," said Monny, "if it's the moon."

She believed that this settled the matter. I believed the exact opposite. But I left it at that, for the moment, as the boat was waiting, and Asiut seemed a long way off.

This was my first lesson in what Brigit called "Monny's little ways"; but the second lesson was on the heels of the first.

CHAPTER III

A DISAPPOINTMENT AND A DRAGOMAN

It was a blow not to see Anthony on the quay. And other blows rained thick and fast. My two consolations were that I was actually in Egypt; and that in the confusion Rechid Bey with the veiled figure of his silent bride had slipped away without further incidents. Their disappearance was regretted by no one save Monny, unless it was Neill Sheridan, and he was discreet enough to keep his feelings to himself. The girl was not. She protested on principle, although she had the Asiut address. But where all men, black and brown and white, were yelling with the whole force of their lungs, and pitching and tossing luggage (mostly the wrong luggage) with all the force of their arms, nobody heard or cared what she said. For once Monny Gilder was disregarded by a crowd of men. This could happen only at the departure of a boat train! But if I was not thinking about her, I was thinking about her fifteen trunks, and Cleopatra's sixteen and Biddy's and Miss Guest's two. The maids were worse than useless, and I had no valet. I have never had a valet. I clawed, I fought, I wrestled in an arena where it was impossible to tell the wild beasts from the martyrs. I rescued small bags from under big boxes, and dashed off with a few samples to the train, in order to secure places. All other able-bodied men, including Sheridan and the artist sculptor Bailey, were engaged in the same pursuit, and our plan was to "bag" a whole compartment between us in the boat-special for Cairo. But we never met again till we reached our destination. One expects Egypt to warm the heart with its weather, but the cold was bitter; so was the disappointment about Anthony. Both cut through me like knives. Darkness had fallen before I was ready to join the ladies—if I could. In passing earlier, I had shouted to the maids where to find the places, grabbed with difficulty, for their mistresses. Whether they had found them, or whether any of the party still existed, was the next question; and it was settled only as the train began to move. The compartment I had selected was boiling over with a South American president and his effects; but as I stood transfixed by this transformation scene, Cleopatra's maid hailed me from the end of the corridor. *Les quatres dames* were in the restaurant car. Why? Ah, it was the Arab they had engaged as dragoman, who had advised the change in milord's absence. He said it would be better, as of course they would want dinner. He himself was looking after the small *baggages*, except the little sacks of the hand which the maids kept.

What, the ladies had engaged a dragoman! And they had trusted him—a stranger—with luggage? Then it was as good as gone! But no, mildly ventured Cleopatra's handmaiden. The dragoman came recommended. He had a letter from a friend of milord.

My thoughts jumped, of course, to Anthony. Yet how could he have known that I was travelling with ladies? And if by some Marconian miracle he had heard, why should he, who prided himself on "not bothering" with women, trouble to provide a dragoman at Alexandria?

I hurried to the dining car, and found Monny with her satellites seated at a table, three of them looking as calmly innocent as if they had not upset my well-laid scheme for their comfort. Biddy alone had a guilty air, because, perhaps, I was more important in her eyes than in the eyes of the others. "Oh, dear Duffer," she began to wheedle me: "We hope you don't mind our coming here? We thought it a good idea, for we're starving, although we're perfectly happy because we're in Egypt, and because it's such a *quaint* train, so different and Eastern. The dragoman who——"

"I think he came from your friend Anthony with an 'H,'" Cleopatra broke in. "He seemed providential. And he speaks English. The only objection is, he's not as good-looking as Monny and I wanted our dragoman to be. We did hope to get one who would be *becoming* to us, you see, and give the right sort of Eastern background. But I suppose one can't have *everything!* And it was I who said your friend Anthony's messenger must be engaged even if his face is—is—rather like an *accident!*"

"It's like a catastrophe," remarked Monny, looking as if she blamed me.

"Where *is* it?" I wanted to know.

"It's waiting in a vestibule outside where the cook's cooking," Biddy explained ungrammatically. "I told it you'd want to see it. And it's got a letter for you from some one." "Did the fellow say the letter was from Fenton?" I inquired.

"No. He only said, from a friend who'd expected to meet you; and Mrs. East was sure it must be from the one you were talking about."

Wasting no more words, I marched off to the fountainhead for information. Near the open door of the infinitesimal kitchen stood a fat little dark man with a broken nose, and one white eye. The other eye, as if to make up, was singularly, repellently intelligent. It fixed itself upon me, as I approached, with eager questioning which melted into ingratiating politeness. Instinct warned the fellow that I was the person he awaited. At the same moment, instinct was busily whispering to me that there was something fishy about him, despite the alleged letter. He did not look the type of man Fenton would recommend. And though his face was of an unwholesome olive tint, and he wore a tarbush, and a galabeah as long as a dressing-gown, under his short European coat, I was sure he was not of Arab or Egyptian blood.

"Milord Borrow?" he began, displaying large white teeth, of which he was evidently proud.

I assented.

"My name is Bedr el Gemály," he introduced himself. "I have a letter for milord."

"Who gave it to you?" I challenged him.

The ingratiating smile seemed to flicker like a candle flame in a sudden puff of wind. "A friend of my, a dragoman. He could not come to bring it. So he give it to me. The gentleman's name was Fenton. My friend, he was sent from him at Cairo." As the fellow spoke, in fairly good English, he took from a pocket of the short coat which spoiled his costume, a colourful silk handkerchief. Unwrapping this, he produced an envelope. It was addressed to me in the handwriting of Fenton, but before opening it I went on with my catechism.

"Then the letter doesn't introduce you, but your friend?"

The smile was practically dead now. "I think it do not introduce any ones. It is only a letter. My friend Abdullah engaged to carry it. But he got sick too soon to come to the ship."

"I see," said I. "You seem to have used the letter, however, to get yourself taken on as dragoman by the ladies of my party. How the devil did you find out that they were travelling with me, eh?" I shot the question at him and tried to imitate gimlets with my eyes. But he was ready with his answer. No doubt he had prepared it.

"I see you all together, from a distant place, before I come there. A gentleman off the ship, he pointed you out when I ask where I find Milord

Borrow. I see you, and those ladies. When I come, you was away already, so I speak to them, and say if I could help, I be very pleased. When I tell one of the ladies I was from a friend of milord's with a letter, she say, is the friend's name Captain Fenton, and I say 'yes, madame, Captain Fenton, that is the name; and I am a dragoman to show Egypt to the strangers. I know it all very well, from Alexandria way up Nile.' Then the lady say very quick she will take me for her dragoman. I am pleased, for I was not engaged for season, and she say if I satisfy her she keep me in Cairo and on from there." "H'm," I grunted, still screwing in the gimlets. "I see you're not an Egyptian. You have selected the name of an Armenian famous in history. Are you Armenian?"

"I am the same thing as Egyptian, I bin here for dragoman so many years. I am Mussulman in faith. But I was born Armenian," he admitted.

"You speak English with an American accent," I went on. "Have you lived in America?"

"One time a family take me to New York and I stay a year or two. Then I get homesick and come to Egypt again. But I learn to talk maybe some like American peoples while I am over there."

It sounded plausible enough, the whole story. And if Mrs. East had snapped the dragoman up under the impression that he came from a man she had determined to meet, the fellow might be no more to blame than any other boaster, touting in his own interest. Still, I had an uneasy feeling that something lay hidden under Armenian plausibility. Bedr el Gemály was perhaps a thief who had courted a chance for a big haul of jewellery. Yet if that were all, why hadn't he hopped off the tram, as it began to move, with the ladies' hand luggage? He might easily have got away, and disappeared into space, before we could wire the police of Alexandria to look out for him. He had not done that, but had waited, and risked facing my suspicions. And he must have realized, while in charge of Monny's and Cleopatra's attractive dressing bags, that he was missing an opportunity such as might never come to him again. This conduct suggested an honest desire to be a good dragoman. Yet—well, I resolved not to let the gimlets rust until Bedr el Gemály had been got rid of. If Mrs. East had really promised him a permanent engagement, she could salve his disappointment by giving him a day's pay. I would take the responsibility of sending him about his business.

Without further parley I opened the letter. It was short, evidently written in a hurry. Anthony had scribbled:

Horribly sorry, dear old Duffer, but I'm wanted by the Powers that Be in Cairo. No other reason could have kept me from Alexandria. I was afraid a wire wouldn't reach you, so I sent a decent old chap by the train I meant to take. He's pledged to find you on the quay, and he will—unless some one makes him drunk. This seems unlikely to happen, as he won't be paid till he gets back, and having no friends on earth, nobody will stand him drinks. Beastly luck, but I shan't be able to see you to-night even in Cairo. Tell you all to-morrow—and there's a lot to tell, about many things.

Yours ever,

A.F.

The messenger had "no friend on earth," according to Fenton. Then the friendship stated to exist between him and Bedr el Gemály must have come readymade from heaven, or—its opposite. I guessed the nature of the "decent old chap's" illness. But I should have been glad to know whether it had been produced by design or accident.

When I went back to the ladies, Bedr went with me, at my firm suggestion, and gave them their handbags to use as footstools. Dinner was ready, and a seat had been kept for me at a table just across the aisle, but before beginning, I explained the real circumstances governing the dragoman's arrival. "Whatever else he may be, he's a shark," I said, "or he wouldn't have traded on a misunderstanding to grab an engagement. You owe him nothing really, but if you choose, give him a sovereign when we get to Cairo, and I'll tell him that I have a dragoman in view for the party. He'll then have two days' pay, according to the guide-books."

With this, I slipped into my seat, thinking the matter settled. But between courses, Monny leaned across from her table (she and I had end seats) and said that she and her aunt had been talking about that poor dragoman. "Aunt Clara raised his hopes," the girl went on, "and now Rachel Guest and I think it would be mean to send him away, just because he's hideous."

"That won't be the reason!" said I. "It will be because we don't know anything about him, and because in his sharpness he's over-reached himself."

"But we do know things about him. He showed Aunt Clara letters from people who'd employed him, lots of Americans whose names we've heard, and some we're acquainted with. The tragic thing is, that he finds difficulty in getting engaged because of his face. I've felt guilty ever since I called it a catastrophe. Of course it *is*; but I said it to be funny, which was cruel. And we deserve to punish ourselves by keeping the poor wretch a few days, or more, if he's good."

"I thought you wanted a becoming dragoman?" I reminded her.

"Oh, that was just our silliness. I *do* like good-looking people, I must say. But what *does* it matter whether a brown person is handsome or homely, when you come to think of it? Besides, we can have another dragoman, too, for ornament, if we run across a very picturesque one."

I laughed. "But you can't go up the Nile on a boat with a drove of private dragomans, you know!"

"I *don't* know, Lord Ernest. And why don't you call them dragomen? You make them sound as if they were some kind of animal."

"Dragomans is the plural," I persisted.

"Well, I shall call them dragomen. And if this poor thing can't get any one else to drag, he *shall* drag us up the Nile, if he's as intelligent in his ways as he is in that one eye, which is so like a hard-boiled egg. You see, Lord Ernest, we're going to have a boat of our own. A steam dahabeah is what we want, so we won't be at the mercy of the wind. And we can have all the dragomen we choose, can't we?"

"I suppose you can fill up your cabins with them," I agreed, because I felt that the Gilded Rose wished me to argue the point, and that if I did I should be worsted. As I should not be on board the dahabeah in question, it would not matter to me personally if the boat were entirely manned by dragomans. Except that there would in that case probably be a collision, and I should not be near to save Biddy—and incidentally the girl Biddy wished me to marry.

After that, we went on eating our dinner and talking of Egypt, Miss Guest doing all the listening, as usual. When we had finished, we kept our places because we had no others. Cleopatra was curious about my friend's failure to arrive, but I put her off with vaguenesses; and said to myself that, for Anthony's sake, it was well that mysterious business had kept him in Cairo. Still, I wondered what the business was: why he would be unable to see me that night: and what were the "many things" he had to tell.

CHAPTER IV

A MAN IN A GREEN TURBAN

I shall never know for certain whether or not our future was entirely shaped by Monny's resolve to breakfast on the terrace of Shepheard's Hotel next morning.

A great many remarkable things have happened on that historic site. Napoleon made the place his headquarters. General Klèber was murdered in the garden. Half the most important people in the world have had tea on the terrace: but, according to a German waiter, there was one deed yet undone. Nobody had ever ordered breakfast out of doors.

Of course, Monny got what she wanted. Not by storming, not by putting on power-of-wealth airs, but simply by turning bright pink and looking large-eyed. At once that waiter rushed off, and fetched other waiters; and almost before the invited guests knew what to expect, two tables had been fitted together, covered with white, adorned with fresh roses, and set forth with cups and saucers. I was the one man invited, and I felt like an actor called to play a new part in an old scene, a scene vaguely, excitingly familiar. Could I possibly be remembering it, I asked myself, or was my impression but the result of a life-long debauch of Egyptian photographs? Anyhow, there was the impression, with a thrill in it; and I felt that I ought to be handsomer, more romantic, altogether more vivid, if I were to live up to the moving picture. It seemed as if nothing would be too extraordinary to do, if I wanted to match my surroundings. I thought, even if I burst into a passionate Arab love-song and proposed to Monny across the table, it would be quite the right note. But somehow I didn't feel inclined to propose. It was enough to admire her over the rim of a coffee cup. In her white tussore (I heard Biddy call it tussore) and drooping, garden-type of hat, she was a different girl from the girl of the ship. She had been a winter girl in white fur, then. Now she was a summer girl, and a radiant vision, twice as pretty as before, especially in this Oriental frame; still I was waiting to see myself fall in love with her, much in the same way that Biddy was waiting. And there was that Oriental frame! It belonged to my past, and perhaps Monny Gilder didn't belong even to my future, so it was excusable if I thought of it more than of her.

It was hardly nine o'clock, but already the wonderful coloured cinema show of Cairo daily life had begun to flash and flicker past the terrace of Shepheard's, where East and West meet and mingle more sensationally than anywhere in Egypt. Nobody save ourselves had dared suggest breakfast; but travellers were pouring into the hotel, and pouring out. Pretty women and plain women were sitting at the little wicker tables to read letters, or discuss plans for the day with each other or their dragomans. Officers in khaki came and talked to them about golf and gymkhanas. Down on the pavement, close under the balustrade, crowded young and old Egyptian men with dark faces and wonderful eyes or no eyes at all, struggling to sell painted post-cards, strings of blue-gray mummy beads; necklaces of cornelian and great lumps of amber; fans, perfumes, sample sticks of smoking incense, toy camels cleverly made of jute; fly whisks from the Sudan with handles of beads and dangling shells; scarab rings and brooches; cheap, gay jewellery, scarfs from Asiut, white, black, pale green and purple, glittering like miniature cataracts of silver, as brown arms held them up. Darting Arab urchins hawked tame ichneumons, or shouted newspapers for sale—English, American, Greek, French, German, Italian, and Turkish. Copper-tinted, classic-featured youths in white had golden crowns of bananas round their turbans; withered patriarchs in blue galabeahs offered oranges, or immense bunches of mixed flowers, fresh and fragrant as the morning; or baskets of strawberries red and bright as rubies. Dignified Arabs stalked by, bearing on nobly poised heads pots of growing rose-bushes or arum lilies, or azaleas. Jet-black giants, wound in rainbow-striped cottons, clanked brass saucers like cymbals, advertising the sweet drinks in their glass jars, while memory whispered in my ears the Arab name "sherbétly." Across the street, clear silver-gold sunshine of winter in Egypt shone on precious stones, on carved ivories, silver anklets, Persian rugs, and embroideries, brilliant as hummingbirds' wings, all displayed in the windows of shops where dark eyes looked out eagerly for buyers. Everything was for sale, for sale to the strangers! The whole clamouring city seemed to consist of one vast, concentrated desire on the part of brown people to sell things to fair people. They shouted and wheedled and besought on the sidewalks; and the roadway between was a wide river of colour and life. Motor cars with Arab chauffeurs carried rich Turks to business, or to an audience of State. Now and then a face of ivory glimmered through a gauzy veil and eyes of ink and diamonds shot starry glances from passing carriage windows. Erect English women drove high dog-carts. Gordon Highlanders swung along in the kilt, more at home in Cairo then in Edinburgh, the droning of their pipes as Oriental as the drone of a räita, or the beat of tom-toms. A wedding party with a hidden bride in a yellow chariot, met a funeral, and yashmaked faces peeped from curtained windows, in one procession, to stare at the wailing, marching men of the other, and to shrink back hastily from the sight of the coffin. Tangled it would seem inextricably with streams of traffic, surging both ways, moved the "ships of the desert," loaded with emerald-green bersím; long, lilting necks, and calm, mysterious eyes of camels high above the cloaked heads of striding Bedouins, heads of defiant Arab prisoners, chained and handcuffed to each other; heads of blue-eyed water buffaloes, and heads of trim white, tasselled donkeys.

None of us talked very much, as we sat at the breakfast table: the novelty and wonder of the scene made the actors forget their words: and if we had been able to talk, we could not have appreciated each other's rhapsodies, over the shoutings of men who wanted us to buy their wares, and harangues of dragomans who wished, as Monny said, to "drag" us. These latter, especially, were persistent, and Bedr the One Eyed, having been forbidden to come till ten o'clock, was not on the spot to give protection. Our method at first was to appear oblivious, but presently in my wickedest Arabic, I would have ordered the troop away if Monny had not interfered.

"Don't!" she said, "they're part of the picture. Besides, they've more right here than we have. It's their country, not ours. And they're so interesting—most of them. That tall man over there, for instance, with the green turban. He's the only one who hasn't opened his mouth. Just to show him that virtue's its own reward, I'm going to engage him. Will you call him to us, please, Lord Ernest?"

Sitting as I sat, I could not see the person indicated. "What do you want him for, Miss Gilder?" I obeyed temptation, and asked.

"Why, to be a dragoman, of course," she explained. "That's what he's for. I told you, I'd have a picturesque one for ornament. This creature's a perfect specimen."

I stood up reluctantly, and looked down over the balustrade. "A man with a green turban?" I repeated. "But that means he's a Hadji, who's been to Mecca and back. I never heard of a dragoman—"

I stopped short in my argument. My eyes had found the man with the green turban.

He stood at some distance behind the pavement-merchants and self-advertising dragomans who pressed against the railing. In his long galabeah of Sudan silk, ashes of roses in colour, he was tall and straight as a palm, gravely dignified with his folded arms and the haughty remoteness of his expression. Dark and silent, half-disdainful, half-amused, he was like a prince compared with his humbler brethren; but there was another resemblance more relevant and intimate which cut my sentence short.

"By Jove," I thought, "how like he is to Anthony Fenton!"

He was looking, not at me, but at Miss Gilder, quite respectfully yet hypnotically, as if by way of an experiment he had been willing her to find and single out the one motionless figure, the one person whose tongue had not called attention to himself.

Yes, I thought again, he was an Arab copy of Anthony, but more as Anthony had been years ago before his moustache grew, than as Anthony had become in late years. Still, there were the aquiline features, the long, rather sad eyes shaded with thick, straight lashes, the eyebrows raised at the bridge of the thin nose, then sloping steeply down toward the temples; the slight working of muscles in the cheeks; the peculiarly charming mouth which could be irresistible in a smile, the stern, contradictory chin marring by its prominence the otherwise perfect oval of the face. I wondered if Anthony had as noble a throat as this collarless galabeah left uncovered, reminding myself that I could not at all recall Anthony's throat. Then, as the sombre eyes turned to me, drawn perhaps by my stare, I was stunned, flabbergasted, what you will, by realizing that Anthony himself was looking at me from under the green turban.

The dark face was blankly expressionless. He might have been gazing through my head. His eyes neither twinkled with fun nor sent a message of warning; but somehow I knew that he saw me, that he had been watching me for a long time. "You see the one I mean, don't you?" asked Monny. "Well, that's the one I want. I'll take *him*."

She spoke as if she were selecting a horse at a horse show.

Anthony had brought this on himself, but I was not angry with Anthony. I was angry with the girl for putting her finger into our pie.

"That's not a dragoman," I assured her. "If he were, he'd come and bawl out his accomplishments, as the others do. He's a very different sort of chap."

"That's why I want him," said Monny. "And if he isn't a dragoman, he'll jump at being one if I offer to pay him enough. He's an Egyptian, anyhow, by his clothes, or a Bedouin or something—although he isn't as dark as the rest of these men. I suppose he must know a little about his own city and country."

"It doesn't follow he'd tell travellers about them for money," said I. "He looks to me a man of good birth and distinction in old fashioned dress. Why he's lingering on the pavement in front of this hotel I can't explain, but I'm certain he isn't touting. Probably he's waiting for a friend."

"He's the best looking Arab we've seen yet," remarked Mrs. East. "Like my idea of an Egyptian gentleman."

"Pooh!" said Monny. "Just test him, Lord Ernest."

"Sorry, but I can't do it," I answered, with a firmness which ought to have been tried on her long ago. "And I wouldn't discuss him in such a loud tone of voice. He may understand English."

"We have to yell to hear ourselves speak over all this row," Biddy apologized for her darling; but she need not have troubled herself. Miss Gilder had been deaf to my implied reproach.

"I'm glad I'm an American girl," she said. "When I want things I want them so dreadfully I just go for them, and surprise them so much that I get them before they know where they are. Now I'm going for this dragoman."

"He's not a drag—" I persisted, but she cut me short.

"I bet you my hat he will be one! What will you bet that he won't, Lord Ernest?"

"I'll bet you his green turban," said I.

"How can you get it?"

"As easily as you can get him," I retorted. "It's a safe bet."

Monny looked excited, but firm. Luckily, as she does it so often, it's becoming to her to look firm. (I have noticed that it's not becoming to most girls. It squares their jaws and makes their eyes snap.) But the spoiled daughter of the dead Cannon King at her worst, merely looks pathetically earnest and Minerva-like. This, I suppose, is one of the "little ways" she has acquired, since she gave up kicking and screaming people into submission. As Biddy says, the girl can be charming not only when she wants to be, but quite often when she doesn't.

The man with the green turban was no longer engaged in hypnotizing. He had retired within himself, and appeared oblivious to the outer world. Yet nobody jostled the tall, straight figure which stood with folded arms, lightly leaning against a tree. The colour of his turban was sacred in the eyes of the crowd; and when Miss Gilder, leaning over the terrace railing beckoned him, surprise rather than jealousy showed on the faces of the unwanted dragomans. As for the wearer of the turban, he did what I expected and wished him to do: paid not the slightest attention to the gesture. Whatever the motive for his masquerade, it was not to attract anything feminine.

I smiled sardonically. "That's a nice hat you've got on, Miss Gilder," I remarked.

"Do you collect girls' hats?" she asked sweetly. "But mine isn't eligible yet for your collection. Let me see, what did you say he was? Oh, a Hadji!" And she shrilled forth sweetly, her voice sounding young and clear, "Hadji! Hadji! Effendi! Venez ici, s'il vous plait. Please come here."

I could have been knocked flat by a blow of the smallest, cheapest ostrich feather in the hands of any street-merchant. For he came. Anthony came! Not to look meekly up from the pavement below the railing, but to ascend the steps of the terrace, and advance with grave dignity toward our table. Within a yard of us he stopped, giving to me, not to Miss Gilder, the beautiful Arab salute, a touch on forehead and heart.

"You devil!" I was saying to myself. "So you walk into this trap, do you, and calmly trust me to get you out. Serve you right if I don't move hand or foot." And I almost made up my mind that I wouldn't. But I was interested. I wanted intensely to know what the dickens Anthony was up to, and whether he would have been up to it if he'd known the sort of young woman he had to deal with.

"It was I who called to you, not this gentleman," said Monny, when she found that Green Turban did not look at her. "Do you speak French or English a little?"

"A little of both. But I choose French when talking to Americans," replied Anthony Fenton, with astounding impertinence, in the preferred language. "I do not know you, Madame. But I do know this gentleman."

Good heavens! What next? He acknowledged me! What was I to do now? What did the impudent fellow want me to do? Evidently he was trying an experiment. Anthony is great on experiments, and always has been. But this

IT HAPPENED IN EGYPT | 41

was a bomb. I thought he wanted to see if I could catch it on the fly, and drop it into water before it had time to explode.

"Why didn't you tell us, Lord Ernest?" asked Monny, with a flash in her gray eyes. "I thought you hadn't been in Egypt since you were a child."

"I haven't, and I didn't recognize him at first," I answered, trying for the coolness which Anthony dared to count upon.

"You remember me now?" he inquired politely.

"I—er—yes," I replied, also in French. "Your face is familiar, though you've changed, I think, since—er—since you were in England. It must have been there—yes, of course. You were on a diplomatic mission. But your name—"

"You may have known me as Ahmed Antoun," said the wretch, not dreaming of that slip he had made.

Cleopatra, who has little French, nevertheless started, and fixed upon the face under the turban a stare of feverish interest. Brigit and the unobtrusive lady with the slanting eyes both showed such symptoms of surprise as must too late have warned Fenton that he had missed his footing, skating on thin ice.

"Antoun!" exclaimed Mrs. East. "Why, that's what you said you called your friend Captain Fenton."

I glanced at Anthony. His profile had no more expression than that of an Indian on an American penny, and, indeed, rather resembled it. If he were blaming me for letting anything out, I had a right to blame him for letting himself in. He was silent as well as expressionless. He left it all to me—diplomat or duffer.

"'Antoun Effendi' was the nickname my friend Fenton got at school," I explained to Cleopatra, "because it sounded a bit like his own name, and because he had—er—because he had associations with Egypt. He was proud of them and is still. But Antoun is a name often heard here. And every man who isn't a Bey or a Prince, or a Sheikh, is an Effendi. I quite remember you now," I hurried on, turning to Anthony once more. "You are Hadji as well as Effendi."

"I have the right to call myself so, if I choose," he admitted. "I am pleased to meet you again. I was waiting for a friend when you beckoned. If you did not recognize my face at first, may I ask what it was you wanted of me?"

There was no limit, then, to his audacity. He had not learned his lesson yet, after all, it would seem.

Monny could not bear tamely to lose her hat, though she must have felt her hatpins trembling in the balance. "I told you before," she repeated, "that it was I who beckoned you." He looked at her, without speaking; and somehow the green turban and the long straight gown, by adding to his dignity, added also to his remote air of cold politeness. How could she go on? Had she the cheek to go on? She had; but the cheek was flushed with embarrassment.

"I—er—I am anxious for a guide, some one who knows Egypt well, and several languages," she desperately blurted out, looking like a half-frightened, half-defiant child. "I thought——"

"There are plenty of dragomans, Madame," Green Turban reminded her. "I can recommend you several."

"I don't want a regular dragoman," she said. "And I'm not 'Madame.' I am Miss Gilder."

"Indeed?" Chilling indifference in the tone. (Monny's hat was practically mine. I thought I should rather value it.)

"Yes. But of course that can't matter to you."

"No. It cannot, Mademoiselle."

"What I want to say, is this. You're a Hadji, which means you've been to Mecca; Lord Ernest Borrow's just told us. So you must be very intelligent. Are you in business?"

"I am interested in excavations."

"Oh! And are you allowed to make them yourself?"

"Not always."

I glanced at him quickly, wondering if he meant that answer more for me than for the girl. But his face told nothing.

"Would you be able to, if you were rich enough?"

"It is possible." "Well, I'd be willing to give you a big salary for showing us about Cairo, and perhaps going up the Nile."

"You do not know who I am, Mademoiselle. Ask your friend Lord Ernest Borrow. Perhaps he may remember something about my circumstances now he has recalled my face."

I was honestly not sure whether this were further deviltry, or an appeal for help. In any case, I thought it time for the scene to end. "I told you," I said to Monny in English, "that he was a man of importance, not at all the sort of person you could expect to engage for a guide. You must see now that he's a gentleman. And a—a—an Egyptian gentleman is just the same as any other."

"Surely not quite!" she answered in the same language, and I realized my foolish mistake in using it, as if I meant her to understand that Antoun Effendi knew it too little to catch our secrets.

"An Egyptian man can't have the same feelings as a European? Why, for hundreds and hundreds of years they've been an enslaved race, like our black people at home. We'd never think of calling even the fairest quadroon man a gentleman, though he might be wonderfully good looking and nice mannered."

Literally, I was frightened. Anthony Fenton is fiercely devoted to the memory of the beautiful princess-mother, for love of whom his father's career was ruined. *Her* mother was a Sicilian woman, and her father was half Greek, so there is little enough Egyptian blood, after all, in the veins of General Fenton's son. He is proud of what there is—proud, because of his mother's fatal charm, and the romance of her story (it was on the eve of her wedding with a cousin of the Sultan that the famous soldier Charles Fenton ran away with Princess Lalla and married her in Sicily): but he is sensitive, too, because, great name as Charles Fenton had made in Egypt, he was asked to resign his commission on account of the escapade. Anthony, sent to England to a public school, had fought bigger boys than himself, who, in a certain tone, had sneeringly called him "Egyptian." I imagined now that through the dark stain on his face I could see him turn pale with rage. He thought, perhaps, that the American beauty was revenging herself for his impertinence, and maybe he was right, but that did not excuse her.

"Be careful, Miss Gilder!" I warned the girl. "This man understands English better than you think. He comes of a princely family and he's got only to put out his hand to claim a fortune—"

"You seem to remember all about me now, Lord Ernest," broke in Fenton, looking dangerous.

"Yes," I said. "It comes back to me. You must forgive Miss Gilder."

"There is nothing to forgive," he caught me up. "I am not a dragoman, to be sure, but I'm enough of an Egyptian to have a price for anything I do. I may put myself at this lady's service if she will pay my price, though I'm not a servant and can't accept wages, even for the sake of pursuing my excavations!"

He continued to speak in French, lest my companions' suspicions should be further roused by the English of an Englishman; and Monny, pale after her blush, answered in neat, schoolgirl French, with a pretty American, accent. "What's the price you wish to name?" she inquired, looking a little afraid of him and ashamed of herself, now that talk of princes and fortunes was bandied about. "Of course," she went on, when he did not answer at once, "if I'd known—all this, I shouldn't have asked you to be a dragoman. At least, perhaps I shouldn't. Anyhow, I shouldn't have made a bet—"

"A bet that I would have a 'price,' Mademoiselle? Then you may win your bet, for I've just told you; I have a price. But I think it unlikely you would be willing to pay it."

"Good heavens, is he going to try and marry the girl?" I asked myself. It would be the last thing to expect of Anthony Fenton. However, he had already done the last but one; the thing I had bet his green turban he would not do. After all, he was a man, and a reckless man, as he had proved on more than one wild occasion. He was in a strange mood, capable of anything; and the Gilded Rose could never have been prettier in her life than at this minute. She had made him furious, and I had imagined that his acceptance of her overtures was the beginning of some scheme of punishment. Now I was almost sure I had been right, yet I could not guess what he would be at. Neither could Monny. But here was the dangerously picturesque Arab who "must be a prince or something," as Cleopatra had expressed it. And he was even more dangerous than picturesque.

"You—you said you wouldn't take wages," she stammered (I enjoyed hearing the self-willed young person stammer): "so I can't understand what you mean. But even though you are all those things Lord Ernest says you are, your price can't be so terribly high as to be beyond my power to pay—if I choose to pay."

"First, Mademoiselle, I must decide whether I choose to be paid."

"Oh!" Monny exclaimed, taken aback. "I thought it was a question of price."

"Not only that. 'I *may* put myself at the lady's service—for a price,' was what I said. I didn't say, 'I will.' I shall not be able to tell you until to-night." The patronizing tone in which Anthony spoke this sentence was worth to me everything I had gone through in the last half hour.

"But—I want to settle things this morning or—not at all," said Monny, reverting to type: that of the spoiled child.

"I am sorry," replied the man of the green turban. "In that case, it must be not at all." And he made as if to go.

The Gilded Girl could not bear this. I and the others would see that she was fallible; that there were things she wanted which she could not get. "Why can't you tell me now what your price is?" she persisted.

"Because, Mademoiselle, I may not need to tell you ever. It depends partly on another than myself." He threw a quick glance at me. "I expect to meet that other at Abdullahi's Café in an hour from now at latest. Everything will depend on the interview. In any case, I will let you know to-night what I can do."

"I may not be in," said Monny. "But if I'm out, you can leave a note."

"If I must refuse to serve you, yes, I can leave a note. If I am to accept, I must see you in person. Should you be out, I'll take it for granted that you have changed your mind and do not want"—he smiled faintly for the first time—"so expensive a guide."

Monny hesitated. "I am not stingy. I'll stay at home this evening," she volunteered at last.

"Bravo Petruchio!" I said under my breath. But if Biddy's plot were to succeed, it was *my* business to play the part of Petruchio to this Katherine. Let the masquerading prince find a Desdemona who would suit his Othello!

CHAPTER V

THE CAFÉ OF ABDULLAH

"Well—you got away from them all right?" began the man with the green turban when, according to his roundabout instructions, I met him an hour later at the café he had named, one of the principal resorts of Cairo, where Europeans can consort with natives without attracting remark.

"The real dragoman came and took them off my hands—at least the realer one than you—a dreadful creature with a game eye, who murdered your messenger last night, and gave me your letter and induced the ladies to engage him on the strength of it. No wonder they want a 'looker' to take the taste of him out of their mouths. And you certainly are a 'looker' in that get-up. Now kindly tell me all about it, and everything else."

"That's what I'm here for," said Anthony, running a match-box to earth in some mysterious Arab pocket. "But hold on, Duffer. Something you said just then may be important. Is it true that my messenger didn't give you the letter?"

"If you'd hung about Shepheard's Hotel ten minutes longer, you'd have seen the fellow who did give it. Bedr el Gemály he calls himself—Armenian Mussulman, a sickening combination, and an awful brute to look at—said your messenger was taken suddenly ill; pretends to be a dragoman."

"What is he like?"

"Rather like a partially decayed but decently dressed goat."

"Don't rot. This may be serious."

I described Bedr el Gemály as best I could, feature by feature. When I had polished them off, Anthony shook his green-turbaned head. "No portrait of him in my rogues' gallery. Just now, I'm sensitive about spies—over-sensitive rather. Of course, you've spotted my game?"

"I confess I was conceited enough to think you'd given yourself all this trouble with the costumier in order to take a rise out of me. But when you speak of spies, I begin to put two and two together—your business in Cairo—the powers that be, keeping you from me last night, etc. I suppose it's an official job, this fancy dress affair?"

"Yes. In my own capacity, I'm not in Cairo. I turned up day before yesterday, jolly glad to get back from Adrianople—though it was good fun there, I can tell you, for a while; and I looked forward to wallowing no end in the alleged delights of civilization. I reported myself, and all seemed well. I took a room at Shepheard's where you and I had arranged to meet, and when I'd scrubbed, I strolled over to the Turf Club to see what the gay world would have to say to a fellow in disgrace."

"Only silly asses swallowed that newspaper spoof! Every one in London who knows anything about you was betting his boots that the story had been spread on purpose to save our face with Turkey." I couldn't resist interrupting his narrative to this extent. But Anthony merely smiled, and watched a long-lived smokering settle like a halo over the head of an Arab at the nearest table. He was not giving away official secrets, but I was sure and always had been sure that he was a martyr, not a rebel, in the matter of the Balkan incident, just closed. What the public were led to suppose was this: that Captain Fenton had asked for two months' leave from regimental duty at Khartum, in order to spend the time with a relative who was seriously ill in Constantinople. That instead of remaining at his relative's bedside, he had used his leave for a dash to the Balkans. That this indiscretion might have been kept a secret had he not capped it with another: a flight with a Greek officer in an army aeroplane which had ended by crashing down in the midst of a Turkish encampment.

What I and friends who knew him best supposed, was that the "leave" had been a pretext—that Fenton had been sent on a secret mission of some sort—and that he was bound to take the blame if anything went wrong. Aeroplanes have the habits of other fierce, untamed animals: they won't always obey their trainers. Thus Anthony and his plan had both been upset. (Or had it really been premeditated that he should fall into that camp?) The remainder of his "leave" was cancelled, in punishment, and he had been "recalled" to Egypt, to be scolded in Cairo before proceeding to Khartum.

"Queer how many silly asses one knows!" Anthony said. "Still, considering what a mess I seem to have made of things, fellows were jolly kind, at the Turf Club. Nobody cut me, and only a few let me alone. Maybe there'd have been still fewer if there hadn't been a hero present who claimed attention: an American chap, Jack Dennis, who knows Miss Gilder and was telling the good news that she was on her way to Egypt. He called her the Gilded Rose and said it was going to be a good flower season in Cairo and up the Nile. All the men with one exception seemed to have heard a lot about her and to find her an interesting subject, and to want Dennis to introduce them."

"I can guess the 'one exception'!" said I.

"Can you? Well, I don't read newspaper gossip about heiresses. Thank heaven, I've something better to do with my time. But the others wanted to meet her, or pretended to, perhaps to chaff Dennis, rather a cocky youth, though I oughtn't to say so, as he was nice to me, according to his lights. He got Sam Blake to introduce us, when he happened to hear my name, and went out of his way to pay me compliments, which I daresay he thought I'd like. When there was a lull in the discussion of what could be done to make Miss Gilder enjoy herself in Egypt—chaps suggesting trips in their motor cars or on their camels and a lot of rot, Dennis remarked that I was the only man who hadn't chipped into the conversation. And hadn't I any ideas for entertaining the Golden Girl? Naturally I said that I didn't know who she was and had never heard of her, and even if I had, entertaining girls wasn't in my line. They all roared, and Dennis wouldn't believe at first that I didn't know of such an important person's existence; but the other men rotted a bit, and described me to him according to their notions of me. So he let me alone on the subject; and having plenty of other things to think of, I forgot all about it till the lady in question introduced herself this morning. Then—well, it struck me as rather amusing at first that I, the only one in the crowd who hadn't made plans to get at her, should have her trying to get at me. That was partly why I came up on the terrace when she beckoned."

"Partly? For purely intellectual reasons I'm curious to know the rest. I suppose it had nothing to do with her looks?"

"As it happened, my cynical friend, it hadn't. I've got eyes in my head and I could see she was pretty, very pretty, though not my ideal type at all. That little sprite of a woman in fawn colour, the one with green eyes and a lot of black lashes, is more what I'd fall in love with if I were frivolous. But apart from the funny side of my meeting with Miss Golder, or Gilder, it popped into my head that I might make her a victim in a certain cause. Don't ask me to explain yet, because there are a lot of things that have got to be explained first, or you couldn't understand. You were right, of course, when you thought I'd stationed myself in front of Shepheard's to take a rise out of you. I gave up my room there yesterday, for reasons I'll tell you. But I knew you'd be in the hotel, and that you'd be bound to show yourself on the terrace, in order to go out. I wanted to see if you'd recognize me, and to have a little fun with you if you didn't. By the way, I'm not pleased that you did. It's a poor compliment to my make-up, which I may tell you has been warmly praised in high quarters!" "Well, you see," I apologized, "I knew you were a nailer at that sort of thing, or you would never have got to Mecca, and earned your green turban. I knew you'd been pretty often called upon to disguise yourself and go about among the natives for one thing or another. And besides, we were chums before you had the shadow of a moustache, so I have an advantage over the other Sherlock Holmeses! But even as it was, I couldn't be sure at first. You must have got some fun out of my expression."

"I did. I took revenge on you for recognizing me by tormenting you as far as I dared. Dear old boy, I knew you'd see me through to the end, bitter or sweet!"

"Which was it?" I inquired.

"Mixed. The girl riled me, rather, so much so that I definitely decided it would be fair play to make use of her as a cat's-paw. But it depends on you, whether she's to lose or win her bet."

"If she loses, I get her hat. If she wins, I've engaged myself to procure for her—your green turban."

"Did you think you could, without my consent?"

"No. I distinctly thought I couldn't. But I would have been willing to bet the head in the turban, served up on a charger, so sure I was that you'd refuse to come near her. I thought I knew you *au fond*, you see."

"You do. I haven't changed. But—circumstances have changed. And that brings me near to the stage of this business which concerns you and me. First, before I go further though, I'll tell you a part of the reason why I'm sporting the green turban. There's been the dickens to pay here, about a new street that had to be made; an immensely important and necessary street. Well, they couldn't make it, because the tomb of a popular saint or sheikh was in the way. To move the body or even disturb a saint's tomb would mean no end of a row. You remember or have read enough about Mohammedans to know that. What to do, was the question. Nobody'd been able to answer it till yesterday, when the sight of me reminded them of a trick or two I'd brought off some time ago, by disguising myself and hanging about the cafés. They wanted me to try it again. Consequently Captain A. Fenton received a telegram and had to leave Cairo at once on business. He gave up his room at Shepheard's, and the only regrettable thing to the official mind is, that the fellow'd been seen about town even for an hour. However, it couldn't be helped. Luckily Ahmed Antoun is not unknown in Cairo cafés. He's made quite an impression upon the public on several occasions since his pilgrimage to Mecca, two years ago. And since yesterday afternoon, he's been drinking enough coffee to give him jaundice, while casually spreading the story of a dream he had. Our friend the Hadji related how he had slept in the mosque of Ibn Tulun after the noon hour, and dreamed of the sheikh whose tomb is so inconveniently placed. In the dream, the saint clamoured to have his tomb moved on account of a bad smell of drainage which he considers an insult to his own memory. Also dogs have taken to howling round his resting-place at night, and you know that to the true believer a dog is an unclean animal. Except for hunting purposes, or watch-dogging in various branches, good Mohammedans class dogs and Christians together in their mind. Well, already the Hadji's dream is working like yeast. The news of it is being carried from one café to another; and I hope that a few more nights' work will do the trick. The votaries of the saint will get up a petition to have his body moved. When it has found another abode, the making of the new thoroughfare will be suggested."

"Very neat! I see it all, except the connection with Miss Gilder. What has your saint got to do with her?"

"Very little, I should say, by the look in her eyes. But though a green turban's as good as an heirloom, and extorts respect wherever it goes, even a Hadji may have jealous detractors. I have mine. Another green turban in this town, whose genuineness is doubted for some obscure reason or other, has sneered at my dream."

"I say! That sounds as if you might be in danger. If one man suspects you to-day, to-morrow————"

"Oh, it's only the dream he suspects—at present. I know all the little prayer tricks so well, and I've invented my own history so ingeniously, with a *patois* to match my province, that I shall get through this incident as I have through others of the sort. There's only one hole in my jebbah. Last night, when my rival sprang a sudden question as to what I was doing in Cairo (I'm supposed to be a Luxor man), on the spur of the moment I replied that I was acting as dragoman to a rich family of tourists. On that, the brute inquired with honeyed accents where they were staying. I said Shepheard's, because I expected you to be there, and thought if I were followed, you might be useful as a dummy."

"Ah, that's where Miss Gilder comes in? A gilded gingerbread lamb, ready for the sacrifice. Why didn't you accept her offer at once, as she seemed so providential?" "I'm coming to that. It sounds complicated, but it isn't. For one thing, though, it may be well to wait and find out a little more about that goat-eyed Armenian of yours."

"He isn't mine. He's—".

"I want to know for certain whose he is. If he has anything to do with my rival Hadji, there's more venom and wit inside that green turban than I've given it credit for. Is there a reason, by the way, except their riches, why one should want to 'get at' a member of the American party?"

"By Jove!" said I, as if I had been pinched—for there was a sharp nip in the thought Anthony's question jabbed into my mind. I had disliked and distrusted Bedr el Gemály, but I had associated my distaste for him with Fenton's affairs. It had not occurred to me that Biddy's fears meant more than a nervous woman's vague forebodings. During the few hideous years of hide-and-seek she had passed in trying to protect the traitor, Richard O'Brien, she had no doubt had real enough reason to dread a spy in every stranger; but I had cheerfully advised her "not to be morbid" when she spoke of herself as a dangerous companion, or stopped me with a gasp in the midst of what seemed an innocent question about her stepdaughter. Could it be possible that her alarms might after all be justified, and that the powerful association betrayed by O'Brien would visit his sins on his widow and daughter? That American accent of Gemály's! He admitted having been in New York. Of course, he had made acquaintances there. My thoughts flashed back to the meeting at the railway train. Could the fellow have found out in advance that I was with Mrs. O'Brien, [alias Jones] and her friends? It seemed as if such knowledge could have reached land ahead of us only by miracle. But there was always Marconi. Perhaps news of Miss Gilder had been sent by wireless to Alexandria, with our humbler names starred as satellites of that bright planet. If this were so, Bedr, instructed from afar to watch Richard O'Brien's widow, might easily have been clever enough to suborn a messenger waiting for one Ernest Borrow.

"What are you mumbling about?" Anthony wanted to know, when I forgot to answer. "Have I put some idea that you don't like into your head?"

"I was turning your question over in it," I explained, "and wondering what to answer. Of course, Miss Gilder's rather important, and I believe her father's obsession used to be when she was a child, that she'd be kidnapped for ransom. The 'little sprite of a woman' you admire so much, knew the Gilders in those days. She says that the unfortunate baby used to be dragged about in a kind of caged perambulator, and that some of her nurses were female detectives in disguise, with revolvers under their white aprons. No wonder the girl revels in emancipation and travel! I should think, now she's grown up to twenty-one years and five foot eight or nine of height, without being kidnapped, there's not much danger so long as she keeps in the boundaries of civilization. Still, one never knows, in such a queer world as ours, where newspapers live on happenings we'd laugh to scorn if they came out of novel writers' brains."

"That's the only incentive you can suggest for spying, unconnected with my affairs?"

I hesitated, for Biddy's secret was not my secret, and it seemed that I had no right to pass it on, even to my best friend. I must ask Biddy's permission before telling Fenton that Mrs. Jones was the widow of the informer Richard O'Brien; that she feared over-subtlety on the part of the enemy might confuse her girl travelling companion with Esmé O'Brien, hidden in a convent school near Monaco. "It's just credible that there may be other incentives," I said. "But I must confess, I'd rather believe that Armenian spies were on the track of Ahmed Antoun, who can take care of himself, than after poor Miss Gilder or—any of her party."

"What's the name of the laughing sprite?" suddenly asked Fenton.

"Mrs.—er—Jones. Brigit Jones."

"Where's her husband?"

"In his grave."

"Oh! Well, his widow looks ready to bubble over with the joy of life, so I suppose we can't associate spies or anything shady with her? That's too much to hope for?"

"Why to 'hope' for?"

"It would make her too interesting."

"Look here, my dear fellow, you can't have them both!"

The dark eyes of Antoun lit with a spark of surprise and laughter. "I don't want either, thanks. I admire flowers, but I never gather them. I leave them growing. However, you might tell me which one you want for your own buttonhole?" "Really, I don't know," I mumbled, taken aback. "All I do know is, it's not likely I can get either."

Anthony stared at me with a curious expression, then abruptly changed the subject. "You've heard of Sir Marcus Lark?" he asked.

"Of course," said I, surprised at this question sandwiched into our affairs. Sir Marcus Lark is a man who has had his finger in many pies, but I didn't see how he could poke one into ours. Everybody knows Sir M. A. Lark, given a baronetcy by the Radicals some years ago in return for services to the party—starting and running a newspaper which must have cost him fifty thousand pounds before it began to pay. He has financed theatres, and vegetarian restaurants; he owns cocoa plantations and factories, and a garden city; he has a racing yacht which once beat the German Emperor's; he owns two hotels; he has written a book of travel; his name as a director is sought by financial companies; he has lent money to a distressed South American government in the making; and though the success of his enterprises has sometimes hung in the balance for months or years, his wonderful luck seems invariably to triumph in the end; so much so, that "Lark's Luck" has become a well-known heading for newspaper columns, in the middle of which his photograph is inset. At the mention of his name, the oft-seen picture rose before my eyes—a big man, anywhere between thirty-six and fifty—good head, large forehead, curly hair, kind eyes, pugnacious nose, conceited smile under waxed moustache, heavy jaw, unconquerable chin, and prize-fighter's neck and shoulders. "What has Sir Marcus Lark to do with us?" "He's in Egypt—in Cairo just now; and—he's got our mountain."

"Good heavens!" I stared blankly at Anthony, seeing not his dark face under the green turban, but that everlasting, ever-smiling newspaper block portrait. Down toppled our castle in the air, Anthony's and mine—the shining castle which had been the lodestone of my journey to Egypt, the secret hope and romance of our two lives, for all those months since Anthony first read the Ferlini papers and began negotiations with the Egyptian Government.

"It's all up then," I said, when I felt that I could speak without betraying palsy of the jaw. "We're done!"

"I'm not sure of that," Fenton answered. "If I had been, I shouldn't have broken the news so brutally. It's on the cards that we may be able to bring the thing off yet."

"But how, if that bounder has got the place for himself? He must have found out the truth about it somehow, or he wouldn't have bothered. And if he knows what we know—or think we know—he certainly won't give up to us what he's grabbed for himself. A beastly shame we should have been let in like this, after being given to understand that it would be all right."

"Lark must have had a pull of some sort, I haven't learned what; but I will. The one hope is, that he hasn't stumbled onto the secret."

"What! You think he hit on our pitch by a mere coincidence—an accident?"

"No. There's not a shadow of doubt that he had a special motive for wanting *our* mountain and no other." "Have you formed an idea what the motive is, if not the same as ours?"

"I've heard his version from his own lips. It's rather astounding. And I want you to hear it from him, too."

"You've met him!"

"Yesterday at Shepheard's, before I went in for this dressing-up business. Lark heard I had wired for a room at the hotel, and was lying in wait for me on the terrace when I got back from the Agency. We had a talk. I'd heard just before, the news about the mountain. But he explained. Now he wants to see you. He's got something special to say, and I've made an appointment for you with him at two o'clock."

CHAPTER VI

THE GREAT SIR MARCUS

The appointment was at the Semiramis Hotel, where Sir Marcus Lark was staying. I went with my mind an aching void, and my heart a cold boiled potato. I can think of nothing more disagreeable! For not a word more would Fenton let drop as to the great man's business with us or the Mountain of the Golden Pyramid.

I sent up my card, and a few minutes later was shown into a private salon more appropriate to a beautiful young duchess than to a middle-aged, bumptious financier. It was pale green and white, full of lilies and fragrance, and an immense French window opened out upon a roofed loggia overlooking the Nile. This would have been the ideal environment for our Gilded Rose; and I felt more venomous than before, if possible, toward the rich bounder who posed against such an unsuitable background. I thought, as the door of the salon was opened for me by the smart Arab servant, that the room was untenanted, and that Sir Marcus Lark meant to keep me waiting; but there he was, on the balcony, gazing in rapture at the shining river. As if he were capable of raptures, he, an earth-bound worm! But there was no mistaking that back, those shoulders, or the face, as the big body turned. He advanced through the open window, holding out a hand as big as a steak. He was exactly like his photograph, except that there was even more of him than I had been led to expect. The pretty room was net small, but entering, he seemed to turn it into a doll's house parlour. "Six foot two, if he's an inch!" I said to myself, longing to play David to his Goliath. "Big, rich, common brute!" I thought. "You snatch our mountain out of our mouths, and then you send for us as if we were servants—men whose boots you ought to be blacking!" I was vindictive. I stared him straight between the eyes—where a stone from David's sling would have fitted in neatly.

The eyes were wide apart, and kinder than in the photographs. They were even curiously innocent, and boyish. His grin of greeting made the large, waxed black moustache point joyously up. He showed teeth white as a child's, and had dimples—actually dimples—in his big cheeks, to say nothing of the one in his chin, with which snapshots had familiarized me. He looked like a huge, overgrown schoolboy with a corked moustache. My glare faded in the light of his smile. No man with a gleam of humour could have kept a mask of grimness. I found my hand enveloped in the pound of steak, and warmly shaken up and down inside it.

"Lord Ernest Borrow, I'm delighted to see you. Very good of you to come, I'm sure!" to David quoth Goliath, in a big voice, mellow despite a slight Cockney accent. "Nice view I've treated myself to here, what? I'm in Egypt on business, but I like to have pretty things around me —pleasant colours and flowers and a view. That's a specialty of mine. I'm great on specializing. And that brings me to what we have in common; a scheme of yours; a scheme of mine."

I wanted to detest the man, but somehow couldn't. To hate him would be hating an overpowering force, like heat, or electricity.

With an old-fashioned politeness he made me sit down, picking out my chair, the most comfortable in the room, then taking the next best for himself. He fitted into it as tightly as a ripe plum into its skin, and talked with one leg crossed over the other and swinging, the points of his brown fingers joined. I was glad they were brown.

"I'm afraid you're sore with me," he began, having ordered coffee and liqueurs, and forced upon his guest a cigar as big as a sausage. "I've got what you and your friend wanted; and I'm going to be frank with you as I've been with him, and admit that I got it because you did want it. Simply and solely for that reason and nothing else. He told you this?"

"He left the telling to you," I said, wondering why I wasn't more furious than curious. But it was the other way round.

"Good egg! He promised he would, and he looks the sort of chap to keep his promise. Well, I see you want me to get down to business, and I will. I'm going to lay all my cards on the table. I came here to Egypt for the first time in my life, to see a scheme through, and I landed on the scene in time to find that I was likely to fail. I haven't told any one else that, but your friend Fenton; for I never have made a business failure yet, and I don't mean to now if I can help it. The scheme had to be saved in a hurry if it could be saved at all; and when I set my wits to work I saw that I must get hold of some such young men as you and Captain Fenton to help me. I don't know how the thought of you two popped into my head, but I suppose it was seeing a lot of stuff about Fenton in the papers, his Balkan adventure, and the announcement that he'd been recalled to his regiment. There were paragraphs about him as a linguist, and an Egyptologist, and anecdotes of him as a smart soldier. You know the sort of thing. And the stories about his parentage caught my fancy a bit. They're romantic. I've got enough romance in me to see that side of life, and to know how it goes down with the women. This scheme of mine depends on women. Most schemes do. At the same time the Egyptian papers were printing paragraphs about Lord Ernest Borrow. I don't know whether you're aware of that or not? No? Would you like to see 'em? I've had my secretary cut 'em out—and the Fenton stuff, too. The minute this idea began to wiggle in my mind like a tadpole in water, I kept everything."

"Don't trouble about the paragraphs, thanks," I said.

"All right. It will save our time not to. But your wish to go in with your friend, for the rights of excavating in the Sudan, was mentioned, and the delay on account of alleged interference with Garstang's pitch."

"By Jove, I wonder how the reporters got onto that?" I couldn't help exclaiming.

"It's their livelihood to get onto everything. 'Well then,' I said to myself, 'Here's my chance, my only one. I want those two young men. They're the right combination nation for me, to give real distinction to my undertaking. I have money, but they ain't the sort you can buy with money. There must be an incentive. If I get what they want, perhaps I can get *them*.' So I went into the job tooth and nail. Neither you nor Fenton was on the spot. I was—very much on it. Nothing was definitely fixed up between the Government and Fenton for the right to excavate at the Mountain of the Golden Pyramid, as they call the little old molehill, and I scored. Now, if you two will do what I want, you can have your mountain, and whatever you find you can keep. You're worth more to me than any beads and broken-nosed statues under the sand of Egypt. I think I've made some impression on your friend. He may be inclined to go in with me, if you will. He's explained that in any case he can't use his own name, on account of his position in the army and so on. That's a disappointment to me, but I'll put up with it for the sake of his accomplishments and his looks. Your name alone will carry the necessary weight as a leader."

"You're very flattering," said I. "But I'm in the dark."

"I'm going to put you wise, as Americans say. My scheme was—and is—to be a rival *de luxe* of Cook on the Nile. Not only that, but all over the near East. You've heard, of course, about my buying the Marquis of Redruth's yacht *Candace*, on his bankruptcy—the second biggest, and the most up-to-date yacht in the world—and turning her into a pleasure cruiser for the Mediterranean?"

"If I've heard, I'm afraid my memory's treacherous," said I, glad to show how unimportant to me were the schemes of financiers, but interested in the yacht's name, which carried my thoughts away to Meröe.

"Great Scout! And I've spent two thousand in advertising! I've taken whole pages of London and Continental papers!"

"I never read advertisements if I can help it, except of new patents in razors. They're a fad of mine."

"Thank goodness you've got fads. Then we've something in common. I make money out of my fads. I call 'em inspirations. I thought the *Candace* business was one of my inspirations, and that I'd have some fun out of it. I advertised her to start on her first pleasure cruise from Marseilles to Gib, Algiers, Tangier, Tunis, Greece, Alexandria, and Jaffa. 'That'll be a smack in the eye for the big liners,' I said to myself. 'I'll skim the top layer of clotted cream off their passenger lists!' I was going to do the thing *de luxe* straight through—bid for the swell set, exclusiveness my motto. Of course I didn't expect to hit the dukes and dollar kings first shot, but I thought if everything went right the passengers would tell their friends at home how much better we did them on board than any one else had ever done, and we'd get a 'snowball' ad, that nothing could stop. All would have worked out first rate, if I hadn't made one mistake. I engaged a retired army colonel for a conductor on board my yacht. I got the man cheap. But I was a fool to economize on him. I ought to have launched out on a belted earl. Folks, especially Americans, don't like retired colonels. The woods are full of 'em over there, crawling with 'em. Most Americans are colonels and not retired. Besides, this chap of mine's no good anyhow —fancies himself as a politician, and is a first-class snob; has no tact; rubs up the passengers the wrong way, and outrages their feelings. We got a lot of people from the north of England, rich and a bit crude, like me. Will you believe it, Colonel Corkran began his job by sneering audibly at 'provincials' to some beastly friend of his, come to see him off at Marseilles? Instead of making his dinner-table lectures a kind of travellogue as he was hired to do, he turns 'em into political tirades, and calls the Liberals scoundrels, half of our folks being red-hot Rads.

Not only that, if the girls and boys talk while the band's playin' any of his favourite airs, he hisses out 'Silence,' through a hole in his mouth where one tooth's missin'. That tooth bein' gone, has got on the girls' nerves worse than anything else, it would seem, except his being down on Suffragettes. And the crisis was reached when he insulted Miss Hassett Bean, the richest and most important woman in the bunch, when she expressed her political opinions. Said to her, 'My dear lady, why do you bother to have opinions? They give you a lot of trouble to collect, and nobody else will trouble to listen. Why not collect insects or stamps instead?' Of course she did think Germany had already invaded England with a large army of soldiers disguised as hotel waiters, which was calculated to rile an old officer; but that's no excuse for a man who's paid to please. And now the fellow's wondering why he's not popular with the passengers!"

I laughed, but Sir Walter had worked himself into a state past smiling point. "It's no laughing matter," he said, "This snob Corkran's killing my scheme. There's a plot on foot for the party to walk off the yacht at Alexandria, and demand half their passage money. Some old grampus on board has started the story that the *Candace* has been down three times———"

"A lie, of course," I soothed him.

"A dastardly lie. She's been down only twice. The first time was a collision, the second a coincidence."

"But I thought she was the most up-to-date yacht in the world!"

"So she is, as the *Candace*. That was the Marquis's name for her: gave it after a trip to Egypt. He bought her second hand, and rechristened her while she was being redecorated. He spared no expense, which he could well afford, seeing that he never paid a penny. I got her at cost price, as you may say. But these plotters are going to claim that they were inveigled on board under false pretences, by my advertising the *Candace* as the newest thing in yachts. I've had a letter and several cypher telegrams from the assistant conductor, a useful chap, telling me the whole story of the plot, which he's nosed out; and I'm faced with humiliating failure unless I can save the situation by a grand coup at the eleventh hour. Now, you can guess why on the spur of the moment I bought up your rights to dig in the Sudan, can't you?"

"I confess I can't," I said.

"Why, I want you to take Colonel Corkran's place on the *Candace* as conductor. And I want you and your friend Fenton to go up Nile in charge of the splendid steam dahabeah I've bought to supplement the Mediterranean trip. There you have my motives in a nutshell!"

I burst out laughing. "A cracked nutshell," I remarked. Sir Marcus' rosy face turned royal purple. "What—you won't undertake it?"

"I couldn't," I assured him. "For one thing, I'd be a fish out of water. My dear sir, perhaps you don't know that my nickname since the age of five has been 'Duffer?' I'm proud of it. I take pains to live up to it——"

"I bet you do. I bet it opens doors and lays down velvet carpets for you. Why, a duffer with a title is exactly what I want! Duffers are the rage nowadays. You and your friend will make a brilliant pair, a fine contrast, especially with your friend's present get up. If you'd both been born for me you couldn't suit me better."

I laughed again. "You said you ought to have launched out on belted earls. We're humble——"

"There's no earls handy, and if there were any, they wouldn't be what you two are in looks and talents, to say nothing of your brother being a marquis. I'm offering you both the softest kind of job. All you have to do is to be agreeable young gentlemen, with a knowledge of society, and history; that means, you can be yourselves. You get a fine trip on high salaries if you don't scorn to accept my money; and as a reward for a good holiday you receive the right to explore your golden mountain. I suppose you must think it *is* a golden mountain, or you wouldn't be such nuts on it. You'd better consult your friend before you refuse my offer, anyhow."

"Haven't you heard that Fenton's left Cairo?" I took the precaution to ask. "That doesn't look as if he were entertaining the idea of going up the Nile on your steam dahabeah." "I have heard that he's left. But I happen to know—it isn't so. I saw him standing in front of Shepheard's Hotel this morning, waiting for you. I got on to what was in that green turban before the pretty girl in white—Miss Gilder, I've found out since—called him on to the terrace. Don't look as if you wanted to eat me, Lord Ernest. I've won my way up from the bottom rung of the ladder by keeping my eyes open, and by putting two and two together. I specialize on that. I don't suppose there's another man in Cairo except me and you, would have recognized Fenton, so you needn't worry. I twigged that he'd dressed up for serious business, not for fun, because I read about some smart coups he'd brought off by going among the natives like one of themselves. I'm not a sneak, and I shan't revenge myself by giving him away, even if you two do show me the frozen face. Captain Fenton encouraged me to think he might consider my proposition if you would, though he refused to influence your decision one way or the other. Naturally I conclude that he could be on my Nile boat if he wanted to, even if not in his own capacity as an officer. I'll take him in his green turban. He makes the best looking Egyptian I ever saw, and he'd go down with the ladies like hot cakes."

"Sir Marcus," I smiled, "you're one of the most amusing as well as the sharpest men, if you'll allow me to say so, that I ever met. Whatever happens I shall not forget this conversation."

"I don't want you to forget it," he grinned, beginning to hope. "Think it over. We're the chance of a lifetime for each other. And remember the Mountain of the Golden Pyramid." I rose, and he got up heavily. "When will you let me know?" he asked.

I was tempted to reply that he must have taken Fenton's seeming encouragement too seriously, that, mountain or no mountain, it was practically impossible for us to accept his amazing proposition. But suddenly I seemed to hear "Antoun Effendi" telling Miss Gilder that she must wait for his decision until evening. He had said afterward, also, that it depended on me. It was evident that he had a scheme of his own, worked by wheels within wheels. He had consoled me after the first blow by saying that all was not lost. And I had four months' leave from duty. A lot could be done in four months. "I will let you know before night," I said to Sir Marcus Lark.

CHAPTER VII

THE REVELATIONS OF A RETIRED COLONEL

Fenton's orders were, when the Cairo business should be finished, to go slowly up the Nile in native dress, and get at the truth of certain rumours which had disturbed officialdom at Cairo. At Denderah, Luxor, and two or three other places there had been "incidents," small but troublesome. English sightseers had complained of being hustled, and even insulted by the inhabitants of several river towns, and it was important to find out whether the Egyptians or the foreigners had been more to blame; whether there were real symptoms of sedition, as reported, or whether the young men of the suspected places had merely resented with roughness some discourtesy of tactless tourists. Fenton had seized upon the idea that, as Egyptian lecturer and conductor—a sort of super-dragoman—on board Lark's Nile boat, he might find a plausible pretext for his secret errand. "Why do you travel?" would be the question he must expect from suspicious leaders of any plot that might be hatching, if he journeyed from one Nile village to another without the excuse of business. As a glorified conductor of a pleasure-trip for a party of tourists his excuse would be readymade for him; but he had been far from sure that I would fall in with Sir Marcus Lark's plan, despite the bribe. He had wanted me to hear the whole story, the whole project, from Sir Marcus' own lips; and in his uncertainty of the result, he had thought of Miss Gilder as an attractive "victim." There she was, as he had said, presented to him by Providence. If I should pour scorn upon the Lark suggestion, he might find it worth while to guide the Gilded Girl and her friends on their Nile pilgrimage. He left the question for me, and I decided to kill as many birds as possible with one stone. The name of the yacht was in itself an incentive: *Candace*— Queen of Meröe—our Meröe. She seemed to call, and to promise good luck. We would accept Lark's terms, and enter his service in return for a written agreement to hand over his ill-got digging rights to us, whether or no we turned out to be satisfactory as guides. We could but do our best, and at all events we should earn the reward which we had looked upon as ours already.

Anthony would play his double part, serving the interests of government and those of Sir Marcus Lark. As for Monny Gilder, why shouldn't she and her party become Lark's passengers? The only reason against this "inspiration" (as Sir Marcus would have called it), lay in the fact that Monny wished to engage a private dahabeah. When she wished for a thing, it appeared that only a miracle or a cataclysm could induce her to give it up for something else suggested by an outsider. But when I mentioned this peculiarity to Fenton, he was fired to punish the girl by forcing her compliance with our will. She had treated him like a servant. She looked upon a man supposedly of Egyptian blood, even though of princely birth, somewhat as she looked upon an American "nigger." True, Anthony Fenton had in his veins but very few such drops. On his father's side he was all English, and his mother had been more than two thirds Greek and Italian. Nevertheless this spoilt girl had struck a blow at the pride which went ever walking about the world with a chip lightly poised on its shoulder. Anthony had no desire to poach on my preserves. At the same time he yearned to show Miss Gilder that he could be her master, not her servant.

Once Anthony and I had made up our minds, everything else arranged itself with lightning speed. Sir Marcus, rejoicing in his ill-got conquest of us, broke to me the news that I must go by the first ship to the Piraeus, to meet the *Candace*, and head off the recalcitrant band of passengers. He flattered me by thinking that, if I took the place of Colonel Corkran as conductor, they would abandon their plot to desert the yacht at Alexandria. It was, according to Lark's secret information, only the "smart and would-be smart set" who had combined to spring this mine upon the management. The rest grumbled no more than it was normal for all pleasure-pilgrims to grumble; and as, roughly speaking, the contented travellers were all going on to Palestine after a week's wild sightseeing in Cairo, the colonel might be allowed to continue his voyage without the interruption of a "row."

"I should have had enough common sense at the start," growled Sir Marcus with crude candour, "to engage a lord for the Smart Set, and a parson for the Ernest Inquirers. There's a world of difference catering for a Set, and a Flock. The art is, to know it, and how to do it. Now I've secured you, I'm all right with the S. S. and thanks be, I've a young reformed missionary on board to shepherd the Flock. Now the Reverend Watts will come in handy, herding his sheep through Palestine, while the colonel swaggers and fancies he's bossing the show. It's the Egypt lot I worry about: girls out for dukes, and dukes out for dollars. Not that there's a darned duke on board, but there are some who think they out-duke the dukes, and it's our business to humour 'em. You just duff all you want to, Lord Ernest, they'll swallow anything you do, like honey. Don't bother about a line of conduct: only be genial. Murmur soft nothings to the women; flirt but don't have favourites. Don't be too political with the men: work in plenty of anecdotes about your swell relations."

I replied that I could confidently promise geniality, except if seasick: but Sir Marcus implored me at all costs not to be seasick. That was the one thing I must not be. My whole time between the Piraeus and Alexandria, on board the *Candace,* must be spent ingratiating myself with the sulky passengers, and obliterating from their memories the crimes of Colonel Corkran. In Sir Marcus' opinion my future charges had taken passage on the *Candace,* and would go up the Nile, not to see sights, but to be seen doing the right things. According to him not two out of twenty cared tuppence for Egypt, but wished to talk about it in sparkling style at home. My friend Captain Fenton and I must make it sparkle. Sir Marcus had resigned himself to the fact that one of his trump cards—Anthony—could not be produced until the arrival in Cairo of the troupe, and that even then, the name of Fenton must not be used as an attraction. Lark felt confident that I was a good enough card to make his hand worth playing, and in spite of the half contemptuous amusement with which I regarded the whole scheme, I couldn't help being "on my mettle." I found myself wanting to succeed, wanting to please the big, common man whom a few hours ago I had been cursing.

I had to start for Greece the night after our decision. Meanwhile, I was anxious to explain the unexplainable to Brigit and Monny, and secure the party for Sir Marcus Lark's alleged dahabeah, which turned out to be one of Cook's old boats bought and newly decorated. Both my tasks would be difficult. I had to hide the secret reason for selling myself to the financier, and at the same time keep the respect of the ladies. As for inducing Miss Gilder to give up her dream of a private dahabeah, I foresaw that it would be like persuading the youngest lioness in the Cairo Zoo to surrender her cherished wooden ball. But I began by giving Monny a present; a fine old turban-box of rare, red tortoise shell inlaid with mother of pearl, which I found at an antiquary's. In the silklined box reposed a green turban; and that green turban told its own story. Miss Gilder flushed with pleasure at sight of it. "I've won my bet!" she exclaimed.

"Yes," said I. "To my astonishment! The man consents. He's a great prize, knows Cairo and upper Egypt like a book. But you'll have to surrender him when you go on the Nile."

In her haste to know why, Monny forgot to ask how I had obtained the green turban; and for this I was glad, because it was only the second best headgear of my smart friend the Hadji. In explaining that the distinguished Egyptian had been engaged by Sir Marcus Lark, I slipped in a word about my own part in the trip, describing it as an ideal rest-cure for a budding diplomat on sick leave. I praised the boat and spoke of the fun on board. I regretted Miss Gilder's preference for a private dahabeah, so obvious, so millionairy! Still, I added, every one to his taste! And anyhow, no doubt all the best cabins on the *Enchantress Isis* were taken.

That was the entering wedge—the mention of an obstacle to overcome. Miss Gilder looked thoughtful, though she kept silence: and next day, when making my adieux before starting for Alexandria, she flung out a careless question. When would the *Enchantress Isis* leave Cairo? How many passengers would she carry? Would there be a rush at the Temples, or would there be plenty of time for proper sightseeing? And was I sure that all the nicest cabins were engaged? No, I was not sure. I could inquire. I tried not to look triumphant, but I must have darted out a ray, because Monny withdrew into her shell. She had inquired out of curiosity, she explained. I had told such stories about the *Enchantress Isis* that she would like to see her. Perhaps Antoun Effendi could get permission for a visit to the boat.

In this state I had to leave affairs, and start for the Piraeus, where I must await the return of the tourists from Athens. I had two days at sea in which to work up an agony of apprehension, and I could have thanked heaven when, arriving on board the big white yacht, I found that I was ahead of the passengers. I was expected, however, and a deck cabin was ready for my occupation. I hoped that I had not turned out my rival from the room, but dared not question the steward. He seemed to know all about me, nevertheless, and said that my name had been "posted up" as conductor of the Nile party. "If I may take the liberty of mentioning it, my lord," he added, "it has made a very good impression." We were to steam for Alexandria the moment the passengers arrived in the special train—having had three days of sightseeing in Athens—and I had just got my possessions stowed away when a wave of chattering voices broke over the ship. My heart gave a jump, as a soldier's must when called to fight on an empty stomach at dawn on a winter's morning. What ought I to do? How was I to make the acquaintance of my future charges? Must it be en masse, or could it be done singly? I had neglected to ask Sir Marcus what would be expected of me, and I was in a worse funk than a new boy on his first day at school. Soon it would be dinner time. I wished that I were ill, but I remembered that the one thing I must not do was to be seasick. Already the ship was beginning to move out of the Greek harbour, or I should have been tempted to get a telegram calling me home. Even the Mountain of the Golden Pyramid seemed not too great a sacrifice to make—but it was too late to make it—and some one was knocking at my door.

I opened it with such courage as I had; and the instant I set eyes on the man I knew that he was Colonel Corkran. He was born to be a retired colonel. What came before the retiring could have been but a prelude. A stout figure of middle height; red face, veined on cheeks and nose; pale blue eyes which looked as if they had faded in the wash; purple moustache and eyebrows; close-cropped gray hair; a double chin clamouring for extra collar space; and a bridge-player's expression. This was the rival whose place I had virtually, though not officially, usurped.

I was prepared to hear him hiss "Viper!" between his teeth, as characters in melodramatic serials do to perfection, their front teeth having doubtless been designed for such purposes. But his look seemed to denote pity rather than hatred. So might a prison-warder regard a condemned man, in coming to announce the hour of execution.

"Lord Ernest Borrow?" said he, in a slightly hoarse voice. "I'm Colonel Corkran. Delighted to meet you. I've met your brother, Lord Killeena. Daresay he wouldn't remember me. I don't think I can begin better than by thanking you for coming to take over my job."

"Oh, I haven't done that!" I hastened to protest, as he sat fatly down in a chair I pushed forward. "As I understand, I'm to take a few people off your hands, and the hands of your assistant, Mr. Kruger, so that you can go to Palestine instead of leaving that important excursion entirely to the chaplain, Mr. Watts."

Colonel Corkran laughed. "Thank you for trying to save my feelings," said he. "But I assure you they're not hurt. I'm sincerely delighted to see you—for my own sake. For yours—well, that's another pair of shoes! My dear fellow, I wonder if you've the smallest idea what you're in for?"

"In for?" I echoed.

"Yes. I'm saying this as a friend. Don't think I'm jealous. Lord, no! I look on you as a deliverer. And don't think I want to frighten you. It isn't that. But I feel it's my duty to prepare you. I might have got on better if there'd been some one to do the same by me. There wasn't. Kruger, my so-called assistant, is a spy. At best, he's a mere accountant, not supposed to look after the passengers socially. I gather that he was some secretary of Lark's. Beware of him. He writes to Lark from every port. As for the passengers, the saintly lot are bad enough. Yet it's only the food and the cabins and the attendance *they* grumble about. I'm shunted off the worldly lot onto them in future. But at their worst, they'll be a rest-cure! and Lark has the decency not to reduce my screw. It's the worldly lot that's going to make you curse the day you were born."

He wanted me to speak, or groan; but I maintained a stricken silence, to which I gave some illusion of dignity. After a disappointed pause he went on: "You'd better know something about these people. Beasts, every one of 'em, young or old, some beastly common beasts, but all beastly rich, except those that are beastly poor, and on the make—to marry their daughters, or cadge for smart friends. Lark was bidding for swells, and got snobs. Thinks his silly title will carry weight in society as it does in the city. 'Lark Pie,' we're called, I hear. I call us a 'Pretty Kettle of Fish!' The girls are the worst of the caboodle, though some of 'em aren't bad looking. You won't believe the trouble I've had with the creatures till you begin to get the same yourself."

"What kind of trouble?" I inquired gingerly.

"Every kind a woman can make. Apart from food troubles, they think they're not being entertained enough on board; think I ought to get up more dances; tango teas I suppose! Don't like the way I organize games; are mad because they can't have music at meals—which they can't because the band's all stewards; blame me because the men don't make love to them, or because they do. And at the hotels where we go on shore, it's Hades. Naturally the people staying in the hotels resent us. They look on us as a menagerie—a rabble. So we are. At least, they are. I don't count myself in with them. What can I do? I'm not omnipotent. Perhaps you are. Anyhow, they're prepared to believe it, for you're a new broom—a broom with a fine handle. I'm only a poor colonel with a few medals given by my country for services that were appreciated. You're brother to a marquis."

"You paint a lurid picture" I said, when he stopped for breath.

"I couldn't paint it lurider than it is. But you'll have to find out for yourself. It won't be so bad while you're a novelty. Don't say I haven't warned you. And oh, by the way, I've announced that you're to be presented to the passengers at dinner to-night, on coming in, before the soup is served."

"As a sort of *hors d'oeuvre*, I suppose," I murmured weakly.

Colonel Corkran stared, without a smile. "As the titled conductor of the Egypt tour," he explained to my dull intelligence, with a slight sneer. "So will you please be in the dining saloon just before the bugle blows the beasts in? I have to introduce you, in a short speech. It's all I can do, except say, God help you! But I don't see how He can. I suppose your friend Sir Marcus told you that you would be expected to deliver a lecture on Egypt, to-night at the dinner table? After you've finished your dinner, of course. I hope the cracking and crunching of nuts doesn't disturb you much? I confess I've found it getting on my nerves."

I was aghast. My mind jumped to the wild thought of eating soap, in order to froth at the mouth and simulate a fit. It seemed my only way of escape, and after that, the Deluge. But my rival was so revelling in the mental havoc he had wrought that I rallied, replying that, as Sir Marcus had not broken the news to me, I didn't see how it would be possible to deliver a lecture.

"Aren't you up on Egypt?" the colonel asked, pityingly. "Neither am I, though I've sweated over Baedeker with my head in wet towels, when I wanted to be at bridge. But I thought that was the excuse for engaging you? That, and your title, of course, which is going to make you popular. As fast as I fag up the names of those beastly Egyptian gods or kings and queens, they run out of my brains like water out of a sieve. Or if I do contrive to remember any, by chance, together with their dates, which is almost more than can be expected of the human intellect, why, I find that I pronounce 'em wrong; or they're spelled another way in the next book. But I suppose as you know Egypt, its d—d history comes natural as breathing."

How I wished it did! And how different was this new programme from the one outlined by Sir Marcus. Just to be genial, and flirt with the girls. "My recollections of Egypt are from some time ago," I admitted. "To give a lecture at half an hour's notice.——"

"In justice to yourself I'm afraid you'll have to," the colonel persisted. "It's been announced that you will give the lecture, and the Egypt lot are looking forward to it as the animals in a zoo look forward to their food. If they're defrauded, they'll think you a slacker, and that you're presuming on your title."

"I shouldn't like that!" my anguish racked out of me.

"I fancied you wouldn't. But what's to be done? Am I to announce, when I introduce you, that your knowledge of Egypt isn't equal to the strain?"

I took an instant for reflection. I knew that he was hoping I might throw myself on his mercy, or else that I would speak and fail; but I determined to do neither. "On second thoughts, I may be able to give some kind of a pow-wow," I replied.

Colonel Corkran's face fell. "That's all right, then!" he exclaimed, getting to his feet. "Well, I must be off. Will you have a cocktail?"

"No, thanks," said I. "I think I can get on without it."

He was at the door. "Kind of hash of gods and goddesses with a peppering of kings and queens, and mixed sauce of history and legend, is what's needed," were his farewell words. Then he shut the door; and I tore my watch from the pocket of my waistcoat. I had twenty-eight minutes in which to prepare the said hash with its seasoning and sauce; and the bugle was inviting my judges to dress for the inquisition.

CHAPTER VIII

FOXY DUFFING

"I'll show you your place," Corkran volunteered, lying in wait for me inside the saloon door, with a cocktail in his hand. "Sorry you wouldn't have one. You'll need it. But no time to change your mind. I've put you at the head of the table that would be the captain's, if he ate with us, which he doesn't—happy man! Place of honour. 'Twas mine, 'tis yours. But I can't go on with the quotation unless I turn it into 'You're slave to thousands.' Sixty odd can be as formidable as thousands."

"Are there sixty odd?" I asked.

"Yes, very 'odd.' The Egypt lot will be about twenty-five. But the whole gang's yours for the present. I give them to you, with the seat of honour."

"Please don't put me in your place," I protested. "I prefer———"

"My poor boy, it isn't a question of what you prefer, as you'll learn if you stick this out. Of course if you funk it—but that's a joke! This table's the only one where you can be heard. Do you see?"

I did see; and accepted the situation, because the dinner bugle began to sound, and I could not be scampering round the saloon like a frightened rabbit as the Set and the Flock began dropping in to dinner. As it happened, they did not drop—they poured into the room in a steady stream, which phenomenon, whispered Corkran, was caused by curiosity for a first sight of me. My heart counted each new arrival, with a bump.

If Corkran had not represented "Lark's Party" as being a menagerie for which I had inadvertently engaged as tamer, I should have thought they looked a harmless crowd. But then, of course, I was not obliged to tame anybody on the *Laconia*, which makes a difference in one's point of view. Miss Gilder needed taming, no doubt, but I hadn't tackled the task. My thoughts flew to Cairo, as I stood struggling to look pleasant; and I wished myself back where Anthony Fenton was now in the taming business. I envied him, for there was only one Monny, whereas in this terrible, bright dining saloon, the air was pink and white with girls, dozens of girls, with eyes fixed on me, glittering eyes, which appeared like the headlights of motor cars. I didn't suppose there could be so many eyes in the world as these people of all ages and every possible sex seemed to own. Sixty odd they were, according to Corkran, but they looked like six hundred; a human miracle of loaves and fishes.

Yes, the creatures might have appeared harmless enough had there been no retired colonel. But there was a retired colonel, and so deftly had he undermined my courage that almost any shock might cause it to explode in a blue flame of funk. His speech of introduction was now to come, and if I survived that, I might hope to live through my own fireworks.

"They've put on their best bibs and tuckers," Corkran mumbled in a stage whisper, as the eight dwellers at our table began to sort themselves for places. Then, in portentous silence he paused till everybody everywhere was seated. Waiting still, until satisfied that eyes and ears were focussed upon us, he rapped on the table with the handle of a knife.

"Ladies and gentlemen," he roared, "I have the pleasure of introducing to you Sir Marcus Lark's Great Surprise, entitled Lord Ernest Borrow, younger brother of the Marquis of Killeena, a peer, as Sir Marcus has reminded us, of the oldest lineage in Ireland. Let me reassure you all by saying that Lord Ernest's last name is as unsuited to his nature as the first is true to it. If you'll pardon the pun it is Sir Marcus who 'Borrows' for your benefit, and he hasn't Borrowed Trouble, but a Blessing—in disguise. I am now left free, as suits my superior age and experience, to devote my attention to the serious minded ones among you, who are to proceed with the Reverend Mr. Watts and myself to Palestine. This young and gallant neophyte will 'lord' it over the fleshpots of Egypt and those about to seek them. I hope you'll help him as loyally as you have helped *me*: and later we'll drink to his health and success, in any beverage we happen to have signed for!"

To have killed Corkran might have been butchery; no jury could have brought in a verdict of murder or even manslaughter, had I stabbed him with the knife he used to pound upon the table. I smiled the smile of a skull in a doctor's waiting-room, and in a sickly voice bleated my pleasure in meeting these new acquaintances. I hoped we might be—er —friends as well as shipmates. Then like a mass of jelly out of its mould I plopped onto my chair. The colonel had sneaked off to his own table and I was left to recover myself as best I might among eight of his enemies. They proved (in whispers) to be the most active of these, and tacitly offered me allegiance which I accepted in the same manner. There was a Sir John Biddell, who informed me in the first five minutes that he had been Lord Mayor of London. He promised to show me a speech he had made in the presence of King Edward which, in the form of a newspaper cutting, he never travelled without. This, however, was his first trip farther than Paris, and he had brought with him, not only the speech, but his wife and twin daughters. The distinguished family occupied one side of my table: the other was given up to a General Harlow, his wife (both with high profiles and opinions of themselves), a youngish newspaper proprietor from Manchester, evidently rich and a "catch," and a maiden lady doubtless of importance equal to her proportions, as she was allowed to bring to the table a melancholy marmoset. These people did their best to raise my spirits. The girls, who copied royalties in their hair-dressing, looked alike, dressed alike, talked and laughed alike, and entertained me with chat about high society in London. They had red cheeks, black eyes, white teeth, and an almost indecent familiarity with the private lives of the aristocracy. The Misses Biddell and fat Miss Hassett-Bean (the lady of the marmoset) hinted that the cream of the yacht's social life had risen to our table, and told me, not only what to lecture about, but how to treat the rival cliques. My brain felt more and more like a blotting-pad. I answered at random and longed for the meal to end —until I remembered my lecture. Then I wished that dinner might go on indefinitely like the tea party of the Mad Hatter. All too soon the glory of a French menu flickered down to a dying spark of nuts and raisins, and hardly had I cracked my first almond (was it an ill omen that there should be a worm in it?) when a steward handed me a twisted note from the executioner. "The rule for conductor's dinner speech is, rise with the raisins! Hope you won't find your lecture too hard a nut to crack. Yours sympathetically, Corkran. Bang on the table to make them stop gabbling. Or shall I do it for you? If you haven't by the time I count ten, I will."

He did. I trust it wasn't my courage that failed. But having a raisin in my mouth I could not on the instant respond to the lash. And as Corkran would have said, it takes more than one swallow to make a speech. Ruthlessly he rapped, seizing what I wished might be his dying chance to indulge a mania for puns and thumping wood.

"Ladies and gentlemen," he bawled from his comparatively obscure corner. "Lord Ernest Borrow will render your last moments the most enjoyable of the meal, by washing down your nuts and raisins with the wine of his eloquence. Take your desserts now. We conscientious conductors hope for ours in heaven."

How ardently I desired that these might indeed be the "last moments" not only of my audience but of Colonel Corkran. If the next second had brought a tidal wave or a collision I should have blessed Providence. But I got to my feet—and nothing happened. I seemed to be in a dream, of having shot up to a gigantic height, and having put on the wrong clothes, or none. My hands weighed two pounds each, and ought to have been at the butcher's. My mouth was the size of a negro minstrel's, and so full of large bones which once had been teeth that I could not utter a syllable. I clacked my jaws, and emitted a hacking cough which fortunately so much resembled that of a professional lecturer that I kept my senses. Not only did I keep them, but they seemed suddenly to become my servants. The thought of a certain fable jumped into my head, and I began thereupon to speak; although I had forgotten everything I had ever read of Egyptian history.

"It happens," said I, in a phonographic voice, "that I was born in Egypt. I played with clay gods and goddesses instead of tin soldiers. I preferred stories of Egypt's past and present to tales of adventure. I confess to you what I fear I didn't confess to Sir Marcus Lark. The trouble is, I'm stuffed too full of facts about Egypt. I want you to help me get them out, and not duplicate yours. No doubt all of you, in travelling to the East, have packed your brains with knowledge as well as your boxes with guide books. Why should I bore you by telling you things that you were born knowing? A plan has occurred to me by which your knowledge can be turned into account. As I said, I beg your help. And permission to drink a cup of coffee would be first aid."

People laughed, whether at me, or with me, I was not sure; yet I felt that I had tickled their curiosity. Coffee was going round. Corkran was unctuously sipping his, and had not expected me to receive mine till after the battle. But I got it in spite of him, and mapped out a programme as I drank. Then I ceased to tremble before the confused assemblage or bird-headed gods, cat-faced goddesses, and sacred vultures that danced or flapped in my brain.

I no longer felt inclined to commit suicide because I could remember nothing about Egypt except that the Delta was shaped like a lily, with the Fayum for a bud, and the Nile for its stem: that Alexander the Macedonian defeated Darius the Persian B. C. three hundred and something; that ancient Egyptians loved beer, but were forbidden to eat beans.

"My proposal is," I went on, "that before I unload any of my knowledge upon you, I gleam some idea of what you know already. Thus I can spare you repetitions. Any one who has anything particularly interesting to say about Egypt, let him—or her—hold up a hand."

Now was the crucial moment. If no hand went up, I was lost. But hardly were the words out of my mouth when there was a waving as if in a wind-swept wheatfield *Place aux dames!* I called upon Miss Hassett-Bean to begin. She rustled silkily up, bowing to me, then directing an acetylene glare upon Colonel Corkran's end of the room. She was, I foresaw, about to kill two birds with one stone, to say nothing of the marmoset, who fell off her arm into General Harlow's coffee and created a brief diversion. As soon, however, as the monkey was rescued and before General Harlow's shirt front was dried, the lady began to speak.

"We all thank Lord Ernest," she said, looking from the colonel to the Reverend Wyman Watts, and back again, "for sparing us one of those commonplace inflictions from which we've nightly suffered on board this yacht. If we didn't know already, such school-book facts as Christianity being introduced to Egypt by St. Mark in Nero's time, and Moses and Plato both studying philosophy at Heliopolis, and things like that, we wouldn't be spending our money with Sir Marcus A. Lark to see Egypt. Never before have we been encouraged to air our views. Those of us with political opinions have been snubbed; and we who are interested in Woman Suffrage have been assured that we'll find nothing to please us in the land of Veiled Women. At last I am given a chance to state without being interrupted that Egypt was once the most enlightened country in her treatment of women. Long before the time of the Greeks, and even before the Shepherd Kings Mr. Watts has told us so much about, using his Old Testament as if it were a Baedeker, the women of Ancient Egypt had rights according to their class. Queens and princesses were considered equal with their husbands. Women were great musicians, playing on many instruments, especially the sistrum, sacred to the goddess Hathor. And weren't all the best gods goddesses, when you come to think of it? Women used to drive their own chariots, as we do our motors, and hold salons, like the French ladies. There was Rhodopis, for instance, who married the brother of Sappho. I wonder if Colonel Corkran could have told you that the story of Cinderella comes from an anecdote of Rhodopis? I hardly think that he's been able to spare enough time from bridge to study Strabo, who was the Baedeker of Egypt for tourists six hundred years before Christ. An eagle saw Rhodopis bathing, and stealing one of her sandals flew with it to Memphis, where he dropped it into the king's lap. It was so small and dainty that King Hophra scoured Egypt for the owner, and when he found her at last, according to Strabo, made her his queen."

"If Strabo was right, she lived long before Sappho's day!" interpolated the colonel's voice.

"Of course, Strabo was right. There were two of Rhodopis. Everybody knows that. The Third Pyramid was built for the tomb of the first one, *not* for King Mycineris, *I* believe. Why shouldn't a woman have a Pyramid to herself? The Sphinx is a woman, as I will insist to my dying day, if it were my last word! I hope Lord Ernest won't ram down our throats any nonsense about that noble and graceful tribute to the Mystery of Womanhood being a stupid King Harmachis, or Horemkhu. I wouldn't believe it if I found a hundred nasty stone beards lying buried in the sand under her chin, instead of one, which could easily have been put there to deceive people. Probably King Harmachis had the Sphinx altered to look like him. No wonder she shuddered at such profanation, and shed her false beard. There you have my theory. And as for Egypt being now the land of Veiled Women, where Suffragettes find no sympathy, I've heard that the prophet's order for veiling has been purposely misconstrued by tyrannical men, with their usual jealousy. Even Mohammed himself was jealous."

With this Miss Hassett-Bean sat down, amid fitful applause; and at my earnest request, Miss Enid Biddell, the prettier twin, stood bravely up. She wished, before the subject was changed, to tell some little things she had read about the girls of Ancient Egypt, how like they were to girls of to-day, in all their ways, especially in—in things concerning love. It was they who first questioned the petals of flowers for their lovers' loyalty. How much they thought about their clothes, too, getting their best things from foreign countries, as women did now, from Paris! It was so funny to read how the girls of Old Egypt had consulted palmists and fortune tellers and astrologers just as girls did in Bond Street now; and that what 'Billikens' and 'Swasticas' and birth-stones were to us, images of gods were to the girls of Egypt who lived before the days of Moses! They had scarab rings with magic inscriptions, and sacred apes for the symbol of Intelligence, and lucky eyes of Horus, wounded by the wicked god Set, and cured by the love of Isis. On their bracelets and necklaces they hung charms, and their dressing-tables were covered with images of favourite gods and goddesses. Hathor, the goddess of Love and Joy, was supposed to give her choicest gifts to girls who wore her special colour (that green-blue in the Temple of Edfu which Robert Hichens calls "the colour of love") and to those who had her pet stones, emeralds, or turquoises. Nowadays, in Egypt, the jewels of the women were only lent to them by their men, and could be taken away as a punishment, or be pawned or sold in case of need; but in old days Egyptian women had all their most beautiful possessions buried with them.

When her sister had finished I urged the other twin to speak, and timidly Miss Elaine repeated to us what a friend of hers, a clergyman (here a blush) had told her. That the Red Sea was not red but a brighter blue than any sea in the world, and called red only because it washed the Red Lands. Her friend had written down for her in verse *such* a sweet legend about the Nile rising every spring from a single tear shed by Isis, a *much* more powerful goddess than Hathor, because she was the goddess of goodness as well as love. And the Nile used to be named Sihor by the Egyptians; and the year separated into three seasons, Flood time, Seed time, and Harvest. Miss Biddell's friend was writing a book about Egypt and was going to divide it in three parts like that. It was to be dedicated to *her*.

Bless the dear creatures, how they kept the ball rolling to please themselves, and—indirectly—to sort out my stock of ideas!

Harry Snell, the newspaper man, was not hard to persuade to his feet. He was studying the resemblance between Arabic and English words. He had found out, among other things, that Tallyho was "Tallyhoon," brought home by the Crusaders. He even had a theory that some of our words came from the early Egyptian. "Amen," for instance, he believed to be derived from "Amon," the name of the great god, father of all the other gods of Egypt, which was cried aloud, he understood, in the temples, during religious services. The parson jumped eagerly up to dispute this theory, and happily forgetful of me, seized the opportunity to spring upon us a few facts from his own store. When, however, Mr. Watts' discourse got him as far as Joseph's Well in the Citadel, General Harlow could bear no more, but sprang up to inform us that the Joseph of the Well in the Citadel was quite another Joseph, some Yusef of the Arab conquerors. The general knew all about that, because his son was stationed in the Citadel. And he proceeded to meander on historically, over a period between the first Arab conqueror Amru, to Haroun-al-Raschid, assuring us that old Cairo was the city of the Arabian Nights. He would, to my joy, have gone on indefinitely from Saladin to Napoleon if Sir John Biddell, as the only baronet on board, had not cut the only general short. He is a square man whose portrait could be properly done only by a Cubist. "Too much history, my friend!" he shouted, getting up with the manner of one accustomed to making dinner-table speeches. "What most of us are coming to Egypt for is *mummies*. Egyptian history is too troublesome, anyhow, for a normal man to grasp. Give me mummies! There's something *in* them. Why, even if you get a king or queen fixed in your head, somebody who's paid to make you know things you don't know" (an eye-shot for Corkran) "comes along and swears they didn't exist. Now, there's Mena. I'd pinned him like a stuck butterfly. I could remember that he was the first known king, and founded Memphis and lived six thousand years before Christ, all because we're going to stay at Mena House, which is named after him. I don't know why I remembered him that way, but I did. Just as I could recall the queen with a name like a sneeze by thinking of her as Queen Hat-and-Shoes. Now Colonel Corkran informs us that we must pronounce her, in a different way. And what's the consequence to me? I've ceased to try and keep track of her. King Mena, too, is lost to me forever, through the over-conscientiousness of our late conductor, who says there never was a Mena, only several kings they've mixed into one. I seem to be the one who's most mixed up! To whet my appetite for Egypt now, I have to have something tasty. Where's the good of stuffing my mind with a string of names which I couldn't mention to any one at home, because I can't pronounce them? The word Dynasty (he pronounced it Die-nasty) makes me sick! Luckily I feel that nobody else will know any more than I do. I'm coming to Egypt for a rest-cure, because I don't have to learn its history. But some lecturers won't let me have a minute's peace. A king named Sneferu couldn't expect to appeal to a man like me, even if he did build the oldest Pyramid, and even if you could show me his mummy, which you can't. But I draw the line at kings without mummies. I don't want to know them. Now, my wife is against mummies on show. She's heard that the malignance of mummies, especially in museums, is incredible. And she thinks it a judgment that some of the most distinguished ones are going bad. She says it's spite. I say its management. But I'm not ready to sit down yet! My wife means to start a society for the Prevention of Cruelty to Mummies, with the object of sending them back to their tombs where they can rest in that state of death it pleased their gods to call them to. Their object was eternal privacy, and they spent more on their tombs than their houses, because they expected to be dead a long tune, and wanted all the comforts of home. But I judge mummies by myself. It wouldn't have taken me these thousands of years to realize how narrow and un-christian my notions had been. I should see that I owed some duty to the world; and as so much posterity had rolled by since my day, I'd feel that lying in a museum at some large place like Cairo, was, after all, the only way to keep my name before the public. Now, that brings me to my tip for Lord Ernest. He asks what there is we don't know, and want to know. I'll answer for us all, being used to feel the pulse of crowds. We want to know what the deuce Ancient Egyptians really believed about death and religion. Had they any sense, or were they just plain fools?"

On the tide of applause which congratulated the boat's only baronet, I rose. I felt that I was on the crest of the wave; for the ancient religion of Egypt appeals to me; and as I now had reason to hope that others were comfortably ignorant of my subject I could spread myself as much as I pleased.

"The Ancient Egyptians were far from being fools," I answered Sir John with the air of being in their confidence. "We who are tempted to think so, don't take the trouble to try the key of their Faith in its door. I might say that its door was the door of the Tomb. If we go through that door into the Kingdom of Osiris, Amenti, which the Greeks renamed Hades, the mysteries which appear tangled sort themselves graciously out. The story of Isis the Great Enchantress, and her search for the body of her husband Osiris, murdered by Set, his wicked and jealous brother, Spirit of Evil, is perhaps the most lovable legend of the world. But in hearing that Horus, the son of Isis, was really the same god as Osiris, modern ideas begin to get mixed, and confuse themselves over Isis, goddess of love and goodness, cow-headed Hathor, mistress of love and joy, cat-headed Pasht and lioness-headed Sekhet, goddesses of love and passion. There's hawk-headed Horus, the youth, too; and Horus the child, represented in statues with his thumb in his mouth. How is one to make sense of them all? But once you have the key, it is easy and even beautiful. The esoteric or secret religion known to the high priests and the instructed ones was different from the animal-worship and adoration of bird-headed deities, which gave the common people such interest in daily life. They would have been lost without their monsters; and the priests would have been lost without the temples necessary for the worship of such a menagerie. For Egypt was a priest-ridden country in old days. The explanation of the many gods and goddesses was this: each was a different phase of the one God, Rā, the Sun, by whom and through whom only the world could exist. Animals and birds were chosen to express the different phases, because animals were considered to be nearer nature, therefore nearer God than human beings; besides, to give a god the head of a man would not set him apart from humanity, as it would to make him appear with the body of a man and the head of some bird or beast. Horus, finished off with the head of a hawk (that sacred bird who could look the sun in the face), became to the uneducated eye a supernatural being, which he would not have been with the face of a smiling youth. The child Horus, or Harpocrates, was not respected as was Horus of the Hawk Head. He was merely petted and loved. Even Set, god of evil, wasn't all bad.

He was the Spirit of Storm and Strife in Nature, and had to be propitiated by the ignorant. Typhon, or Typhoon, and he were one. Red was his colour, and red-haired people were his children. There were a hundred phases of the one god, each made incarnate, given his own mission, and worshipped in a different place. It's an ill wind (of Set) that blows nobody good, and animals had a gorgeous time in those days. Very few weren't sacred for some reason or other. It was death and destruction to kill a cat. And I don't think that cats have forgotten to this day the importance they had in Egypt. It's made them the most supercilious of animals.

"If Amon-Rã were angry he could become Menthu, the war god. If he were inclined to be gentle, he could shrink to the dimensions of Horus, child-god of the Rising Sun. If he were weary, he could rest as the old god Tum, of the Setting Sun. Probably gods and goddesses never enjoyed themselves so much as in Ancient Egypt; and though it does seem a drawback from our artistic point of view for Hathor to have the head or ears of a cow, for wise Thoth to have the long beak of an ibis, and so on, it was for them only an amusing kind of masquerade or 'tête' party, on the walls of the temples and tombs. At home, they could be what they liked. Think how interesting for the Egyptians to have all these queer gods, and what variety it gave to their lives. Perhaps the priests really meant well in keeping the secret of the One God for themselves and the kings, as the people weren't fitted to bear its solemnity. Fancy how amusing it was for the children to be told, on silver-bright nights, about Khonsu, god of the moon, always young, wearing the curled lock of youth on his brow—who staked five nights of his light playing draughts with Thoth, father of Magic. But he had a more serious phase, for when he was not a gambler he was an Expeller of Demons, a most popular accomplishment. Indeed, almost every god had several thriving businesses, conducted under different aliases. Khnum the Creator, dweller at the Cataracts, is my favourite, and is still busy, as he looks after the rise and fall of the river. Hekt, goddess of birth, was a pal of his, in spite of her appalling ugliness; and she used to kneel by his potter's wheel. While he fashioned the clay she would hold the Sign of Life, so that spirit might enter into the formed body when Khnum got it to the right state. For very important babies, royal ones or geniuses, she held a Sign of Life in each hand, which made them extraordinarily vital. When you arrive in Egypt, the first thing you'll be asked to buy will be the Sign, or Key of Life, in the shape of paper knives or brooches or what not, and it will be pointed out to you in tombs till you're tired and sick of it. You can buy Hekt, too, and funny old Bes, nurse-goddess of children, quite the golliwog of her day; and all the other gods and goddesses will be offered to you, to say nothing of the kings who were entitled to worship themselves as gods if they wanted to.

"It's easy, you see, to make fun of the ancient religion, and other nations did make fun of it. But to be serious, the priests were nearer right than it would seem; for they believed that God was All: that there was nothing in this or any Universe which was not part of God."

That note was my highest, and I stopped on it. Besides, I could think of nothing more to say. I ventured to sit down; and because the people were glad to hear the last of me, or because I had helped them finish their almonds and raisins, they applauded. Secretly I shook hands with myself, as the monkey must have done, when, with the catspaw, he had pulled the hot chestnuts out of the fire. I had carefully selected my chestnuts—and waited till they were cool. Also, I had disappointed Colonel Corkran.

CHAPTER IX

WHAT HAPPENED WHEN MY BACK WAS TURNED

Three letters for me, brought out by the pilot! One I had expected from Anthony; but my heart gave a bound as I recognized Brigit's handwriting, not seen for years; and instinct told me that the third was from Monny Gilder.

My one thought for the last two days, steaming back from the Piraeus to Alexandria, had been that I was drawing nearer to Cairo, and to those whose doings in my absence pulled at my curiosity and keyed my interest to breaking point. But if you think that I tore open those envelopes and greedily absorbed their contents the moment they were put into my hands, you have never been a conductor or even an observant passenger on a "pleasure yacht." When the letters arrived I was engaged in persuading breakfast-lingerers (they of the eggs-and-bacon habit, who ought never to leave their peaceful English homes) that it would give them more real pleasure to be first in the shore boats than last at the table. Then to get them into the boats; then to hypnotize Lady Biddell and Mrs. Harlow into the belief that they would not, could not, be seasick on the dancing waves which bobbed us up and down. No time to think of the letters; much less to feel the strangeness of fate which brought me back in such queer circumstances to the port I had entered on the *Laconia* eight days ago.

"As soon as we get on shore," I soothed my gnawing impatience, "I'll steal a minute somehow." But each moment was so conspicuously labelled that I could not be a thief of time—my time, which was my charges' time, bought and paid for by Sir Marcus Lark.

This was not the first occasion on which I'd heard the clanking of my chains, for, although I flattered myself that I was a popular success, popularity had penalties. On the night of the lecture I had used the passengers. Since then they had used me. Old ladies appealed to me on questions of etiquette, health or religion, and retailed my answers, not always correctly. Girls asked my advice about keeping up flirtations, and men wanted my help in getting out of them. I was expected to spout pages of Strabo or Pliny at an instant's notice; I must know why Plato went to Egypt, or how long he stayed; and be umpire between American and British bridge-players. I must be able to explain the true meaning and age of the Sphinx; invent new deck games; and show those who hadn't learned, how to dance the Tango. But with those three letters burning over my heart the duties of conductor became infuriating.

It was an awful day; for what was Pompey's Pillar to me while I remained ignorant of my friends' adventures? As I discoursed (more or less) learnedly about Diocletian, and Ptolemy's plot to drown Pompey in the Nile, something inside was asking, "Has Anthony fallen in love with Monny Gilder?" "What scrapes has that blessed girl got into?" "Has anything happened to worry Biddy?" Even that nameless but incomparable tomb on the hill of Kom esh-Shukafa could not distract my thoughts from the sealed envelopes; and three very modern handwritings came obstinately between my eyes and the matchless wall-paintings—paintings as fresh in their underground hiding-place as if finished yesterday instead of in days when it was dowdy to be pagan, fashionable to be Christian.

Corkran, as a soldier, had to guide a band to Aboukir, and chat about Nelson; point out the medieval fort of Kait Bey, and dash with hired motors to Adjemi, where Napoleon landed. Kruger took a few studious pilgrims to that unspoiled Oriental Nile town where the Rosetta Stone gave the secrets of Ancient Egypt to the world. It was mine to pilot the "frivolous lot"; to escort them in carriages round the Italian-looking city when they had absorbed its two chief sights; to give them a glimpse of the Museum, and to let them see the beauty and fashion of Alexandria driving out to San Stefano in the late afternoon. Still I had no chance to read my letters; but, thought I at the hotel, "Now at last, it has come!" Not at all! People's trunks were missing, or in the wrong rooms. It was I who had to sooth alarms, and calm rising storms. It was I who must assure Mrs. Harlow that her room was really preferable to that of Lady Biddell; and Lady Biddell that she, and not Miss Hassett-Bean, had the best in the hotel. Still, I had ten minutes to dress for dinner. Like Mr. Gladstone, I could do it in five, and have five left for my letters. But hardly had I slipped a paper knife under the flap of Monny's envelope (I should have felt a vandal to tear it) when one of the hotel managers knocked at my door. A gentleman was being very angry in the dining-room. He insisted on seeing me. He said he had been Lord Mayor of London, and ought to have a window-table. All these were previously engaged. What was to be done? Would I kindly come at once?

I persuaded Sir John that window-tables were the least desirable, owing to draughts, and returning to my room, had four minutes to dress or risk further rows. After dinner Miss Hassett-Bean burst into tears because she was alone in the world owing to the marmoset's death from seasickness; and now that she was growing old nobody cared to talk to her. I argued that people were shy because she was more important than they, and had a reputation for satire. It took half an hour for the lady's nose to go from red to pink (I think she had papier poudré in her handkerchief); and then I was obliged to walk on the beach with Miss Enid Biddell to keep Mr. Watts from proposing. As Snell relieved me from sentry duty, I was called by Kruger to discuss certain details of next morning's start for Cairo; and at midnight, when I crawled to my room a shattered wreck, the letters were still unread.

"I'm incapable of caring now," I groaned, "what has happened to any of them. If an earthquake has swallowed up our mountain, and Anthony's married Monny, and Brigit's been abducted, or vice versa, and Miss Guest has gone off with the jewels, it will leave me calm."

That was the spirit in which I tossed up a coin to see which letter to read first. Heads, Monny's; tails, Anthony's; but the penny rolled away, far under the bed where collar-buttons go, and so—I opened Biddy's. She began:

MY DEAR GOOD DUFFER!

For any sake hurry back. Make an excuse to leave your pilgrims the minute you get this, and take the first train to Cairo. Surely the late conductor can be your understudy, and trot the people round Alexandria for a day? We need you more than they do. I picture you reading this early in the morning, with Alexandria still in the distance; for you said you'd arrange to have letters come out to the yacht by the pilot. I shall expect a telegram saying by what train you'll arrive here in the afternoon. You'll understand when I've told you everything, why it's *necessary* for you to hurry.

We have done and seen so many things, it seems years instead of days since you left us in care of that handsome Hadji of yours. I wonder if really you didn't suspect that I guessed who he was; or *did* you suspect; and didn't care? I caught the look in your eyes, when you first saw him standing under the terrace at Shepheard's, and then, when the name "Antoun Effendi" came up in the conversation, I put two and two together. Mrs. East guesses, also. I don't know if she did from the first, but she does now. It isn't a question of "guessing" with either of us, really. It's a certainty. Not that she's said anything to me or I to her. That is the malady of us all since you went. We are boiling with secret thoughts, and keeping them to ourselves, which is bad for us and for each other in the long run. I haven't told Monny that the "Egyptian Prince," as Rachel Guest has nicknamed him, is your friend Captain Anthony Fenton playing some deep game, partly connected with us, partly connected with a secret of his and yours; the secret you said was a "dusty" one in which women would not be interested. I haven't told her, because I don't want her to know. She is always talking and thinking about him, and is vexed with herself for doing so. She tries to stop, but can't. If she knew who he was, she wouldn't try to stop. She'd let herself go, and feel she was living in a beautiful romance. So she is living in a romance, but I want you to be the hero of it, not your Anthony Fenton. That's why I don't open her eyes to the game that's going on. The man is a perfect devil. Not a bad devil, but a wild devil.

Mrs. East doesn't tell Monny that Antoun is "Anthony with an h" because she is enjoying the thought that she alone knows the wonderful truth. She imagines that she is in love with him. She believes Fate has brought them together—that he is a "reincarnation," as she is, and that they ought to belong to each other. Well, let them! She isn't more than six or seven years older than he, and she's rich (though poor compared to Monny, of course), and every day she grows handsomer. So does Monny. As for Rachel Guest—but she is in another part of my story. Yet no, come to think of it, I'll bring her in now, because if it weren't for developments concerning that young woman, I might be able to wait one more day without begging you to come to us. She is taking Monny away from me; and something odd is going on, I can't make out what. Anyhow, that horrid Bedr el Gemály is in it. And there's to be a climax, I'm sure, to-morrow night. You'll get this letter to-morrow morning, for I'm writing it early, with my hair down my back, and my coffee not ordered, though I'm starving. We've left Shepheard's because Monny wanted to live for a few days in a hotel close to the Nile; and we were all pleased with the plan, for this was once a palace of Khedive Ismael, and his furniture's still in it, the wildest mixture of Orientalized French taste. There's a garden, with paths of vermilion sand brought from somewhere in the desert. But the most convulsive things live along the Nile Valley and spend their nights braying, hooting, cooing, whining, bellowing, and barking. If only the donkeys and dogs and birds and a few other sacred animals of Egypt would be a little more reticent, especially after dark, the country would be faultless. But what with worrying myself, and listening to furred and feathered creatures worrying themselves, I couldn't sleep last night, and I want you to help me! You'll be here to-morrow afternoon, and I shall stay in to receive you instead of going to the bazaars with the others, chaperoned by that dark-eyed devil of yours, "Antoun." I was there all yesterday, watching crowds of tourists buy beautiful expensive things for themselves, and horrid inexpensive things to take to their friends. Cleopatra purchased some disgracefully cheap pearls no self-respecting *mummy* would be seen in; and my prophetic soul tells me that she's going to try and dissolve them in wine.

There's to be a fancy dress ball at this hotel to-morrow night—or rather in the adjacent Casino, which is one reason we migrated here; and praise the saints you'll be in time for it because if anything's going to happen, you'll be able to stop whatever it is. If I were supposed to know that Antoun was Anthony Fenton, I might take him into my counsels. As it is, I can't. And anyhow, it wouldn't do much good, at present, because a silent duel is going on between him and Monny. He is bent on compelling her to acknowledge his authority. She is bent on resisting it—which is a great compliment to his power—but he doesn't know that, for he doesn't know Monny yet. It would be fun to watch them together, if I hadn't your interests to think of.

He hasn't got rid of Bedr el Gemály; but he would have done so, I'm sure, if it hadn't been for an unexpected turn of the wheel, by the hand of Fate in the person of Rachel Guest. Her hand is never *off* the wheel just now! The few days since you have been away have brought out the true inwardness of her. *Felis Domestica* with very little *Domestica!* Perhaps it's the air of Egypt which is having a really extraordinary effect on all of us; perhaps it's the fact that Monny has given Rachel a lot of lovely clothes which have rejuvenated and apparently revitalized her. But you will see for yourself, and talk things over with Your old friend, Biddy.

This was a nice letter to read, heaven knew how many hours too late!

My fatigue had slipped off like the skin off a grape. I felt energetic enough to start out and walk to Cairo. What could be in Biddy's mind? And what must she have thought when afternoon and evening passed without even a telegram? The evening paper, if she had happened to look, would have told her that the *Candace* had reached Alexandria in the morning, as she expected; and she could neither have guessed nor believed that the whole day would pass without my having a chance to read her letter. I ransacked the writing-table drawers for a telegraph form; and finding one had begun to address it, when I stopped. The message could not go out until morning. Meanwhile there were Monny's and Anthony's letters to read. One or both might give me some clue to the "climax" Biddy feared for to-night at the ball. I cut open Monny's envelope, which had on it an alluring sunset picture of the Pyramids and the name of the hotel. Hastily I ran through the pages. Not a hint of anything disquieting! If I had read her letter instead of Brigit's I might have gone to my well-earned rest without a qualm.

"Dear Lord Ernest," Miss Gilder addressed me, in a handwriting which to any "expert" would reveal some originality, more pride, still more conscientiousness, any amount of self-will, and singularly little conceit. An odd combination! But the Gilded Rose is that. She went on:

You asked me to write to you while you were away, and tell you the news, and what I thought about things. But I'm thinking so much and so fast that I can't sort out my thoughts. I suppose it must be so with every one who comes to Egypt for the first time. Everything fascinates and absorbs me, even more than I had hoped it would—almost too much, I feel sometimes. Your Antoun Effendi is a very good guide, and I am not sorry that we have him—except once in a while. And now and then I'm glad. We're proud of his looks when we go about, for every one stares at him and envies us for having him to take us about, instead of being condemned to a mere dragoman. Oh, talking of dragomen (you see I *will* call them that!), we still have Bedr, though I know you thought we ought to give him up, and I don't see how we are ever to discharge him now, for he has attached himself to Rachel G. in the most wonderful way. It is *pathetic*. It began with a talk they had the day you left, about his having been in America, and about *religion*. She found him half inclined to be converted, and of course, her goodness and unselfishness made her long to snatch him like a brand from the burning. He thinks no one ever talked so wonderfully about religion as she does, which she, dear thing, attributes to the fact that she taught Sunday-school in Salem. She says, if she can have him to work upon even for a few weeks, she is sure to make him a convert.

We haven't wasted a minute since you went away, but have seen sights from morning till night, so as not to have missed anything when we leave Cairo on the *Enchantress Isis*. I hope you'll be pleased that I've given up my dream of having a private dahabeah, and that we shall be with you on Sir Marcus Lark's boat. She is really a beauty. Antoun took us over her, and on board we met Sir Marcus, who was showing some friends round. Antoun introduced him to us. I think Sir M. asked him to do it. We had great fun, for Sir Marcus seemed to take the most violent fancy to Aunt Clara, who didn't like him at all. She says now that she believes when she was Cleopatra he was Caesar, and that it's a pity he can't wear a wreath to hide his baldness, as she remembers his doing then. It's only a *very* little bald spot, really, and Rachel

Guest says it reminds her of a tonsure on the head of a fine-looking monk. Aunt C. quite resents Sir Marcus being able to engage the services of you and Antoun. She wants you both to be there, but she doesn't like Sir M. to have a superior position to Antoun's. That day on the *Enchantress Isis* Sir M. invited us to have tea on the deck, and it really was enchanting; a deck like a huge open-air drawingroom, or one of our biggest verandas at Newport, or somewhere, with jolly green wicker chairs and tables and sofas with heaps of cushions. But I forgot—you've seen the boat. The best rooms *were* engaged, but when we talked to Sir Marcus, he called a man who can speak many languages in bits—broken English, cracked German, fractured French, and goodness knows what all. Between them, they arranged it somehow that we should have our choice, and the other people were to take what was left. I would have refused, because it didn't seem fair, but it was for Aunt Clara's sake, evidently, that Sir M. wanted to make the exchange, and *she* accepted. She was as haughty as a queen, but in rather a fascinating, soft way that I think men like. And she was looking beautiful. So is Rachel, as even Biddy admits. I do believe Rachel looks younger than I do, in some new dresses and hats she has. I never noticed before, but I fancy now that we're rather alike. I'm so delighted to see her enjoying herself so much, for you know, she's *wonderful*. Think what courage it must have taken to break with her tiresome old life, because she felt she must see the glory of the world, when a tiny legacy gave her the chance she'd longed for. She wouldn't have had a penny left, after she'd finished her trip, if Aunt C. and I hadn't been able to help her out. It's a privilege to do anything for such a brave creature. And I can't bear to think of her having to go back when this is over, to the dull round. Perhaps some way out will be found for her.

I've fallen in love with Cairo, although—or perhaps because—I still feel as if I were moving in a marvellous picture. Antoun does make it live for us! I will say that for him, though he can be so annoying that at times he spoils everything, and makes me wish you'd won my hat instead of my winning his green turban. I'm dying to find out how you got it. But, of course, I can't ask him: it would be *infra dig*. You *must* tell me when you come. I think the one he wears now is handsomer though. I wish I could change it for mine.

We have been to heaps of mosques, and I can't help wishing we were the only tourists in Cairo. Of course, this is a selfish wish; and as dear Biddy says, it's quite funny to think how each tourist feels that *he* is the only spiritual-minded, imaginative person travelling—that he alone has the right to be in Egypt—that all the others are offensive, vulgar creatures, who desecrate the beautiful places with their presence. But really, you know, it gets on one's nerves, meeting droves of silly men in pith helmets with little white lambrequins looped up, when it would be so much more appropriate to wear the kind of hats they have at home. And some of the women are *weird!* They have the queerest ideas of what is suitable for Egypt. One friend of Bedr's refused to go about and be seen with the ladies who'd engaged him, as he was the smartest dragoman in Cairo and had his reputation to keep up. Don't you *like* that? Even Antoun laughed—which he hardly ever does. He's so dignified I wish his turban would blow off or something. I *wonder* how he'd look without it, and if most of the charm would be gone? Almost, I hope so. One doesn't like to catch one's self feeling toward an Egyptian, even for a minute, as one does toward men of one's own blood —I mean, on the same level, or even as if a person like that were *above* one. It's just the picturesque dignity of the *costume,* and the *pose,* perhaps. And then, this strange glamour of the East is over everybody and everything, here. I used to wonder why people wrote and spoke of the East as *mysterious.* Why should it be more mysterious than the West? I would ask. Nobody could explain exactly. They said only, "It is." Now I know why—at least I *feel* why. Without his green turban, or in European coat instead of his graceful silk robe, and away from these luminous sunsets of pale rose and gold and emerald, Antoun would be nothing extraordinary, would he? He says he is considered old fashioned in his way of dress. Most of his friends wear European clothes, and the tarboosh which Egyptians love because it never blows away or falls off when they pray. He *does* make me angry, because he wants to banish the beggars and poor men who sell things in the street, instead of letting me give and buy. What am I *for,* with all my money, except to do things for people? And it's such fun making them happy by saying "I *want* a cat-necklace—" or a scarab, or whatever they have, instead of pushing past with a stony glare as if they were dust under our feet. Of course we're attended by great crowds whereever we go, because it's got round that we don't refuse any one, consequently it takes a *little* long to arrive anywhere. But what does that matter in Egypt? Already I'm losing my American hustle. I want to eat lotuses, which seem out of season in Egypt now! I've asked for them everywhere but can't get them. I want to feel back in the Middle Ages, in Cairo, which, as Antoun says, is an Oriental and Medieval Gateway to the Egypt older than history. And how I am looking forward to the *Desert!* Sir Marcus tells us that *you* are to take the people of the *Candace* for a desert trip before they go up the Nile; so of course you must count us among your "trippers," and Mr. Willis and Mr. Sheridan, who have settled to go on the *Isis*. You didn't mention the desert plan before you went away!

No news of that poor, beautiful child, Wretched Bey's wife though I've written twice. I'm worried about her. Mabel she used to be. Now she's Mabella Hânem! Biddy says you'll arrive for the ball to-morrow night. But somehow I don't *feel* you will. I don't know why you should. Men don't care for such things much. And of course I shall not dance, as I'm still in half mourning. I shall only look on, and then—Rachel and I have an amusing plan for the end of the evening. But even if you came, we couldn't let you into the secret, as you would think it silly.

Yours sincerely,

ROSAMOND GILDER.

Mine "sincerely, Rosamond Gilder!" So she ended her letter, with youthful and characteristic dignity, childishly unaware, apparently, that there was more to read between the lines than in the lines themselves.

Had I read this Rosamond letter first, the last four or five sentences would have meant little for me. As it was, I would have given a month out of my future for the gift of an astral body which could go this minute to the ball at the Ghezireh Palace. I was lost in the mystery of that "amusing plan."

In Anthony's letter lay my last hope of a clue. But in it there was none. He did not even mention Monny's name. It was all about that "desert trip" which, from her, I hadn't taken seriously. Sir Marcus was actually planning it. Kruger had written that some of the passengers were clamouring for a few days' camping, and the idea was to send them off in my care, after three days in Cairo, while the others remained in charge of Antoun, who wasn't yet ready to leave. Fenton said:

Somebody's trying to defeat my scheme for getting the sheikh's tomb moved. I don't know who it is yet. Meanwhile my time and my head are so full, that in the few hours of the night I put aside for sleep, I dream queerer dreams than the visits of ghostly sheikhs. Apropos of dreams, do you know by chance a man who answers this description: elderly, stoutish, red face, gray hair, black moustache, pale eyes with sharp look in them. Sounds commonplace, doesn't it?

But I have a recurring dream of such a man, whose face I never saw elsewhere. For the last three nights, as soon as I shut my eyes, he comes. He seems to interrupt some scene between you and Lark, and myself, and I see him looking over Lark's shoulder. Then he turns quickly away, and tiptoes off to a very low, closed door in a deep recess. There he disappears into shadow—and I wake up with a jump, or slide off into another dream—but generally this rouses me, for there's an impression of something stealthy in the shadow round the door. That so ordinary a type of person should be in a dream. You'll laugh at my asking if you've ever known such a man, and say that I'm back at my old tricks again, as a dreamer of dreams. Never mind, I scored, dreaming of our Mountain of the Golden Pyramid the night before I got your letter with Ferlini's papers. I can't help feeling that there may be something in dreams—in mine, anyhow, though I never have any except in Egypt. This one about the red-faced man and the closed door in the deep recess is getting a bit on my nerves.

Excited as I was over the patchwork of news, I laughed scornfully at Anthony's dream. For the man he described might be Colonel Corkran.

CHAPTER X

THE SECRET MONNY KEPT

Cairo at last! My watch said that the journey took only three hours; but my nerves said six.

I had telegraphed Biddy first thing in the morning the hour of my arrival with the "*Candace* crowd," and I half expected to see her at the big white and red station, but there was no familiar form in the throng, the gay throng which excited my charges. Everything interested them; the black face of the Sudanese engine driver who looked down from his huge British locomotive, the display of English, French and German literature mingled with Greek, Italian, Arab, or Turkish papers on the bookstall; the ebony and copper-coloured luggage carriers who seemed eager to take one another's lives, but in reality desired no more than to snatch each other's jobs, under the eyes of the uniformed hotel-porters. To me, the busy place was a desert, lacking one face.

Even outside the station-yard, and in the streets and squares where silent camels looked their contempt of electric trams, soldiers in khaki uniforms jostled Bedouins in khaki robes, and drivers of arabeahs made the way one long procession of shrieks, I still glanced at passing carriages in hopes of a belated Biddy. All in vain! And destitute of news I resigned myself to the task of piloting the Set out to Mena House. The moon would be full that night—and it's "the thing" to be a neighbour of the Sphinx while the moon feeds her with honey.

The Flock, under the guidance of Mr. Watts, had now definitely parted from the Set, chieftained by me. They went meekly off to the cheaper hotels, where they would live before boarding the *Candace* again for Palestine, and Colonel Corkran, who was supposed to have joined that party, had announced that he was "bound for a long talk with Mark the Lark." Mr. Watts, refused by Enid Biddell and separated from her, had relapsed into melancholia. He had ceased to brilliantine his once sleek hair, and dust and crumbs were allowed to collect in each fold of his clerical waistcoat. As we of the Set buzzed richly away in taxicabs, I saw him in a shabby arabeah between two old ladies, gazing wistfully after us. He was envying me Enid!

It is a wonderful drive through Cairo to the Pyramids, whether you spin out there in a motor, or trot on a donkey, or lilt on a camel, squatting cross-legged on a load of green bersím. Past the great swinging bridge, and the Island of Ghezireh (the word that in itself means "island") begins the six-mile dyke, which is the road made by Ismaïl to please the Empress Eugénie. Since her visit, in the days when the Suez Canal was opened, it has pleased two empresses, and more queens than I have time to count. Under the deep shade of lebbek trees it goes on and on, toward the Pyramids, a dark cool avenue, high above cultivated fields flooded by the Nile when the river is "up." The emerald waves of grain flow like green water to the foot of the broad dyke-road, and canals like long, tight-drawn blue ribbons are threaded through it, their ends lost to sight at the shimmering horizon.

Even at this noon hour when the world should have been eating lotuses or luncheon, the interminable arbour was crowded with strings of camels, forever going both ways, into Cairo and out, one wondered why —and there were flocks of woolly brown sheep, and donkeys drawing sideless carts in which whole families of veiled women and half-naked children were seated tailor fashion. On we spun, past the Zoo, past scattered villas of Frenchified, Oriental fashion which might have been designed by a confectioner: past azure lakes left by the ebbing Nile, and so into sudden dazzling sight of three geometric mountains in a tawny desert—two, monsters in size, and one a baby trying to catch up with them.

"Oh!" everybody breathed. For these things were beyond words.

Then in a moment more the Great Pyramid had grown so big that it loomed over us, and ate up half the sky—a pyre of yellow flame against a flame of blue.

We were at the end of the shadowy road that leads like a causeway to the desert, and on the verge of the golden, billowing sea which flows round the Pyramids and engulfs the distant Sphinx. Oriental life encircled us, in the foreground of the picture—a long row of waiting camels gaily saddled and tasselled, delicately nibbling bersím green as heaped emeralds—donkeys white and gray, beribboned and beaded—small yellow sandcarts; little white, desert horses and tall brown, desert men; camels snarling, donkeys braying, horses whinnying, and men touting. "Very nice sandcarts—very nice camels!

Take ladies and gentlemen quick to Pyramids and Sphinx or Petrified Forest!" Farther on, the big, modern hotel, rather like an overgrown Swiss chalet built by Arabs—a vast, confused building the colour of sand or brown heather honey, with carved mushrbiyeh work lending an Eastern charm to windows, balconies, and loggias, and enough green, flowery garden to give a sensational effect of contrast with the tidal wave of desert poised ready, it would seem, to overwhelm palms and roses. Clustered near, the tiny mushroom village which huddles under the shelter of Cheops' Pyramid. Beyond, the immense upward sweep of golden dunes, culminating in the Great Pyramid itself.

I stayed in the picture only long enough to settle my big children into their quarters, and to see most of them making for the dining-room, agreeably Oriental with its white and red walls, its dome and windows of mushrbiyeh work. Then I darted back to Cairo, in a taxi driven by a Nubian youth, so black that he was almost blue, like a whortleberry. He wore a scarlet tarboosh, a livery of violet, and the holes for silver rings in the tops of his ears were so large that the light shining through gave the effect of inserted diamonds. Unconsciously he made a nice contrast with his modern motor.

He drove with such reckless speed that camels "rubber-necked" to look at us—and whirled me past the fat black gate-keeper into the Ghezireh Palace garden of scarlet paths, moonlike lamps, Khedivial statues, and spreading banyans where each tree continued itself in its own "next number," like an endless serial romance.

I nearly asked for Mrs. O'Brien, but turned her into Jones at the danger point. The face of the concierge, as he said that she was at home, conveyed nothing, yet I could not resist adding, "Are the ladies well?"

"Mrs. East is not very well to-day," he replied. "We have had the doctor; but the young ladies have been out spending the night with friends, I believe. They have not yet returned."

It was a long five minutes before Biddy and I were wildly shaking hands in a huge private sitting-room all red-and-gold brocade and crystal chandeliers, as it had been in the days of Ismaïl. I knew I should be delighted to see her, but I didn't realize that it was going to be quite as good as it was.

"Anyhow, *you're* all right and safe," I heard myself blurt out.

"I'm safe, but not all right!" she reproached me. "My messenger who went to the train didn't find you from my description, I know, because he came back with my note——"

"Too flattering, was your description, or the other way?" I asked, trying to buoy her up with frivolity.

"You wouldn't joke if you'd read the note. Oh, Ernest, Monny and Rachel have disappeared!"

"Good gracious! But Anthony——"

"He went to look for them, of course; and he's disappeared, too."

"By Jove!" The exclamation sounded inadequate, but I was so taken aback that I had nothing else to say. It seemed impossible that Anthony, instead of averting danger, could be involved in it himself. It was unlike his resourcefulness. I could not believe it of him, and so, when I had time to control mind and tongue, I said as much to Biddy.

"Yes, I felt like that, too, at first," she admitted. "He gives one the impression of being so infallible in any emergency, somehow, as if he'd be above it, and look down on it from his height. But it's more than twelve hours since he went, and he promised to send me word how things were going on if he couldn't get to me himself. No word has come."

"What have you done?" I asked. "Have you communicated with the police?"

"Sir Marcus Lark has. He was at the ball, and has been very good. But it's for Mrs. East's sake, mostly. One feels he's glad it happened, to give him the chance to win her gratitude—or something. He's been back and forth all day; and I'm expecting him any minute. Mrs. East has been fainting and hysterical, and everything early Edwardian, so I sent for a doctor. But she's better on the strength of *sal volatile* and eggnog, and she's promised to see Sir Marcus."

"Now tell me what happened, from the beginning," I said, when I had made Biddy sit down by me on the sofa, and was trying to warm a cold little hand in mine.

What it all amounted to, told disjointedly, was this: Since Monny had had an inspiration the day after our arrival in Cairo, to give Rachel Guest a lot of her new unworn clothes, Rachel had become quite girlish and "flighty." She had lost her puritan primness, and behaved more in accordance with her slanting eyes than with her bringing up. She giggled like a schoolgirl rather than a schoolmistress, tried to make herself look young, and copied Monny in the way she tilted her hat and dressed her hair. No harm in this; but it had seemed to Biddy that Rachel deliberately incited the girl to do things which "Antoun" disapproved. Brigit fancied that Bedr's influence had been at work, for knowing as he did that "Antoun" would gladly have given him marching orders, he took pleasure in thwarting his superior when he could do so with safety. Bedr had been clever in enlisting the girls' sympathy for his soul. As for Biddy, she had disliked him from the first, and imagined that he had tacked himself onto our party as a spy, upon the receipt of orders from America, he having learned most of his English there. The idea appeared so far-fetched that she had abandoned it. Now, however, it was again hovering at the back of her mind.

Bedr had told Rachel stories of the fascination of hasheesh smoking, and had said that no stranger knew Cairo who did not visit one of the "best houses" where hasheesh, though forbidden, was still secretly smoked. He had assured her that there were several which were "perfectly respectable," even for the "nicest ladies and gentlemen;" and Rachel, probably at his suggestion, had tried to persuade Monny to make the expedition. Monny had mentioned it to "Antoun," in the presence of everybody; and as Rachel and Bedr had looked guilty, Biddy guessed that they had wished to keep the plan a secret.

"Antoun" had perhaps too brusquely vetoed the idea. He said that there were no such houses, which could be visited by ladies, and that it was absurd to think of going. That word "absurd" stung Monny. She began to protest that Bedr knew Cairo as well as Antoun did, and was as likely to be right. "I don't see why we shouldn't go, if others do," she persisted, "and I've always longed to know what a hasheesh dream was like, ever since I read De Quincey. A little, just once, could do us no harm, and Rachel says——"

But what Rachel had said was evidently not for publication. Miss Guest stopped her with a hand on hers, and a "*Dear* Monny, please don't let us think of it any more, if Antoun Effendi disapproves. Maybe it was a silly idea, and we've plenty of amusing things to do every minute."

Monny was apparently contented to let the idea slip, and Brigit had thought that, in the excitement of getting ready for the ball, she and Rachel had really forgotten it. Then, before writing me, she had overheard Rachel say to her friend, "It's for twelve o'clock sharp." And Monny had answered, "Won't it be *great!* Does Bedr think——" But she had stopped short at sight of Brigit.

Even this did not suggest to Biddy a visit to a "hasheesh den," for various other plans had been broached and discouraged by "Antoun." She did not feel that, as she was not supposed to know his real status, she could go "blabbing" to him; and fearing that mischief was on foot, she had wished for me. When

I didn't arrive, she soothed herself by reflecting that, after all, she need only keep a sharp watch over Monny when midnight drew near. None of the party intended to dance, and so it would be easy, Brigit thought, to "have an eye upon the girls."

Monny had bought Oriental costumes for herself and Rachel. They were rather conspicuous, luckily for Biddy's plan, for among the many gorgeous dresses in the Casino she had no difficulty in tracking those two. Until half past eleven, she told herself, she need not be on the alert every instant; but therein had lain her mistake. Sir Marcus Lark had appeared, dressed (more or less) as a Roman officer of the Occupation days, he having heard Mrs. East remark that, "whatever *anybody* said, it was her favourite period." The lady, of course, had not missed such an opportunity to appear as Cleopatra. She had brought a costume with her from New York; and while Biddy "lost herself" in watching the effect of this magnificence on Sir Marcus, the girls vanished.

Without alarming Mrs. East, Brigit had begun to search. She asked everybody she knew in the ballroom if the girls had gone out, and inquired in the cloakroom; but the two had been seen by nobody. It was as if they had melted into air; and Brigit began to suspect that they must have covered up their brilliant dresses with dominoes smuggled into the Casino. Willis Bailey was at the ball, but he had developed a flirtation with Miss Guest, and Biddy felt that he was not to be trusted as a confidant. Perhaps, too, he had helped the girls to disappear. It seemed cruel to frighten Mrs. East, when the scheme, whatever it was, might be no more than an innocent freak; so Biddy said nothing to Queen Cleopatra or her Roman attendant. She slipped across the garden to the hotel, and sent an Arab messenger off in a taxi with a note to the address "Antoun" had told her would find him. In less than an hour he arrived, and when he had listened to her account of what had happened, he said after a minute's reflection that the ladies had almost surely gone with Bedr to some hasheesh den, or a place masquerading as such. "Antoun" consoled Biddy as well as he could, by saying that no harm would come to Miss Gilder or Miss Guest. Bedr would know too well on which side his bread was buttered to take his clients where insult or danger could reach them. Off "Antoun" went to look for the missing ones though, and assured Biddy that she should have news as soon as possible.

It was not till three o'clock that she had begun to be very anxious, and had disturbed the harmony of Sir Marcus Lark's duet with Mrs. East. Even then she would not have spoken had she not feared that the ball would break up, and there would be no man to appeal to!

Sir Marcus had been inclined to smile at the notion of danger; but he, like Anthony Fenton, was ignorant of any private qualms which troubled Brigit O'Brien. She could not tell him who she was, and that she considered herself far from being a "mascot" to her fellow-travellers. If she had told, and added that she feared enemies who might for certain reasons make a mistake in Monny's identity, he would have laughed his hearty laugh, and said that such melodramatic things didn't happen, even in Egypt.

"But *you* know," Biddy appealed to me, "that melodramatic things *have* happened to me and those near me. I'm not even *sure* that poor Richard's death was natural, though I watched over him like a hawk in those dreadful days when he was fearing every shadow, and we were flitting from pillar to post, with Esmé. Through Richard two men were electrocuted. He used to get threatening letters forwarded from place to place, always signed with the same initials, and he wouldn't tell me what they meant. It was because of them that he hid Esmé in a convent-school before he died; for she was threatened as well as he. I, too, for the matter of that! Not that the child or I had done the organization any harm; but Esmé is of his blood, and they may have thought I had more of their secrets than I really have. I've not used the name of O'Brien for years now, and I've moved about so much that sometimes I have felt I must be safe. Still, I ought perhaps not to have gone to visit Esmé, though she wrote and begged me to, for special reasons I needn't bother you with: a curious little love romance which I fear must end badly. I didn't think of danger to Monny; but you see, as I've told you, the convent isn't far from Monaco. I got off the *Laconia* there, to visit Esmé, and when I came on board again, Monny and Mrs. East and Rachel came with me. They'd been in Italy and France, and had picked up Miss Guest, who was only too enchanted to batten on Monny's kindness and dollars. It was I who had engaged their staterooms, on a cable from Monny, long before. And if there were a spy anywhere, he might have the idea that I wanted to smuggle Esmé out of her convent by a trick, and—"

"But almost every one must know Miss Gilder's face from her photographs in newspapers," I broke in, on a stifled sob of Biddy's. "She couldn't be mistaken for another girl, as an unimportant young person might."

"I'm not sure. Those photographs were snapshots, and very bad, as you must know if you've ever seen any. Monny never gave a portrait of herself to a newspaper, and it's years since they got hold of a good one. Besides, if she weren't mistaken for Esmé O'Brien, that wretched Bedr might have made up a plot to have her kidnapped for ransom. It was the thing Monny's father was always afraid of—absurdly afraid of, I *used* to think."

"I think so still," I said. "Such things don't happen—anywhere, to a grown-up girl."

"What about Raisuli in Tangier?" Biddy challenged me. "He used to kidnap people whenever he liked. And so do lots of brigands."

"We haven't to do with brigands."

"Oh, what's in a name? And I wouldn't put *anything* past that horrid Bedr."

"As Anthony said to you, he knows which side his bread's buttered."

"But if he hopes some one will give him more butter for being wicked than he can get from us for being good?"

"Let's not think of far-fetched contingencies, dear," said I. "Now you've told me all, I will try to do something—"

"May I come in?" boomed a big voice at the door. "I knocked and nobody answered, so I thought the room would be empty—"

Biddy dropped my hand like a hot potato. She had jumped up so quickly from our sofa that Sir Marcus Lark's observant eyes could hardly have seen us sitting there together.

"Of course, come in," she said. "Have you anything to tell? But I'll call Mrs. East. She won't like you to begin without her."

Biddy darted off to an adjoining room, leaving me alone with my employer.

"What do you think of this affair?" I wanted to know. "Well," said he, "I can only judge other men by myself. If I had such a chance to appear a hero in the eyes of a pretty woman as Fenton has, I'm afraid I'd be tempted to take advantage of it, even if I had to play some trick to make myself indispensable. Now you see in a nutshell what I think. Captain Fenton will certainly rescue those young ladies from a trap if he has to make the trap himself."

I was disgusted, and shrugged my shoulders. "You have a poor opinion of Fenton," I said.

"On the contrary, I think very highly of his intelligence. I'm not worrying about any one of the three, though don't mention it to Mrs. East or Mrs. Jones that I said so. I've come to tell them that my men have searched Cairo and found nothing. Not the police, you know; I haven't applied to the police after all. I thought Fenton would be furious. And anyhow it might make talk. But I've paid the best dragomans in town to look sharp; and they know as much about this old place as the police do, if not more. By the way, Lord Ernest, did Corkran say anything to you about an intention to throw over his job on the *Candace*?"

"No. He said he was going to call on you, that's all."

"He did call. I was out—on this business, as it happens. He waited, and I found him, making himself at home in my sitting-room—which I use as a kind of office. I wish I knew how many of my letters and papers he'd had time to read."

"Surely he wouldn't—"

"I shouldn't say 'surely' was the word. I'd gone out in a hurry and left things scattered about—which isn't my habit. When I came back, it struck me that my desk looked a bit tempting for a man with a retired conscience. I was going to keep him on the *Candace*, rather than fuss, because it wasn't so much his fault as mine that he was the wrong man in the place. He couldn't do any harm in Jerusalem, it seemed. Let him wail in the Jews' Wailing Place, if he'd any complaints, said I to myself. I thought he was too keen on money to resign because his silly pride was hurt. But to my surprise, he informed me that he'd come to 'hand in his papers,' as he called it. So much the worse for his pocket and the better for mine! Only it struck me as d—d queer, considering Corkran's character. I wanted to ask if he'd spit out any venom to you."

"Not a drop," said I. But I, too, thought it queer, considering Corkran's character, and the fact that having resigned of his own free will, he could hardly expect Lark to pay his way home. It even occurred to me to wonder if the resignation were not a sudden thought of the Colonel's. He had spoken several times of going on to Palestine, and had mentioned the trip that morning. Had Sir Marcus said something inadvertently, which had so piqued Corkran that he threw over his appointment on the impulse? Or had he perhaps been dishonourable enough to glance at a letter, in which Lark referred to him in terms uncomplimentary?

As I asked myself these questions, Mrs. East came in with Brigit, and Sir Marcus forgot me. His face said "What a woman!" And anxiety was becoming to Cleopatra. It gave to her that thrilling look which only beautiful Jewesses or women of Latin race ever wear: a look of all the tragedy and mystery of womanhood since Eve. "What news of *them*?" she asked Sir Marcus, when she had given a ringed hand and an almond-eyed glance to me.

"No news exactly," said the big man, "but I feel sure your niece and her friend are safe—"

"My niece and her friend!" exclaimed Cleopatra, ungratefully frowning. "Why do you say nothing of 'Antoun?' Does nobody care what becomes of him?"

As she spoke, there was a knock at the door. One of the Arab servants of the hotel announced that a man had a letter for Mrs. Jones.

"Mrs. Jones?" cried Biddy. "I am Mrs. Jones. Where's the letter?"

"That man not give it to us. He say he see you or not give it at all."

"Well, why didn't you send him up?"

"Arab mans not let in hotel, if peoples don't ask for them."

"An Arab! Not—not—is he a stranger?"

"Yes, Missis. Very low man. Never comed before."

"Bring him here—quick!"

Five minutes passed. We tried to talk, but could think of nothing to say. Then the servant returned, ushering in a dwarfish Arab in a dirty white turban, and the shabby black galabeah worn only by the poor who cannot afford good materials and the bright colours loved by Egyptians.

"From Antoun Effendi?" asked Biddy, in excitement, as he held out a piece of folded paper, not in an envelope.

The man shook his head. "He spik no English," explained the servant who waited.

"*You* talk to him," Biddy appealed to me, while Cleopatra told the hotel footman that he might go. But I had no time to question the messenger. Biddy cried out as she unfolded the paper. "Why, Duffer, inside it's addressed to you! It says:

"'For Lord Ernest Borrow. To be opened by Mrs. Jones in his absence.'"

Within the outer wrapping was a second folded paper, of the same kind. They looked like sheets torn from a notebook. And I saw that the address, scrawled in pencil, was in Anthony's handwriting.

CHAPTER XI

THE HOUSE OF THE CROCODILE

The letter had evidently been dashed off in a great hurry. It was short and written in French, the language in which "Antoun" chose to talk with foreigners.

Give the bearer two hundred piastres and let him go. Don't try to make him speak. I have promised this. Then quick to Jarvis Pasha and get him to raid the House of the Crocodile. Question of hasheesh. We must be smuggled out when arrests are made—also Bedr, to save scandal.

Not a word as to whether all were safe, or in danger! But I realized that, for some reason, each instant had been of value. And each instant was of value now.

Anthony was one who knew precisely what he wanted and why he wanted it. I obeyed his instructions implicitly. Two hundred piastres went from my pocket into the hand of the withered Arab, and he was allowed to take his departure despite a burst of protest from my companions, who naturally wished the man to be catechised. Once the door had shut behind the bent blue back, I handed round the letter, which had to be translated for Sir Marcus, who professed contempt for "foreign gibberish."

Jarvis Pasha is at the head of the police, has been for many years, and is the most interesting man in Egypt after the well-beloved "K." Leaving Sir Marcus to go on with his task of consoling Mrs. East, I dashed off in my waiting taxi with the Nubian of the silver earrings. We drove to the Governorat, a big house in a square near what was once known as the Guarded City, the very heart and birthspot of Cairo: Masrel Kahira, the Martial, founded under the planet Mars.

I scribbled a line to Jarvis Pasha, and sent it to him in an envelope with my card. This combination opened doors for me; and three minutes later I was shaking hands with a tall, thin, white moustached, hawk-featured Englishman who looked all muscle and bones and brain. Jarvis Pasha being in the secret of "Antoun's" identity and business in Cairo, simplified the explanation, and did away with the necessity for a preface. All I had to tell was the brief story of the girls' disappearance with Bedr el Gemály, and Fenton's following them into space; then, how word had come after fourteen hours.

"The House of the Crocodile," Jarvis Pasha said, when he had taken and read the letter. "H'm! Do you know anything about that house?"

"I know the old stories connected with it," I answered. "If it's reputation to-day is as sinister as ever——."

"Not at all. Figuratively speaking it has been whitewashed. It's become a show place—*a monument historique*. This is interesting information which Fenton sends, but if it came from any one else, I should say he had dreamed it. He may be giving us the chance of an important *coup*. Wait a few minutes, and I'll have this thing attended to, Lord Ernest. But you look upset. Is it that you haven't had lunch, or are you worrying about the ladies?" "Both," I answered with a sickly grin. "Not that I mind about lunch. I couldn't have eaten if I'd had the time."

"You haven't as much belief as I have, in your friend," remarked Jarvis Pasha, "if you think he'd let them come to harm." "They're all in the same box, apparently," I excused my lack of faith.

"Trust Fenton!" said the Head of the Police. "He was sharp enough to find the needles in the haystack, and he's smart enough and strong enough to take care of them when they're found."

On this, Jarvis Pasha went out and left me to my reflections, which rushed to the House of the Crocodile. Every one who has read or heard stories of native Cairo, knows the House of the Crocodile, in the Street of the Sisters, and how, in the later days of Mohammed Ali, people scarcely dared to name it aloud. The "Tiger" Defterdar Ahmed built it, for that beautiful Tigress, Princess Zohra, favourite daughter of Mohammed Ali, who married her off to the fierce soldier when she became too troublesome at home. Zohra had loved a young Irish officer who was murdered for her sake, and had no true affection to give Ahmed or any other. She hated all men because of the murderer, her own nephew, and vowed that since her love had cost the life of the one who had her heart, others who dared to love her must pay the same price. When Ahmed died suddenly, soon after the wedding, those who had heard of Zohra's vow (and there were many in the harems) whispered "poison." Never again did the Princess drive out to see the women she knew; and those who had been her friends were sent away from the door of the dead

Ahmed's palace, over which he had suspended for "luck," a huge crocodile killed in the far south. But Zohra was beautiful, with strange eyes which drew love whether she asked for it or not; and sometimes a small lattice would open in a bay of one of those windows of wooden lace whose carving was known as mushrbiyeh work because shirib, or sherbet, used to be placed there to cool. Out of the lattice would look a wonderful face, as thinly veiled as the moon by a mist, and then it would vanish so quickly that a man who saw, half believed that he had dreamed. But the eyes of the dream seemed to call, and could not be forgotten, any more than the song of a siren can cease to echo in ears which once have heard.

After the beginning of Zohra's widowhood, the noblest and handsomest youths of Cairo began mysteriously to disappear. They would be well and happy one day, and the next they would be gone from the places that knew them. By and by their bodies would be found in a canal; always the same canal, near the water gate of the House of the Crocodile. Then the vow of the Princess was remembered: but there was no English rule in those days, and the police shut their ears and eyes where a daughter of Mohammed Ali was concerned. Mothers and sisters of handsome young men shuddered and begged those they loved never to pass through the dark Street of the Sisters (Sharia el Benât) where the crocodile grinned over the door, and the vision of a face looked down from a latticed window. The women thought of the water gate at the back of the house; the little children, who had heard secret words spoken, thought of the crocodile, and ran crying past the house; but the handsome young men thought only of the face, and each one said to himself, "She will not make *me* pay the price." Still, as years went on, bodies were seen in the water from time to time, with a tiny purple spot over the heart to show the curious that death had not come from drowning. And some, who looked for lost ones, could not reclaim them from the canal, for bodies were not always found. As time passed, it seemed to people who hurried by the house in the narrow street, that the crocodile grew larger and larger. It was said that it had been fed on the children of men Tiger Ahmed had murdered in Sennaar.

None dared to say what they believed of Princess Zohra, but when, after a long imprisonment by her nephew Abbas, in the House of the Crocodile, she escaped to Constantinople, nobody would live where she had lived, and the palace fell almost into ruin.

This was the story of the house where Monny Gilder and Rachel Guest and Anthony Fenton were now. I had heard it talked about by our Arab servants when I was a child, and had never forgotten, though scarcely since then had I thought of the tale, until the remembered name and the horrors attached to it jumped into my mind on reading Anthony's letter. What had happened in the House of the Crocodile since Zohra's day, I did not know; but because of the old story it seemed more sinister that my friends should appeal for help from that place than from any other in Cairo.

I was not left long alone. Five minutes after Jarvis Pasha went out of the room to "arrange things" according to Fenton's request, he sent me a man with whiskey and soda, and biscuits. I drank gladly, and ate rather than seem ungrateful. But there was a lump in my throat which would stick there, I knew, until those three were away from the House of the Crocodile. I was still crumbling biscuits when Jarvis Pasha came briskly back.

"Well," he asked, "are you braced up now? If you'd like to be in this business, you can. I'm sending a white superintendent with my police to raid the house, on the strength of Fenton's letter to you, though until now the place hasn't been suspected. As I said, it's been a 'show' house, for some years—ground floor and first story in repair, just as in Zohra's day—upper floors ruinous, and the public not admitted there. If anything queer's going on, it must be in the forbidden part: and the caretaker is mixed up in the show. A pity you felt bound to let Fenton's messenger off! You can go with my superintendent, Allen, and reach your friends as soon as my men do. Allen has instructions to let Fenton and the ladies, if they're found there, slip away, and it's best for you to be on the spot to save mistakes in identification. Also I've ordered a closed arabeah to wait for you, as near as possible—my men will show you where. You'll know it for certain by a red camellia on the Arab driver's European coat. And by the way, take this Browning, in case of an attack; which I don't anticipate."

As Jarvis Pasha spoke, he opened the door, and summoned in a brown young Britisher wearing the tarboosh which denotes "Gyppy" officialdom. Evidently Allen was prepared for me as I for him, and we started off together on foot, for it seemed that our destination was not far away. We walked swiftly through the crowded Mousky (once the fashionable part of Cairo, before the tide flowed to the modern Isma'iliya quarter), and after a few intricate turnings plunged into a still, twilight region. The streets through which we passed were so narrow, and the old houses so far overhung the path that the strip of sky at the top of the dark canyon was a mere line of inlaid blue enamel flecked with gold. The splendid mushrbiyeh windows thrust out toward each other big and little bays, across the ten or twelve feet of distance which parted them, as if to whisper secrets; yet the delicate wooden carvings skilfully hid all that they wished to hide, and only suggested their secrets.

"Now we'll soon be coming to the House of the Crocodile," said Allen. "By Jove, it's a joke on us, and a smart one, if it's been turned into a hasheesh den, under our noses. But it must be something new, or we should have got onto it. The Chief thinks already he can guess who's at the bottom of the business and who has put the money up: a certain Bey, in whose service the caretaker was—a rich old Johnny, very old fashioned, who lives not far off in a beautiful house of the best Cairene period. He's keen on antiquities, and has been of service to the government in several ways, though he's a reformed smuggler; and his only son, dead now, was a hopeless hashash; that's what they call slaves of the hasheesh habit. I suppose you've read all about the 'Hashashseyn' of the Crusaders' days, whom we speak of as Assassins? Well, ever since then the Hashasheyn have had a bad reputation; but this old man I speak of has been pitied for his son's failings, which he pretends to think a 'judgment for his own past, repented sins.' Now, Lord Ernest, saunter, please, as if you were a tourist in my charge, admiring the old doorways."

Two native workmen appeared in front of us, with pickaxes on their shoulders. Stopping, they threw down their tools. One produced a cord which he stretched across the street from house to house; and in the middle he hung a small red flag. Then the pair began to pick in a leisurely way at the surface of the road, and before we reached the barrier, an Arab policeman stationed himself by the cord. Glancing ahead, I saw that the farther end of the narrow lane was blocked in the same manner.

"This is one trick we have of doing our work quietly," said Allen. "It always answers pretty well."

I said nothing, but used my eyes. Coming from nowhere apparently, there were twenty men in the street. A few had crowbars in their hands. Others, native policemen, carried the canes with which they control the movements of the people. From the shaded doorway of a large house a native sergeant of police stepped out as we approached, and saluted Allen. Over the closed door, a large, dryly smiling, ancient crocodile hung.

"Have our men come and taken their places?" asked my companion in Arabic.

"Yes, Effendi," the sergeant answered. "All has been done according to order. The back entrance which was the water gate before the old canal was filled up, is surrounded, and the adjoining houses with which some communication may have been established are watched. Not a rat could have crawled out since we came, nor could one have gone in. To-day is the feast of a saint, and these people have their excuse not to open the house to visitors, for so it is with other show places. Look, it is written up, that until to-morrow there is no admission." As the man pointed to a card hanging from a hook, he and Allen smiled at the cleverness of this pretext for closing the door. In English, French, and Arabic, the reason was announced in neat print. Probably this was not the first time the same excuse had been used in the same way.

"They must have taken alarm at something, and thought they were being watched," Allen said to me. "That's why they've sported their oak. I expect we shall make a haul, as—for everybody's sake concerned—they wouldn't dare let their clients out, to fall into a trap. Yes, that's why! Or else—"

He stopped, and I did not ask him to go on, for I knew that to ask would be useless. Yet I guessed what he had meant to say, and why he had stopped. He didn't wish to alarm me, but it was in his mind that the house had teen closed because of something planned to happen inside. And that something might be connected with my friends. We should soon know!

My first thought was that we were to get through the door, by breaking it in, or by forcing those on the other side to open for us. In an instant, however, I realized that my idea was absurd. It would take an hour to batter down that thick slab of old cedarwood, and Allen had said that he wanted to do things quietly. No, the brown sergeant was not here to open the door, but to see that it did not open unless for our benefit.

Two of Allen's men were unfolding a curious ladder like a lattice, which they made secure with screws when they had stretched it to full length. Then, up it went to one of the beautiful mushrbiyeh windows which, on the level of the story above the ground floor, bayed graciously, overhanging the street. One man standing below held the ladder firmly in place, while another, small and lithe as a monkey and enjoying the task as a monkey might, ran up to the top that leaned against the window. Evidently he was a skilled worker, for before I knew what he would be at, he had with some small, sharp instrument, prized out without breaking it, one of the sections of carved lattice. This he tossed lightly down to a man who caught it, and as he and four others after him slipped through the opening, the sergeant knocked on the closed door, under the swinging form of the crocodile. Nobody answered. But three minutes passed, and then suddenly there was the sound of a falling bar, and a very old, very dark man, with a white turban and a white beard, peeped out.

"Thieves!" he cried in Arabic. "Thieves break in at the windows!"

He was making the best of a bad business, I guessed, and hoped somehow to justify himself to the police. But though he was gray with fright, he forgot to look surprised.

My Arabic was not equal to the strain of catching all the gabble that followed: the old man protesting that it was right to close the house to-day; that if it were the police and not thieves who broke in, it was unjust, it was cruel, and his son Mansoor, the caretaker, would appeal to all the Powers. Before he had come to the end of his first breath, he was hushed and handcuffed, and hustled away; and another man sprang forward from behind the angle of a screen-wall inside the entrance. He was young, and looked strong and fierce as an angry giant, but at sight of Allen and the rest of us, he stopped as if we had shot him. Perhaps he had not expected so many. In any case, he saw that there was nothing he could hope to gain by violence or bluster. All he could do was to protest as his father had done, that this visit was a violation of his right to close the house on a holiday.

"Don't be a fool, Mansoor," said Allen, who evidently knew him. "You understand very well that isn't why we are here. You've jot a hasheesh den upstairs, above the public show rooms. A nice trick you thought you'd played us, but you see you didn't bring it off."

By this time we were inside the house, having thrust the caretaker in again, and passing the three tortuous screen walls of the entrance, into a courtyard. Several young Arabs dressed as servants stood there, large-eyed, and stricken at sight of their giant master held by four policemen. But there was not a sign of our men who had crawled through the window, and I was impatient to go where they had gone.

There was no sound of scuffling, no sound at all, except the crying of some startled doves, and Mansoor's voice, swearing by the Prophet's sacred beard that if anything were wrong he was not the one to blame. There were those above him who must be obeyed or he and all that were his would be put out of life; but I cared too little for him, or what might become of him and his, to listen much. I looked up and saw at the left of the courtyard, with its several closed doors, a short flight of steps with a mounting-block, and a doorway leading to a winding staircase. Round the court went a gallery, supported with old marble pillars, and underneath on one side was a large recess, the takhtabosh, raised slightly above the level of the courtyard, and having a row of wooden benches round its three walls. Here the caretaker and rough, evidently but lately put up. It was not so strong as the old one; and it yielded in a few minutes to the furious industry of our men with their crowbars. They lifted the door from its broken hinges, leaning it against a wall; and as we passed through, an Arab pulled aside a thick curtain which filled in a doorway. He was evidently a servant, and seeing the police, showed no sign of surprise, but only of a most humble resignation which disclaimed responsibility and begged for mercy.

In silence the man was taken into custody; and Allen and I, with three of the four policemen, passed into the region behind the portière. There, all was dusk, save for the faint light sifting down from a carved wooden dome in the ceiling, partly curtained; and a dark lantern flashed out a long revealing ray. The men ran to pull back heavy cloth hangings which entirely covered the latticed windows, and would allow lamps to be lit at night without being seen from street or courtyard. Instantly sunshine pierced the carved interstices, and let us see what Enterprise had done for his clients. We were in the antechamber of a long, beautiful room. The old, coloured marble of the durkááh—the lower level of floor nearest the entrance—had been repaired with new; the dilapidations of a fountain were almost hidden by pink azaleas in pots; the liwán, on the next level, had a good rug or two; and the diwáán, at the farthest and highest end, was furnished with red-covered mattresses and pillows. The low wall-benches of marble were set here and there with glass bowls of roses and syringa; and tiny cedarwood cupboards high in the tiled walls were open to show coffee cups, tobacco jars, and pipes made of cocoanut shells with long stems of cane.

Four men, who had apparently been lying on the mattresses, stood up and faced us, not fiercely, but with something of the attendant's resignation. Two were in European clothes, with the inevitable tarboosh; and two, equally well dressed, were old fashioned and picturesque in the long, silk gown and turban style which "Antoun" and other lovers of the ancient ways affected. They were of the "Effendi class," and might be merchants or professional persons. A turbaned man with a black beard Allen knew, and greeted in Arabic, "Hussein Effendi! Who would have thought to see you here!"

"Why not?" answered the other, with a melancholy smile and shrug of the shoulders. "There is no harm, really, but only in the eyes of the English. We are caught, and we cannot complain, for we have had true delight: and we have known, since the alarm came last night, that we might have to pay for our pleasure."

and his male relatives and friends had evidently been smoking their nargilehs and drinking coffee; our arrival had disturbed them in the midst.

Suddenly, into the frightened mourning of the doves, broke a sharp sound of cracking wood. "Come along!" cried Allen. "They'll be past the barrier in a minute!" And leaving Mansoor and the others to be dealt with by subordinates, he led the way up the steep stairs, at a run.

We did not stop at the first story, the "show" part of the House of the Crocodile; but catching a glimpse of a latticed balcony off the landing, all lovely mushrbiyeh work, and a great room of Persian tiled walls and coloured marble floor, beyond, we dashed up another flight of stairs to the story above. These stairs were of common wood, and somewhat out of repair. At the top was a door of carved cedarwood like those below, but rough in execution, faded, and with here and there a starpoint or triangle of the pattern missing, leaving a hole in the thick wood. On this door was nailed a large card with the notice in English, French, and Arabic, "Forbidden to the Public."

"What a grand idea to install a hasheesh den here!" I could not help thinking as I followed at Allen's heels to the head of the stairs, where two of his men worked with crowbars to prize open that theatrically dilapidated door. Behind the pair who worked were the others who had entered by the window below; and hardly had we taken our places in the strange *queue*, when with a loud groan the door gave way. The couple in front almost fell into a dark passage on the other side, and my heart leaped, for I half expected to see them driven back upon us by an attack with knives or pistols. But the dim vista seemed to hold only silence and emptiness as I peered over men's shoulders; and as we crowded in, Allen pushing ahead to take the lead, nothing stirred.

The passage was but a gallery, like that below, but instead of being open it was closed in with lattice of mushrbiyeh work, so that, though those within could look through, it was as secret for those outside as if it had been enclosed by a solid wall.

The darkness was patterned with light, like ebony thinly inlaid with gold, for the afternoon sunlight trickled into the delicate loopholes of the carving and we began to see what Enterprise had made of this ruinous upper story. The floor had been dilapidated and unsafe; but new boards had been laid over it, covered with Egyptian-made matting and rugs to deaden sound and give an appearance of comfort. We walked quickly along to the end of this closed gallery turned at right angles, and there found another door.

and his male relatives and friends had evidently been smoking their nargilehs and drinking coffee; our arrival had disturbed them in the midst.

Suddenly, into the frightened mourning of the doves, broke a sharp sound of cracking wood. "Come along!" cried Allen. "They'll be past the barrier in a minute!" And leaving Mansoor and the others to be dealt with by subordinates, he led the way up the steep stairs, at a run.

We did not stop at the first story, the "show" part of the House of the Crocodile; but catching a glimpse of a latticed balcony off the landing, all lovely mushrbiyeh work, and a great room of Persian tiled walls and coloured marble floor, beyond, we dashed up another flight of stairs to the story above. These stairs were of common wood, and somewhat out of repair. At the top was a door of carved cedarwood like those below, but rough in execution, faded, and with here and there a starpoint or triangle of the pattern missing, leaving a hole in the thick wood. On this door was nailed a large card with the notice in English, French, and Arabic, "Forbidden to the Public."

"What a grand idea to install a hasheesh den here!" I could not help thinking as I followed at Allen's heels to the head of the stairs, where two of his men worked with crowbars to prize open that theatrically dilapidated door. Behind the pair who worked were the others who had entered by the window below; and hardly had we taken our places in the strange *queue*, when with a loud groan the door gave way. The couple in front almost fell into a dark passage on the other side, and my heart leaped, for I half expected to see them driven back upon us by an attack with knives or pistols. But the dim vista seemed to hold only silence and emptiness as I peered over men's shoulders; and as we crowded in, Allen pushing ahead to take the lead, nothing stirred.

The passage was but a gallery, like that below, but instead of being open, it was closed in with lattice of mushrbiyeh work, so that, though those within could look through, it was as secret for those outside as if it had been enclosed by a solid wall.

The darkness was patterned with light, like ebony thinly inlaid with gold, for the afternoon sunlight trickled into the delicate loopholes of the carvings, and we began to see what Enterprise had made of this ruinous upper story. The floor had been dilapidated and unsafe; but new boards had been placed over it, covered with Egyptian-made matting and rugs to deaden sound and give an appearance of comfort. We walked quickly along to the end where this closed gallery turned at right angles, and there found another door, new and rough, evidently but lately put up. It was not so strong as the old one; and it yielded in a few minutes to the furious industry of our men with their crowbars. They lifted the door from its broken hinges, leaning it against a wall; and as we passed through, an Arab pulled aside a thick curtain which filled in a doorway. He was evidently a servant, and seeing the police, showed no sign of surprise, but only of a most humble resignation which disclaimed responsibility and begged for mercy.

In silence the man was taken into custody; and Allen and I, with three of the four policemen, passed into the region behind the portière. There, all was dusk, save for the faint light sifting down from a carved wooden dome in the ceiling, partly curtained; and a dark lantern flashed out a long revealing ray. The men ran to pull back heavy cloth hangings which entirely covered the latticed windows, and would allow lamps to be lit at night without being seen from street or courtyard. Instantly sunshine pierced the carved interstices, and let us see what Enterprise had done for his clients. We were in the antechamber of a long, beautiful room. The old, coloured marble of the durkááh—the lower level of floor nearest the entrance—had been repaired with new; the dilapidations of a fountain were almost hidden by pink azaleas in pots; the liwán, on the next level, had a good rug or two; and the diwáán, at the farthest and highest end, was furnished with red-covered mattresses and pillows. The low wall-benches of marble were set here and there with glass bowls of roses and syringa; and tiny cedarwood cupboards high in the tiled walls were open to show coffee cups, tobacco jars, and pipes made of cocoanut shells with long stems of cane.

Four men, who had apparently been lying on the mattresses, stood up and faced us, not fiercely, but with something of the attendant's resignation. Two were in European clothes, with the inevitable tarboosh; and two, equally well dressed, were old fashioned and picturesque in the long, silk gown and turban style which "Antoun" and other lovers of the ancient ways affected. They were of the "Effendi class," and might be merchants or professional persons. A turbaned man with a black beard Allen knew, and greeted in Arabic, "Hussein Effendi! Who would have thought to see you here!"

"Why not?" answered the other, with a melancholy smile and shrug of the shoulders. "There is no harm, really, but only in the eyes of the English. We are caught, and we cannot complain, for we have had true delight: and we have known, since the alarm came last night, that we might have to pay for our pleasure."

"If no harm has come, that's not due to you, but to a very different man, as you well know," I said. And as I spoke, the man I had in my mind appeared before my eyes. "Hullo!" I exclaimed, joyously.

Anthony's eyes and Allen's met; but I could not tell if they knew each other, nor could I ask then. It was enough for Allen in any case, however, that this magnificent Hadji was one of the friends for whom I searched. He turned to Bedr. "You brought two ladies here, I understand," he said quickly and sharply. "Then you must have acquaintance with the place. For good reasons which have nothing to do with you, I shall not arrest you, but you will have to report at the Governorat inside the hour, or you will regret it. Do you know the way out at the back of the house?"

"I do, gracious one," Bedr responded with businesslike promptness.

"Then take these gentlemen, and the ladies, whom I do not need to see, out by that door, and you will all be allowed to go, because my men who are there have seen Lord Ernest Borrow, and they have my instructions."

We waited for no more, but followed Anthony, who made a dash through the further room, and into another. There, on a mattress, crouched two forlorn figures, veiled as if in haste, and muffled in black satin *habberahs* such as Turkish ladies wear in the street.

"Lord Ernest! Oh, how glad I am!" cried one of these creatures, while the other, less vital or more miserable, whimpered and gurgled a little behind her veil.

"Come along, quick!" I said; and they came. Bedr led the way, thankful to show himself of use. Anthony followed as if to protect or screen the girls from sight. I brought up the rear, and so, scuttling through a rabbit warren of little unfurnished, dilapidated rooms, we found a narrow side staircase, and tumbled down it, anyhow, in dust and dimness. Then two more staircases, and we were in a cellar which looked as if it might once have been used as a prison. Up again, and rattling at a chained door. Then out, into light and air, into the midst of a group, which for an instant, closed threateningly round us. But the sergeant I had seen was among the alert brown men. A glance, a gesture, and we were allowed to pass, a youth running with us, to show the promised carriage and the Arab driver with the red camellia. So it was over, this adventure!

Yet was it over?

That remained to be seen. And remained also, to see what it meant, if indeed there were a meaning underneath the surface.

"So you had the alarm last night?" said Allen, looking as if there were nothing surprising or puzzling in that.

"Yes, why should we not admit it now? Word came that a watch had been set outside, both back and front, and none of us dared leave the house. We consented to be locked in, though there is one in another room who wished to get out and run the risk. That was not permitted, for the sake of others; and to prevent him from taking his own way in spite of prudence, we let ourselves be shut in, with only one attendant who took through the holes in the door such little food as we needed. We had begun to hope that it had been a false alarm, or, since no inquiries seemed to have been made below, that the watchers had gone and would not come again. We planned as soon as night fell to go to our homes; but it was not to be. And if any are to blame, it is not those who come to take pleasures provided for them, but rather they who cheat the coastguard of the swift-running camels, and bring what is forbidden into Egypt."

"The blame will be rightfully apportioned," said Allen. "Meanwhile, I am sorry to say, Hussein Effendi, that you and those in your company are subject to the law. I must now leave you, and go farther to see what others we have to deal with."

The four Effendis were politely left in charge of two policemen who would have been equal to twice their number, and our one remaining man went on with Allen and me.

"Your friends, and perhaps two or three who can afford to pay big prices, will have had their smoke in private rooms," Allen explained. "We can guess *who* it was, who wanted to break out! There are probably no more doors, only curtains, so we shall have no trouble. But don't forget that, if anything unexpected should happen, you have a pistol. Of course, you understand that it could be used only in an extreme case."

A curtained doorway led out from the diwáán into a small anteroom, and there, on the floor, sat Bedr el Gemály, the picture of dejection. Had I raised my voice in the next room, he would perhaps have ventured in to see what I could do to help him; for now, at sight of me, he scrambled up in shamefaced eagerness.

"Oh, my lordship!" he began to cackle. "Praise be to Allah you are come! I was persuaded to bring the young ladies here. They would make me do it. Yes, sir. It is not my fault. They pay me. I have to obey. Then we get caught, like we was some rats. No fair to punish me. The ladies all right. No harm come, except a little sick."

CHAPTER XII

THE NIGHT OF THE FULL MOON

"It seems too good to be true that it should end like this," said Monny.

She said it on the roof of Mena House, in the kiosk-room made of mushrbiyeh work, which I had engaged for a little private dinner-party that night. You see, it was the night of the full moon, the magic night of the Sphinx-spell, which must not be wasted, no matter how tired you may be or how many excitements you may have lived through.

Anthony and I had had our explanations. He had told me that one night in a café, where he was spreading the news of his dream, he had heard two men talking in low voices about the House of the Crocodile. The word "hasheesh" had not been mentioned, but Anthony had imbibed a vague impression of something secret, and had wondered, and been interested. Then the matter had slipped his mind; but, summoned in the night from the writing of letters, to advise Mrs. Jones, he had recalled Monny's wish to visit a hasheesh den. He knew of none, but suspected the existence of one or two. How to find out in a hurry? he had asked himself. And with that, the remembrance of those few whispered words in the café had come echoing back to his brain. He acted upon the suggestion; went to the door of the swinging crocodile, knocked, and knocked again; had the door opened to him as if in surprise by an apparently sleepy man. Announced the motive of his coming as if it were a foregone conclusion that hasheesh could be smoked in that house by the initiated. His disguise was not suspected. It never was, when he played the Egyptian; and when asked who had sent him, he had the inspiration to utter the name of that Bey who had been Mansoor's master. This gave him entrance. He was taken upstairs, passed through the door "Forbidden to the Public"; and the first person he saw in the long room as he entered, was Bedr smoking a gozeh, one of those cocoanut, cane-stemmed pipes in which hasheesh is mingled with the Persian tobacco called tumbák.

Bedr was accused of treachery, and defended himself. The ladies had insisted. It was his place to obey. He had done no wrong in engaging a carriage to wait outside the Ghezireh Palace gardens, and bringing his employers to the best place in Cairo for the hasheesh smoking. The ladies were safe and happy, in a private room where they had tried their little experiment, and now they were sleeping. As soon as they waked and felt like going home, he was ready to take them. It was for Miss Gilder, not for Bedr, to beg pardon of her friends if they were frightened. And all the time, it had seemed to Anthony, that the man was expecting some one to arrive. He watched the doorway half eagerly, half anxiously; when a servant came or went, he started, and betrayed emotion which might have been disappointment or relief. But when Anthony questioned him, he said, "I expect no one, Effendi. It is only that I shall not be easy till we get the ladies home, now you tell me their people are alarmed."

Just then, and before Anthony saw the girls, a servant had come running in to say that there was an alarm. Something had happened in the street, and the police were there. Mansoor feared that it was a ruse, and that the house was being watched, back and front. Where the forbidden thing is, no precaution can be too great. For their own sakes, and Mansoor's sake, no one must go out, perhaps not till the next night; but luckily a saint's day would give peace for the morrow, and all doors could be shut without causing remark. The news that there was no escape for many hours to come distressed no one apparently, except "Antoun." He had gone to the door, and tried to open it, but found that already it was locked on the other side. Then he knew that it was useless to struggle, for he was unarmed, the door was thick, and no one outside could hear if he shouted. He must use his wits; but first he must make sure that the two girls were safe. He forced, rather than induced Bedr to show him the room they had engaged—a small one, closed only with a portière, and looking over the court, down into the open-fronted recess where Mansoor's family-life went on, like a watch dog's in his kennel.

It was true, as Bedr had said; the girls slept on a cushioned mattress, wrapped in black habberahs, their faces turned to the wall. As they could not be taken out, Anthony did not wake them, but let them get, in peace, their money's worth of dreaming. His next thought was to try and bribe the Arab attendant to smuggle out a letter; but acceptable as a bribe would have been, the man explained his helplessness to earn it, at least for the time being. He could do nothing till one of his fellow-servants came up from below, to pass the food for the imprisoned smokers through a hole in the door, made purposely in case of just such an emergency. Probably no one would appear till morning, for who would be hungry before then? Even with the morning, it might be Mansoor himself who would bring the food, and inquire again at the door if all were well within. But if the noble Hadji wrote the letter, it should be sent when opportunity arose. One of the servants below stairs, said the man, was his father, who might during the next day be able to slip out as if on some errand. Then he would perhaps take a letter, if he could be sure of good pay, and that he would not be delivered up to the police. So Anthony had written on a sheet torn from his notebook, and made an envelope of another sheet. The address of the Ghezireh Palace had helped the man to believe that no evil would reach his father; and a "sweetener" in the shape of all Anthony's ready money had done the rest. But evidently the old man had not succeeded in finding an excuse for an errand until after the noon hour, and meanwhile time had seemed long in the House of the Crocodile. When the girls waked, wanting to go home, they were ill. They found the game not worth the candle—but Anthony's presence had given them comfort. They were humble, and remorseful; and Bedr was so conspicuously a worm that Monny consented to his discharge. "It would take more time than we've got to make him worth converting," she said to Rachel when the Armenian had carefully laid all the blame of the expedition upon her shoulders.

Never were two runaway children more glad to be found and restored to their anxious relatives than Monny Gilder and Rachel Guest. As for Bedr, he took his dismissal, with a week's wages, submissively; but the gravest question concerning him still lacked an answer. Had he merely been officious and indiscreet in guiding the girls secretly to the House of the Crocodile, and there procuring hasheesh to buy them dreams, or had he wanted something to happen, in that house, which had not happened? A certain amount of browbeating from "Antoun," and bullying from me, dragged nothing out of him. And perhaps there was nothing to be dragged. Perhaps it was through oversensitiveness that Brigit and I dwelt suspiciously upon Bedr's motives, and asked each other who it was he had expected at the House of the Crocodile. Even Anthony did not accuse the Armenian of anything worse than slyness and cowardice, according to him the two worst vices of a man; but he volunteered to find out what mysterious night-disturbance in the street had caused the sudden closing of the doors. It was Biddy's thought that the person Bedr wished to meet might fortunately have been prevented by this very disturbance from keeping his appointment, and Monny saved a serious ending to her adventure. It began to seem rather a worry, travelling with so important a young woman as Miss Gilder: and a vague dread of the future hung over me, as it hung over Brigit, who loved the girl. We felt, dimly, as if we had had a "warning," and did not yet know how to profit by it. The atmosphere was charged with electricity, as before an earthquake; and we felt that the affair of the hasheesh den might be but a preface to some chapter yet unwritten. Still, it was impossible not to forgive Monny her indiscretion. Indeed, she became so honey-sweet and childlike in her desire to "make up" for what we had suffered, that the difficulty was not to like her better.

She besought us to forget the episode. If we only *knew* how sick she and Rachel had been, we'd see why they never wanted to think of those hours again! And when I chanced to mention that to-night would be full moon—the night of nights when the Sphinx and the Ghizeh Pyramids held their court—Monny begged to have the bad taste of her naughtiness taken out of her mouth by a dinner at Mena House. We might dine early, and plunge into the desert later, when the moon was high. Of course, I proposed that all should be my guests—all except "Antoun" who, though recognized as a gentleman of Egypt, was considered by Miss Gilder an alien, not exactly on "dining terms." He was supposed to go home, "to his own address." At eight-thirty he was to take a taxi to Mena House, where he would arrive before nine, in time to help me organize my expedition.

I explained to Monny that, though we should dine privately, it would be my duty to see that the *Candace* people paid their respects to the Sphinx, and gazed upon her as she ate moon-honey. If they missed this sight, or if anything went wrong with their way of seeing it, I should never be forgiven. But the much chastened Monny graciously "did not mind." She thought it would be fun to watch the sheep-dog rounding up his flock. Useless to explain to her the subtle social distinction between a "Flock" and a "Set" (both with capitals)! To her, the blaze of the Set's smartness was but the flicker of a penny dip. We could drive the crowd on ahead, and look at *our* moon when they were out of its light.

So there's the explanation of Monny's presence in the mushrbiyeh kiosk on the roof of Mena House, on the night following the great adventure, which would have put most girls to bed with nervous prostration!

Part of our programme, to be sure, had failed; but it was not a part which could interfere with my selfish enjoyment. Mrs. East had changed her mind at the last moment, and had decided not to dine, although I had invited Sir Marcus on purpose for her. According to Biddy, Cleopatra had "something up her sleeve," something her excuse of "seediness" was meant to cover. Maybe it was only a flirtatious wish to disappoint Sir Marcus—maybe it was something more subtle. But it did not matter much to anybody except Lark, who was obliged to put up with Mrs. Jones in place of Mrs. East; for Rachel Guest and the sculptor, whom we nicknamed "Bill Bailey" were to be paired off: and, urged by Biddy, I intended to monopolize Monny.

I suppose there could scarcely be a more ideal room for an intimate dinner-party on a moonlight night than that kiosk on the flat roof of Mena House. Through the wide open doors, and the openwork walls like a canopy of black lace lined with silver, the moonlight filtered, sketching exquisite designs upon the white floor and bringing out jewelled flecks of colour on the covering and cushions of the divans. There was no electricity in this kiosk, and we aided the moonlight only with red-shaded candles, and ruby domed "fairy lamps," the exact shade of the crimson ramblers which decorated the table. For the corners by the open doors, I had ordered pots of Madonna lilies, which gave up their perfume to the moon, and looked, in the mingling radiance of rose and silver, like hovering doves.

"Oh, I could hug and *kiss* that moon!" sighed Monny, tall and fair in her white dress as the lilies I had chosen for her.

I was relieved that the Man in the Moon has now been superseded by a Gibson Girl; for Monny was beautiful at that moment as a vision met in the secret garden which lies on the other side of sleep.

"And the stars," Monny said, as I watched her uplifted face, wondering just how much I was in love with it, "the little stars high up at the zenith twinkle like silver bees. Those that sit on the edge of the horizon are huge and golden, like desert watch-fires. Oh, do you know, Lord Ernest, if quite a dull, uninteresting man, or—or one that it would be madness even to *think* of—proposed to me on such a night, I should *have* to say yes. It would seem so prosaic and such a waste, of moonlight, not to. Wouldn't you feel like that if you were a girl?"

"I'm sure I should," I replied with extraordinary sympathy. "I *do* feel like it, even as a man. I warn you not to propose, or I shall snap at you."

She laughed; but I was wondering if I were dull and uninteresting enough to stand a chance. It seemed as if Providence were actually *handing* it to me. But just then Biddy and Sir Marcus came to the doorway which so becomingly framed Monny's form and mine. Naturally that put the idea out of my head; and two such opportunities don't come to a man in a single night.

Dinner was not ready yet, and we sauntered about on the flat roof, white as marble in the moonlight. The sky was milk—the desert, honey —far off Cairo with its crowned citadel, pale opal veined with light, and faintly streaked with misty greens and purples; the cultivated land a deep indigo sea. The fantastically built hotel (in its ancient beginnings the palace of a Pasha) was like a closely huddled group of châlets, looked down on from its central roof. On the fringe of the oasis-garden the cafés and curiosity-shops buzzed with life, and glittered like lighted beehives. Outside the gateway, donkey-boys and camel-men and drivers of sandcarts chattered. To-night, and on a few moonlight nights to come they would reap their monthly harvest. They were all ready to start off anywhere at a moment's notice; but apart from them and their clamour, reposed a row of camels previously engaged, free, therefore, to enjoy themselves until after dinner. As we gazed down as if from a captive balloon, at the line of sitting forms, they looked immense, like giant, newborn birds, with their huge egg-shaped bodies and thin necks. Along the arboured road from Cairo, flashed motor-car after motor-car, their lights winking in and out between the dark trees, now blazing, now invisible, their occupants all intent on doing the right thing: dining at Mena House, and seeing the full moon feed honey to the Sphinx. Some, wishing to save time, or to dine later in town, or to take a train, for somewhere, later, did not turn in at the hotel gate, but swept past with siren shrieks, and tore on, hoping to "rush" the steep hill to the Pyramid platform at top speed. Only a few of the strongest succeeded, and, with a dash instead of an ignominious crawl, triumphantly fanned their lights along the base of that vast monument in which King Cheops vainly sought eternal privacy. What would he say, we wondered, could he see the crowds of tourists tearing out to pay him a call, on their way to the Sphinx? Would he blight them with a curse, or would he remember pearly nights of old, when his subjects assembled in multitudes for the feast of the Goddess Neith when the moon was full, and all the white, brightly painted houses along the Nile reflected their flowerlike illuminations in the water? Anyhow (as Sir John Biddell would have said), this was helping to keep his name before the public; and nothing could succeed in vulgarizing his mountain of gold in its gleaming waves of desert, under pulsing stars and creamy floods of moonlight.

Anthony had told me that the great "tip" was to go out while the less instructed sightseers ate their dinner. Then, the desert was comparatively empty; and, more important still, instead of having the moon on her head, and her face in shadow, the Sphinx received its full blaze in her farseeing eyes. Of this advice I meant to avail myself, feeling vaguely guilty as I thought of the giver, who was absent from the feast: Anthony Fenton, one of the finest young soldiers in Egypt, who could be lionized in drawing-rooms at home if he would "stand for it"! Anthony who, would he but accept the repentant overtures of that tyrannical old prince, his maternal grandfather, might inherit a fortune and a palace at Constantinople! Yet as Ahmed Antoun in his green turban, he was "taboo" at our little party.

He was due later, however, and I rather expected to find him waiting below, when I excused myself to descend to the Set. But I had not left the roof when a note for Monny was brought up by an ebony person in livery. I watched her as she read, one side of her face turned to marble by the moon, the other stained rose by the red-shaded candles. I thought that the rosy side grew more rosy as she finished the letter.

"There's a—message for you, Lord Ernest," she said. "Aunt Clara wants me to tell you that 'Antoun' can't meet you at the hotel, because she — changed her mind about not coming out, and sent for him. She felt better, it seems, and got thinking what a pity it would be to miss the full moon, so she suddenly remembered that 'Antoun' wasn't with us, and decided to invite him. She writes in a hurry and didn't know where they would dine, but says anyhow they'll meet us by the Sphinx between nine and ten."

"Where '*they'd*' dine!" echoed Sir Marcus, pricked to interest. "Was she going to let Fe—I mean 'Antoun,' take her out to dinner?"

"Apparently she was," replied Monny, rather dryly.

"Why not?" asked Brigit. "He's perfectly splendid. And Mrs. East—not that she isn't a young woman, of course—is old enough to go about without a chaperon."

"If we're to meet them between nine and ten at the Sphinx," said Monny briskly, "don't you think, Lord Ernest, you'd better hurry and get your people off, so we can set out ourselves?"

"I'm going," I assured her. "But I thought we planned to give them a long start, in hopes that they might be ready to come back by the time we arrived?"

"Oh, well," she said, "that will make it very late, won't it, and we may miss Aunt Clara? Anyhow, lots of other creatures just as bad as yours will be there, for we can't engage the desert like a private sitting-room."

That settled it. I dashed downstairs and sorted out my charges. They had got themselves up in all kinds of costumes, for this "act." One man had on a folding opera-hat, which he had thought just the right thing for Egypt, as it was so easy to pack! Girls in evening dress; men young and old in helmets and straw hats, ancient maidens, and fat married ladies, in dust cloaks or ball gowns, climbed or leaped or scrambled onto camels, with shrieks of joy or moans of horror: or else they tumbled onto donkeys which bounded away before the riders were well on their backs. And men, women, and animals were shouting, giggling, groaning, gabbling, snarling, and squeaking; an extraordinary procession to pay honour to the Pyramids and the lonely Sphinx.

We of the roof-party considered ourselves, figuratively speaking, above camels, far above donkeys, and scornful of motor-cars, in which it was irreverent to charge up to the Great Pyramid as if to the door of a café. We walked, and Monny still lent herself to me; but she no longer bubbled over with delight at everything. A subdued mood was upon her, and her eyes looked sad, even anxious, in the translucent light which was not so much like earthly moonlight as the beginning of sunrise in some far, magic dreamland. She had the pathetic air of a spoiled child who begins suddenly, if only vaguely, to realize that it cannot have everything it wants in the world. And she merely smiled when I told her how, to insure the peace of the desert, I had offered a prize of a large blue scarab as big as a paperweight, for that member of the Set who did not even say "Oh!" to the Sphinx. "Antoun" had "vetted" the alleged scarab and pronounced it a modern forgery; but nobody else knew that, and as a prize it was popular.

The sky had that clear pale blue of dawn, when day first realizes that, though born of night, it is no longer night. Casseopeia's Chair and Orion were being tossed about the burning heavens like golden furniture out of a house on fire; and one great star-jewel had fallen on the apex of cruel Khufu's Pyramid. I should have liked to believe it was Sirius, the "lucky" star sacred to Isis and Hathor; but Monny's schoolgirl knowledge of astronomy bereft me of that innocent pleasure. No wonder that the ancient Egyptians, with such jewels in their blue treasure-house, were famous astrologers and astronomers before the days when Rameses' daughter found Moses in the bulrushes of Roda Island!

The stars spoke to us as we walked, soft-footed, through the sand; and the pure wind of the desert spoke other words of the same language, the language of the Universe and of Nature. Here and there yellow lights in a distant camp flashed out like fireflies; far away across the billowing sands, rocks bleached like bone gave an effect of surf on an unseen shore; now and then a silent, swift-moving Arab stealing out of shadow, might have been the White Woman who haunts the Sphinx, hurrying to a fatal tryst: and the Great Pyramid seemed to float between desert sand and cloudless sky like the golden palace of Aladdin being transported through air by the Geni of the Lamp. There never was such gold as this gold of sand and pyramids, under the moon! We said that it was like condensed sun rays, so vivid, so bright, that the moon could not steal its colour. Cloudlike white figures were running up Khufu's geometric mountain; Arabs expecting money when they should come leaping down, whole or in pieces. And the khaki uniforms of British soldiers mounting or descending for their own stolid amusement, made the Pyramid itself seem to be writhing, so like was the colour of the cloth to that of the stone. No use being angry because the monument was crawling with Tommies! The Pyramids were as much theirs as ours. And probably Napoleon's soldiers spent their moonlit evenings in the same way; a thought which somehow made the thing seem less intolerable.

We climbed to the vast platform of the Ghizeh Pyramids, and then plunged into the billows of the desert, in quest of the Sphinx. Sir Marcus was entitled to call himself the pioneer, but we needed no one to show us the way. It was but too clearly indicated by the bands of pilgrims, going or returning. And among the latter were those whom Monny callously referred to as "poor Lord Ernest's crowd." Miss Hassett-Bean and the Biddell girls made us linger, with sand trickling over the tops of our shoes, while they poured into our ears their impressions of the Sphinx. Miss H. B. thought that She (with a capital S) was a combination of Goddess, Prophetess, and Mystery. Enid thought she was like an Irish washerwoman making a face; and Elaine said she was the image of their bulldog at home. Monny (after a sandy introduction) listened to these verbal vandalisms in horrified silence. I could see that she was exerting herself, for my sake, to be civil to my charges (who were more interested in her than they had been in the Sphinx), and that, if she could have done so without hurting their feelings, she would have struck them dead. But my fears that their mental suggestions might obsess her were baseless. She did not speak when the golden billows parted to give us a first vision of the great Mystery of the Desert. I had led Monny by a roundabout way, and instead of seeing the Sphinx from the back, we came upon her face to face, as she gazed with her wonderful, all-knowing eyes, straight into that world beyond knowledge which lies somewhere east of the moon. Veiled by the night in silver and blue, with a proud lift of the head, she faced past and future, which were one for her, and the present, nothing. The moon gave back for a few hours all her lost loveliness, of which men had robbed her, seeming miraculously to restore the broken features, whole and beautiful as they had been in her youth before history began. It was as if in the moon's rays were silver hands, mending the marred majesty, giving life to the eyes and to the haunting, secret smile. I thought of the story of King Harmachis: how he dreamed that the Sphinx came to him, saying that the sand pressed upon her, and she could not breathe. Nobody since his day had for long left her buried!

"What does it mean to you?" I broke the silence to ask.

"I don't know," Monny said. "All I know is that she's more wonderful than I expected, and as beautiful as the loveliest marble Venus of Italy, though a thousand times greater—if one perfect thing can be greater than another. She's so great that I don't think she can be meant to be a woman—or even a man. She is like a *soul* carved in stone."

"All in a moment you have guessed the riddle!" I exclaimed, liking and understanding the girl better than I had liked or understood her yet. "I believe that's the secret of the Sphinx. The king who had this stupendous idea, and caused it to be carried out, said to some inspired sculptor, 'Make for me from the rock of the desert, a portrait, not of me as I am seen by men, in my mortal part or Khat, for that can be placed elsewhere; but an image of my real self, my soul or Ka, looking past the small things of this world into eternity, which lies beyond this desert and all deserts.' Then the sculptor made the Sphinx, and gave it such grandeur, such mystery of countenance that instinctively the souls of people recognized the *soul look*. You have a soul, and it told you the secret. Only those who have no souls find the Sphinx heavy or hideous, or utterly beyond their comprehension."

"Have I a soul?" Monny asked, dreamily. "Men I've known have told me I haven't. Yet sometimes I've thought I felt it fluttering. And if I have a soul, I shall find it in Egypt. Oh, I shall! Something—yes, the Sphinx herself!—tells me that."

I was tempted to ask "What about a heart?" And then—in a violent hurry, before anybody came—to mention my own, into which the moon seemed pouring a little of the honey it had brought for the Sphinx. I did feel that some one owed a moonlight proposal under the Sphinx's nose (or the place where its nose had been) to such a girl as Monny. Her Egyptian experience could never be perfect and complete unless she were proposed to on the night of the full moon, with the Sphinx's blessing; and as no better man was here to do it, I could not be thought conceited if I took the duty upon myself. Besides, Brigit would so thoroughly approve!

"Look here, Biddy, I mean Monny," I began hastily, "there's something I want to tell you, something very important you ought to know, because matters can't go on much longer as they are—"

"Is it something about 'Antoun'?" she broke in, with a little gasp, as I paused for breath and courage. "If it is, maybe I know it already!"

Extraordinary, the relief I felt! I ought to have suffered a shock of disappointment, because I couldn't possibly finish a proposal after such an interruption. But instead, my spirits went up with a bound. Probably, however, that was because her hint was a whip to my curiosity. "*What* do you know about 'Antoun'?" I asked.

Perhaps I forgot to lower my voice; or perhaps voices carry far across desert-spaces, as across water. Anyhow the clear tones of Cleopatra answered like an echo. "Antoun—Antoun! I hear Lord Ernest calling."

Biddy—dear little matchmaking Biddy—had managed Sir Marcus, Bill Bailey and Rachel, as a circus rider manages three spirited white horses at one time. The desert was her ring, and she had reined her steeds to her will, keeping them out of my way and Monny's at all costs, no matter whether they saw the Sphinx in back view or noseless profile. But Mrs. East's principal occupation in life was not to get me engaged to the Gilded Rose. And either she lost her presence of mind, or else she was not so much enjoying her moonlight tête-à-tête with Fenton, that it was worth while to hide from us behind a sand dune.

The two emerged from a gulf of shadow, Anthony very splendid under the moon, a true man of the desert. I thought I heard Monny draw in a little sharp breath as she saw that noble incarnation of Egypt (so he must have seemed, unless she knew the British reality of him) walking beside Cleopatra.

Then up came the others, Sir Marcus impossible to restrain; and we all talked together as people are expected to talk when they have come thousands of miles to see these monuments of Egypt. Yes, yes! Wonderful—incredible! Which do you find more impressive, the Sphinx or the Pyramids? Isn't it a pity they let the temple between the paws remain buried? And aren't the Pyramids just like Titanic, golden beehives? And can't you simply *see* the swarming builders, like bees themselves, working for twenty years?

Thus we jabbered; and others, many others, appeared to dispute the scene with us, to break the magic of the moonlight, and to puncture the vast silence of the desert with their cooings and gurglings and chatterings in German, English, Arabic, and every other language known since the Tower of Babel.

Arab guides lit up the Sphinx with flaring magnesium, an impertinence that should have made hideous with hate the insulted features, but instead turned them for a thrilling instant of suspense into marble. Indeed, none of our petty vulgarities could jar or even fret the majestic calm of the desert and the stone Mystery among its billows. The Sphinx gazed above and past us all. She was like some royal captive surrounded by a rabble mob, yet as undisturbed in soul as though her puny, hooting tormentors had no existence. It was not so much that she scorned us, as that she did not know we were there.

When we sorted ourselves out, to escape Sir Marcus, Cleopatra deigned to make use of me, having first observed (with burning interest) that Monny and Rachel were with Bailey, and that "Antoun" was pointing things out to Brigit O'Brien, as it is Man's métier (in pictures and advertisements) to point things out to Woman.

"It's been a wonderful evening," Mrs. East said. "It has made up for everything I suffered last night. We brought dinner out into the desert, in that smallest tea-basket, you know, and ate it together, he and I—Antony and I. There! I may as well confess that's what I call him to myself, for I've guessed your secret—and his. But don't be afraid. I won't tell a soul. It's too romantic and fascinating for words—or to put into words. He let me have my fortune told by an Arab sand diviner, who came while we were at dinner. I can't repeat to you what the fortune-teller said. But I feel as if I were living in a book. Oh, if only I were writing it myself and could make everything happen just as I want it to happen! Do you know one thing I would put into the story?"

"No, I can't think," I said, rather anxiously.

"I would have *you* propose to Monny."

"Oh—by Jove, Mrs. East!"

"Why—don't you admire her?"

"But of course. She's irresistible. Only she's so horribly rich. And besides, she doesn't think of me in that way."

"You can't be sure. Now, Lord Ernest, I'm going to whisper you a secret. I believe—I really do—that Monny would be *glad* if you'd propose. If I were in your place, if I *liked* her, I would do so as soon as possible. It might save her from humiliation—from a great trouble."

Being a duffer, I could only say once again, "By Jove!"

CHAPTER XIII

AN UNDERGROUND PROPOSAL

I didn't sleep much that night, for thinking of Monny; and when I did sleep, I dreamed of her; tangled dreams, in which she was Monny Gilder with Brigit O'Brien's eyes. Could it be possible that she liked me? Mrs. East ought to know. I made up my mind that to-morrow I would begin by feeling my way, but when to-morrow came I had no time to feel anything which concerned my private affairs.

It seemed, or so I was told "for my own good" by Miss Hassett-Bean, that the Candace people thought it "snobby" for me to have indulged in a private dinner-party, and to have hustled them off in a drove to the Sphinx while I went leisurely with my smart friends. They knew all about the feast on the roof, and were of opinion that they ought to have been there. Did I consider my American heiress better than they, better even than the family of an ex-Lord Mayor? If I wished to make up lost ground, I must devote myself to duty, and be nicer than ever to everybody.

This was one of the moments when I was tempted to throw over my job; but I remembered the reward, and set myself once more to the earning of it. For the next few days I scarcely saw Monny or Brigit, or even heard what was happening to them—for they had "done" the principal sights of Cairo, and I (at the head of the *Candace* crowd) was "doing" them. As if in a game of "Follow my Leader," I led the band from mosque to mosque; not indeed visiting the whole two hundred and sixty-four, but calling on the best ones. To begin with, I collected the Set on the height of the Citadel, which commands all Cairo, the platform of the Pyramids (not only the Ghizeh Pyramids but the sixty odd others, which newcomers don't talk about): the tawny Mokattam Hills, and the silver-blue serpent of the Nile. From this vantage place I pointed out the things we had to see in the city spread out below us, so that on the vaguest minds the picture might be painted in its entirety, before they began to absorb details on that mosaic map which was

Cairo. The tombs of the Mamelukes, strangely shaped monuments, vague and white as squatting ghosts; the graves of the Caliphs; the historic gates of el-Kahira; and the many ancient mosques, whose minarets soared against the blue like tall-stemmed flowers in a palace garden.

Mentally fortified by this bird's-eye view from the Citadel (of course, I had to trot them up again for the sunset), my charges let themselves be led from mosque to mosque, from tomb to tomb. Some, possessed with a demoniac desire to get their money's worth of Egypt, were unable to enjoy any sight, in their nervous dread of missing some other spectacle, which people at home might ask them about. These strained their wearied intelligences to see more than they possibly could at any one moment, unless they had eyes all round their heads; and others, of an even more irritating type, never lifted the few eyes they had from the pages of guide-books. I liked better those who, like Monny, frankly said that they didn't wish to have their minds tidied up, and be told a string of things about Egypt. They just wanted to *feel* the things, and let them slowly soak in. And the nice, lazy, Southern Americans, who said they were "tomb shy," and loitered about, betting from one to six scarabs on the speed of fleas, or donkeys, while I whipped forth for their tired companions a dull drove of facts fattened for their benefit.

Mosques and churches and tombs had to be visited, but did not appeal to all tastes. The Bazaars did. So did the Zoo, more fascinating than any other zoo, because each animal has its trick, or pet, or plaything.

As an excuse to see Monny and the rest of my friends, I got up a moonlight digging expedition at Fustat, those great mounds of rubbish and buried treasure near Egyptian Babylon where a city was burnt lest it should fall into the hands of the Crusaders. Monny and her party were invited to join us, and accepted the invitation, piloted by "Antoun." And concerning this entertainment, I had an idea. Those who choose to dig among these desert-like sandhills, between the Coptic churches of Babylon and the tombs of the Mamelukes, may chance on something of value, especially after a windstorm or a landslip: bits of Persian pottery, fragments of iridescent glass, broken bracelets of enamel, opaline beads, or tiny gods and goddesses. Why should I not (thought I) apportion off to each member of the band his or her own digging patch? This would save squabbling, and would provide an opportunity for me to propose in a unique way to Monny.

Regarding the idea as an inspiration, I carried it out scientifically. Helped by Anthony, after the sun had set and the mounds were deserted, I staked out the most promising "claims," and marked each space with the name of the "miner" for whom I intended it. In Monny's patch, near the surface where she could not possibly miss it, I buried a letter wrapped round a cow-eared head of Hathor which I had bought at the Egyptian Museum-shop. Now, in justice to myself, I must tell you that this letter was no common letter, such as any Tom, Dick, or Harry may write to the Mary Jane Smith of the moment. It was a missive which cost me midnight electricity and brain-strain; for not only must I appeal to my lady, I must also suit an environment.

Monny had taken up the study of hieroglyphics, in order to appreciate intelligently the tombs and temples of the Nile. She had bought books, and was learning with the energy of a stenographer, to write and read. She wrote out exercises, and submitted them for correction to "Antoun" who, as an Egyptian, was to be considered an authority. "Of course," she explained to me, "one comes here thinking that all Egyptians nowadays, even Copts, are Arabs. But *he* says that Egyptians are as Egyptian as they ever were, because Arab invasion has left little more trace in their blood than the Romans left in the blood of the English. It interests me *much* more to feel when I'm in Egypt that I'm among real Egyptians."

With this in my mind, I was convinced that a love letter in hieroglyphics, unearthed by moonlight in the mounds of Fustat, would please Monny.

The difficulty was that, though I could speak Arabic fairly well, I hardly knew the difference between hieroglyphic, hieratic and demotic forms; but the limited symbols I was able to employ were so strong in themselves that a few would go a long way: and if they were not as correct as the sentiments they expressed, Monny was not herself a mistress of hieroglyphic style. I could find no hieroglyphic suit in which to clothe the name Ernest; but since I had become keeper of men, mice, and morals in Sir Marcus Lark's floating zoo, Monny's craze for Egyptianizing everything had suggested the nickname of Men-Kheper-Rā. She sometimes called me Rā for short, therefore I now ventured to divert to my own uses a sign and cartouche once the property of a "son of the Sun," and King of Egypt:

Translation: Beautiful Queen, Star (of) My Heart (and) Soul. Give Me (your) Love. Become My Wife (and) Goddess (for) Eternity.

Men-Kheper-(Ka) Rā.

I patted myself on the back, put the letter in the ground; and the digging party was a wild success; but time passed on, and I had no answer. What I expected was a reply in kind, an hieratic acceptance or a demotic refusal; either one would be good practice for Monny. But not a hieroglyph of any description came. I had to go on as if nothing had happened. To be ignored was less tolerable than being refused. Monny's silence began to get upon my nerves; and to make matters worse, there was that desert trip hanging over my head. I knew even less about organizing a desert trip than I knew about hieroglyphics; yet it had to be done. As Sir Marcus said it was "up to me" to do it so well that Cook would look sick. Anthony was absorbed in secret official duties and open, unofficial duties. His was a great "thinking" part, and our occupations kept us apart rather than brought us together. On the one occasion when we were alone, he devoted four out of five minutes to telling me what he had learned of the night disturbance in front of the House of the Crocodile. "A Britisher of sorts" had come into the street, guided by an Arab. There had been some dispute about payment, and the Britisher had slapped the dragoman's face. This had been followed, as he might have known it would, with a stab; a crowd had assembled, and scattered before the police; the stabbed one had gone to hospital, the stabber to prison. Altogether it was not surprising that Mansoor, the suspicious caretaker, had feared a trap, and closed his doors. Bedr el Gemály, now one of the great unemployed, had been seen near the hospital where the injured man lay; but he had taken the alarm and departed without inquiring for the invalid's health; or else his being in that neighbourhood was a coincidence. The name of the man knifed was Burke, and London was given as his address. He was between thirty-five and forty, and according to the arrested dragoman was "not a gentleman, but a tourist." His hurt was not severe: and as the Arab had been exasperated by a blow, the punishment would not be excessive.

When at length I had seized the last remaining minute to put the question, "Do you think Miss Gilder has found out who you really are?" Fenton seemed astonished.

"I hadn't thought of it at all," he answered simply. "She's giving me too many other things to think of."

"What kind of things?" I stealthily inquired.

"Oh,"—with an evasive air—"I don't know what to make of her yet. But I haven't given up my silly scheme."

"What silly scheme?"

"Antoun" looked almost sulky. "Well, if you've forgotten, I won't remind you. It's absurd; it's even brutal; and I'm ashamed of it. But I stick to it."

CHAPTER XIV

THE DESERT DIARY BEGUN

I found out why Monny paid no attention to my buried letter. But the way in which I found it out (and several other things at the same time) is part of the desert trip.

I am not a man whose soul turns to diaries for consolation; but I did keep up a bowing acquaintance with a notebook in Egypt—it helped me with my lectures—and in the desert it relieved my feelings. Looking over the desert pages, I'm tempted to give them as they stand:

Black Friday: Morning. The start's for Monday, and nothing done! Could I develop symptoms of creeping paralysis, and throw the responsibility on Anthony? But too late for that now; and he may have to stay on in Cairo for a day or two. Why did I leave my peaceful home? It's the lure of the Mountain of the Golden Pyramid. Last night before I went to bed, read over my copy of Ferlini's letters, to gain courage. Gained it for a little; but when I think of that desert I'm supposed to turn into a happy playground for trippers, and not a tent hired or a prune bought, or an egg laid, for all I know, I wish Anthony and I had let Lark stick to our mountain.

This is Lark's fault anyhow. He sprang the thing on me. Said it would be easy as falling off a log. Said Cairo was full of Arabs whose mission in life was supplying tents and utensils for desert tours. People would be charmed with simple life, and me as universal provider. All I had to do was to supply cheap editions of "The Garden of Allah," and plenty of dates; and hint that it was considered vulgar in the Best Circles to put on Pêche Melba airs in the desert. With a few quotations, I should make them content with a loaf of bread, a cup of wine, and Thing-um-Bob. Why, they'd be falling in love with each other under the desert stars, and my principal occupation would be saying, "Bless you, my children!"

Sounded neat; and I remembered that, according to Brigit, Monny wanted the "desert to take her." Thought it might be useful if I were on in that act. Abyssmal beast of a dragoman who lurks round Mena House buoyed me up with false hopes. Said he had a fine outfit which he let, and threw himself in as guide. Plenty of everything (including cheek) for fifteen people, the exact number who have put down their names to go. (Some girls and parents are staying for a ball at the Semiramis, where I've tearfully persuaded the only soft-hearted officers I know to dance with them—otherwise the lot would have been on my hands in the desert.) Had so much to do yesterday taking the crowd to Matariyeh, where the Holy Family hid in a hollow tree, that I had no time to look at the Arab's outfit. Was inclined to save trouble and trust him, but saw Anthony a minute last night; he urged me to inspect everything. Did so early this morning. Rotten outfit: tents like old patchwork quilts, pots and pans, etc., probably bought job lot from Noah when the Ark was docked. Those keenest on desert "taking" them, will be mad as hatters if it takes them in. Suppose I'll have to interview half the Arabs in Cairo to-day. Wish I had a Ka or Ba or whatever you get for an astral body in Egypt, and I could say to it, "Here, my dear chap, I trust you to do this job while I stay in Cairo and rest my features." Then he'd get the blame, and I'd disappear, never to be seen again. Or if he were a Ka with Cook accomplishments, maybe he'd bring the thing off all right, in which case I could turn up and take the credit and marry Monny. Happy thought! Cook! Why shouldn't I sneak to Cook, and inquire in a careless way if they publish any pamphlet on "How to Do a Desert Tour."

Later: Have been to Cook. No pamphlet, but a friend in need. Talk of casting bread on the waters! In Rome I cast a crust which I didn't want, and it's come back in Cairo with butter and sugar on it.

Must have been two years ago in Rome when a young chap wrote to me to the Embassy. Said he'd been disappointed in getting work he'd come abroad for, had seen my name, recognized it, was from my county; and could I use him as a stenographer or anything? I couldn't; but I found him some one who could; and forgot him till I saw him this morning a fully fledged clerk at Cook's. Checking the impulse to fall on his neatly striped blue and white bosom, I invited him to lunch; and as a reward for what he calls "past and present favours," he had given me new life. What I mean to say is, he's promised to provide me not only with tents, but camels and camel-boys and a camp chef, and waiters and washbowls and a desert dragoman, and thousands of things I'd never thought of. It seems practically certain that since Napoleon no such genius has been born as Slaney. Cleopatra would say that S. is the reincarnation of Napoleon; but neither Cleopatra nor any one else —above all, Sir Marcus Lark—is to know of his existence. Such is the disinterested self-sacrifice of this buttered-and-sugared Crust, that it will do everything for me, while keeping itself and the Organization which controls it, completely in the background. The Organization is too great to mind; and the Crust, alias T. Slaney, thinks itself too small.

Lark, Ltd., considers himself a budding rival of the firm of Cook; but a deadly bud. If, however, Sir M. should come to hear that I had flown for succour to the enemy's camp, I fear it would be all over with the bargain for which Anthony and I are selling our souls. T. Slaney says he never shall know. He guarantees that Cook labels and other telltale marks shall be removed from everything, though time is short and there is much to do. He will be the power behind the tents, and I will be in them, absorbing all the credit.

Saturday: All *couleur de Rose*, thanks to Slaney. Should like to get him canonized. Many less worthy men, now deceased, have been given the right to put Saint before their names. He has handed me a list, something less than a mile long, of articles which Biddy and I, as children, used to call eaties and drinkies. He has told me where the things can be bought, and has written a letter of introduction which secures me "highest consideration and lowest prices." Also he has suggested a medicine-chest, packs of cards, the newest games, cigarettes suited to European and Arab tastes, picture post-cards of desert scenes; ink, pens, and writing paper. "People forget everything they want on these trips, but you mustn't," said he. I have acted on all his suggestions, and feel as proud as if I had originated them myself.

Sunday: My precious friend Slaney has made a large collection of Arabs, camels, tents, etc., and ordered everything, animate and inanimate, to assemble in the neighbourhood of Mena House this afternoon, in order to be inspected by me, and to be ready for a start early to-morrow morning. We are to have a sandcart with a desert horse for Cleopatra, who has tried a camel and found it wanting. I fancy she thinks a sandcart the best modern substitute for a chariot; and at worst, it ought to be as comfortable. Slaney has promised a yellow one —cart, not horse. The horse, by request, is to be white. The other ladies are having camels. I daren't think of Miss Hassett-Bean at the end of the week. The men, also, will camel. There is, indeed, no alternative between camelling and sandcarting—sandcarting not recommended by the faculty but insisted upon by Cleopatra. Hope it will work out all right; and am inclined to be optimistic. A week in the desert and the flowery oasis of the Fayum, with the two most charming women in Egypt! There will be others, but there's a man each, and more. I shall have to look after Monny and Brigit, as Anthony is having his hands full with Cleopatra lately, and, besides, he can't start with us. Something keeps him in Cairo for two days more, and he will have to join us near Tomieh.

Sunday Evening: Back from Great Pyramid, where I went to inspect the assembling army. Magnificent is the only word! The camels fine animals, but Anthony has provided the three best, borrowing these aristocrats of the camel world from Major Gunter of the Coast Guard. They have chased hasheesh smugglers, and have seen desert fighting. Were snarling horribly when I was introduced, but a snarl as superior to the common snarls of baggage-camels as their legs are superior in shape. Biddy, Monny, Mrs. East, and Rachel Guest were there with Sir M. and "Antoun," having been inside the pyramid and up to the top. Monny on her high horse because "Antoun" says it will be better for the ladies to ride the baggage-camels. The others take his word, meekly, but she persists, and Anthony agrees to give her the camel he had meant to ride, the one supposed to be the most spirited. When he joins us, he will have the animal intended for her. When this bargain was struck between them I thought his eyes looked dangerous, but she didn't notice or didn't care. Fenton tells me he has dreamed again of the red-faced man with the purple moustache. I laughed at his bugbear and flung Colonel Corkran in his teeth. By the way, nothing has been heard of C. by any of us since the day he handed in his resignation. Suppose he has gone back to England in the sulks.

Monday Night: I am writing in my tent, which is to be shared with Anthony when he arrives. I feel years older than when we started this morning. Middle age seems to have overtaken me. If I keep on at this rate, shall be a centenarian by the time we get back to Cairo.

We made a splendid caravan at the start. Besides the train of camels ridden by my party from the *Candace* and Monny Gilder with her satellites (it goes against the grain, though, to call a bright particular star like Biddy a satellite), there were over thirty gigantic beasts laden with our numerous bedroom, kitchen, luncheon, and dinner-tents, tent-pegs, cooking-stove, food for humans, fodder for animals, casks of water, mattresses, folding-beds, other tent furniture, tourists' luggage, and so on. I was happy till after the baggage-train had got away, each camel with its head roped to the tail of the one ahead, all trailing off toward the distant Pyramids of Sakkhara well in advance of us. Each camel looked like a house-moving. On top of the kitchen-camel's load was perched the chêf, a singularly withered old gentleman with black and blue complexion, clad in a vague, flying blanket. (Has been Turkish-coffee man in Paris hotels.) Many other negroid persons in white with large turbans; a few café au lait Arabs; these all counted beforehand by Slaney, for me, and identified as assistant-cooks, waiters, bed-makers, and camel-men, enough apparently to stock a village. But we had one surprise at the moment of starting in the form of a bright black child, clad in white, with a white skull cap and a flat profile evidently copied from the Sphinx. I don't know yet why this Baby Sphinx has come or who he is; but he rode on the kitchen-camel's tail, hanging on by the bread (our bread!) which was in a bag.

When this cavalcade had wound away, the camels making blue heart-shaped tracks in the yellow sand, it was our turn to start. Not one of us would have changed places with any old Egyptian king or queen, and we did not feel vulgar for doing this trip in luxury, because ancient royalties had done the same, and so do the great sheikhs of the desert even now. As I put Cleopatra into the sandcart with its broad, iron-rimmed wheels, she was recalling the days when she travelled with a train of asses in order to have milk for her bath. I suggested a modern condensed substitute, but the offer was not received in the spirit with which it was made. Now to get the ladies on their camels, after which we men would vault upon our animals, and wind away among billowing dunes full of shadowy ripples and high lights, like cream-coloured velvet!

But just here arose the first small cloud in the blue. It was bigger than a man's hand, for it was the exact size and shape of Miss Hassett-Bean's hat. It was a largish hat of imitation Panama trimmed with green veiling, just the hat for a post-card desert all pink sunset and no wind. As she was about to mount the squatting camel, a breeze blew the flap over her eyes. This prevented Miss H.B. from seeing that the camel had turned its neck to look at her; and so, as she reached the saddle and the hat blew up, lady and camel met face to face. It was a moment of suspense, for neither liked the other at first sight. The camel began to gurgle its throat in a threatening manner, and at the same time to rise. Miss Hassett-Bean, staring into two quivering nostrils shaped like badly made purses, shrieked, forgot whether she must first bend forward or bend back, bent in the way she ought not to have bent, and fell upon the sand. I don't quite see why I was to blame for this result, but she *saw*, and said I ought to have warned her what a vile creature a camel was. Nothing would induce her to try again. She would go to any extreme rather than ride a beast with a snake for a neck, and a nasty unsympathetic face full of green juice which it spit out at you. She was used to being liked. She simply couldn't go about on a thing which would never love her, and she wouldn't want it to if it did. She would go home or else she would have a sandcart. All the neighbouring sandcarts were engaged; but fortunately "Antoun Effendi" appeared at that instant (he'd taxied out to see us off), and he persuaded Cleopatra to let Miss Hassett-Bean drive with her. The desert horse, feeling this extra weight, looked round almost as unsympathetically as the camel had; but nobody paid the slightest attention except his attendant, who was to lead him: a type of negro "Nut," who had a snobbish habit of reddening his nails with henna.

By this time a crowd had assembled, kept in check by the tall, blue-robed sheikh of the Pyramids. It consisted mostly of Arabs determined to take our photographs or sell us scarabs—which Miss Hassett-Bean refused on the ground that she disliked things off dead people. But on the fringe lurked a few Europeans, amused to see so large a caravan setting forth; and the men of our party, hitherto proud of their curtained helmets and desert get-up, became self-conscious under a fire of snapshots.

"Hello, my Boy Scout!" I was hailed by Sir Marcus, arriving three minutes behind Anthony, and on the same errand. This blow to my self-esteem fell as I was leading Monny to the white camel which was hers and should have been Anthony's. She laughed—I suppose she couldn't help it. I couldn't myself, if it had been Harry Snell or Bill Bailey; but as it was, my pride of khaki helmet, knickers, and puttees collapsed like a burst balloon. I seemed to feel the calves of my legs wither. It was in this mood that I had to put Monny on that coastguard camel, while "Antoun" stood looking on. He did not offer to help the girl, as their talk yesterday on the subject of baggage-camels versus running camels had not conduced to officiousness.

Monny was in white: broad white helmet such as women wear, white suede shoes, white silk stockings, and a lot of lacy, garden-party things that showed frills when she flew, birdlike, onto the cushioned saddle. "*That's* the way to do it!" I heard her cry, exultantly—and what happened next I can't say, for the white camel knocked me over as it bounded up, jerking its nose rope from the leader's hand, and the next thing I knew it was making for the horizon. I hadn't been on a camel since I was four, if then, so it was useless to follow. But while I stood spitting out sand, Anthony flung himself onto one of the swift coastguard beasts, and was after her like a streak of four-legged lightning. None of us had the nerve to continue our operations until, a quarter of an hour later, they appeared from behind the Great Pyramid, coming at a walk, "Antoun" holding the bridle of Monny's camel.

I saw by Fenton's face that he intended to make no suggestions, and I guessed that he was practising his chosen method. If Miss Gilder wished for anything she must ask for it, and ask for it humbly if she expected to get it.

Her face, too, was a study. She was pale and even piteous. I thought there were tears in the blue-gray eyes; and if I had been Anthony I could not have hardened my heart. Pride or no pride, I should have begged her to abandon this praiseworthy adventure, and deign to mount the baggage brute. Not so Anthony. He led back the camel, with Monny limply sitting on it, and when it had calmed down at sight of its friends he retired into the background.

"How wonderful that you kept on, darling!" exclaimed Biddy.

"I didn't," said Monny. Then she turned to "Antoun," who remained on his beast, in case of another emergency, or because he did not wish to be looked down upon by her. He was rather glorious enthroned on his camel, the only one of our party who was truly "in" the desert picture. I didn't blame him for stopping up there on his sheepskin, eye to eye with the girl.

For a moment Monny did not speak. She was evidently hesitating what to do, but common sense and natural sweetness got the better of false pride. "Antoun, you were right, and I was wrong," she admitted. "I said yesterday that you were selfish, keeping the coastguard camels for yourself and Lord Ernest and General Harlow, and giving us women the baggage ones. Now I'm sorry. I was silly and hateful. I wouldn't ride another fifty yards on this demon for fifty thousand dollars. He's nearly broken my back, and if it hadn't been for you, he would quite have done it. Please help me off, and put me on any old baggage thing that nobody else wants."

Anthony's eyes lit for an instant, from satisfaction as a man, or from Christian joy in her moral improvement. He sprang off his sky-scraping camel, brought Monny's animal to its knees, helped her off, and motioned to the Arab attendant of the Ugly Duckling of all the other creatures. It gave the effect of being a cross between a camel and an ostrich, and had been chosen by "Antoun" as his own mount, when he surrendered the aristocrat to Monny.

"Oh, dearest, I can't have you ride that grasshopper!" cried Biddy. "'Antoun' took it for himself very kindly because it's the worst. And I don't care any more than he did. Give the thing to me, and take *my* one, that dear creature with the blue bead necklace."

But Anthony answered for Monny. "Mademoiselle Gilder made a bargain with me yesterday," he said. "If she failed in what *she* wanted to do, she was to do what *I* wanted her to do. I think she will wish to keep her bargain."

"I'm *sure* I wish to," added Monny.

With a chastened, not to say shattered air, she curled herself up on the sheepskin-covered cushion which was the ugly Duckling's saddle. This time it was "Antoun" who settled her into place, with her feet meekly crossed; and the caricature of a camel rose like a sofa at a spiritualistic séance. Strange to say, however, when all were ready to start, Monny appeared more comfortably lodged than any of the camel-riding ladies; and the thought entered my mind that perhaps Anthony had, with extreme subtlety, taken this roundabout way of benefitting Miss Gilder.

After this we got off with only a few minor mishaps. The one remaining incident of note was the arrival on the scene, as we left it, of another caravan—a small caravan consisting of two Europeans—a few laden camels, and camel-boys marshalled by one dragoman. The dragoman was Bedr el Gemály, and he smiled at us as affectionately as though we had not driven him from us in disgrace.

"How forgiving Arabs are, even when they're not converted!" remarked Rachel Guest, by whose side I happened to be riding.

"He isn't an Arab," said I. "He's an Armenian. And both are supposed to be the reverse of forgiving. But he's found another job quickly, so he can afford to let bygones be bygones."

"Oh, he would *anyway*!" Miss Guest exclaimed, warmly. "Poor fellow, you've all done him a great injustice, but I'm thankful he's not going to suffer for it. I wonder if he and his people are bound the same way we are?"

I feared that this was likely to be the case, as we were going the conventional round, sticking—as one might say—to suburban desert, on our way to the Fayum. But, as Monny observed the other night, we couldn't engage the desert like a private sitting-room. I would, however, have preferred sharing it with most people rather than Bedr and his clients, though the two latter looked singularly harmless, almost Germanic.

We went on more or less happily, though I noticed that whenever a camel changed its walk for a trot, each one of the ladies reached back a desperate hand to clutch the saddle and save her spine from the bruising bump! bump! which smote the bone with every step. As for me, that feeling of middle age began to creep on while my coast-guard camel and I were getting acquainted. I tried to distract my thoughts from the end of my spine, by concentrating them in admiration upon the scene. There was the Sphinx welcoming us with an immense smile of benevolence, as suitable to the sunshine as had been her mysterious solemnity to the moonlight. There, far away to the left, the spire-crowned Citadel floated in translucent azure. Its domes and minarets, and the long serrated line of the Mokattam Hills were carved against the sky in the yellow-rose of pink topaz. Shafts of light gave to jagged shapes and terraces of rock on the low mountains an appearance of temples and palaces, very noble and splendid, as must have been the first glimpse of Ancient Egypt to desert-worn fugitives from famine in Palestine. Between us and the Nile, hiding the sparkling water as we rode, went a dark line of palms, purple, with glints of peacock-feather green, in the distance. Hundreds of tiny birds flew up into the burning blue like a black spray, and the sand was patterned by their feet, in designs intricate as lace. Wherever lay a patch of white and yellow flowers or of rough grass no bigger than a prayer rug, a lark soared from its nest singing its jewel-song; and here and there a gentle hoopoo reared the crown which rewarded it for guiding lost King Solomon and his starving army to safety.

All this was beautiful; but I wondered painfully if Monny could be happy in spite of the bumps, now that the desert was taking her. Strange, how a disagreeable sensation constantly repeated at the end of a mere bone can change a man's outlook on life! If Monny had come to my camel-side and whispered, "I found your buried letter, oh, Men-Kheper-Rā. Behold that bird now flying toward you. It is my Ba—my Heart or Soul-bird carrying the gift of my love:" I should with difficulty have prevented myself from snapping out, "Thanks very much; but, my good girl, I'm in no mood to talk tommy-rot."

It was sympathy, kind, friendly sympathy I yearned for, not spoken in words, but given from soft, sweet eyes, as little Biddy had given it when I tore my hands and barked my shins birds'-nesting on the rocks a hundred years ago.

I think we should have liked the excuse to stop and gaze at the ruinous Pyramids of Abusir; but the dragoman-guide supplied by Slaney urged us on to the great plateau of the Pyramids and Necropolis of Sakkara. There, on the terrace of Marriette's House, we saw a crowd of Cook's tourists from Bedrachen, and I had some moments of guilty fear lest my Secret should leak out, as their dragoman rushed down and warmly greeted ours. But in the throes of rolling off their camels for the first time, the ever-wakeful suspicions of the Set were submerged under physical emotions. It's an ill camel that bumps no one any good!

I was only too glad to lure my charges away from danger-zone; and luckily it was so early that the influential ones who never lunched until two "at home," gave the word, "Tombs before food." Girding up its aching loins, the procession allowed itself to be led by me and my dragoman down inclined planes into dark, mysteriously warm passages where our lights were wandering red stars. Now and then a face would start suddenly out of the gloom, haloed with candle-light: and in this way, Biddy's flashed upon me, starry-eyed. "Oh, I'm glad to see you!" she whispered. Bedr and his two tourists are here. I'm afraid!"

"My dear child," I said soothingly, but not as soothingly as if I hadn't had toothache in the spine, "you may be afraid of Bedr, but hardly of two stout Germans in check suits."

"Not if they *are* Germans. But are they? Just now one of their candles almost collided with mine, and his eyes stared so! Then they looked over my head at Monny, who was behind me. And where she is now, heaven knows!"

"Nothing can happen to either of you here," I assured her. "And probably our fuss about Bedr is much ado about nothing. We have no evidence—"

"The man who stared at me over his candle has a scar on his forehead," said Biddy. "Maybe he got it in that row in front of the House of the Crocodile. Maybe he is Burke, and has just come out of the hospital."

"Most likely he is Schmidt, and adorned himself with the wound in a student duel," said I.

"It's too fresh-looking. He must be over thirty," she objected, but at that moment Miss Hassett-Bean loomed into sight; and in the stuffy atmosphere of the tomb felt the need of my arm to keep her from fainting.

We "did" the Pyramid of Unas, dilapidated without, secretively beautiful within. We went from tomb to tomb, lingering long in the labyrinthine Mansion of Mereruka who, ruddy and large as life, stepped hospitably down in statue-form from his stela recess, to welcome us in the name of himself and wife. Almost he seemed to wave his hands and say, "Look at these nice pictures of me and my family and our ways of life, painted on the walls—our servants, our dwarfs, our mountebanks and acrobats, our flocks and herds. Sorry there's no refreshment at present on my alabaster mastaba, or table of offerings, but you see I didn't prepare for visitors outside my own immediate circle of Ka's and Ba's. Still, as you *have* come, make yourselves at home, and take pot luck. I think when you've examined everything, you'll admit that you haven't a Soul-House in Europe to touch mine which, if I do say it, is the best thing this side of Thebes."

Next came the Tomb of Thi; but by this time, mural representations of fish, flesh, and fruit began to be aggravating. It would be past two before we could reach our luncheon-tent; and somehow it seemed less desirable to feed after than before that sacred hour, though the custom be sanctioned by royalty. "Another tomb to see before lunch?" groaned Sir John Biddell, when the dragoman firmly insisted on the Apis Mausoleum. "Oh, darn! *Need* we? What? Where they buried *Bulls*? I'd as soon see a slaughter house, on an empty stomach. Lady Biddell and I will go sit in the shadow of our camels."

And they did; nor would they believe the twins' assertions that the dark Mausoleum, with its cavernous rock chambers and granite vaults, was the most impressive thing they had seen in Egypt. "You say that to be aggravating, because we weren't there," I heard Lady Biddell snap, over the grumbling of the camels.

The sky blazed down and the sand blazed up. The desert was white-hot, with a silver whiteness hotter than gold, and the foreshortened shadows were turquoise blue. It was heaven to arrive at a miniature oasis, and see the open-fronted, awninged luncheon-tent reflected with its green frame of palms, in a clear lagoon, thoughtfully left by the receding Nile. At sight of this picture, my popularity went up with a bound. It really was a lovely vision: the big tent lined with Egyptian appliqué work in many colors, the porchlike roof extension supported by poles, and in its shadow a white table loaded with good things and guarded by Arab waiters waving beaded fly-whisks. As we lingered over our chicken-salad, fruit, and cool drinks, and lazily watched our camels munching bersím, all our first enthusiasm for these interesting beasts streamed back. The ladies called them poor dears, and sweet things; and the men marvelled at their calm endurance, or the number of their leg-joints.

Monny was gay and charming, and looked at me so kindly that I thought she must mean to give a favorable answer to the buried letter. I blessed Cleopatra for the "tip" she had given, though I wondered what was the "humiliation" from which I could save her niece. "After all," said I, "the desert trip's going to pan out a success." But it must have been about this time that the wind rose. It blew Miss Hassett-Bean's hat up instead of down, and other hats off, when we had started again—and it blew into our eyes grains of sand as large as able bodied paving-stones. Also, as we passed through a picturesque mud-village which ought to have pleased everybody, it blew into our noses smells which Lady Biddell knew would give us plague. As if this were not enough, the sandcart nearly turned over in a rut, and Miss Hassett-Bean said that she must go home or be left to die in the desert. I had to lead the little stallion before she would consent to go on, and realized when I had ploughed through fifty yards of sand, that the manicured snob of a leader was a thin brown hero. By the time I had had a mile or two of this, the dark Pyramids of Dahshur were visible, and I knew that our camp was to be pitched not far beyond. My first emotion was pleasure; my second, panic.

What if Slaney had forgotten his promise to remove the Cook labels?

Since remounting Farag (only the coastguard camels had names; the baggage-beasts smelt as sweet without) Monny and I had been bumping along side by side, and she had just said, "If I tell you something, you'll never breathe it to a soul, will you?" when I saw those Pyramids, and was smitten with the fear of Cook.

"Never!" I vowed, torn between the desire to hear her secret, and to dash ahead of the caravan into camp.

"It's about 'Antoun,'" Monny went on. "You know I said to you the other night, that perhaps I knew something about him?"

"Yes—er—oh, yes!"

We were within a few hundred yards of the Pyramids now. At any instant the camp might burst into sight.

"You don't look interested!"

"But I am, awfully!"

"You're *sure* you won't tell?"

"*Dead* sure."

(Was that a flag fluttering on the horizon?)

"Well, then—it isn't *my* business, of course. But one can't help being interested in him, he's such a—such a romantic sort of figure, as you said yourself. And there's something so high and noble about him—I mean, about his looks and manners—that one hates to be disappointed."

"You *would* have him with us, you know!"

"I know. And—and I'm glad I—we—*have* got him. It's a—it's an experience. I suppose he's rather wonderful. But don't you think he ought to remember that he isn't *exactly* a prince? He isn't even called Bey. And if he were, its not the same as being a prince of Ancient Egypt."

"In what way has he presumed on his—er—near—princehood?"

"I believe he has—fallen in love with Biddy!"

"By Jove! *Let* the flag flutter!"

"What flag?"

"Oh—er—that was only an expression. They use it where I live. Why shouldn't he fall in love with Biddy, when you come to think of it?"

"He's of a darker race. Though—he does seem so like *us*. Of course she couldn't marry him. It wouldn't do. *Would* it?"

"I don't know. I must think it over. Is that all you were going to tell me?"

"No. I suppose it's natural he should fall in love with Biddy. She's *so* attractive! But the worst part about it is that he has *proposed* to Aunt Clara."

"Not possible!"

"Yes. He has. I saw part of the letter—the first part. She's the only one of us who thinks it would be right to marry a man of Egyptian blood, because you know she believes she's Egyptian herself—and she's always talking about reincarnations. *I* don't see that It's such a wonderful coincidence his name being 'Antoun.' It wouldn't be so bad if he were in love with her; but it's Biddy who is always right in everything she says and does, according to him—just as I am always wrong. Aunt Clara is richer than Biddy. I can't bear to fancy that's why he has proposed; it would take away all the romance"

"Don't strip him of his romance yet," said I, again torn between interest in Monny's incredible statement, and excitement which grew with the growing in size of those flags on the horizon. "You may wrong him. If you saw only the *first* part of the letter—"

"There could be no mistake. It was in hieroglyphics, and who but 'Antoun' would have written such a letter to Aunt Clara? She asked me to translate it, the night she dug it up at Fustât—"

"Dug—"

"And when I'd read as far as, 'Beautiful Queen, Star of my Heart, be my wife,' she snatched the paper away, and put it inside her dress, saying she'd look up the rest in one of my books."

"Good heavens! You must have changed places at Fustât. That letter couldn't have been for her!"

"It couldn't have been for any one else. 'Beautiful Queen' meant Queen Cleopatra. She said so herself. I don't know what she's going to do about it."

"Do about it?" I echoed desperately. "Why—" and just then my straining eyes saw that on the middle flag in the fluttering row were four large red letters on a white ground. Slaney had betrayed me! Everything depended on getting that flag down before those letters declared themselves to other eyes. "Excuse me," I finished my sentence with a gasp.

Monny must have gasped also, as she saw me suddenly dash away from her at full speed of one-camel power. But I had no time to think about what she might think. I suppose I must have done something to the steering-gear of that camel, which coastguard camels do not permit. Whatever it was, it got me into the midst of camp before I could draw breath; but I have a dim recollection of being caught by Arab arms, and seeing suppressed Arab grins, as mechanically I felt to see how far the end of my spine stuck out at the top of my head.

"That flag! Pull it down!" was my first gasp, pointing convulsively to the banner which shrieked, "Cook!" "Quick—before they come!"

Dazed by my vehemence, several Arabs scuttled to obey the order, but there were too many of them. Each hindered his neighbour, and as I danced about, making matters worse, out pounced our withered chêf from the kitchen-tent.

"It was *he* brought that flag, wrapped round something," explained one of the men, in Arabic. "When he saw we had other flags, but none of Cook, he gave it to us to put over the biggest tent, because he thought it shameful to have no flag of the master's."

"Cook isn't the master. I'm it," I burbled, with a leap to catch the telltale square of white as it reluctantly came down. But I was too late. Sir John Biddell and Harry Snell, the newspaper man, came gallumping up on their camels before I could stuff the flag into my pocket.

"What's the matter?" they asked, as their animals squatted to let them down. "Were you run away with? What are you so mad about? Hullo! What flag's that—C-O-O-K!"

"It should be over the kitchen-tent," I heard myself explaining. "Don't you see? C-O-O-K! It's the cook's special flag. He brought it himself, but these chaps went and flew it over the dining-tent in place of the Union Jack. That's why he and I are mad."

And I thanked all the stars on Monny's tent flag that none of the Set understood Arabic.

After this, how could I hope to explain to Monny that the hieroglyphic proposal was mine, and that she, not Cleopatra, ought to have dug it up? She isn't a girl used to having men run away from her, on camelback or anything else—so naturally she thought me a rude beast, and showed it. Besides, even if I'd dared, I should have had no chance to straighten matters out; for though the flag-episode was after all no fault of Slaney's, there were a few little things which had escaped even his Napoleonic memory; and it was only by combining the feats of an acrobat with those of a juggler that I saved my reputation during the next half hour.

No sight could have been more beautiful in our eyes than that village of white tents in the waste of yellow sand. Our wildest imaginings could have pictured nothing more perfect, more peaceful.

Tea was ready, in the huge dining-tent, where folding chairs were grouped round a white-covered table. The floor of sand was hidden with thick, bright-coloured rugs, and it was finding "T. C. and Son" on the wrong side of one which Miss Hassett-Bean's foot turned up, that filled me with renewed alarms. Hastily I laid the rug straight, placed a chair upon it, and persuaded everybody to have tea before inspecting their bedroom tents. While they drank draughts and dabbed jam on an Egyptian conception of scones, I hurried like a haggard ghost from tent to tent, seeking the forbidden thing. Cook on the backs of the little mirrors hanging from the pole hooks!... Will it wash off?... No! Cut it out with a penknife! Down on your knees and tear off the label from the wrong side of another carpet! (Memo: Must do the one in the dining-tent when the people are asleep for the night.) Cram three Cook towels into my pockets. Hastily pin a handkerchief over the name on a white bit of a tent wall. Must have it cut out, and patched with something, later. Shall have to pay damages when I settle up with Slaney. Lady Macbeth wasn't in it with me! All she needed was a little water. I have to have pins and penknives and pockets all over the place.

I didn't get any tea. But that was a detail. And everybody was so delighted with everything that my spirits rose, despite a snub or two from Monny—for which Biddy tried to make up. People took desert strolls, or sat on dunes, and gazed into the sunset which couldn't have been better if I had turned it on myself. Along the western horizon ran a pale flame of green blending with rose, rose blending with amethyst, and in the distance the Pyramids of Dahshur burned with the red of pigeon-blood rubies.

The wind had died among the desert dunes, and it was not till after dinner that any one realized the arctic fall of temperature. It was too cold to enjoy playing bridge or any of the games I had brought; and the only hope of comfort was in bed. People said good night to each other in the comparatively warm dining-tent, and then gave surprised shrieks or grunts (according to sex) at the piercing cold. Several of the elder ladies fell over ten-tropes, despite the large lanterns illuminating the desert, and had to be escorted to their bedroom tents, and soothed. After this, silence reigned for a few minutes, and I had stealthily begun to work on the biggest rug-label, when arose a clamour of voices and presently appeared the dragoman lent by Slaney.

"Eight ladies wishing hot-water bottles," he explained.

But there were no hot-water bottles. We had thought of everything, it seemed, except hot-water bottles.

"I tell them very sorry but can't have?" Yusef suggested, looking pleased.

"Let me think!" I groaned. "What about the mineral water bottles we emptied at lunch and dinner? Let the cook boil water, and we'll supply the bottles."

This was done; and I was proud of the inspiration, with the pride that comes before a fall. When I began to write, in my bedroom tent, wrapped in all the blankets of the bed that should be Anthony's, I had the place to myself. But about midnight a head was unexpectedly thrust through the door-flap. It looked ghostly in the haze of colour made by the gorgeous appliqué work of high roof and octagon walls, which gave an effect of sitting at the bottom of a giant kaleidoscope.

"Who's that?" I hissed, in a whisper meant to be discreet, but which roused a camel or two in the ring outside the tents.

"Biddell—Sir John Biddell," replied the head. "I saw your light, and remembered you had your tent to yourself to-night. Those hot-water bottles have been leaking. There's one at least gone wrong in most of the ladies' tents. The married men have given their beds to girls who are drowned out. 'Twas *your* idea about those bottles, wasn't it? I expect you'll hear from it in the morning! Three of us want to come and camp in here with you."

"All right," I sighed, with a sinking heart. "I *like* sitting up, and you can toss for the cots."

At this moment Sir John Biddell reposes in one of them, General Harlow in the other. These gentlemen were so affected with the cold that they went to bed in their clothes, then got up to put on their overcoats, then got up again and put on their hats. On the floor lies a certain Mills of Manchester, rolled in all the rugs, except one which I have on, after surrendering my blankets. He has his head in a basket, to keep off the icy draught; and in the ruggy region of his spine, as he rests on his side, are the letters C-O-O-K. I wonder if I could rip them off without waking him up?

CHAPTER XV

THE DESERT DIARY TO ITS BITTER END

Tuesday: The principal water-cask has leaked; consequently not enough water to go round. Chêf said it was a question of baths, or soup. Considering the cold, most of the people voted for soup. Some washed in Apollinaris. Others douched with soda siphons. We can get more water to-night. Can't think why the north wind doesn't stop and warm itself while traversing the Mediterranean or the hot sands! It seems to be in too fierce a hurry and consequently cuts across the desert, like a frozen scythe, the moment its rival the sun has gone to sleep. I hear that Miss Hassett-Bean cried with cold as she dressed, and put on two of everything; but she is luckier than the younger women. Monny and Mrs. East, though warned that nights would be chill, have come clothed in silk and gossamer, and have brought low-necked nightgowns of nainsook trimmed with lace. This was confided to me soon after sunrise by a blue-nosed Biddy, hovering over the kitchen fire and — incidentally—ingratiating herself with the cook. It wouldn't be Biddy if she weren't ingratiating herself with some one!

Nobody yearned to get up early (I speak for others, as *I* passed my night in the attitude of a suspension bridge between two folding chairs); but in camp where sleep is concerned, men may propose, camels dispose.

Their nights they spend in a ring of camelhood, huddled together for warmth; and if they do not have nightmare or bite each other in their sleep, mere humans in neighbouring tents may hope for comparative silence in the desert, if not near a village full of pi-dogs. At sunrise, however, a change comes o'er their spirit. They are given food, and made as happy and contented as it is their nature to be, which apparently is not saying much. Judging by the strange, inarticulate oaths they constantly mutter, they are equally accursed in their sitting down and their getting up. It is only when they are actually "on the move," floating and swaying through the air—legs, tail, neck, jaws—that they have nothing disagreeable to say. Immediately after dawn this morning, our camels began to imitate every animal they could have met since the days of the Ark, when one had to know everybody. They mewed like cats, hissed like snakes, bleated like sheep, roared like toy lions, grunted like pigs, barked like dogs, squawked like geese, and bellowed like baby bulls. Also they gargled their throats like elderly invalids. It was useless trying to sleep; and when I had accomplished such bathing as the chêf permitted, I went out to see what was the matter. Nothing was the matter, except that the creatures had the sunrise in their eyes, and could see the camel-boys preparing their loads; but I was glad I had come out, because Biddy was there and the scene was beautiful. Shivering, we chuckled over the morning toilet of the camels, who turned their faces disconcertingly upon us, sneering with long yellow teeth, and bubbling as if their mouths were full of pink soapsuds, when they realized that we were laughing at them.

Incidentally we learned why the Baby Sphinx accompanied our caravan uninvited. His name is Salih; and he came because there's a very important camel (the property of his father) who refuses to eat or stir without him. It is a most original and elaborate camel. It has a neat way of turning its ears with their backs to the wind, in order to make them sand-proof. If any person other than Salih touches it, an incredible quantity of green cud is instantly let loose over their turbans; but at the approach of Salih it emits a purring noise, preens its head for the nose-strap ornamented with a bunch of palmlike plumes, and playfully pretends not to want the bersím which the little black Sphinx thrusts down its throat in handfuls. This, it seems, is good camel table-manners. And it is to the tail of this animal that Salih clings on the march. If he is not there, the animal looks round, stops, or turns to charge at any Arab who jestingly misuses its idol.

Yesterday the miniature Sphinx was in a white robe. To-day he is in black. All the Arabs have changed their clothes, although they have brought no visible luggage except vague pieces of sacking. The dragoman is exquisitely arrayed, galabeah and kaftan gray-blue, with a pink petticoat, and a white one under that. I suspect that he sleeps beneath the dining-table—and the other Arabs among the kitchen pots—yet they are smarter than any of us Europeans, all of whom have a frayed air. This, I suppose, would not be so in desert-fiction. Nothing would be said about hot-water bottles leaking, or beetles beetling (one doesn't come to Egypt to see live scarabs), or draughts raging, or camels gobbling, or flags flapping all night. (Memo: Abolish flags, even at expense of patriotism.)

Despite every desert drawback, however, Biddy and I agreed that the sunrise alone was worth the journey, and the pure air of dawn which, though cold, seemed perfumed by mysterious rose-fields. Just at sun-up the desert was lily pale—then, as the horizon flamed, a dazzling flood of gold poured over the dunes. The sun was a fantastic brooch of beaten copper, caught in a veil of ruby gauze, while here and there a belated star was a dull, flawed emerald sewn into the veil's fringe. Shadows swept westward across the desert like blue water, showing a glitter of drowned jewels underneath; and though last night it had seemed that we were alone in a vast wilderness, now there were signs that a village lay not far off. A group of children in red and blue, staring avidly at the camp, were like a bunch of ragged poppies in the sand. Their mangy pi-dogs had ventured nearer, to smell sadly at the meat-safes hanging outside our kitchen-tent. A gypsy-woman with splendid eyes and a blue tattooed chin, breakfasted on an adjacent dune with her husband. Men like living hencoops passed in the distance. Patriarchal persons blew by, in that graceful way in which people do blow in Egypt, driving a flock of sheep, with a black lamb "for luck." These men were dressed as their ancestors had dressed in the time of Abraham, and Biddy and I envied them. How nice, said she, to wear the same clothes for a hundred years if you happened to live, and never be out of fashion. If a few of your things dropped off by degrees, you were still all right, and nobody would be rude enough to notice!

Our faded family revived after breakfast, and even those who vowed they hadn't closed an eye all night enjoyed the scene of striking camp. The big white tents fell to the ground like pricked soap-bubbles; whereupon their remains were deftly rolled up and tied on to the backs of bitterly protesting camels. Beds, mattresses, tables, chairs ceased to be what they had been and became something else. Camels made faces and noises. Arabs tore this way and that, doing as little work as possible. The cook fluttered about in his blanket, brandishing a saucepan. Yusef the dragoman made noble gestures of command, and our little desert city ceased to exist except on camels' backs. It was shaved off the surface of the earth, and went churning and swaying along toward the next stand; the procession rising and falling among swelling dunes, under a sky which seemed to trail like a heavy blue curtain, where at the horizon it met the gold.

We travelled over pebbly plateaus, scattered with jewel-like stones. Sand-pyramids rose out of the glistening plain. Here and there were rocks like partly hewn sphinxes pushing out of the sand to breathe; other rocks like monstrous toads; and still others dark and dreadful in the distance as ogres' houses.

Altogether the desert gave us a truly Libyan effect, which made the Set feel that after all they were getting what they had paid for, with an introduction to a beauty and heiress thrown in. But apropos of this latter boon, it is dawning upon me that Rachel Guest is receiving more attention than Monny. This strikes me as inexplicable. There are more men than women in our party, all young except Sir John Biddell, General Harlow, and Mills of Manchester, a soft, fat sort of fellow whose first name you can never remember. It occurred to me on starting, that the desire of so many unattached young men to spend a week in the desert and the Fayoum, might not be unconnected with Miss Gilder's intention to join the party. Not being jealous, I expected to see a little fun, and laugh over it with Biddy, who is a heavenly person with whom to share a joke. But if there is a joke, I haven't seen the point yet, nor has she. There's no disputing the fact that Miss Guest, the poor, brave school teacher on holiday, is the belle of the desert.

Of course, if Monny had stopped in Cairo, Rachel's success with our men wouldn't be astonishing. As Brigit and Monny warned me in their letters to the *Candace*, she grows better looking every day; but though she is distinctly of Monny's type, despite those slanting eyes, she will never be a real beauty, or a Complete Fascinator, like our Gilded Girl. Besides, Monny has millions, and Rachel hasn't a cent. Yet there it is! Miss Guest is having the "time of her life" in spite of leaky water bottles and bumping camels, while Miss Gilder might be an old married woman, for all the attention she gets from any man on this trip except me. What can be the explanation? Even those two exaggeratedly German-looking men with Bedr stared at Rachel from their respectful distance. It turns out that they camped not far from us last night. Yusef heard this from one of our camel-boys. But they kept to themselves, and didn't come within a mile of us, so there's nothing to complain of. Every one except Sir John delighted with to-day's desert. He can't see anything beautiful in yellow lumps that keep you sawing up and down, though he has no doubt the desert is full of other fools doing what we're doing; and we could all see each other doing it if it weren't for those darn dunes.

Later: Adventure for sandcart on one of the biggest plateaus. Looked all right from the top; but a shriek from Mrs. East put me to the dire necessity of sliding off Farag and running to the rescue. The plateau was broken off in front and became a precipice which, Cleopatra seemed to think, would not have existed had "Antoun" arrived in tune to arrange it.

Great wind came roaring up again about noon. Feared to learn that it had been impossible to get luncheon-tent in position. But when the time came to find it, there it was with its back to the blast, and its shady open front, of tile-patterned appliqué, offering the hoped-for picture of white table and smiling brown waiters.

While we lunched, the fierce gusts striking the back canvas wall were like the frightened flappings of giant wings, and the beating of a great bird's heart. Otherwise we might have forgotten the elements as we ate, save for a slight powdering of sand on our food. But even that wasn't bad, if we selected only the port side of our bread and chicken, leaving windward bits to the Arabs.

Our night camp was in shelter of the two vast dunes which hide the ancient city of Bacchias, now called Um-el-Atl, where we found "Antoun" awaiting us. He had started from Cairo in the morning on a coastguard camel, coming quickly along the camel route between Bedrashen and Tomieh, and the extra few miles to our encampment. Before we arrived he had sent the camel back with the mounted Arab who accompanied him; and somehow the camp seemed all the smarter and more ship-shape for the presence of the handsome Hadji, in his green turban. The Set are all extremely interested in him; and on hearing my version of his history, sketchily told, have taken to calling him "the prince." Enid and Elaine almost fawn upon him, in their admiration of so romantic and splendid an addition to our party: a real, live Egyptian gentleman, with enough European blood in his veins to justify nice-minded maidens in cherishing a hopeless love for him, when he has safely vanished out of their lives.

Mrs. East made Anthony pick up pre-historic oyster shells in the desert, between flaming sunset and twilight, when the sky became a vast blue tent hung with a million lamps. And at dinner she was not nice to Enid and Elaine who admired her hero too frankly. She has developed an embarrassing clearness of vision as to other people's former incarnations, especially their disagreeable or shocking ones. "Ah, it has *just* come to me!" she exclaimed, her elbows on the table, looking dreamily into Elaine Biddell's face "You were *Xantippe*. I knew I'd seen you somewhere."

As for Enid, it seems that she was Charmian or Iris, Cleopatra can't be sure which; but the girl has come to me saying that, if Mrs. East doesn't stop calling her "My dear handmaiden," one or the other of them will have to give up starting on the Nile trip next week.

Wednesday: We had lobster á la Newburgh for dinner, in mid-Libyan desert, and drank the chêf's health in champagne. I don't know which was to blame, or whether it was the combination; but in the windy middle of the night when tent flaps stirred like a nestful of young birds, there were demands for ginger and for peppermint. Now, ginger and peppermint happened to be the only two medicaments in the whole pharmacopoeia left out of the medicine chest. But nothing else would do. The more the things weren't there, the more they were wanted; and all the people who had made notes to remember me in their wills, scratched me out again. Then, to pile Ossa on Pelion, the dogs of Tomieh arrived to pay a visit. They barked, of course; but they barked so much that the noise was like a silence, and nobody minded after the first half hour. The worst was, that they did not confine their demonstrations to barking. In order to signify their disapproval of our stingy ways, they took the boots we had confided to the sand in front of our tents to be cleaned, and worried them at a considerable distance. Some of the boots were past wearing when found, and some were not found. Judging from cold glances directed at me by those obliged to resort to pumps or bedroom slippers, one would imagine me the trainer of this canine menagerie. It has been hinted, too, that a conductor worth his salt would have filled up interstices of the medicine chest with toothbrushes. Several members of the party forgot to pack theirs in moving camp and they are now the property of jackals. A stock of toothbrushes is the one other thing besides peppermint and ginger and hot-water bottles that Slaney and I left out of our calculations; still, I do think bygones ought to be bygones. Anthony is the hero now, because it occurred to him to buy in Cairo flannelette nightwear, male and female, of the thickest and most hideously pink description. Had these horrors been suggested at the start, they would have been rejected with fury, in favour of lace and nainsook; but the contribution has made a *success fou*, at a crisis when vanity has been forgotten, and the girls are employing their prettiest frocks as bed covering.

Another Day: Have now forgotten which, or how many we've had. This is Anthony's hour—but he may take such advantage of it as he chooses—I'm indifferent. On top of my troubles I've contracted Desert Snivels. Whether the habit of using sand for snuff has produced the malady, or whether I've caught something (despite the tonic air) from nomads or oasis-dwellers, all of whom emit a storm of coughs and sneezes, I do not know. All desire to use this grand opportunity of taking Cleopatra's advice and winning Monny's love while for once she's neglected by others, has died within me. My one wish is to keep away from her and the rest, except perhaps Biddy, and suffer alone, like a cat. Biddy has got Desert Snivels, too. It makes another link between us, like the memories of our childhood. We swop stories of symptoms. Both feel that sense of terrible resignation which desert babies have when their eyes are full of flies and no one takes them out.

The sky lowers. Big black birds flap over our heads like pirate flags that have blown away. They are the vultures which used to be sacred to Egyptians, and seem to labour under the delusion that they are sacred still. The sand blows into our back hair, and the Arabs make scarves and veils of their turbans. Apparently these Moslems never say any prayers, and the *Candace* people feel they've been cheated of a promised sensation of desert life. The only religious thing the men do is to bawl "Allah!" when they lift the heavy, rolled up tents onto the camels.

People are beginning to grumble about their meals, which at first seemed to them miracles of culinary art. "Same old desert things we've been eating ever since Moses," I heard Harry Snell mutter. And Sir John Biddell is sick of h. b. eggs. I suppose he means hard-boiled. I should like to feed him on soft-shell scarabs!

Tea is the only incident in the desert which has palled on no one yet. Very jolly, having finished the day's exertion, and sitting on folding chairs inside tent door, teacup in hand, watching the winged shadows sweep across the dunes! One feels like Jacob or Rebecca or some one. There may be a fine saint's tomb standing up, marble-white, against the rose-garden of a sunset sky, but one doesn't bother to walk out and examine it at close quarters. There's nothing like sitting still after a windy day on camel back.

We lack interest in history ancient and modern, although Egypt is the country which ought to make one want to know all other history. There may be a European war or an earthquake. We don't care what happens to any one but ourselves. It is all we can do to keep track of our own affairs. As for ancient history, we content ourselves with wondering if Anthony and Cleopatra, when picnicking in the desert, dropped orange peel and cake to feed the living scarabs of their day.

We seem to be lost to the world, yet now and then we're reminded that we have neighbours in the desert. We've had glimpses of a distant caravan which must be Bedr's; and when we came in sight of our own camp last evening, we were just in time to catch a party of Germans being photographed in front of it, with our things for an unpaid background. Ever beauteous picture, by the by, your own encampment! White tents blossoming like snowy flowers in a wilderness; a dense black cloud, massed near by on the golden sand, which might in the distance be a plantation of young palms, but is in reality a congested mass of camels. You sing at the top of your voice "From the desert I come to thee, on a stallion shod with fire!" hoping to thrill the girls. But they are thinking about their tea. Girls in the desert, I find, are always thinking about their tea, or their dinner, or their beds. You would like (when your Desert Snivels improve) to walk with a maiden under the stars; but no, she is sleepy! She wants to get to bed early. Even the camels are most particular about their bed hours. It would be irritating, if you didn't secretly feel the same yourself. But what a waste of stars!

Some old Day or Other: Interesting but dusty dyke road into the Fayoum oasis. Every one enraged with Robert Hichens because "Bella Donna's" Nigel recommended The Fayoum. "No wonder she poisoned him!" snarled Mrs. Harlow. Our Arabs riding ahead look magnificent, seeming to wade through a flood of gold, the feet and legs of their camels floating in a rose-pink mist. But alas, the flood of gold and the rose-pink mist are composed of dust—that reddish dust in which presumably the boasted Fayoum roses grow; and it blows into our noses. This upsets our tempers, and prevents our enjoying the pictures we see in the sudden transition from desert to oasis. Biblical patriarchs on white asses, disputing the high, narrow "gisr" or dyke road; women with huge gold nose rings; running processions of girls, in blowing coral and copper robes, large ornamental jars on their veiled heads, thin trailing black scarves and slim figures dark against a sky of gold. Blue-eyed water-buffaloes—gamoushas—and exaggerated brown-gray calves, with wide-open, boxlike ears in which you feel you ought to post something. Canals stretching away through emerald fields to distant palm groves; here and there a miniature cataract; children playing in the water, imps whose red and amber rags ring out high notes of colour like the clash of cymbals; now and then a jerboa or a mongoose waddling across the path; travelling families on trotting donkeys or swinging camels who pass us with difficulty. Camels everywhere, indeed, on dyke or in meadow; even the clouds are shaped like camels who have gone to heaven and turned to mother o' pearl. There are horses, too; not little sand stallions like ours, but ordinary, plodding animals whose hoofs know only Fayoum dust or mud. Our desert creature, however, does not spurn them. On the contrary, though he pretends not to notice camels, cows, or buffaloes, he whinnies and prances with delight when he meets anything of his own shape, and assumes hobby-horse attitudes, much to the alarm of Cleopatra and Miss Hassett-Bean. Also, just to remind everybody that sand is his element, he shies at water, and almost swoons at sight of the Fayoum light railway.

Much wind again. But thank goodness out of Fayoum dust, and in desert sand for lunch! Prop up tent with our backs, leaning against the blast. However, we have now a special clothes-brush for the bread, and a moderately clean bandanna for the fruit. Plates, we blow upon without a qualm. Scarabei gambolling in the sand around our feet we pass unnoticed. This is the simple desert life!

But ah, what an encampment for the night! It makes up for everything, and a sudden realization of abounding health is tingling in our veins. We adore the desert. We want to spend our lives in it. Thank goodness we have two nights here, on the golden shore of the blue Birket Karun, all that's left of Lake Moeris of which Strabo and Herodotus raved. From the dune-sheltered plateau where our white tents cluster, the glitter of water in the desert is like a mirage: a mysterious, melancholy sheet of steel and silver turning to ruby in the sunset, with dark birds skimming over the clear surface.

Suddenly the Bible seems as exciting as some wonderful novel. Not far from here ran Joseph's river, making the desert to blossom like the rose. In tents like ours, perhaps, Abraham rested with Sarah, planning how to save himself by giving her to the Egyptian king. To see this lake is like seeing a bright, living eye suddenly open in the face of a mummy, dead for six thousand years!

Our best sunset; romance but slightly damaged by an Arab waiter wrapping up his head in a towel with which he had just dried our teacups and no doubt will again.

Another Day: (Merely slavish to look it out in the calendar, and besides there is none.) All I know is, we've had two on the shore of Birket Kurun (I spell it a different way now, because no books ever spell anything in Egypt twice alike), "The Lake of the Horns"; and we've been on the water in some very old boats, in order to see things which may have existed once, but don't now; and at present we're encamped near Medinet-el-Fayoum, a kind of lesser Cairo: originally named Medinet-el Fâris, City of the Horseman, because of a Roman equestrian statue found in the neighbouring mounds of "Crocodilopolis." We have just arrived, hot and dusty, with more dust of more Fayoum than we had before Lake Moeris. "Fayoum" means Country of the Lake it seems; and it really is a great emerald cup sunk below the level of the Nile —as if to dip up water for its roses.

However, the Set is happy despite the state of its clothes and its hair. None of us quite realized what the Fallaheen were really like before, or that the word Fellal meant "ploughman." This has been market-day, and we met an endless stream of riding men, and walking women with black trailing garments. They had bought sheep, and goats, and rabbits, and quantities of rustling, pale green sugar cane, which they carried on their shoulders.

There were wild adventures for the sandcart, and watery spaces across which Cleopatra was carried (at her own urgent request) by Anthony; Miss Hassett-Bean by me and the strongest Arab. There were the wonderfully picturesque squalid mud towns of Senoures and two or three others, honey-yellow in a green mist of palms, against an indigo sky with streaks of sunshine like bright bayonets of Djinns. And then Medinet, through which our caravan had to pass *en route* to camp, much to the ribald joy of smart, silk-robed Egyptian "undergrads" who strolled hand in hand along the broad streets near the University. They were big, fantastic houses to suit modern Oriental taste, painted pink and green, and set in shady gardens. And between high brick embankments we saw the river Joseph made—swiftly running, deep golden yellow like the Nile, with ancient water-wheels pouring crystal jets into enormous troughs.

This was our most fatiguing day, and we wanted our last encampment to be the best. We found the worst: a suburban meadow inhabited by goats and buffaloes. "Can't we move somewhere else?" Cleopatra besought Anthony, to whom she appeals when he's within appealing distance. "Isn't this tour for our *pleasure*, and can't we do what we *like*?"

Anthony absolved the camp-makers, explaining that we must be near the town in order to get carriages and see the sights we had come to see. Also our water supply had given out, and we must beg some from the "government people." He hinted that it would be well to make the best of things; but Cleopatra, with her royal memories, is not good at making the best of what she doesn't like. She wants what she wants, especially in her own Egypt, where things ought to know that they once belonged to her. Miss Hassett-Bean is quite as *exigeante*, in a different way, more Biblical, less pagan. Her criticism on the encampment was that it, and all her oasis experiences, are destroying her faith in hymns. "By cool Siloam's Shady Rill," for instance, used to be her favourite, but she doesn't believe now that Siloam ever had a rill.

Later: 11 p. m. Fallahcen and Fellahah (doesn't sound female, but is) pretended to have things to do on the frontier of their field and ours, as we were settling in, and stared unblinkingly at us, whenever we stuck a nose outside a tent. Also they laughed. Also they brought their dogs. But they couldn't spoil the sunset, and Medinet was a colourful picture of the Orient, towering against the crimson west. I took Monny and Biddy into the town to see the bridge and dilapidated Mosque of Kait Bey, with its pillars stolen from Arsinoë. Anthony took Cleopatra, and most of the other unmarried men took Rachel Guest. When Brigit remarked rather sharply upon the ex-school teacher's popularity, Monny laughed an odd, understanding little laugh. "I believe you think you know *why* they're all so mad about that girl!" exclaimed Biddy.

"Perhaps I do," smiled Miss Gilder.

"*What* is her fascination?"

"Bedr could have told you," Monny cryptically replied. "He told several people."

"What do you mean, child? I'm eating my heart out to know!"

"Don't eat it, dearest. You can't eat your heart and have it, too. And it's your most important possession."

"I wish you wouldn't tease me when I'm tired. Is it part of the secret you and Rachel were always giggling over, when we first got to Cairo?"

"Yes, dear, it is, if you must know. But I don't want to tell even you what the secret is, please! You might think it your duty to spoil Rachel's fun, and she and I are both enjoying it *so* much."

"Can you guess what she means, Duffer?" Biddy appealed to me. "You know I wrote you that Monny and Miss Guest had a secret. I thought afterward it might have been only their plan to see the hasheesh den; but since then I've realized it was something else."

"Even if I could guess, ought I to give Miss Gilder away, when she has just told you she doesn't want you to know?" I asked innocently.

They both turned on me in a flash. (I expected that.) "*Do* you guess?"

"I don't see, if I do, why I shouldn't have *my* little secret," I mildly replied. I knew that, after this, Monny would give me a good deal of her society, even though she might not have forgiven me for bolting to haul down the Cook ensign, in the midst of her confidences. But in truth I have not guessed the secret! My wits go wheeling round it, like screaming swallows who see a crumb. I get a glimpse of the crumb, and lose it again. In my present mood I almost regret that Bedr and his supposed Germans have not dumped themselves down in our field. It would have been like them to do so, judging by the aggressive checks on those mustard tweeds; but as a matter of fact the party has disappeared from view since just before Birket Karun. They may have turned back to Cairo; they may have been swallowed up by a palsied sand dune; they may have been eaten by jackals (we saw a dead one), or they may have taken to the fleshpots of a Greek hotel in Medinet; but the fact remains that, just when he might be useful, Bedr is not to be had.

In our tent to-night, I took advantage of our friendship to try and draw Fenton out a little on the subject of his feelings. It seemed the right hour to open the door of the soul. The Fallaheen having taken their families home, our tent-flaps were up, and only the stars looked in—stars swarming like fireflies in the blue cup of a hanging flower; but Anthony would speak of nothing more intimate than the Mountain of the Golden Pyramid, or his tiresome sheikh's tomb. I yearned to tell him of the *contretemps* about the hieroglyphic letter, but something stopped the confession on the end of my tongue, though perhaps in the circumstances, I owed it to Mrs. East. If he had mentioned her name the story might have come out; but the one drop of Eastern blood which mingles with a hundred of the West in Anthony's veins makes him singularly reserved, aggravatingly reticent where women are concerned. I used to think that this was because he was not interested in them. But something—I can't explain what, unless it's instinct—tells me that this is no longer the case. Another interest has come into his life, rivalling his soldier interest, and the secret hope buried deep in our Mountain. I see it in his eyes. I hear it in the *timbre* of his voice. It means Woman. But what woman? Is Monny right? Is he falling seriously in love for the first time in his strenuous life with Biddy, whom he picked out for admiration the moment he set eyes on her? Or is it Monny herself? I must be a dog in the manger, because I don't like the idea of its being either.

He is asleep on the other side of the tent as I write. Desert dogs do not disturb him. He's great on concentrating his mind, and when he goes to sleep he concentrates on that.

I wish he'd talk in his sleep! But even in unconsciousness, he is discreet as a statue.

The Last Day. Evening: I am in disgrace, and am left alone to bear it, so I may as well finish my Desert Diary. It's all an account of a lamb, just an ordinary, modern lamb you might meet anywhere. But I mustn't begin with that, though it haunts me. In spirit it's here in the tent, sitting at my feet, staring up into my face. Avaunt, lamb! Thy blood is not on *my* head. Go to those who deserve thee. I wish to write of Crocodilopolis. Shetet, the city was called in the beginning of things; Shetet, or the "Reclaimed," for the Egyptians stole land from the water, and made it the capital of their great Lake Province, which Ptolemy Philadelphus renamed to please his adored wife. Queen Arsinoë was charming, no doubt; and the Greek ruins and papyri of her day are interesting, but it is the city sacred to the crocodile god Sebek which can alone distract my thoughts now from the tragedy of the black lamb. If his Ka refuses to go I shall set crocodiles at it —ghosts of crocodiles mummied somewhere under the desert hills which separate the Fayoum from the Nile Valley.

We drove out to the ruins in a string of hired carriages, at an incredibly early hour this morning. As the night was one long dog-howl, and the dawn one overwhelming cockcrow, people were thankful to get up. But what a waste of hardly obtained baths before the start! Between Medinet and Crocodilopolis rose a solid wall of red dust. We had to break through it, as firemen dash through the smoke of a burning house; and when our arabeahs stopped at the foot of a mountainous mound, about a mile out of Medinet, the dust had come too. Scrambling up, with the wind on our backs, we began to breathe; but it was not until we had ascended to the old guard house on top of the pottery strewn height, that we could draw a clean breath. Then the reward was worth the pains.

Down below us, seen as from a bird's-eye view, lay a vast, unroofed honeycomb. It's size was incredible. The thing could not really be there. It was a startling dream, that endless gold-brown city of regular streets, and mud brick buildings, big and small, shops and houses, theatres and libraries, lacking only their roofs, deserted save by ghosts for thousands of years, yet looking as though it had been destroyed by a cyclone yesterday. Down there in the devastated beehive myriads of bees still worked frantically, human bees, which Cleopatra said were reincarnations of those who had owned slaves and killed them with forced labour, when Shetet was among the richest cities of the "Two Lands." These bees of to-day worked to destroy, not to recreate, for the crumbling brick is the best of fertilizers—and fertilizing their land is the one great interest in life for the Fellaheen of the Fayoum. Furiously they tore at the remaining walls; furiously they packed away their treasure of dried mud in sacks; furiously they piled it on backs of donkeys and rushed away to make room for others. Each instant hundreds of wild figures in dusty black or blue scampered off, beating loaded donkeys, only to be replaced by hundreds more doing the same thing in the same manner. Yet always a few forms remained stationary. They were police guardians of the ruins, men armed with staves, whose business was to oversee each worker's sack, lest some rare roll of papyri, some rich jewel which once adorned a pampered crocodile of the lake, should be found and stolen. Glimpsed through the red flame of blowing, ruby dust, the scene was a vision of Inferno; we on our mount looking down on it were in company of Dante and Virgil.

The rest of the day we gave to a light-railway excursion to Illahun and the brick Pyramid of Hawara. There was much laughing and shrieking among the girls of the Set (I don't count Monny, who shrieks for nothing less terrible than the largest spiders) as Arabs pushed our trolley cars along the line; and we were frivolous even on the site of the labyrinth which was, perhaps, copied from the Labyrinth of Crete.

The Set were frankly disappointed in the few remains of granite columns and carvings; but vague memories of jewels seen at the Egyptian Museum waked an interest in the brick pyramid tomb at Hawara where King Amenemhat and his daughter Ptah-nefru lay for a few thousand years. All of us were eager for the "last camp tea," when we got "home" from our expedition, and it was then that the tragedy happened: the tragedy of the black lamb.

How could I guess, when Yusef said the camel-boys wanted money to buy meat as a feast for the last day, that they meant to buy it alive?

When we arrived in camp, an idyllic scene was being enacted. A woolly black lamb with a particularly engaging facial expression was being hospitably entertained by all our men with the exception of the chêf. They formed an admiring ring round it, taking turns in feeding it with bersim, and patting its delightfully innocent head. It was difficult to say which was happier, the charming guest or its kind hosts.

"How *sweet* of them!" said Miss Hassett-Bean. "I must write a few verses about this, for our home paper!"

Everybody joined with her in thinking the Arabs sweet, and Enid Biddell went round and took up a collection. The men arranged a football match for our benefit, to show their gratitude, and played so well and were so picturesque that Sir John and other ardent sportsmen pressed more money upon them. It was altogether a red-letter day for the camel-boys, quite apart from the fact that they would get rid of their noble benefactors to-morrow; and by way of a climax they had what we supposed to be a bonfire at dark.

"Aren't all those white figures wonderful, grouped round the blaze?" asked Monny, who appeared on the whole satisfied with the way in which the desert had taken her. "And look, the flames are reflected on the clouds. I do believe it's going to *rain*, if such a thing can happen here! I hope it won't spoil the poor darlings' celebration. Why, they seem to have something big and black hanging over the fire. What *can* it be? Oh, it looks awful!"

"It is not awful, mees," Yusef, standing near, good naturedly reassured her. "It very naice. It is the lamb, they cook for their supper. The genelman, milord, he give them money to buy it."

"Lamb?" shrieked Monny, in a wild voice which brought a crowd round us. "*Lamb*! Not—oh, not—"

"Yes, mees, you all see it feeded when you come home, when you say it so sweet. Camel-boys find sweeter now!"

"Oh!" the girl exclaimed. "Fiends! They invited that lamb here, and brought it in their arms and played with it and did everything they could to make it think it was having a pleasant afternoon, and then —they *killed* it!"

"Of course, yes, mees," said Yusef, puzzled. "Why else for milord tell they can buy it? They kill and pound it up to make it good, and soon they eat in honour of the genelmen and ladies who have been so kind this naice trip."

"I should like to kill *them*!" gasped Monny, preparing to cry, and flinging herself into Biddy's arms. "Oh—*somebody* give me a hanky —quick!"

We all felt mechanically in our pockets; but I, being nearest, was first in the field. It was a shock to see Monny wave my handkerchief away with a gesture of horror, and bury her face in a far inferior one tendered by Anthony.

"No *wonder!*" exclaimed Miss Hassett-Bean, who is not, as a rule, a Monny-ite. "You're *quite* right, Miss Gilder. Lord Ernest Borrow, I don't see *much* difference between you and a murderer!"

For a minute, I did not know what she meant. Then it broke upon me that the Arabs' monstrous breach of hospitality to the lamb was laid at my door. I jabbered explanations, but no one listened; and just then the rain, which nobody had believed in, seized the opportunity of coming down in floods. The camels roared with rage and surprise; the camel-boys swore Arab oaths; the fire sputtered, and what became of the half-cooked lamb I shall never know. We rushed for the dining-tent, all soaked in an instant, with the exception of Brigit and Monny, whom "Antoun" protected with a long cloak.

Dinner was a gloomy feast, which might have been composed of funeral baked meats, though the chêf himself came to the door and vowed by all his saints that the lamb cutlets were not from *that* lamb. So well did he exonerate himself, so eloquently did he protest that he had nothing to do with the camel-boys' orgy, that another special collection was taken up for him.

"Poor, dear old gentleman!" sighed Miss Hassett-Bean. "I shall never be able to forget him. When I'm out of this awful country of *cannibals*, and safe in my own home, he will simply haunt me, passing his respectable old age, black though he is, chasing across deserts on camels, wrapped in a blanket and covered with chicken coops, at the mercy of any queer Christian who can afford to pay for him. It's a *tragedy!*"

Perhaps she wrote her poem about the cook instead of the camel-boys. Luckily, however, at the last moment I remembered a superstition of the Ancient Egyptians. They were in the habit of sacrificing a black lamb to propitiate Set, the sender of storms. Our lamb *was* black: and at the hour of his untimely death a storm was coming up. The dreadful deed, therefore, was turned into a Rite.

CHAPTER XVI

AN OILED HAND

That is where my diary of the desert stopped; for the adventure that ended our trip was not of the sort that mixes well with tragedies of lambs.

Before dinner Monny had apologized for refusing my handkerchief, I really believe because she was sorry she had misunderstood, *not* because the rain had leaked through her tent, and she wanted me to give her mine. In fact, she and Biddy refused pointblank at first when Anthony and I suggested the change. They would not have told us that the water had come in on their beds if they had thought we would suggest such a thing. All they wished for was to have the tent-roof somehow mended before matters got worse. But we insisted, especially Fenton; and he is difficult to disobey. A look from him, and a drawing together of the black eyebrows has the same effect on the mind of a rebellious woman as an "Off with her head!" from an Arabian Nights Sultan, while I might vainly exert my ingenuity to achieve the result he gets by sheer mysterious magnetism.

It was bedtime when the leak showed itself, but the change of quarters was accomplished with military quickness and precision, as Fenton's undertakings generally are; and almost before they knew what had happened, Monny and Brigit, who had been tent-mates during the tour, found themselves transferred bag and baggage to our tent, with the last clean sheets in the bedroom-Arab's possession.

Transferred, we set ourselves to making repairs, and soon patched up the leaks. Rain at this season comes so rarely, it was not surprising that a stitch or two had been neglected.

Only the pillows and upper blankets had had time to get wet, and we had but to remove the coverings and turn the pillows. We both did this simultaneously, and simultaneously exclaimed "Hullo!"

"They've left their treasures" said Anthony, not with quite the masculine scorn of feminine weaknesses I was used to noticing in him. Indeed, he spoke almost tenderly, as a father might speak at finding the forgotten doll of an absent child.

Each of us stood with a wet pillow in his hand, gazing at his borrowed bunk. In the one I had selected, lay a small chamois-skin bag, attached to a narrow pink ribbon. In the bed chosen by Fenton, was a tiny white enamelled watch, on a platinum chain. Both these things had been covered by their respective owners' pillows, and forgotten in the hasty change of quarters. The watch was Monny's. She wore it round her neck every day—therefore the chamois-skin bag on the other bed must be Brigit's. I told myself that in it she probably kept her pathetic store of money, hidden under her bodice by day, her pillow by night; and beholding this intimate souvenir of my childhood's friend, my heart yearned over her.

"Too late to rouse them up now," said Anthony.

"Yes," said I. "We must have been twenty minutes or half an hour getting the roof to rights. They may be asleep, and if not, they won't worry anyhow. They'll know that their things are safe till to-morrow morning."

Fenton agreed with this verdict, and each keeping charge of his own treasure trove, we went to bed and to sleep.

I am a champion dreamer. So much so, that I often find the life of dreamland rivalling in interest the life this side of sleep. I look forward to my dreams, as some people look forward to an interesting dinner-party; but that night I was too tired to inspect the dream-menu, before lying down to it. The first thing I knew, a handsome Egyptian god with crystal eyes, like those which Bill Bailey means to make the fashion, stood by my bedside. I asked him politely whether he were Rā or Osiris, deliberately picking the two best gods of the bunch in order to flatter him; but without answering, he pointed a bronze hand to the mat on which he stood. It was a white mat, and on it I read a word which evidently he meant me to take as his name: TAM HTAB. For an instant it seemed to me a fine name for an Egyptian god, though I hadn't met it before. Then I burst out laughing disrespectfully. "Why, you're only a Bath Mat wrong side out!" I heard myself sneering; and the god disappeared as a flash of lightning comes and is gone. In going, however, he stumbled slightly against the bed. It was a mere touch; but that, or my own voice, half waked me up.

"TAM HTAB," I mumbled dreamily; and was just reminding myself before dropping off to sleep again that I must tell Biddy about the new bath god, when I realized that he had not quite gone. No, not quite gone! It must be he who still lingered by the bed, for it could be nobody else. Anthony would not come and hover silently at my bedside in the middle of the night. Besides, I was almost awake now, and I could hear the gentle, regular breathing of a man asleep: Anthony's breathing.

"Go away, TAM HTAB," I tried to say, but I was not awake enough to speak. He was bending over the bed. His face was near to mine. I felt rather than saw it. "How could I see in the dark?" sleepily, even fretfully, I asked myself. And yet, *was* the tent dark?...It had been, I remembered that. I remembered that Anthony had got to bed first, and I had extinguished the two candles on the washhand-stand. Afterward, I had had to grope my way to the bed. Now, however, there was a light...a very faint, rather curious light. There seemed to be only a square of it, a square sloped off at the top. It was opposite my eyes, which really were open now, I felt sure. I couldn't be dreaming this. It was like a queer-shaped window in the blackness, a window full of starlight, but close to the floor. Then the rain must have stopped. The stars must be out. Yes, but how could I see that? There was no window in the tent.

This thought dragged the last film of sleep off my tired brain, like a veil snatched away by impatient fingers on an unseen hand.

Odd! Those very words said over themselves in my head: "Fingers on an unseen hand." And that was because a hand was being slipped cautiously, inch by inch, under my pillow. It was the Egyptian god's hand. But I knew suddenly that the dream-god had turned into a thief: that the silver-glimmering square of light was one of the tent flaps unbuttoned and turned back. That the man must stealthily have pulled up a peg or two while we slept our heavy sleep, must have crept into the tent, soft-footed over the thick rugs, and now here he was, trying to steal.

After that, I did not go on with the thought. My dull reasoning snapped off as short as a dry stick. I made a grab for the hand under my pillow, seized a wrist, held it for an instant in a grip which must have hurt, then had the shame and disappointment of feeling it slip out of my grasp, like a greased snake. There was a stifled exclamation of pain or surprise, scarcely louder than a sigh, and I was out of bed and after a shadow that ran for the low square of starlight. Something caught and tripped me as I reached the opening. What it was I did not know then and don't know now, but I had a vague impression that it was warm. If I had stumbled against a bare leg thrust out to stop me, it would have felt like that. Yet it could not have been the leg of the man running away. He was using both his, and must have used them well, for I was up and out from under the lifted tent flap which had fallen on top of me as I tumbled, before I could have counted five. Very wide awake now, I stood in the rough, sandy grass, under a sky encrusted with stars, and could see no one. Barefooted, I pattered this way and that, searching every shadow, but the whole camp seemed an abode of peace. There was not a sound or movement even in the black ring of sleeping camels. Rain had driven to shelter the roving dogs which had troubled us last night. The camp lanterns burned clear and strong, yellow and crude in the silver flood of starlight which dulled their radiance. The smell of earth and grass after the heavy shower was like the fragrance of tea roses. Could it be that an evil, stealthy presence had but just broken this sweet serenity with its vile intention, or had the whole incident been after all a singularly vivid dream? I should have believed so, if my hand which had clutched that other hand, had not been slippery with oil.

No, I had not dreamed. And suddenly a troubling thought leaped into my mind. "Biddy!" The name sprang to my lips and spoke itself aloud.

If this were for her! I had laughed at her forebodings. Sensational revenges such as she feared seemed so incongruous, so utterly unsuited to those laughing, long-lashed eyes of hers! Yet she had in her past life lived side by side with fear and tragedy for more years than I liked to count. And as she said, men such as those whom Richard O'Brien had betrayed had been known to reach out very far to take revenge. Biddy had done nothing. Surely they owed her no grudge. But she had known things. Perhaps they thought that she knew even more than she did know. Their organization was rich as well as powerful. It had many branches. Yet why should men use its power to hurt the widow of a dead enemy, now that they—or fate—had put him underground?

In a flash I remembered the chamois-skin bag, which she had forgotten under the pillow: and lifting the loosened canvas flap with its dangling pegs, I stooped to go back into the tent. Inside, I expected to find darkness, but instead I found light; Anthony up, setting a match to a candle wick, and looking a tall, dark silhouette in his pyjamas.

"What's the row?" he calmly wanted to know—too calmly to suit my ruffled mood.

"A thief, that's all," I answered, hastily searching under the pillow where the unseen hand had been. Sheet and pillow-case were slimy with oil, yet the chamois-skin bag was safe. "But he didn't get what he wanted!" I finished.

"Good," said Anthony, who had lighted both candles. "Let's go look for him."

"I've been, and couldn't see anything."

"I know. I heard a sound. I sang out, and you didn't answer, so I thought something must be up. Let's have another try. I've got Miss Gilder's watch."

I slipped Biddy's bag into the pocket of my pyjamas, and pulling on our boots we went out into the night.

"It's *their* tent I'm thinking of," I said, though I'd never talked of Brigit O'Brien's affairs to Fenton. "If some one had planned to rob them, not knowing of the change we made at the last minute—"

"All our Arabs did know—"

"I'm not talking of them. We've been here two days. Any one could have spied on us enough to find out which tent was Mrs. Jones' and Miss Gilder's."

"You're thinking of Bedr?"

"Well, yes, I suppose I am. Biddy never believed they were Germans."

"Who, those chaps in checked clothes he had in tow? By Jove! yes—I heard her speak of a scar on the forehead of one."

"She thought he might have been Burke, the fellow in the street row, that night at the House of the Crocodile."

"These things happen to heiresses in old-fashioned story books," said Anthony. "But there's nothing that happens in a story which can't happen in real life, I suppose—especially to *such* a girl. She—"

"Oh, but I wasn't thinking of her!" I began, then stopped, shocked because it was true, and also because I was unwilling to tell why my thoughts had turned to "Mrs. Jones."

"We must find out if they're safe," I went on. "The thieves seem to have got clear away and we're not likely to find them, unless they've gone to our old tent—"

"Come along," said Anthony. "We'll slip on something, and call the ladies as softly as we can, not to disturb the others and have the whole camp buzzing like a beehive. When we're sure *they're* all right, we can attend to such details as searching for tracks."

He seemed as eager as I was, to know that the two women were safe; but there was no sign to tell me about which one he chiefly concerned himself.

A minute transformed him from a pyjamaed Englishman into a robed Egyptian of that old-fashioned order which despises things European. Only, he forgot to put on his turban. I didn't think of the omission myself at the time, but I recalled it later.

Going to the tent which had been ours, I scratched on the tight drawn canvas near the spot where I knew one of the folding iron bedsteads was placed. "Biddy—Biddy!" I called gently, and after a few repetitions I heard her voice, rather sleepy, a little anxious, cry, "Is that you, Duffer?"

"Yes," I whispered, seeing the tent quiver in the region of some big cushiony buttons. "'Antoun' and I are both here. But don't be scared. Could you come and peep out from under the door flap a minute?"

"Yes," said she. "Go round there, and I'll come."

There was not much delay, for Biddy's crinkled black hair needs no night disfigurements by way of patent curlers. In a few seconds the door flap waved, and Biddy looked out into the starlight, the yellow glimmer of a candle flame within the tent silhouetting the Japanesey little figure wrapped in a kimono. Behind her dark head and above it, floated a mist of bronzy gold, which I took to be Miss Gilder's hair. There seemed to be quantities of it, and I should have been feverishly interested in wondering how long it was, if I had had time to think of anything but my thankfulness that Biddy and Monny were both safe.

"Are either of you ill?" asked the creamy Irish voice which had never sounded half so sweet as now, in the starlight and fragrance of this strange night. "Because if you are, I've some lovely medicine—"

"I wouldn't frighten them any more than I could help, if I were you," I heard Fenton mumbling advice in muffled tones at my back.

For obvious reasons I made no audible answer; but I had just been resolving not to tell Biddy my suspicions unless it were necessary to do so.

"No, we're not ill," I assured her. "But there's been a silly sort of scare about a sneak thief: may have been a false alarm, and we won't say anything about it to-morrow, if others don't. We're horribly sorry to disturb you and Miss Gilder, but we couldn't rest without making sure you hadn't been worried."

"*You* heard nothing, did you, Monny?" Brigit threw a question over her shoulder to the floating mist of gold.

"No, and I wasn't asleep either," Miss Gilder's voice answered. "I was lying awake thinking about its being our last night—and lots of things."

"I was lying half awake, too, thinking of 'lots of things,'" Biddy mimicked her friend, "or I shouldn't have heard you so easily when you scratched on the canvas. Oh, by the way, Duffer, did you or Antoun Effendi find a little chamois-skin bag under the pillow?"

"I found it," said I, and this gave me a chance I had been wanting but hadn't quite known how to snatch. "I was rather worried over the responsibility. Of course you knew that we'd take care of your treasures."

"It's all my money, and—and just *one* other thing!" Biddy answered, with an odd little hesitation in her manner and a catch in her voice. "I should hate to have anybody open that bag. I'm thankful it's safe. With you, I know it's *sacred*. All the same, I'd like to have it, if you don't mind the bother."

"You oughtn't to carry the thing about with you, if it's so important," I scolded her. "Why not leave your secret treasure, whatever it is, and most of your money, in Cairo, when you come off on an expedition like this?"

"I don't know," she mumbled evasively. "I'm used to having this thing with me. I can't think how I forgot it under my pillow. I never have before. It isn't the sort of—of valuable one keeps in a bank. Monny embroidered the bag when she was a little girl. It was her first work. I taught her how to do it, and she gave it to me for a birthday present. I wouldn't lose it for the world."

"You shan't," I said soothingly. I had heard what I had been afraid to hear; but why should Biddy's trip be spoiled by another worry if I could shield her? We could not *know* that the oiled hand had been groping for that bag; and I resolved not to distress Brigit by putting the idea into her head at present. "Go to sleep again in peace, both of you," I went on. "All's well, since *you* are well. Probably some prowler has been sneaking round the kitchen-tent."

"Yes. The news of the lamb has gone forth!" said Biddy. "Good night!"

"Good night!" I answered.

Down went the tent flap, and hid the sparkle of eyes in starsheen, and mist of gold in wavering candle-light. We trusted that the two had crept back into their beds; but we did not return to ours. We took one of the camp lanterns and searched for footprints—those which were freshest after the rain. The rough grass growing sparsely out of the sandy earth was not favourable to such attempts, however; and even at dawn, when we looked again before the camp was stirring, we made no notable discoveries such as amateur detectives make, in books.

Our next expedition, as soon as light came, was to the town, where we inquired at the few hotels, and put questions to the police. Nobody answering the description of Bedr and his two companions had been seen in Medinet, and we had to go back to camp baffled.

There was our adventure; and when we reached Cairo by train, the mystery of the oiled hand was still unsolved.

CHAPTER XVII

THE SHIP'S MYSTERY AGAIN

I expected a black mark for the lamb and every little desert difficulty, but, to my surprise, only our joys were remembered. Those who had stayed in Cairo exchanged tales with the desert travellers, and it was astonishing to hear what a marvellous week we had had. Each day had been better than its brother. In fact, our trip had been one long, glorious dream of golden sands and amethyst sunsets; the camels were as easy to ride as sofas, and combined the intelligence of human beings with the disposition of angels; the camp was as luxurious as the Savoy or the Plaza; and to me and that wonderful Antoun Effendi all credit was suddenly due. Not to be outdone, the stayers in Cairo had had the "time of their lives." They had not been herded together like animals in a menagerie, as in Colonel Corkran's day. The girls had not only been to dances, but had danced with darling pets of officers, friends of Ernest Borrow; while their mothers had been asked to those fascinating picnics they get up in Egypt, don't you know, where you dig in ancient burial grounds and find mummy beads and amulets. Somehow or other, all these people attributed their pleasures to me, as they had blamed me for their mishaps; and my spirits were at the top of the thermometer three days later when, after some hard work, the *Enchantress Isis* was ready to start "up Nile."

Sir Marcus wanted "his tours to be different from every other Nile tour, and a little better." He wanted to "show what he could do," and he was beginning well. Though the *Enchantress Isis* had had a past under other owners, she looked as if this were her maiden trip, and she was as beautifully decorated as a débutante for her first ball. Her paint was new and gleaming white; her brass and nickel glittered like jewellery; and even those who thought nothing quite good enough for them, uttered admiring "Ohs!" as they trooped on board.

"The Highway of Egypt" was a silver-paved road, leading to adventure. The masts of native boats lying along the river bank were etched in black lines crowding one over another, on the lightly washed-in background of blue. Near by, the great Kasr-el-Nil bridge gleamed with colour and life like a rainbow "come alive"; and the *Enchantress Isis* looked as gay and inviting as a houseboat *en fête* for Henley regatta. She was smaller than the most modern of the Nile boats, for she had been sold cheap to Sir Marcus by another firm: but she was big enough for his experiment, though he had turned some of her cabins into private baths and sitting-rooms. Her three decks towered out of the water with a superior air of stateliness, such as small women put on beside tall sisters; and her upper deck was a big open-air sitting-room. There were Turkish rugs on the white floor, and basket chairs and sofas with silk cushions. On the tables and on the piano top there were picture-books of Egypt, and magazines, and bowls of flowers. From the roof, sprouted electric lamps with brass leaves and glass lotuses; and smiling Arabs in white from turban to slippers had blue larks flying wide-winged on their breasts. Oh, yes, Sir Marcus was "doing" his clients well, that was patent at first glance, and became even more conspicuous to the eyes of the Set as they wandered into the dining saloon, drawing-room and library, or peeped into each other's cabins. Sir Marcus himself had come on board ostensibly to see us off, really to watch the effect of his boat upon Cleopatra. He lay in wait for her outside the door of her suite (the best on board), pretending to engage me in conversation, but forgot my existence as she appeared. The ecstasy on his big face was pathetic, as his brown eyes fixed themselves on a quantity of artificial blue lotuses she held in her hands.

"Do you like 'em, Mrs. East?" he ventured.

"Do I like what?" she inquired, that quiver of impatience in her tone which she kept for her unfortunate adorer.

"The—those flowers," he stammered. "I—"

"They're *awful!*" she exclaimed. "The rooms are lovely, but these dreadful artificial things some *silly* person has stuck all over the place spoil the whole effect. I want to find an Arab to take them away. Or do you think I might throw them overboard? No one *could* like them, I'm sure."

"Of course, chuck 'em overboard—or hand 'em to me, and I'll do it," said Sir Marcus, looking ready to cry. "But—they're *lotuses*, I suppose you know? I heard you say you'd give anything to have some."

"Not artificial ones," explained Cleopatra, *belle dame sans merci*. "I can't stand artificial flowers even on hats, much less in rooms. Who could have put such horrors all over my *salon*?"

"I don't know," Sir Marcus lied stoutly; "but it shan't happen again. There ain't any real lotuses to be got, so maybe the—er—the decorator—" his meanderings died into silence, as he took the bunch of flowers from Mrs. East, and viciously flung them as tribute to the Nile.

"After all, we oughtn't to do that," said Cleopatra. "In the beautiful old days real lotuses were given to the Nile. These are an insult."

"They aren't meant as such," the big man apologized, all joy in his fine boat and the compliments he had received crushed out of him. I knew now that he had hovered at Cleopatra's door hoping for a cry of pleasure. Probably he had ransacked Cairo for the lotuses, or telegraphed to Paris, before his cruel lady went from him into the desert. I was sorry for the "boss," though a snub or two would be good for him, no doubt, and perhaps were being specially provided by a wise Providence. But I had other things to think of than Sir Marcus Lark's love-troubles: Monny, for instance, who at last had found a letter from "Madame Wretched" in Cairo, and had wonderful schemes in her head. On board the *Laconia* I should have thought such schemes obstinate and headstrong, the wish of a spoiled child to do something dangerous, to meddle in matters which did not concern her, and to have "an adventure." But I understood the Gilded Rose a little better now. I began to see the real Monny as Biddy saw her, bright with the flame of courage and enthusiasm and passionate generosity, behind the passing cloud of superficial faults. She wanted everybody to be as fortunate and happy as she, and was prepared to be exceedingly trying and disagreeable in the effort to make them so.

We had not been on board ten minutes when Biddy told me about the exciting letter, and escorted me to find it and Monny. Miss Gilder was in the act of insisting that General and Mrs. Harlow should accept her suite, and that she should take their cabin. The matter had to be argued out before she could spare attention for anything else; but as she made it clear that the Harlows were not to pay extra, their scruples were soon conquered. "The baggage hasn't been put into the cabins yet," she explained breathlessly to me, "so that's all right!"

In my astonishment, I forgot Madame Wretched. "But why," I adjured Monny in my professional tone, as conductor, "why on earth should you sacrifice yourself to these people? What have they done for you? I thought you didn't like them?"

"I don't," she replied, calmly, while Biddy listened, smiling. "That's why I gave them my suite—at least, it's partly why."

"I should think the other part of the 'partly' is more convincing," I remarked; and Monny blushed.

"Perhaps you know that your friend Antoun Effendi thinks me the most selfish as well as the most obstinate girl he ever saw," she said. "And I don't intend to have foreigners like him go on doing American girls an injustice. Besides, maybe he's right about me—and I want him to be wrong. I hate having all the best things there are everywhere, just because I'm rich. The Harlows wanted a suite, and they couldn't afford to take one. They were looking sadly through the door at my rooms and envying me, so I thought I would change. I was *determined* to change, whether they would let me or not. They are old; I'm young, and I shall enjoy thinking I've done something nice for people I thoroughly dislike, as much as *they* will enjoy having their own bathroom."

"If Mrs. Harlow could hear you calling her old!" gurgled Biddy.

"Well, she *is* old. And she's perfectly horrid, much more horrid even than Miss Hassett-Bean; so I'd rather give my suite to her and her husband than any one else. Biddy and Rachel are together, and Aunt Clara is alone. I'm robbing no one but myself."

"How do you know Antoun Effendi thinks you selfish and obstinate?" I inquired. "Surely he wasn't rude enough to say so?"

"He was indeed, the day I *would* have the coastguard camel, and he came after me when it ran away," she confessed. "And you're not to tell him about the suite. I didn't give it up to please him."

"I thought you did," I ventured, "in order that Egyptian princes shouldn't do injustice to American girls?"

"I meant," she explained hastily, "that I like to know they're *wrong* about us. And now what was it that Biddy and you wanted to say? Oh, poor Mabel's letter! How thankful I am to get it! I've been wondering if I dared write, and thinking of all sorts of desperate plans. But, Biddy thought we must wait till Wretched was off his guard. You see, we shall have to rescue her when we get to Asiut."

I would have answered, but a look from Biddy enjoined silence. And so we were in touch with the "Ship's Mystery" again! I took the envelope, which was addressed to Miss Gilder in a distinctively American handwriting, strange to see coming from an Egyptian harem.

The letter began abruptly, and showed signs of haste:

"You were so good, I know I can appeal to you, but I'm not sure if there's any way to help me. I began to be frightened on the ship, when *he* behaved so queerly, just because I talked about the most ordinary things to one or two men. He made me stay in my cabin—but you'll remember that. Already it's like ages ago! I tell myself now that I was almost happy then. At least, I believed I was his *wife*, and that it was better than being poor, and a governess to hateful French children in Paris. He was kind, too—he seemed to love me; and I thought it was like living in a romance to marry a Turk. He swore he'd never loved any one except me, that he'd never been married, and that he wouldn't try to convert me or shut me up like Turkish women. But everything was untrue and different from what he said. I hardly know how to tell you, for you will think it horrible, yet I must tell. When I came here, I found he *had a wife already*, and a perfectly fiendish little girl. It is legal in this dreadful country to have four wives, but I don't care about the law. I want to get away. I've been cheated. This isn't marriage! I don't know what will become of me, for I haven't any money, but I'd rather starve than stay. I heard Mr. Sheridan say on board ship that it was easy to get a divorce in Egypt or Turkey. Maybe he meant me to hear, thinking some day I might be glad to know. But I can't get a divorce while I'm shut up in this house and watched. Now, *he* suspects I want to leave him (since a scene we had about the wife), and he won't let me go out, even into the garden. You are my only hope. You'll wonder why I don't try appealing to the American Consul here, instead of to you. I suppose there must be a consul—Asiut seems a big, important town. I'll tell you why I don't. For one thing, there mayn't be a consul. For another thing, the woman who has promised to post this wouldn't do so if she guessed I was writing against my husband, who is her brother-in-law, and she would guess if she saw an envelope addressed to a consul, although she knows scarcely any English. I have to talk to her in French. He thinks she is devoted to him, and that she's explaining the Mussulman religion and ideas of a woman's life to me, or he wouldn't let her come. It's true, she is loyal to him, in a way. She wouldn't help me to escape. But I think women in the harems like to have secrets with each other, which they hide from their men. I've told her about you, how pretty you are, and a great heiress and she's so interested, she's dying to see you. She hopes, if she posts this letter, that you will call on me on your way up the Nile. She can perhaps find out what day your boat is to arrive, through her husband, and then she'll try to come to our house on the chance of meeting you. I'm almost sure she'll keep her promise and post this letter. If not —if she sees it, maybe he will kill me. I believe now he would do anything. But I must run the risk. Do come. Do think of some way to help.

"MABEL.

"I don't feel I have the right to any other name, for surely as he has a wife I'm not truly married."

"Well?" asked Monny, as she saw me finish and fold up the letter. "You were horrid about her at first, but just at the last minute on the ship, you were good, and kept Wretched Bey talking, so I might have my chance with Mabel. If you hadn't, I shouldn't like you as much as I do. And I'm sure even you'll be anxious to do something now."

"Yet we don't wish Ernest or Antoun Effendi to run into danger, do we, dear?" Biddy suggested, coaxingly. "When you wanted to show the letter, I said yes, but—"

Monny listened no longer. Her eyes were sparkling, as they looked straight into mine. "Antoun Effendi!" she repeated. "Tell me first —because, you know, you are his friend—what would he think about a case like this? Whatever he is, he's not a Mussulman, I'm sure. Still, he's not one of us—"

"You're sure he's not a Mussulman?" I echoed. "What makes you sure, when you know he's been to Mecca, unless somebody has put the idea into your head?" "His own head put it there," she answered. "I saw it without his turban, the night of the alarm in camp. It wasn't shaved, as I've read the heads of Moslem men are. It was a head like—like the head of every Christian man I know, except that it was a better shape than most! So, as he isn't Mussulman, he might not mind our trying to help this poor deceived girl?"

"Shall I ask his advice?" I inquired, rather drily perhaps.

She hesitated for an instant, then said "Yes!"

"You seem certain that whatever he thinks, he won't betray your plan."

"I am certain," she replied, looking rapt. "He's not the kind of man who betrays."

"You're right," I said. "He's not the kind of man who betrays. He's the kind that helps. Though in such a case as this—you know, the very meani' or "forbidden." Still—we shall see!"

We could not "see" at once, however, because Anthony had not come on board. Even when the hour for starting arrived, there was no Anthony, no message from Anthony. "Your friend isn't going to leave us in the lurch, is he?" asked Sir Marcus, watch in hand. He had meant to travel with us as far as Beni Hasan, our first stop, and return to Cairo by donkey and train, but had changed his intention and was going off at once—I thought I could guess why. "The *Enchantress Isis* ought to be under way this minute, but Antoun and you are our chief attractions. We can't leave him behind."

I agreed. We could not leave Anthony behind, but I was not worrying. If he had to drop down out of an aeroplane, I felt sure that having said he would come, he would keep his word. So, while Sir Marcus stared at his watch and fumed, I rushed usefully about among the ladies who clamoured for their luggage, or complained that their cabins were too small for innovation trunks. I showed them how these travelling wardrobes could be opened wide and flattened against the walls, taking up next to no room; I assured each woman in confidence that she had been given the best cabin on the boat; I dealt out little illustrated books about the trip; I advised people which tables to choose in the dining-saloon, and consoled them when the places they wanted were gone. Still, the *Enchantress Isis* had not stirred, and a rumour was beginning to go round that something had happened, when suddenly I saw Antoun Effendi's green turban.

"Thank goodness!" muttered Sir Marcus, putting his watch into his pocket. And then Mrs. East came swiftly across the deck from the door of her own suite, where she must have stood watching, hidden behind the portière. "Oh, Antoun Effendi!" she cried, and though her face was turned toward us, she did not seem to know that we existed. How Anthony looked at her we could not judge, for we saw only his back; but her eyes must have told Sir Marcus a piece of news. He glanced from her to Fenton, and from Fenton to her, with the expression of a school-boy who has been punished for something he hasn't done. Then he turned to me as though to ask a question; but shut his mouth tightly, as if gulping down a large pill, wheeled, and left me without a good-bye. I wondered, Cleopatra-fashion, what he had done in his last incarnation to deserve these heavy blows in the hour which should have seen his triumph. "What if he changes his mind and doesn't want Fenton and me after all?" I asked myself. To my surprise, I realized that it would be a genuine disappointment not to be wanted by Sir Marcus Lark. The Mountain of the Golden Pyramid had nothing to do with this. It was borne in upon me that I had begun to enjoy the rôle of conductor; and certainly I was learning lessons in high diplomacy which might be useful in my career.

Anthony, who was free as an eagle from questions of innovation trunks and how to give everybody the best cabins, and places at table, looked as if he were bound for the Island of Hesperides, on a voyage of pure romance. The air of gravity and responsibility he had worn in Cairo and in the desert was gone with the starting of the boat. I knew suddenly, without asking him, that his mission had been of a far more serious nature than the transplanting of a sheikh's tomb; that there had been something else, and that it had finished at the last moment in success.

"Sir Marcus was worrying about you," I said, when the importance of unpacking left the deck empty save for Anthony and me.

"You weren't, were you?" He was smiling at me in a friendly, confidential way that showed a happy mood.

"Not I! I knew you'd turn up, as you'd said you would."

"Thanks, my good Duffer. But now it's over, I don't mind telling you that it was a toss up."

"You mean there was a chance of your failing us—in spite of the Mountain?"

"Well, I meant to bring this off somehow. But my first duty was to finish up the Cairo business. I simply had to finish it, and I did. It was a—rather bigger job than the sheikh's tomb racket, though of course that was on the cards, too. Everything's all right now; but I spent last night in getting the full details of an Arab plot to blow up the house of a rich Copt, who's been of great service to the Government. Some of the young Nationalists think that the Christian Copts are put ahead of Moslems by the British, and there are jealousies. The whole set of men concerned in this affair were arrested an hour ago, so all's well with the world! I'm free to turn my face toward the Mountain of the Golden Pyramid—free to enjoy myself, although I must stick to my turban still."

"Are you getting tired of it?" I asked.

"I've been tired of it since the first day I put it on. I don't like play-acting for long. But it was necessary. And it has had its advantages as well as disadvantages for me."

I should have liked to ask another question then, but dared not, so instead I told him about the letter from Bechid Bey's beautiful American bride, Mabella Hânem, the "Ship's Mystery" of the *Laconia*. Anthony listened, as the *Enchantress Isis* slipped past the Island of Roda, past Ghizeh, past old Cairo and still older Babylon, then out on to the broad bosom of the river where the Nile Valley lay bathed in sunshine from Gebel Mokattam in the east, to the Libyan hills—haunt of departed spirits—in the west.

"Miss Gilder wants me to help, does she?" he asked at last. "She told you to tell me about this?"

"I warned her that you mightn't approve," I explained. "I said you had more knowledge of Egypt in your little finger than I had in all my gray matter, and you might think that nothing could be done—"

"Tell her I think something may be done," he interrupted me. "And before we reach Asiut we'll plan out how best to do it."

"You and I?"

"You and *she* and I. She has brains as well as courage."

"She?"

"Of course I mean Miss Gilder."

"Oh! Is it 'of course'? There are others who answer that description."

Fenton smiled. "But it's going to be her show."

"She is under the impression," I reminded him, laughing, "that all Egypt, including the Nile, and you and your green turban, are her 'show'."

Anthony did not answer. Perhaps already he was thinking of something else. I should have liked to be sure exactly what his smile meant. Was it for Monny? Was it for Biddy? Or only for an adventure which he saw in the distance?

CHAPTER XVIII

THE ASIUT AFFAIR

Nothing could be less appropriate to the Spirit of the Nile than our spirit in setting out. We had turned our backs upon medieval Cairo, and our faces toward Ethiopia. Our minds should have teemed with thoughts of early gods, and the mysteries of their great temples. But not at all. Medieval or prehistoric, it was all one to us in our secret hearts, which throbbed with passionate excitement over our own small affairs of to-day, and to-morrow. Little cared we, as our white boat bore us southward, on the bosom of the sacred river—little cared we for the love-story of the Great Enchantress—pupil of Magician Thoth, —fair Isis, in whose honour that boat was named. Her tragic journey along this river, whose stream she could augment by one sacred tear, should have been followed by our fancy. We should have seen with our minds' eyes the lovely lady asking news of the painted boat which carried the dead body of her murdered husband Osiris, asking always vainly, until she thought of questioning the little children. But instead we thought of our own love-stories and amusements. We played bridge, and danced the Tango on deck; we drummed on the piano, or warbled the latest musical comedy airs. Above all, we flirted, or gossiped about those who flirted, if for any reason we were off the active list of flirters ourselves.

To be sure, we had brought learned books, and took pains to leave them in our chairs, open at marked passages of deep interest to students. We even scribbled heterogeneous notes, if for a moment there were nothing more amusing to do; and bits of paper scampered wildly about the deck informing those who retrieved them that "Nub" was ancient Egyptian for "gold," that Osiris created men and women from the tears he wept over his own body, cut in pieces by Set; that the ivy was his favourite plant; or that "scarabeus" was the Greek word for a blue-green beetle, which created itself from itself, becoming the symbol of eternal life. All this, however, was affectation. Each hoped others might think that he or she was not an ordinary tourist: each wished to pose as a devotee of some phase of history concerning gods, temples, or portrait statues, anything not difficult to "study up." But life was too strong for us. The colour and glamour of the Nile got into our blood. Hathor, goddess of Love, bewitched us into doing queer things which we should not have dreamed of doing if we hadn't drunk "Nile champagne." Yet after all, what did it matter? We were absorbing what our hearts, if not our minds, called out for: the enchantment of Egypt.

More or less conscientiously I performed the duties Sir Marcus Lark had bribed me to perform. I gave neat little lectures, and tried to remind people, whether they liked it or not, that almost every moment the boat was taking us past places of astonishing interest.

The so-called tombs of "Beni Hasan," the *Enchantress Isis* stopped for us to see, in order that we might admire wall-paintings in rock chambers, and gabble about Queen Hatasu or King Seti and his mother Pakhet, the "Beautiful Lady of the Speos." But it was difficult to rouse emotion concerning things which we glided by without visiting.

Ruined temples were everywhere, "thick as flies," as I heard Harry Snell say to Enid Biddell; but why bother about them, when finer ones were waiting further down on the menu-card of the Nile-feast? Especially when there was a pretty girl to walk the deck with, meanwhile? As for Tell el-Marna, the Heretic King's great city, the general vote went against a visit to the ruins. Antoun Effendi praised it as one of the most interesting places near the Nile, because with the exception of Queen Hatasu and Rameses the Great, Amen-hetep IV was the most human personality in Egyptian history. But only Monny, who was making a hero of Aknator, really wished to delay at the Disc Worshipper's Utopia. It must have seemed strange to the Gilded Rose not to have her will prevail; but there was a "clique" on board who appeared to find pleasure in thwarting Monny. Her sacrifice to the Harlows was misunderstood. She had made it, said those who did not like her, in order to gain credit for unselfishness, or to have an excuse for displaying herself *en route* to the public bath, in a dream of a dressing-gown, and a vision of a cap, carrying a poem of a sponge bag. Rachel Guest was still mysteriously more popular than Monny, and was said to have had two proposals on the first day. She didn't want to get off the boat to see irrelevant painted pavements, in the harem of Aknaton's royal palace, and her laziness won, when the vote was taken. But what did anything matter, if the glamour of the Nile was in our blood?

Not one of us but thrilled to the droning cry of the shadoof men on the brown banks, as the dripping water jars went up and up, tier after tier above the river level. Not one but felt a strange allurement in the passing scene; the dark mystery of palm groves, whose slender stems were prison bars against the shining sky; the copper glow of the mud-bricks in piled-up villages; the colour of the flowing water, where secret gleams as from flooded gold mines seemed to glint through masses of dead violets, that floated with the tide. No eye so dull that it could not see how the shadows on land and water were painted at evening with a blue glaze, like the bloom on old scarabs and mummy beads, and broken bits of pottery that art cannot copy now.

In her way, even Miss Hassett-Bean felt the charm of the Nile, and its shores of brown and emerald and peacock-purple. "I don't call it *scenery*," she explained. "Except when the light is different, or there's some green stuff for cattle growing on the banks, everything's the same yellow-brown; and nothing happens but palms and mud villages, and shadoofs, and a few Arabs, or camels, or those ugly water buffaloes they say the devil made, to show what he could do. But the funny thing is, you can't bear to shut your eyes for a single minute for fear of missing a tree, or a mound, or one of those tall-masted gyassas loaded with white and pink pottery: they all seem so ridiculously *important*, somehow! Then, there's that bothersome north wind following you, and trying to freeze your spine, unless you pounce on the best seat where it can't reach. If you put on your fur coat you're too hot; if you don't you're too cold. At night your bed creaks, and so does everybody else's. You hear a creaking all down the line when people turn over, which gets on your nerves: but you soon forget; and the whole experience is so perfectly wonderful that I'd like to spend the rest of my natural life going up and down on a Nile boat!"

Through the opalescent dream of these first days and nights, shot the fiery thought of our mission in Asiut. I had been surprised at first that Anthony, who knew so well the dangers and mysteries of the East, encouraged Miss Gilder to meddle in so delicate an affair; and there had never been any explanations between us. But I told myself that his motive was sympathy with Monny's desire to help: or else he had been tempted to associate himself with her in an adventure where again, as once or twice before, he had been able to win her gratitude. Perhaps both motives combined.

As for Mrs. East, she frankly sulked. Intuition told me that she had never dared speak to "Antoun Effendi" about the proposal in hieroglyphics (so difficult for me to explain) which she attributed to him. Never had she dared say: "You have written me a love letter. Why don't you follow it up, and give me a chance to answer it, one way or the other?" But it was puzzling her, disappointing her, if not breaking her heart, that he avoided rather than sought her, on this glorified houseboat where "the Egyptian Prince" was more or less a hero with romantic women. While we four planned, in thrilling whispers, how to rescue the "Ship's Mystery," and Rachel Guest walked the deck with Bill Bailey or Harry Snell, Cleopatra was reduced to writing picture post-cards. I thought, if Sir Marcus had but the inspiration to reappear at some stopping place farther on, she might be ready to forgive him the false lotus flowers: and perhaps he would come, for the Lark type is as difficult to snub as Cleopatra's Needle. I was half inclined to send him a telegram, on some excuse or other.

We came to Asiut in the morning, and it was to be a long stop, for there was much to see, and every one was excited at the thought of our first Nile town, a town already of Upper Egypt, which made it seem that we had come a tremendous way from Cairo. For us, Egypt existed no longer as a country, but as a golden brown, purple-green river-bed and a flowing stream of history on which we floated; so it was fun for those having no special mission, to feel that once again bazaars and more or less sophisticated "Sights" awaited their pleasure. I had given my after-dinner lecture the night before, trying to behave as if I were not boiling with emotion, and had told those who deigned to listen that Asiut, "City of the Wolves," was the capital of a province. I had babbled, too, about the tombs which self-respecting tourists must see, even if they hurry over the inspection of carvings, cartouches, and representations of very small queens smelling very large lotuses (most Egyptian queens apparently spent much of their time, lightly clothed, and smelling lotuses, a ladylike pursuit for those about to have their portraits taken); in order to find time for the mummied cats, the bazaars, the silver scarves, the red and black pottery, and the images of wolves, crocodiles, and camels cheap enough to be freely bought for poor relations at home. "Antoun" and I hinted at business which must prevent our joining the sightseers, who would be chaperoned by the dragoman. Luckily, they got the idea into their heads that our affairs were connected with Sir Marcus, and the "trip." We were pitied, rather than blamed, but our real difficulty was with Mrs. East, as Monny did not wish Cleopatra to be let into the secret. If she knew, she would want to be in the adventure, and in Monny's opinion, Aunt Clara was a dear, but unfitted for adventures.

We planned that Brigit and Monny should call upon the wife of Rechid Bey, whose house would be easy to find. If they were admitted, they would try to bring her out, as if for a drive, for it seemed a case of now or never if she were to escape. In case she were able to come, they would take her straight to the American Consulate, which I was to visit meanwhile, in order to explain matters. But if the rescuers were refused admission, the Consul must be entreated to give active help. I, as a "diplomat," was considered a suitable person to deal with this side of the affair; and Antoun Effendi was to keep unobtrusive guard within sight of Rechid's house until Brigit and Monny, with or without a companion, should come forth safely. As I said, however, the difficulty was Mrs. East. She would expect her niece if not Brigit to go about with her, and would not be easily persuaded to join any other party. As for Rachel, we need not think of her, as she had been annexed by the Biddells, who would otherwise have lost Harry Snell. But Cleopatra! What to do with Cleopatra? It was Anthony who had an inspiration.

There lived near Asiut, it seemed, an Italian who bred Sicilian lap-dogs, said to be like those which had been favourite pets in the day of Cleopatra the Great. Indeed, Antony was supposed to have given one to the Queen. Now, Fenton asked permission to present a Sicilian lap-dog to Mrs. East, a dog so small, so polite, that he could be taken anywhere. Anthony could not go himself to select the gift, but would find an interpreter as a guide to the kennel and bring her back to the exploring party. Cleopatra, delighted with her hero's thoughtfulness, caught at the idea: and when the Set went tearing furiously away in arabeahs or on donkeys, Mrs. East followed sedately in a carriage with the elderly Greek interpreter, and Miss Hassett-Bean, who also fancied the idea of a Sicilian lap-dog, to replace the lamented Marmoset.

Everything glittered at Asiut. The sun glittered on the water; palm trees in gardens glittered as the wind waved their big green fans; the white or pink facades of large, square houses glittered, those fine houses along the Nile, in one of which Rechid Bey was known to live. But brighter than all glittered the silver scarfs which Arabs begged us to buy. Hanging over arms raised to show them off, the shining folds glittered like cascades of running water in moonlight. "Very cheap! very beautiful!" cried the merchants. "Ladies, see here! Your gen'lemen, they buy for you!"

In spite of "Antoun's" dignified refusals, putting the men off till our return, they ran after us, waving scarfs and shawls and robes, white as scintillating hoarfrost, pink as palest roses, purple as sunset clouds, green and golden as Nile water, or sequined black as a night of stars. Their vendors feared that if we did not buy of them, others might beguile us, and saw danger ahead in a distant group of rivals crowding round some tourists from another boat. This group we had to pass, and as we did so, who should break out from the glittering ring but Bedr.

He came toward us, humble and cringing, giving the beautiful Arab salute. "Dear gen'lemen and ladies!" he exclaimed. "I am very happy to see you again. Won't you shake hands, to forgive, because I meaned no harm, and did no wrong thing but obey the sweet ladies' wish when they would go to that House of the Crocodile. I too much punished when I been sent away."

"That's past now, and forgotten," said Monny, shrinking slightly from the outstretched hand. "Perhaps it wasn't your fault, that trouble we got into, but we didn't need you afterward, anyhow, and probably the people you are with now are nicer to you than we were."

"Oh, no peoples could be nicer, though they are very nice, my two gen'lemens you seed with me in the desert. They travel with me yet. We go everywhere by trains, because it takes not so much time as the boats. And Miss Guest, that nice good young lady, is she well?"

"Yes, she is very well," replied Miss Gilder, beginning to be restless, her beauty-loving eyes avoiding Bedr's face, as had been her habit when the man was in our employ. She did not like to hurt his feelings (Monny can't bear to hurt the feelings of any one below herself in wealth or station, though apparently she doesn't consider that one is bound to be kind-hearted with the rich); but I could see that she wanted to escape. Never had she liked Bedr. He had been Rachel's man from the first. "Miss Guest has gone to see the tombs," Monny explained.

"You not go there, and to the bazaars? I take my gen'lemen in a few minutes."

"We shall go by and by; just now we've other things to do," said the girl evasively, rather too evasively, perhaps. But in the hope of killing two birds with one stone (luring the man to betray his secret if he had one, and then shunting him), I broke in.

"How have you been getting on," I inquired, looking into the squint eyes, "since that night I saw you at Medinet-el-Fayoum?"

But the eyes opened wide, with a stare of innocence.

"You see *me* there, milord? I thought your party had not come when we went away. My gen'lemen not like that camping place, and we stay there not even one night. You must make mistake, and think some other man me. Sure!"

We could not help laughing at the "Sure!" It was spoken in so truly an American way that it was funny on those lips. Afterward, however, it struck me in remembering the scene, that the man's accent in speaking English was even more distinctly American than it had been. This was odd, if he had been associating with Germans; but natural if his new clients were Americans.

Another question was on my tongue, but before I had time to speak, Monny cried out: "Oh, there's Wretched Bey, in a carriage, all alone with some luggage! I hope he's going away!"

Naturally we turned, but I saw Biddy raise her eyebrows warningly. The girl looked puzzled, as if, for an instant, she did not see what she had done that was wrong. But I guess that Biddy's distrust of Bedr as a possible spy was still alive in her breast. She did not know of my suspicions concerning the "camp thief," for the affair at Medinet, thanks to a white fib or two, had never assumed serious proportions in her mind. It did not need that, however, to make her feel that Bedr's ears were not fit receptacles for secrets.

Monny had not been mistaken. It was Rechid Bey, leaning comfortably back in an old-fashioned but not badly appointed open carriage, drawn by two very decent horses, and driven by a smart, red-sashed, white-robed negro. We saw him in profile as he passed along the road at some distance, but he was reading a paper with an expression so placid that I felt sure he had not seen us. On the seat beside him was a suitcase with the air of having been made in France; and circumstantial evidence said that Monny's wish was to be granted.

I glanced hastily at Bedr, to observe, if I could, whether the girl's impulsive exclamation had aroused undue interest; for it was not unlikely that he had seen Rechid Bey and Mabel landing at Alexandria the night of his first meeting with us. But the ugly face showed nothing.

"If you have things you want to do, my ladies," he said, "please excuse that I have keeped you. I go to my gen'lemen or they give the men with the silver shawls too much money."

The "gen'lemen" in question were more interested in observing our movements than in completing any bargain with the street vendors; nevertheless Bedr hastened back as if in great fear that they might be cheated.

An arabeah waited for them; and having bought a scarf or two, they drove off before we had parted to go our several ways. An arabeah was in attendance upon us, also, and we put Brigit and Monny into it alone, for Rechid Bey's house, the driver informed us, was not far off.

"Good luck!" I said encouragingly, and Brigit smiled gayly at me; but Monny was looking at Fenton. She was telling him something with her eyes; and, with a significant little gesture, she touched the small leather handbag she carried.

"One would think she was a suffragette with a bomb," I remarked to Anthony, trying to speak easily, as though I were not at all anxious, when the carriage had turned its back on us.

"Instead of which," said Anthony, gazing at the dark head and the fair head, as earnestly as if he never expected to see them again, "instead of which, she's merely a brave girl with a pistol that she knows how to use. Or, anyhow, she says she does."

"Great heavens! Has she got one in that bag?" I gasped.

"She has. My Browning."

"Jove! You gave it to her?"

"I did. Last night."

My heart began suddenly to feel like a cannon ball, in my breast. I felt that I had not understood the situation, and that now I did not understand Anthony—though that was far from being a new sensation.

"I thought that *you* thought there was no danger?" I bleated. "You know Egypt and I don't. I didn't want them to go in for this thing, but when you said it would be all right, I yielded. I wish to heaven I hadn't!"

"Do you think if you hadn't given in, Miss Gilder would have given up?"

"You and I together could have kept them both out of the business."

"Only by sheer force. You see, Miss Gilder was interested in this girl and fond of her before she met you. So was Mrs. East. As Rechid tricked the pretty little governess by making her believe she would be his first and only wife, they don't look upon her as married to him: And I think they're right. Don't you glory in them both for knowing there's a risk, yet taking it so gayly for that foolish child's sake?"

"I glory in them, but I wouldn't have let them go if—"

"You've changed your mind, just because I gave Miss Gilder my Browning? Honestly, Duffer, I don't think there's actual danger. But, anyhow, don't you see, they *had* to go, and they had to go alone. They would have hated us and themselves and each other if they hadn't answered the girl's appeal. And *we* couldn't do the thing, unfortunately, as it deals with the harem. If it can be done at all, it's woman's business. These two are the right ones, as they felt bound to do it, and you and I can but see them through, from the outside."

CHAPTER XIX

"IF AT FIRST YOU DON'T SUCCEED"

Now that we were thoroughly launched on this somewhat quixotic adventure, I envied Anthony because his part in the drama kept him "in the wings," within sight of the stage. He was to watch the house of Rechid Bey, and if the rescue party of two did not appear after an hour's absence, the true story of the affair and Mabel's appeal was to be laid before the Inspector General of Upper Egypt—laid before him not by "Ahmed Antoun Effendi," but by Captain Anthony Fenton, officially on leave, secretly on a special mission for the British government.

My rôle, less exciting but perhaps no less important, was to play the diplomat in beguiling the American Consul to stand by the wife of Rechid Bey, if the attempt at rescue succeeded, or—if possible—even if it failed.

"Antoun" accounted for his presence in front of Rechid Bey's high garden wall, by attracting a crowd, and lecturing them in his character of Hadji, while I dashed off in a jingling arabeah, to the American Consulate. As in Cairo, my progress was one long adjuration of the crowd by the driver, who would have revelled in conducting the car of Juggernaut.

"Shemalak, ya welad!" ("To the left, oh, boy!"), or "Yeminick!" ("To the right!"), he roared, while men dived and dipped under his horse's prancing feet. A hawk flew by on my right side, and my right eyelid twitched, as we neared the Consulate. In Egypt these were good omens. Besides, there had been a red sunrise, which in the Nile country had meant, since Egyptians superseded the prehistoric "new race," that Rā had conquered his enemies, and stained the sky with their blood. Therefore all should be well with me and the world; and it did seem as if my hopes bade fair to be fulfilled, when in the Consul I recognized a man I had been able to advise in a small official difficulty in my early days at the Embassy in Rome. This was even more fortunate than the case of Slaney. We shook hands warmly, and as soon as was decent, I interrupted a flow of reminiscent gratitude by flooding Mr.

James Bronson with the story of Rechid Bey's unhappy American bride, Mabella Hânem, ill treated as well as cruelly deceived, if her story were true. He knew Rechid slightly, but the marriage was news to him. With interest he listened to my account of the lonely little governess in Paris, bewitched by the love-making of a handsome Turk as white as herself. But when I asked for help, the Consul shook his head.

"Lord Ernest," he said, "there's nothing I'd like better than to pay my debt by doing you some favour. But you're asking me the one thing that's hardest, as you probably know. You understand as well as I do that when a girl marries a man, she ceases to be a subject of her native land. And to interfere with the inmate of a harem is just about impossible. But I'll tell you what I will do for your sake. If you can get the girl out of Rechid Bey's house—which, mind you, I doubt—you may bring her to my wife, and we'll cook up some story about her being a relative of mine. So she is, I guess, through Adam and Eve! If you think she's been badly treated, we'll stand by her, once she's under this roof (which means she'll be on American soil), through thick and thin, whatever the consequences. I can't go farther, and I don't believe you expected that I would."

I admitted that I had not, and thanked him for his promise.

By this time, I thought that Brigit and Monny might be on their way to meet me at the Consulate, as arranged, escorted by "Antoun," and perhaps bringing Mabel. Even the route they were to take was planned, so that I could not miss them if I started.

Meanwhile, Mr. Bronson was to interest his wife in our protégée. Back I flew, my ears deafened by more "Ya Welads," but though I met many things and many creatures on the congested road, there was no arabeah containing the desired ones. I made my driver slacken pace as we neared the big, square pink house of Rechid Bey, set far back in its garden of palms and impossible statues, on the bank of the Nile. No green turban was in sight, and I wondered what could have happened, as we drove slowly past the ponderous black gate-keeper, apparently half asleep on his bench. There was nothing to do but crawl along at a snail's pace, lest that droop of the crocodile-lids should be assumed for effect. I went on, meaning to turn presently; but when the arabeah had taken me beyond eyeshot of Rechid's gate-keeper, an Arab sacca, or water seller, ran forward, striking his musical gong. From his brass jar, protected by crimson-dyed horse hair to keep out dust, he offered a draught; and his look said that he had something more for me than a drink of water. I beckoned him close, stopping the arabeah; and under the tumbler he handed up was a folded bit of paper. None save the water seller had attention to spare for me just then, as a wedding procession was approaching, with a crude but gorgeous curtained litter drawn by camels, and a number of musicians with räitas, darabukas, the "key and bottle," and other Eastern instruments which may have been ancestors of the Highlanders' bagpipes. The street crowd followed, enchanted by the plaintive, monotonous notes, grotesque to newcomers from the west, but enthralling to those who have fallen under the spell of their melancholy magic.

"Failure for the present, but Miss G. and Mrs. J. safe," Anthony had scrawled in pencil. "Couldn't wait in front of R.'s house, but you'll find us at an Arab restaurant to which the messenger will guide you. All you have to do is to discharge your arabeah, and walk in the direction the man takes, keeping your distance in case you're watched."

I obeyed instructions, and in the town of Asiut, far from the gardens along the Nile front, I came to a house between the mosque of the tallest minaret, and the great market whither Arabia as well as Egypt sends her wares. It was a house of some pretension, though in a narrow unpaved street, lined with humble native dwellings. I guessed that it must have been built for a rich man who had died or failed in business, but now a sign in Arabic announced that it was a restaurant. A nod from the water seller told that I had reached the end of the journey. Nubian servants salaamed in the big room where once the master of the house had held receptions, and in a smaller room beyond I saw Antoun, Brigit, and Monny. They were seated at a low table where no forks or knives or even plates were laid. In the centre of the white cloth stood a large dish of something sweet and rich-looking, from which everybody pretended to eat; but at sight of me, Brigit and Monny began talking together. They told me breathlessly how they had been informed by the gatekeeper that "Mabella Hânem" was not well. Having insisted that they were intimate friends whom she would desire to see, they had been bidden to return in an hour. Reluctantly coming away, they had as soon as was prudent been joined by Antoun. He had then taken them to the bazaars, hoping to give them a glimpse of the shops before the Set returned from the Tombs; but they had met Neill Sheridan, who had something to tell. He had caught sight of Bedr running after the carriage of a Turk strongly resembling Rechid Bey. The carriage had stopped near the railway station; and after an instant's conversation the horses had been turned to gallop off in the direction whence they had come.

"Of course we were sure the Turk *was* Rechid," said Monny, "so Antoun Effendi thought we'd better go back to watch his house. When we got there, it was too late, for already some time had passed since Mr. Sheridan saw Bedr. Rechid's gate-man said that Mabella Hânem was suddenly better, and had gone away with her husband. He could talk a little French, so we understood perfectly—and, anyhow, you know I'm studying Arabic. It's *so* discouraging when Arabs answer me in Cockney English, or say "Sure" in American! We believed the fellow, because it seemed exactly what Wretched *would* do—come back and grab Mabel away at a minute's notice. So unfortunate about Neill Sheridan! Wretched was idiotically jealous of him on the *Laconia*; and if he caught a glimpse of him to-day he's certain to think Mr. Sheridan's here to try and see Mabel. We tore to the railroad depot, but the train was just going out. No doubt Rechid and his wife were both on it. Isn't it heartbreaking?"

I sat mute, thinking things over, but Anthony tried to give consolation by saying that he still had some hope. He had found out that Rechid Bey owned a sugar plantation, with a house on it, near Luxor. The train which had left Asiut was bound for Luxor. In a very few days our boat would land us there, and we would try our luck again.

"Not much doubt," Fenton added, speaking as always in French, "that this is Bedr's revenge on us. He must have told Rechid that Miss Gilder had mentioned his name saying she hoped he was leaving home. That hint of danger would be enough for any Turk."

"It will be my fault, then," moaned Monny, "if he kills Mabel. He's deceived and shut her up and tried to convert her. Worse than all, he has another wife. The next step will be murder. Oh, how can we bear the delay of going on to Luxor by boat! Hadn't we better take a train? Better miss all the things we've come to Egypt to see, rather than leave Mabel to her fate."

"Rechid isn't the sort to have her put out of the way,"! said Anthony. "He's not a bad fellow, as such men go, and he's hardly had time to tire of his conquest yet. According to his lights, he's right not to allow any interference with his harem from Europeans. He was jealous on board ship, of one or two men of your acquaintance, you've told me. This attempted visit of yours will revive his interest in his wife, inconveniently for us; but if I know his type it will die down again, the minute he thinks he has covered his tracks. For a day or two he will be a dragon. Then he'll begin to think we're discouraged, or that we haven't found out about his sugar plantation, or that nothing more than a visit to his wife was intended, and he'll turn his attention to other things than watch-dogging. It's far better to go on by boat, and make a dash when he's off guard again."

After a few arguments, we agreed with "Antoun," as we usually ended by doing, and soothed our restlessness by visiting Mr. Bronson to tell him of our disappointment. If it hadn't been for Monny, I think the Consul would have taken the point of view that he was now "out" of the affair, but Monny, sapphire-eyed with generous zeal, is rather irresistible. Fired by her enthusiasm, as he had not been by my beguiling, he volunteered to go to Luxor on two or three days' leave, with his wife, to visit a Syrian friend who had often vainly invited them to his villa, and arriving if possible about the time our boat was due. If we succeeded in our quest, we might bring Mabel to them, and they would smuggle her back to the American Consulate at Asiut.

Our great adventure thus postponed, we let the Nile-dream take us once more; and though we had moments of impatience, the dream was too fair to be resisted. Besides, we were all four dreaming it together. Poor Cleopatra was the only one outside, for Rachel Guest was dreaming her own dream, with an extremely practical side to it, unless Biddy and I were mistaken. She wore Monny's clothes, and used her special perfume, and took advantage of the same initials, to accept gifts of filmy handkerchiefs and monogrammed bags and brushes. Also she had firmly annexed most of the men on board who would, in normal states of mind, have belonged to the Gilded Rose. But they all seemed to have gone mad on the subject of Miss Guest. Even Harry Snell, who had been the property of Enid Biddell on board the *Candace*, on the *Enchantress Isis* was gravitating Guest-ward, lured by that meek, mysterious witchery which I was trying hard to understand.

We got past Sohâg, and the famous White and Red Coptic Monasteries built by Saint Helena, without jarring notes of any sort in the Nile-dream (save for the failure of our rescue plot): past Akhmin, which Herodotus wrote of as Chemmis: past Girgah, where once stood ancient This, that gave the first dynasty of kings to Egypt: but when we arrived at Baliana to visit Abydos, between Enid Biddell and Harry Snell I had an interlude of nightmare. It was Rachel's fault, but it was I who had to suffer for her sins. I, who had engaged as Conductor of the Set and found myself their Arbiter as well.

Other tourists on other boats do not see Abydos until the return trip; but the aim of Sir Marcus was originality as well as "exclusiveness." This was a special tour, and everything we were to do must be special. Some passengers might wish to stay longer than others at Khartum, or from there go up the White or Blue Nile after Big Game. Or they might tire of the Nile, and wish to tear back to Cairo by train. Sir Marcus was boldly outdoing his rivals by allowing clients to engage cabins for "up Nile" only, instead of paying the return also: and they were not to miss any temple because of this concession. "I consider it an advertisement, and a cheap one," he had explained to me, in saying that we were to visit at Abydos on our way south.

Beautiful smiling donkeys, adorned with beads and amulets, met us at the boat-landing. We ought to have called it Al-Balyana, but we didn't. We called it Baliana, and we pronounced Abydos according to our education. We had a ride of an hour and a half from the boat to the temple; and having sent off Cleopatra and Lady Biddell in a carriage, my conscience was free, my heart light. The sun shone on tawny desert hills, like lions creeping stealthily out from the horizon toward the Nile to drink. There were sweet smells of unseen flowers, and herbs such as ancient Egyptian doctors used, and I looked forward to keeping my donkey near Biddy's. Of course I ought to have preferred Monny's, but then, I could talk of Monny to Biddy, and we had had so many subjects in common since childhood that it was restful to ride even the most energetic donkey at the side of "Mrs. Jones." No sooner, however, had I begun to urge my gray animal after her white one, than I was called by Enid Biddell. "Oh, Lord Ernest! I *must* speak to you!" she pleaded so piteously that I couldn't pretend not to hear.

When we were ambling side by side, separated from the rest of the party by a gleaming cloud of copper dust, a few long-haired, brown sheep, some blue-eyed water buffalo, and a plague of little birds, Enid turned upon me a pair of tear-wet eyes.

"Why, Miss Biddell, what is the matter—or is it a cold in your head?" I asked anxiously.

"It's not a cold in my head," she confessed. "It's a dreadful, dreadful pain in my heart. And you're the only one who can cure it."

For a fearful moment I thought that she was going to propose. One hears of these awful visitations. But I need not have trembled.

"I feel as if I could say anything to you," she murmured. "You are so understanding, and so sympathetic."

It was on the tip of my tongue to reply that it was my duty as Conductor to be so, and that, if I succeeded, a mountain full of hidden treasure might perhaps reward me. But just in time I realized that this speech would not be tactful. Instead of speaking, I looked at her and let her go on.

"It's Harry Snell," she said. "You have influence with him. He thinks you such a great swell, he'd hate to do anything you would call unworthy of a gentleman. He—he's making me so unhappy. He's done —everything—to win my love and now—now he's gone over to that Miss Guest." The donkey having begun inopportunely to trot, the words were jolted out, one after another, like a shower of pebbles. And they fell on my feelings like paving stones. She expected *me* to do something about it! Horrible! I should almost have preferred the proposal.

"My dear Miss Biddell," I soothed her in my best salad-oil voice, cultivated at the Embassy, "you are much prettier than Miss Guest, and you can win Snell back easily if you want him. Probably he's only flirting, to make you jealous."

"It's me he was flirting with," she moaned. "But I *don't* believe he cares for Miss Guest. It's only a case of 'follow my leader,' because other men like her so much. Nothing succeeds like success, you know. And other men's admiration is the most becoming background a girl can have. He told Mrs. Harlow it was haunting him, that Elaine and I would get fat like our mother, and the men who married us would have to spend dull years seeing us slowly grow into mother's likeness. Wasn't it cruel? And we eat scarcely *anything* except pickles on purpose to keep thin. But that's only his excuse. It's the romance of the situation, and the *secret* that appeals to him."

"What secret?" I felt entitled to inquire.

"Why, the secret between those two girls, Miss Gilder and Miss Guest. You *know* what all the men believe about them, don't you? But of course you do."

"But of course I don't."

"Why, that they've changed places, to deceive people, just as heiresses and poor girls do in old-fashioned plays or books. They think Miss Gilder (I mean the girl we *call* Miss Gilder) is really the school-teacher, and the one we call Miss Guest, and that all the men are after, is Rosamond Gilder the cannon heiress."

"Whew!" I whistled, bumpily, as my donkey kept up with Enid's. "For goodness' sake, what makes them think that?"

"I don't know exactly how the story started, but it seems *authentic*. Have you known them long?"

"Only since Naples. But—"

"Then you can't be certain whether it's true or not?"

I paused, swallowing an answer. So *this* was the explanation of the Monny puzzle! Yet it was but the first word of another enigma. *Who* was responsible for the wild story? There was more than met the eye—or ear—in this. I could hardly believe that Monny would have chosen, or Rachel dared, to start this rumour, though it might have amused the real heiress, and suited the false one, to watch it run. I dared not contradict it flatly, without consulting Brigit or the Gilded Rose herself. It was not my business to be a spoil-sport, if there were sport to spoil, no matter how sternly I might disapprove.

"In the matter of actual knowledge, I have very little about Miss Gilder," I decided to reply, "except that she's charming enough and pretty enough for any man to fall in love with, if she hadn't a penny. As for Miss Guest"

"Miss Guest is a cat! And if *only* you'll tell Harry Snell so, I'll bless you all my life."

"Good gracious! I couldn't do that."

"I mean, tell him you think she isn't the heiress, that she's only what she seems to be, and nothing mysterious or interesting. He'll believe *you*! Why, she *can't* have any money, or even a nice mind. She always writes 'No,' with her finger on top of her cold cream at hotels, she told me so herself. Not that it's any good with Arabs, they don't want to steal cold cream. But such a trick would never occur to a rich girl, would it? She grows vainer every day, too, till one can just see vanity spouting from the top of her head. She intends to use this mistake people are making about her, to bag a rich man like Harry Snell, or a successful one with a big, growing reputation like Mr. Bailey the American sculptor. You *will* help me save Harry from her, and bring him back to me, won't you? You're the only one he'll listen to. If you don't speak, I shall simply jump overboard into the Nile, and Sir Marcus Lark would *hate* that."

"So should I, dear Miss Biddell," I assured her. "But what can I possibly do in—in such a very intimate matter?"

"Why, you're a diplomat, aren't you? I thought they always knew what to do. You make us all dance to your tune like puppets, and imagine we're prancing about to please ourselves. Tell him he's breaking my heart."

"By Jove! You're not in earnest?"

"I am. Oh, he must come back! I thought on board the *Candace* we were as good as engaged. I—I submitted to his kisses, and now—"

"'Submitted' is a good word," I sneered to my inner self, but outwardly I submitted a handkerchief to the lady, as she had lost hers in one of the last donkey jolts, and ventured to insert sympathetically into a pause a small suggestion. It was usual, I reminded Miss Biddell, if a gentleman's intentions had to be asked, that the father did the asking. This hint, however, fell flatter than a flounder; and all the way to Abydos, most sacred temple of ancient Egypt, I was persecuted with Enid Biddell's woes, when I should have been free to meditate upon the tragic history of Isis and Osiris. It was here that the head of the murdered god was buried, and perhaps his whole body, when the magic secret of Thoth had enabled Isis to collect the fourteen separate pieces Set had hidden. Many temples claimed the sacred body of Osiris, ruler over departed spirits and Amenti, their dim dwelling place beyond the western desert; Philae and Memphis among others; but it was Abydos to which the Egyptians give their most reverent faith, as the true burial place of the Beloved One. It was there they wished to lie when they died and were mummied, in order to rest through eternity near the relic of their most precious god. Thus a necropolis grew like a poppy-garden of sleep, round the temple; and a city rose also. But even in the long-ago time of Strabo, the city was reduced to a village, and all traces of the shrine had vanished. The great white jewel of the temples—temple of Seti I, and the temple of his son Rameses II—remain to this day, however, with the Tablet of Ancestors which has helped in the tracing of Egyptian history. Therefore is it that this treasure of the Nile-desert is still a shrine for travellers from the four corners of the earth.

After the long, straight road, and a high, sudden hill, we came face to face with the marble-white columns of the outer court. If I had been with Brigit or Monny, I could have run back into the past, hand in hand with either, to see with my mind's eyes the white limestone palace of Memnon, copied from the Labyrinth, standing above the city between the canal and the desert. I should have peered into the depths of its fountain; and with a hand shading my eyeballs from the sun I should have gazed at the grove of Horus' sacred acanthus trees, dark against the burning blue. I should have found the Royal tombs which Rameses restored, grouped near the buried body of Osiris. But bad luck gave me Enid Biddell for my companion. She would not let any one else come near me, even had the Right Somebody wished to dispute my battered remains with her. "Antoun Effendi" had the others hypnotized, and I wondered if they noticed how like his boldly cut profile was to certain portraits of the youthful Rameses carved on the glittering white walls. So splendid were they that had I been a woman my spirit would have rushed back along the sand-obliterated, devious paths of Egypt's history, to find and fall at the feet of their original. But—there was Antoun, much easier to get at, and perhaps better worth the gift of a woman's heart than Rameses the Great with all his faults and cruelties!

Crowds of birds lived in interstices of the broken columns, and their tiny faces peeped out like flowers growing among rocks, their eyes bright and arresting as personal anecdotes in long, dull chapters of history. They seemed to look at me, and sympathize, cocking their heads on one side as if to say, "Poor, foolish, modern man, why don't you make a virtue of necessity and get rid of this still more foolish modern maid, by promising her anything she asks? Then you can go listen to that princely looking person in the green turban, who might be descended from the kings our ancestors used to behold. He does seem to know something about the history of this place, on which *we* are authorities! The dragomans who bring crowds of tourists to our temple and gabble nonsense, put us really off our feed. Peep, peep! Just hear him tell about the staircase we're so proud of. Did *you* know there was a picture of it in the Book of The Dead, with Osiris standing at the top, like a good host waiting to receive his guests? Well, then, if you didn't, do anything you must to escape from that lovesick girl, while there's time to hear a real scholar talk of 'Him who is at the Head of the Staircase!' Peep, peep! Hurry up, or you'll lose it all, you Silly. Of course, the real staircase is in Amenti, which your Roman Catholics call Purgatory; and no doubt Osiris is standing on it to this day."

So I took the birds' advice, and promised Enid to have a "heart to heart" talk with Harry Snell. Satisfied that she had got all that was to be got out of me, she powdered her nose (in the same spirit that David anointed his head) and attached herself to Rachel, in whose train was the Desired One. Thus basely did I free myself to enjoy the society of Biddy and Osiris, with lovely carved glimpses of Isis thrown in, to say nothing of Seti I and Rameses II. Trying to push into the background of my mind the nauseating thought of my vow and its fulfillment, I helped Brigit and Monny take snapshots of King Seti showing his son Rameses how to lasso, and also to catch by its tail the most fascinating of bulls. They were on the wall, of course (Rameses and Seti, I mean, not Brigit and Monny), but seemed so real they might leap off at any instant; and so charmed was Monny with Rameses' braided "lock of youth" that she resolved to try one over her left temple in connection with an Egyptian Princess costume she was having made for some future fancy-dress ball. "I can't take a grain of interest in any one but Egyptian Princes and

Princesses and their profiles," she exclaimed; then blushed faintly and added, "I mean Princes and Princesses of the *past*."

We got some good pictures of the temple of Seti, for Monny had an apparatus for natural colour photography which gave sensational results in ancient wall-paintings—when any one except Monny herself did the taking. It was better still in the Seven Chapels, the holy of holies at Abydos, and in the joy of my first colour photography I forgot the doom ahead. Appropriately, the sword I had hung up over my own cranium descended in the Necropolis, at that place of tombs called Umm el-Ka'ab, "Mother of Pots." Nobody wanted to see the fragments of this mother's pots, but I insisted on a brief visit, as important discoveries have been made there, among the most important in Egypt. It was a dreary place where Harry Snell strolled up and caught me alone, gazing at a desolation of sandy hillocks, full of undiscovered treasure.

"Look here," said he. "You're supposed to know everything. Tell me why they call seats outside shops in bazaars, and tombs of the Ancient Empire by the same name: mastaba?"

I explained that mastaba was an Arab word meaning bench. Then, realizing that it would be flying in the face of Providence not to get the ordeal over while my blood was up, I spoke of Enid. Among the shattered pots and yawning sepulchres, I racked up her broken heart and blighted affections. I talked to Snell like a brother, and when he had heard me through in silence, to the place where words and breath failed, I thought that I had moved him. His eyes were downcast. I fancied that I saw a mist of tears, a man's slow tears. Then suddenly he opened his eyelids wide, and glared—a glare stony as the pots, and as the desert hills. "Borrow," he said, "I thought you were a good fellow and a man of the world. I see now that you're a damned sentimental ass."

With this he stalked off, and I could not run after him to bash his head, because what he said was perfectly true. I was almost sorry that evening, on board the boat, when he apologized and the Nile-dream went on as if I hadn't broken it by being the sort of fool Snell had said that I was.

In the dream were Nile cities, with crowding houses whose walls were heightened by tier upon tier of rose-and-white pots, moulded in with honey-coloured mud. There were stretches of sandy shore, and green gloom of palm groves. There were domed tombs of saints, glittering like snow-palaces in the sun. There were great golden mounds inlaid with strips of paler gold picked out with ebony. There were sinister hillsides cut into squarely by door-holes, leading to cave-dwellings. There were always shadoofs, where giant soup-ladles everlastingly dipped water and threw it out again, mounting up from level to level of the brown, dyke-like shore. The wistful, musical wail of the men at the wells was as near to the voice of Nature as the sighing of wind, or the breaking of waves which has never ceased since the world began. Sometimes the horizon was opal, sometimes it throbbed with azure fire, or blazed ruby red, as the torch of sunset swept west and east before the emerald darkness fell. When our *Enchantress* landed, great flocks of kites, like in form and wing to the sacred vulture of Egypt, flew to welcome us with swoopings of wide purple wings. Their shadows on the water were like passing spirits; and at night when the Nubian boatmen danced, their feet thudding on the lower deck to the cry of the darabukah, the Nile whispered of the past, with a tinkling whisper, like the music of Hathor's sacred sistrum. Gyassas glided by, loaded with pots like magic melons, long masts pointing as though they had been wands in the hands of astrologers: and the reflection of the piled pots as they moved gave vague glimpses as of sunken treasure.

Denderah meant work for Fenton. There had been trouble there, and tourists had complained of insults. It was the Hadji's business to find out whether natives or Europeans had been more to blame, and whether there were wrongs to right, misunderstandings to adjust. But to the rest of us, Denderah meant the sacred temple of Hathor, Goddess of Love, in some ways one of the most beautiful of all the Nile temples; though, being not much over two thousand years old (it was built upon ruins more ancient than King Menes) archeologists like Neill Sheridan class it as "late Ptolemaic," uninterestingly modern.

Mrs. East had been looking forward to the temple of Denderah more eagerly than to any other, because she had read that on an outer wall was carved the portrait of Cleopatra the Great. That of Cæsarion was there also, as she must have known; but Cleopatra's son was never referred to by her reincarnation, who chose to ignore the Cæsar incident. Mrs. East had not yet deigned to mount a donkey, but to reach the temple she must do so or walk, or sway in a dangerous looking *chaise à porteur*. Rather than miss the joy of seeing herself on a stone wall as others had had the privilege of seeing her for two thousand years, she consented to accept as a seat a large gray animal, tasselled with red to keep off flies and evil eyes. "Won't you ride with me, Antoun Effendi?" she asked. "I'm afraid. This creature looks as large as an elephant and as wild as a zebra. I feel *you* could calm him." But Antoun Effendi was not going to ride. He had other fish to fry; and poor Cleopatra's luminous dark eyes were like overflowing lakes, when he had politely excused himself on the plea of a pressing engagement. I felt sure that she would have been kind to Sir Marcus if at that moment he could have appeared from behind the picturesque group of bead-necklace sellers, or emerged from one of the huge bright-coloured baskets exposed for sale on a hill of brown-gold sand.

I don't know whether it made things better or worse that the gray donkey should be named "Cleopatra," but it was evidently a blow when the animal's white-robed attendant announced himself as Anthony.

"I can't and won't have the creature with me!" she murmured, as I helped her to mount when she had pushed the boy aside. "Thank you, Lord Ernest. You're very kind. But Antoun ought to have been here. Fancy seeing *this* temple, of all others, without an Anthony of any sort on the horizon! A pity it isn't *your* middle name! If you could spare time to ride with me, that would be better than nothing!"

"I'll be delighted," I said hypocritically, for I had been dying to talk with Brigit about the Monny and Rachel imbroglio which, as a hard-worked Conductor, I had not since Abydos found a chance to discuss. Besides, Biddy had whispered in passing that a letter just delivered at Denderah, had brought exciting news of Esmé O'Brien: But I was sorry for Cleopatra, and wondered whether I could manage after all to hint an explanation of the hieroglyphic love-letter—that fatal letter of mine which had stealthily made mischief between Mrs. East and Anthony. I didn't quite see how the subject was to be broached: still, some way might open. "I'm sorry about the middle name," I said. "But if I assumed it—like a virtue which I have not—I should be the third person connected with this trip, labelled the same fashion."

"Who is the second person?" she asked abruptly, as all the animals of the party started to trot vivaciously through the blowing yellow sand.

"Sir Marcus. Surely you've heard that his 'A' stands for Antonius?"

"Good heavens!" she gasped: and I hardly knew whether it was the shock of my news, or a jolt of the donkey which forced the exclamation. Whatever it was, the emotion she felt bound her to silence after that one outburst. She said not a word, and did not even groan or threaten to fall off when both our beasts broke into a thumping gallop. In silence we swept round that great bulk of rubbish heap, Roman and early Christian, under which lies An, the town of the Column. Cleopatra did not cry out when suddenly we came in sight of Hathor's temple, honey-gold against the turquoise sky, and vast as some Wagnerian palace of the gods. The tasselled donkey (or I) had given her cause to think. Or perhaps she did not consider me worth talking to, as we approached the temple toward which all her previous travelling had been a mere pilgrimage. Still silently, when we had left our donkeys and were following the crowd up the dromos (Harry Snell actually with Enid, thanks to me and the wisdom of second thoughts), Cleopatra's eyes wandered over the Hathor-headed columns with their clinging colour; and over the portal with its brilliant mass of yellow, of dark Pompeian red, and the green-blue sacred to Hathor, whom Horus loved —Venus-Hathor, whose priestesses danced within these walls in Cleopatra's day. "Oh, this red and this green-blue were my colours, I remember," she murmured, and then hardly spoke when I walked with her in the gloom of the temple itself—the rich gloom under heavily ornamented ceilings. She wanted to save the portrait till the last, she announced, until after she had seen everything else: and she didn't care *what* Mr. Sheridan said about her temple; it was wonderful. I tried to interest her in the crocodiles, which had been detested and persecuted at Denderah in the late Cleopatra's time as ardently as they were worshipped at Crocodilopolis and other places. I joked about Old Egypt having consisted of "crocs and non crocs," just as the inhabitants of Florence had to be Guelphs or Ghibellines. I explained carefully the geography of the place, or rather, "reminded" Cleopatra of it, adding details of the canal which once led to Koptos, where the magic book of the Wisdom of Thoth lay hidden under the Nile. I could not waken Mrs. East from reverie to interest, as Antoun would have had the power to do; but my vanity was not hurt. It was only my curiosity which suffered, for I wanted desperately to know whether the donkey had seriously jolted the lady's spine, or whether the news that Sir M. A. Lark was Marcus Antonius, not a more obvious Marcus Aurelius, had fired her imagination.

In any case I devoted myself to her while Monny and Brigit frolicked with others; and I had a reward of a kind. When we had seen all the halls and chambers, and the crypt with its carvings all fresh as if made yesterday; when we had been on the roof where chanting priests had once awaited the rising of Sirius; when I had taken her outside the temple, where blowing columns of dusty sand rose like incense from hidden altars of Hathor, we stood at last alone together, gazing up at the figures of Cleopatra and her son. The wall on which they were carved rose behind the Holy of Holies, where the golden statue of the Goddess had been kept; but alas, the figures themselves! Alas! I knew how Cleopatra must be feeling; and I dared not speak. Perhaps she was even blushing: but I did not look. Instead, I gazed helplessly up at that exposed, misshapen form, that flaccid chin.

"Thank heaven it's only *you* who are with me!" breathed Mrs. East.

That was my reward. Or should I call it a punishment? Anyhow, it made it easier for the insignificant person in question to unburden his conscience about the hieroglyphic letter. I stammered it all out, on the way back, apropos of the rubbish-heap which had been Tentyra. I let it remind me of Fustât and our digging expedition. I had meant to follow Mrs. East's advice and propose to Miss Gilder, I explained, but Monny had not found my buried love-letter. What had become of it I—er —had never been told. All I knew was that it hadn't come into Miss Gilder's hands; and I should never have as much courage again.

"Oh!" Cleopatra exclaimed, with a curious light in her eyes, more like relief than disappointment. "You really do want to marry my niece? You delayed so, that I wondered. I wasn't sure, sometimes, if it were Monny or—but I am on your side, Lord Ernest. It isn't too late yet *for any of us*, perhaps. Trust in me. I'm going to help you."

I could have bitten my tongue out, though I had blundered with the best intentions. "Mrs. East," I protested almost ferociously, "you mustn't do anything. I said before I began, that I was going to tell you a *secret*."

"I won't betray your confidence. But I *will* help. I want to. It would be a good thing for Monny to accept you, Lord Ernest, a very good thing in more ways than one. Mrs. Jones wants it too, or did. I promise you, I'll be discreet."

With that, we arrived in sight of the boat. Once more, necklaces and scarabs and baskets were thrust under our noses. Anthony had returned from his mysterious whisperings in cafés or mosques in the new town, and was waiting for us. Cleopatra called him, with a note of gayety in her voice, to help her off "the elephant." He came. I felt she was going to hint to him that I was in love with Monny—hint to Brigit also.

Virtue may be its own reward, but it makes you very lonely!

I hadn't another easy moment for dreaming the Nile-dream. And we all woke out of it when, with the pink dawn of a certain morning, we saw a vast temple, repeated column for column, in the clear river, as in a mirror of glass.

We were at Luxor; and somewhere not far off, Mabella Hânem was praying for release.

CHAPTER XX

THE ZONE OF FIRE

Just at the first moment of waking, when I was moved by my subconscious self to roll out of my berth and bound to the cabin window, I forgot that we had anything more active to do at Luxor than worship the glory of sky and river and temples. I had room in my mind only for the dream-beauty of that astounding picture, into the foreground of which I seemed to have been thrust, so close upon my eyes loomed the line of lotus columns. It was as if the ancient gods had poured a libation of ruby wine from their zenith-dwelling into the translucent depths of the Nile. Even the long colonnade of broken pillars was deep rose-red against a pale rose sky, repeated again in deeper rose down in a magic world beneath the pink crystal roof of shining water. Then, suddenly, bright windows of sky behind the dark rose-columns flamed to the colour of primroses, were shot with pansy purple, and cleared to the transparent green of unflawed emerald. The thought came as I gazed at the carved wonder (reflected flower for flower and line for line in the still river) that here was illustrated in unearthly beauty the chief religious legend of ancient Egypt. As each human soul was believed to be a part of the World-Soul, Osiris, reunited with him beyond the western desert, after death, so did these columns made by human hands unite themselves at sunrise with the soul of the Nile, the life of Egypt. I caught a glimpse as if in an illuminated parable, of the Egyptian Cosmos, the Heavens, the Earth, the Depths, three separate entities, yet forever one as is the Christian's Trinity. Almost I expected to see the sun-boat of the gods steered slowly across the river from the city of Kings, westward to the tombs of Kings; and the little white-breasted birds, which promenaded the deck of our boat as though it belonged to them, might have been Heart-birds from the world of mummies across the Nile, escaped for a glimpse of Rameses' gayly painted, mosaiced white palace with its carved brass balconies, its climbing roses, its lake of lotuses and its river gardens. I was sure that, if I told these tiny creatures that the Pharaohs and all their glories had vanished off the earth except for a few bits in museums, they would not believe the tale. I wasn't even sure I believed it myself; and deliberately blotting out of sight the big modern hotels and the low white line of shops away to the right of the temple, I tried to see with the Ba-birds, eastern Thebes as it must have been in the days of Rameses II. I pictured the temple before Cambyses the Persian, and the great earthquake felled arches and pillars, obelisks and kingly statues. I built up again the five-story houses of the priests and nobles, glistening white, and fantastically painted in many colours: I laid out lawns and flower beds, and set fountains playing. Then, with a rumbling shock, a chasm many thousand years deep yawned between me and ancient No, the City of Palaces:

It was the voice of Sir John Biddell which opened the ravine of time, and let the Nile pour through it. He was on deck, in pyjamas and overcoat, with General Harlow, holding forth on his favourite topic of mummies—an appropriate subject for this neighbourhood of all others; yet, I should have preferred silence.

Poor Sir John! He had been disappointed in Cairo because a villain had not lurked behind each of the trees in the Esbekîya Gardens, and notes tied with silken black hairs had not tumbled on his respectable bald head from the mystery of latticed windows; but he was thoroughly enjoying his Nile trip, and learning something every day to tell at home. Lady Biddell had humiliated him twice, once by asking me if "those old hieroglyphics were written in Arabic?" again by inquiring whether the stone-barred temple windows had been "filled in once with pretty stained glass?" But he had forgiven her because yesterday had been their silver-wedding day, and he meant to buy her a present at some curiosity-shop at Luxor. "A pity it isn't the wooden wedding," I heard him say to General Harlow, "for I might give a handsome mummy-case. I suppose silver will have to be Persian or Indian, unless I can get hold of one of those old bracelets or discs the Egyptians used for money: but that's too good to hope for."

It certainly was: though no doubt some industrious manufacturer of antiques would cheerfully have made and dug up any amount on the site of Rameses' palace, could he have known in time.

We were to have three days at Luxor—three days, when three months would have been too little!—and the second attempt at abducting an ill-used lady from the harem of her treacherous lord would take place as soon as we could learn that our auxiliaries, the Bronsons, had arrived. Until they were on the spot, even a success might prove an anti-climax. Meanwhile I had plenty to do in playing my more obvious part of Conductor, and arranging the last details of our excursion programme. Every one had bundled out early to see the sunrise. Consequently most members of the Set were cross or hungry, or both. Nothing could be less suitable than to clamour for porridge on the Nile, but they did it, and called for bacon, too, in a land where the pig is an unclean animal. They were the same people who played "coon can" and bridge on the deck at twilight, when moving figures on shore were etched in black on silver, or against flaming wings of sunset, and in gathering darkness the blue-robed shadoof-men who bent and rose against gold-brown dykes, were like Persian enamels done on copper.

"Hundred gated" Thebes, the dwelling of Amen-Rā whom Greece adopted as Jupiter-Amon, used to lie on both banks of the Nile; the east for the living, the west for the dead and those who lived by catering for mummyhood.

I had arranged to take our people first round Luxor, making them acquainted with the temple which had already introduced its reflection to us. As for the town, they were capable of making themselves acquainted with that, its hotels and curiosity-shops, when there was nothing more important on hand. Next was to come Karnak, the "father of temples," once connected with the younger temple at Luxor as if by a long jewelled necklace of ram-headed sphinxes. And for those whose brains and legs were intact, by evening I thought of a visit to the thrilling temple of Mût. This last would be an adventure; for Mût, goddess of matter, the Mother goddess, has apparently not taken kindly to Moslem rule. Any disagreeable trick she, and her attendant black statues of passion, fierce Sekhet, can play on a devout Mohammedan, are meat and drink to her: but she can work her spells only after dusk, therefore none save the bravest Arab will venture his head inside her domain, past sunset. I was sure we could get no dragoman to go with us, and equally sure that the adventure would be more popular for its spice of horror.

The second and third days I allotted to western Thebes, the city of the dead: the tombs of the Kings, the tombs of the Queens and the Nobles; then the Ramesseum, the "Musical Memnon" with his companion Colossus, and the great temples wrapped in the ruddy fire of the western desert, where Hathor receives the setting sun in outstretched arms.

As I was about to unfold these projects at breakfast, a telegram was handed to me. I read it; and while bacon plates were being exchanged for dishes of marmalade, I cudgelled my brain like a slave to make it rearrange the whole programme without a hitch.

The American Consul wired from Asiut that he was detained by an Important Personage, who wanted to know things about Egyptian Cotton and its enemy the boll worm. But Mr. and Mrs. Bronson would arrive at the Villa Sirius, Luxor, day after to-morrow, "ready for emergencies."

Of course, being Conductor of a tour, and next a man, I ought to have put the interests of Sir Marcus and his "Lark Pie" (as we were called by rival firms) ahead of personal concerns. I ought to have immolated myself in the western Mummyland with the consciousness of duty done, while on the eastern side of the Nile, Anthony Fenton and Monny Gilder and Biddy played the live, modern game of kidnapping a lady. But I determined to do nothing of the sort. I gazed at the telegram with the air of committing to heart instructions from my superior officer; and without sign of inward tremour, announced that we would explore the wonders of the west before visiting those nearer at hand. The weather being cool and the wind not too high (I said), it would be well to seize this opportunity for the Valley of the Tombs of the Kings, an expedition trying in heat or sand storms. To-morrow also would be devoted to the west, and our third day would belong to Luxor and Karnak. As a *bonne bouche*, I dangled the adventure of the Temple of Mût, to sweeten the temper of grumblers: but there were no grumblers. The Set listened calmly to my honeyed plausibilities; and the alarmed stewards dared not betray their consternation at the lightning change.

No doubt they thought me mad, or worse, because a day in western Thebes meant a picnic: magical apparition at the right moment, in a convenient tomb, of smiling Arabs and Nubian men with baskets of food and iced drinks.

Somehow the trick had to be managed, however; for I must be in eastern Thebes, alias Luxor, on the day when the Bronsons' presence would render our second attempt at rescue feasible. I had to interview the chêf—a formidable person—hypnotizing him and the stewards to work my will, and above all, I had to make sure of boats and donkeys for the party at short notice. Only by a miracle could all go well; but I set my heart upon that miracle. "Antoun," hurriedly taken into my confidence, volunteered to arrange about the boats, and the donkeys for the other side. Fortunately there was no rival ahead of us; and with juggling of plans and jingle of silver, Anthony's part was done. Just at the moment when, by dint of bribes and adjurations I had induced chêf and stewards to smile, Fenton dashed on board to cry "Victory!" Somehow, less than an hour later than we should have started, we got off in two big boats with white sails and brown rowers. The canvas did its work in silent, bulging dignity; but the rowers exhausted themselves by breathlessly imploring Allah to grant them strength, and shouting extra prayers to some sailor-saint whose name was calculated to pump dry the strongest lungs.

On the mystic western side, where once landed with pomp and pageant the sun-boat of the gods, and the mourning boats of the dead, we scrambled on shore with that ribald mirth which always made the Set feel it was getting its money's worth of enjoyment. Many donkeys and a few carriages awaited us: the whole equipment previously engaged for to-morrow! and in opaline sunshine which stained with pale rose the Theban hills and piled the shadows full of dark, dulled rubies, we started across an emerald plain, kept ever verdant by Nile water. The touch of comedy in the dream of beauty was the queer, mud-brick village of Kurna, with its tomb dwellings of the poor, and immense mud vases shaped like mushrooms, standing straight up on thick brown stems before the crowded hovels. In each vase reposed sleeping babies, brooding hens, dogs, rabbits, or any other live stock, mixed with such rubbish as the family possessed: and the most ambitious mushrooms were decorated with barbaric crenellations.

Almost as far as the Temple of Seti I flowed the green wave like a lake in the desert, but beyond, to join the Sahara, rolled and billowed a waste of rose-pink sand, shot with topaz light, and walled with fantastic rocks, yellow and crimson, streaked with purple. In the heart of each shadow, fire burned like dying coals in a mass of rosy ashes: and the light over all was luminous as light on southern seas at moonrise and sunset. Before our eyes seemed to float a diaphanous veil of gilded gauze; and white robes and red sashes of donkey-boys, animals' bead necklaces, and blue or green scarfs on girls' hats, were like magical flowers blowing over the gold of the desert.

Everything blew: above all, sand blew. We found that out to our sorrow, after we had seen the Temple of Kurna, with its noble columns, and its fine fragment of roof, where squares of sky were let in like blocks of lapis lazuli. I rushed here and there on donkey-back assuring people that this was not *wind* we felt: it was only a breeze. We could not have a more favourable day for our excursion into this world of the dead. Why, if we'd waited till to-morrow we might have met a *real* wind, perhaps even Khamsin, alias Simoom, the terror of the desert. To make Miss Hassett-Bean and Cleopatra forget the smarting of their eyes, I told them what a true-sand-storm was like, and how its names in Arabic, Turkish, and Persian all came from the fiend "Samiel," who destroyed caravans, just as "devil" came from the Persian "div." *Our* little breeze was from the east, which at Thebes in old days was considered lucky.

The west wind used to bear across the river evil spirits disguised as sand-clouds. And these wicked ones had not far to travel, because the Tuat, or Underworld, was a long narrow valley parallel to Egypt, beginning on the west bank of the Nile. Red-haired Set was ruler there, the god who had to be propitiated by having kings named after him. But Rä, greater than he, could safely pass down the dim river running through that world: could pass in his golden sun-boat, guided by magic words of Thoth instead of oars or sails; and the guardian hippopotamus (whom Greeks turned into the dog Cerberus) dared not put out a paw.

Mrs. East remembered that Thebes was Tape in "her day," at which Miss Hassett-Bean snorted: and when out came that familiar story about Cleopatra making red hair fashionable, Miss Hassett-Bean stared coldly at the lady's auburn waves. "I wonder if the queen got the colour at her hairdresser's, as people do now?" she murmured. "I've read that they had beauty-doctors in those days, and used arsenic for their complexion, and all sorts of mixtures. Besides, I can't imagine anything natural about Cleopatra, except the asp wanting to bite her!" Upon this, Mrs. East retaliated by calling her companion Miss Bean without the Hassett.

I shall always think of the Valley of the Tombs as a place of terror and splendour, meant to be hidden from mortals by the spells of Thoth, who circled the rock-houses of the dead with a zone of fire, as Wotan hid Brunhilda, and decreed that they should be lost forever in the blazing desert. Despite Thoth and his magic, men have burst through the blazing belt and found in the gold-rose heart of the rocks, sacred shrines the wise old god would have protected. They have found many but not all: for in the breast of some one among Thoth's sleeping lions which masquerade as rocks, may yet be discovered a tomb, better than all those we know with their buried store of jewels, and their painted walls like drapings of strange tapestry.

We broke through the zone of fire, and it pursued us with burning smoke of sand, pink as powdered rubies. Always it was beautiful and terrible as we rode in the blowing pink mist: and still it was beautiful and terrible, when half dazed we slipped off donkeys or slid out of carriages, to enter the tombs which the desert had vainly striven to hide. It was hot and breathless in those underground chambers, scooped out of solid rock thousands of years ago, that great kings and their queens and families and friends might rest with their kas in eternal privacy. Enid Biddell waited until Harry Snell happened to be exactly behind her, and then fainted, with dexterity beyond praise. Cleopatra, however, was in her element. She felt at home, and did not turn one of those auburn hairs scorned by "Miss Bean," at sight of the royal mummies lit up by electricity in their coffins. These gave the rest of us a shock, our nerves being already in the condition of Aladdin's on his way down to the Cave of Jewels. When the guardian of the Tomb of Amenhetep (the king had several other names, which annoyed Sir John Biddell) darkened the painted, royal chamber of death, and suddenly lit up several white, sleeping faces, the ghostly dusk was alive with little gasps. There lay Amenhetep himself, in a disproportionately large sarcophagus of rose-red granite from Suan; and in companion coffins were a woman and a girl, all three brilliantly illuminated. They had the look of the light hurting their poor eyes, and being outraged because, against their will, they were treated as if they had been paintings by old masters.

The dreadful rumour ran that the woman was none other than the great Queen Hatasu (never mind her more scientific names), her mummy never having been found, or, at any rate, identified: and it was pitiful seeing her so small and female, when in life she had wished to be represented with a beard and the clothing of a man. Our dragoman, who read English newspapers and whose idea of entertaining his crowd was to make cheap jokes (just as his family doubtless manufactured cheap scarabs), announced that Hatasu was the "first suffragette." But even those who thought her downtrodden nephew, Thothmes III, justified in erasing every trace of her existence wherever possible, did not smile at this jest. In fact, having Antoun and me to refer to, the Set as a whole sat upon the unfortunate dragoman, trying to talk him down in tombs and temples, or ostentatiously reading Weigall, Maspero, Petrie, Sladen, and Lorimer when he attempted to give them information. A few with kinder intentions, however, interrupted his flow of historical narrative by exclaiming, "Why, yes, of *course!*" "I thought so!" and "Now I remember!" He revenged himself by advising everybody to buy antiques from an extraordinary old gentleman, extremely like a galvanized mummy. The antiques were extraordinary, too, so everybody took the dragoman's advice, neglecting the other curiosity merchants of the squatting row near the luncheon-tomb and the glorious three-tier temple, in that vast copper cup of desert and cliff which is called Der el-Bahari. The sale in mummied hawks, gilded rams' horns, broken tiles with beetles flying out of the sun, boats of the gods, and gods themselves, was brisk round this ancient gentleman, who advertised a blue mummy-cap by wearing it on his bald pate, and seemed to possess as many royal scarabs as a dressmaker has pins. Afterward I learned that he was our dragoman's father; but I was loyal and did not tell.

It was a wonderful day, all the more wonderful perhaps because it left in the mind a colourful confusion; pictures of painted tombs hidden deep under red rock and drifted sand, tombs which we should perhaps never reach again through their guarding zone of fire—tombs of kings and queens and nobles forgotten through thousands of centuries save by their kas and has, their friends and servants, painted or sculptured on the walls with the sole purpose of caring for or entertaining them eternally.

Already we had ceased to remember which was which. And back on the boat, in the hour of sunset, when dazzling tinsel and pale pink cloud-flowers sailed over a lake of clear green sky, the Set argued whether the King with the Horses, or the Queen with the Retroussé Nose was in this or that tomb. Sir John Biddell recalled the fact that Egyptian horses had been celebrated, and that it was "as swell a thing to be a charioteer then as it was now to be a Vanderbilt with a coach and four." As for a retroussé nose, it didn't matter *where* it was, on a tomb-wall or on a girl's face.

Monny thought differently. She and Biddy were glad that the sand and rocks would still hide many secret treasures, while the world lasted. It would be dreadful to think that everything was dug up, for tourists to pry into, or to cart away to museums, and no mysteries left. As for Mrs. East, she was doubtful whether to rejoice or grieve that Cleopatra's mummy had not been found. If, however, it were like the incised wall portrait at Denderah, it would be well that it should share the fate of Alexander's body and remain lost forever.

The next day gave us another trip to the west of the Nile: not again in the burning desert, but only as far as the Ramesseum, and then to see the Colossi, seated side by side on their green carpet of meadow, looking out past the centuries toward eternity.

We had a dance on board that night; and next morning it came out that Rachel Guest, who had disappeared during a "turkey trot" and a "castle walk," had got herself engaged to Bailey. I was not as pleased about this event as was Enid Biddell, who now saw her "title clear" to Harry Snell; for I had "bagged" Willis Bailey and Neill Sheridan for Sir Marcus in order to gain Kudos for myself: but Biddy, appealed to, consoled me by saying it served Bailey right if he were mercenary: and that both men would have come in any case.

The third day was to be the Great Day for us, the day big with fate for Mabella Hânem; and the first thing that happened was a letter sent by hand from the Bronsons at the Villa Sirius. They had arrived. The fireworks could begin.

CHAPTER XXI

THE OPENING DOOR

Not half an hour after the first word from Bronson, came another hurried note. An unexpected obstacle had cropped up. So confident had he and Mrs. Bronson been of their friends' cooperation, that rather than put such important matters on paper, they had waited to explain by word of mouth. The owner of the villa was a rich Syrian with a French-American wife. He was a Copt in religion, hating Mohammedanism in general and the father of Rechid Bey in particular. This had seemed to the American Consul a providential combination: but to his disgust he found that there had been a reconciliation between the families. Dimitrius Nekean would not betray the Bransons' confidence, but he could not allow his roof to be used as a shelter for Rechid's runaway wife—no, not even if Rechid had three other wives in his harem.

Here was a situation! And as Monny remarked, in neat American slang, we were "right up against it." She thought that, if Antoun and I "put our heads together," maybe we could think of "some way out." So we did, almost literally put our heads together across a table no bigger than a handkerchief, in my cabin: and decided that the visit to Rechid Bey's harem must be made by Brigit and Monny in the late afternoon. They must time their departure from the house at about the hour when the Set would arrive at the Temple of Mût. "Antoun" would be waiting for them, and they would drive in a closed arabeah to the temple, where Mr. and Mrs. Bronson would happen to be "sightseeing." If Mabella Hânem had been rescued, she would then be put in charge of the American Consul, whose very footprints created American soil around him as far as his shoes could reach. Rechid would be unlikely to search at the Temple of Mût, nor could he induce any Arab servant to accompany him there after sundown. We would escort Mabel and her two protectors to the town, and to the train for Cairo, Mr. Bronson promising to take the girl to Alexandria, whence she could sail for "home."

It was the best plan we could think of in the circumstances, and Monny approved it, though her patience was tried by having to wait through nearly all of another day. Mabel must have begun to believe that we had ignored her prayer and meant to do nothing. I argued that the girl would believe we were working for her in our own way. I said, too, that if Rechid were spying, his suspicions would be disarmed by seeing us go the ordinary round of tourists. Every one came to Luxor. We had come, leisurely, by river, and were sightseeing every moment. Even Bedr, if he were on the spot, intending to finish his revenge as neatly as it had been begun, could have noticed nothing suspicious in our actions. The mention of Bedr in this connection seemed to startle Biddy, and I was sorry I had let his name slip. But, as I had said, every one came to Luxor. Bedr had with apparent frankness explained that he was travelling up the Nile by rail with his two clients: and if that were true, he would arrive at all our destinations in advance of us. Probably it would depend on "the clients" whether they lingered at Luxor long enough for us to run across them again.

"What are you afraid of," I asked Biddy when I had a chance with her alone, "even if Bedr is a spy? Surely you kept your promise and left that chamois-skin bag in a Cairo bank?"

"It wasn't a promise," she reminded me. "I only said I'd think about it. Well, I did think about it, and I couldn't put it in a bank. I told you it was the sort of thing one *doesn't* put in banks."

"You didn't tell me what it was—I mean, what was in it besides money."

"No, I couldn't."

"Will you now?"

"Oh, no!"

"Well, then, will you give it to me to keep till we get back to Cairo?"

"No, *indeed*! But Duffer dear, honestly and truly it isn't for myself I'm afraid. You *know* that, don't you?"

"Of course. Yet if people are believing that Monny Gilder is Rachel Guest, a poor little school teacher, then no one who heard the gossip would bother to risk kidnapping her for ransom. And, also, there'll be no further danger of those you fear mistaking her for—"

"Oh, don't speak the name!"

"I wasn't going to. I was merely about to use the word 'another.'"

"Good Duffer! Yours is a consoling argument. Still, I never liked Bedr or wanted him with us. And even now, there seems something mysterious about Rachel thinking so much of him. As if there were a secret arrangement between them, you know! I've never got over that, or understood it a bit."

"He flattered Miss Guest, perhaps. She loves flattery. But she's made her market now, and all through Monny's charity. She couldn't want to do her benefactress harm."

"No-o, I suppose not. Unless it were to do herself good. Don't those eyes of hers say to you that she'd sacrifice any one for herself?"

"I've been thinking more about a different pair of eyes. And there were such a lot of men crowding round Rachel's—for some reason or other."

"*Now* we know what the reason was—as she and Monny must have known all along, since their joke together began. Oughtn't *you* to tell Bill Bailey the truth?"

"No, my dear girl, I must draw the line somewhere! I've gone about at people's beck and call, telling other people disagreeable truths, till I'm a physical and mental wreck. Bill Bailey knows all about statues, with and without glass eyes. Let him find out for himself about a mere girl—"

"With cat's eyes." Biddy snapped.

If one triumph leads to another, Anthony could afford to be hopeful for the ending of our stay at Luxor. He had not done as much sightseeing as the rest of us, but when we had been asleep in our beds or berths, dreaming of temples—or of each other—he had been out whispering and listening, in places where his green turban opened doors and hearts. He had traced the mysterious "trouble" to its source, and learned the inner history of that regrettable incident which, like a dropped match, had lit a fire hard to extinguish. A party of young men travelling with a "bear leader" had laughed at some Arabs prostrating themselves to pray, at that sacred moment, just after sunset, ordained by Mohammed lest his people should appear to worship the orb itself. One of these youths, fancying himself a mimic, had imitated the Moslems. They were old men, unable to resent with violence what they thought an insult to their religion; but they had told their sons, and the story had spread. Later that night the joyous tourists with their near-sighted "bear leader," had been attacked apparently without reason, on coming out of a native café. Having forgotten the sunset prayer, they honestly believed that they had been set upon by men to whom they had given no provocation. They had uttered statements and complaints; and disgusted with the "beastly natives" had pursued their journey up Nile, visiting their grievances on the innocent, and making more mischief at each stopping place. Murmured threats, with dark looks, insulting words and jostlings of strangers by the inhabitants of Upper Nile villages, had occasioned anxiety at the British Agency. It had proved impossible to get at the truth, and the influence of the Young Nationalists had been suggested. Our Hadji had now turned the green light of his sacred turban upon obscurity, and those in power at Cairo would know how to set about repairing damages. In spite of private anxieties, those which I shared and others which I didn't share but suspected, I think Anthony was happy on that third morning at Luxor. He must have been tired, for much of his work had been night work, but he showed no fatigue. The true soldier-look was in his eyes, the look I knew far better than the new and strange expression which had said to me lately, "A woman has come to be of importance in Anthony Fenton's life."

We spent our morning and a good part of the afternoon at Karnak, lunching irreverently but agreeably in the shade of fallen pillars Cambyses or the great earthquake had thrown down. Neill Sheridan, who had been to California, likened the ruddy columns of the Great Hall to the giant redwoods. He was enjoying Karnak because there was practically nothing "modern and Ptolemaic about it," but I thought how quickly he would lose this calmness of the student if some one blurted out a word about our plan for that evening. According to Monny, he had been "taken" with poor Mabella Hânem on board the Laconia—admiring her so frankly that Rechid had banished his bride to her cabin. If Sheridan regretted her, as a man regrets a woman vainly loved, he had confided in no one, not even Monny, who had risked seeming to seek his society in order to reach the secret of his heart. He had, however, been graver in manner than at first, so said the girl, who had been much with him before my appearance on the scene. Whether it was intuition, or sheer love of romance which inclined her to the opinion, she believed that Sheridan was unhappy. It would make things worse for Mabel (if our scheme failed) were Neill Sheridan mixed up in the plot; therefore, even impulsive Monny admitted the wisdom of keeping him out of it. But I could see by the way she looked at him—almost pityingly—when he discoursed of lotus and papyrus columns, how she was saying to herself: "You poor fellow, if only you *knew!*"

The "thing" being to see the Temple of Luxor at sunset, we gave it the afternoon, as if condescending to do it a favour. When I remembered how I had meant to linger here week after week, I felt that I was paying a big price for my share of the Mountain of the Golden Pyramid, making a knockabout comedian of myself, rushing through halls of history followed by a procession of tourists, as a comet tears past the best worth seeing stars, obediently followed by its tail. Still, I had Brigit and Monny as bright spots in the tail; and my old dreams of Luxor had been empty of them.

These ideas were in my mind, while on donkeys and in arabeahs we dashed as if our lives depended on speed, from the Temple of Karnak to the Temple of Luxor, along the dusty white road trimmed with sphinxes. This description was Enid Biddell's, she being happy and therefore frivolous. She rode with Harry Snell, as queens may have ridden along that way, guarding a captive prince who had been subdued forever.

Sunset illumined the world, as for a New Year's festival of Amen-Rā in his ruby-studded boat of gold, when we were ready to leave the glorious temple, and turn to the region of little bazaars and big hotels, fair gardens, and girls with tennis rackets whose shape reminded our Egypt-steeped minds of the key of life. Monny and Brigit had slipped away. Their *real* day was just beginning.

My heart was with them; Anthony's, too, and his work permitted him to conduct *his* heart along the way that they must take, while I had to conduct the Set to the Winter Palace Hotel, and give them tea on the terrace.

When everybody was rested and had had enough strawberry tarts, view and flirtation, we were to make for the Temple of Mût: and, having returned at last to the *Enchantress Isis*, were to steam away just as tourist boats and dahabeahs were lighting up along the shore. We were to dine late, after starting, and anchor in some dark solitude, so as to enjoy a peaceful, dogless night on the Nile. But—what would have happened to Brigit and Monny before the sounding of that dinner gong?

What did happen at the beginning I must tell as best I can, because I was not there, and can speak for myself only from the Temple of Mût.

When they stole almost secretly away from Karnak, they took an arabeah which was waiting and drove to the sugar-plantation of Rechid Bey. This place of his is not prepared for a lengthy or luxurious residence; but as I have said, there is a house. There is also a small gatehouse, in a somewhat neglected condition; but a gatekeeper was there: the usual stout negro. Monny and Biddy were quivering with fear lest they should be refused admission, as at Asiut: but this time their coachman was Ahmed Antoun, carefully disguised as a common driver of an arabeah, a rather exaggeratedly common driver perhaps, for his face and turban were not as clean as the face and turban of a self-respecting Moslem ought to be. He had been helped to play this trick by one of the secret friends he had made in some café or other, the cousin of an uncle of a brother of him who should have sat on the box seat. But the motive he had alleged was not the real one. The two beating hearts in the arabeah had confidence in him. If the gatekeeper tried to send them away, Antoun would bribe him, or threaten him with black magic, or say some strange word which would be for them as an "Open Sesame."

The fat creature at the gate had no French, but the driver of the arabeah addressed him in Arabic, and translated his answers. Yes, the great lady had come hither with her husband the Bey. Word should go to her. It should be ascertained whether it was her pleasure to receive these friends who had journeyed from a far country to pay her a visit.

Monny and Brigit sat in the arabeah to wait, but they dared not talk to the dirty-faced driver, lest some spy should be on the watch, where every group of flowering plants might have ears and eyes. Even if the big gatekeeper came back with an excuse, as seemed too probable, there was hope from Antoun's diplomacy; but the chances were two to one against success. Rechid Bey had almost certainly been put upon his guard by the revengeful Bedr who had shown himself all grinning friendliness to us. Rechid might have tired of playing dragon, as Antoun prophesied; yet it would be strange if he had not given instructions that no European ladies were to visit his wife. Mabella Hânem had been snatched in haste from Asiut, but if she were still in Luxor with her husband, she and her women in the harem would be guarded by eunuchs, as in the more ambitious villa which Rechid called his home.

I suppose Anthony, slouching on the box seat in his unattractive disguise, must have been as much astonished as Monny and Brigit when the gatekeeper returned with another big negro to say that the ladies would be welcomed by Mabella Hânem. The two girls were wildly delighted. Fenton's emotions were mixed. He wanted to save the American bride from the consequences of her tragic mistake, but he cared more for his friends' safety than for hers.

He knew that Monny and Brigit were brave, and that Monny had his Browning, but the thought that she might need to use it could not have made him comfortable on the box seat of his borrowed arabeah, outside Rechid's gate. It was arranged that he should give Mabel's visitors one hour, thus allowing for delays and emergencies; but if they did not appear at the end of that time, he would dash off to tell the Luxor police that two ladies were detained against their will in the house of Rechid Bey.

Once in charge of the chief eunuch, who had come to take them to the harem, Brigit and Monny might almost as well have been deaf and dumb. Brigit knew practically nothing of Arabic; and Monny, though she had been vaguely studying since her arrival, had been too passionately occupied with other things to give much time or attention to the language of Egypt's invaders. Her blood was beating in her veins now, and she could think of no words except "Imshi!" "Malish!" and "Ma'salama!" These buzzed in her head, like persistent flies, as she and Biddy followed their silent, white-robed and turbaned conductor along a narrow pink path, toward a modern villa almost shrouded with bougainvillia. And they were the last words she needed. She didn't want to tell the ponderous negro to "get out." On the contrary, she wished to be polite. So far from saying "no matter," everything mattered intensely. And, unfortunately, it was not time yet to bid the creature "farewell."

Behind the white house with its crimson embroidery of flowers, rose a thick growth of tall sugar-cane, the shimmering green pale as beryl, in the dreaming light which precedes sunset. The dark red of the bougainvillia looked like streaming blood against such a background.

Though the villa appeared to be comparatively new, it was built according to Turkish, not European ideas, as it might have been were the owner a Copt instead of a Mohammedan. The building was in two parts, entirely separating the *selamlik* from the *haremlik*. The latter was small and insignificant compared with the former, for this was not a place prepared for family life: it was but a temporary dwelling, where the master would more often come alone than with the ladies of his harem.

The eunuch opened a door leading into the women's building, and Brigit and Monny entered the same secretive sort of vestibule they must have remembered in the House of the Crocodile. A screen-wall prevented them from seeing what was beyond; and the dead silence frightened them a little, so easy was it to make of this place a trap.

In the vestibule was a long, cheaply cushioned bench, the resting-place of the women's custodian; and upon it lay spread open the eunuch's well-used koran, which he had deserted to meet the visitors. Who had given him the order to go, and why it had been given, the guests began to ask themselves.

Beyond the screen-wall they entered an anteroom. Through a big window-door they could look into a small, grassy court that served as a garden: and opening from the anteroom was a second room much larger, which also gave upon the garden court. At the door of this, the eunuch bowed himself away; but an involuntary glance which Monny threw at him over her shoulder showed that he was grinning. The grin died quickly as a white flash of heat-lightning fades from a black night-sky: but though the heavy face composed itself respectfully, there remained a disquieting twinkle in the full-lidded eyes. It struck Monny that the negro was amusing himself at the expense of the visitors, because of something he knew which they did not know.

"We're not going to be allowed to see Mabel!" she thought, with a jump of her pulses; and even when a negress, smiling invitingly, beckoned her and Biddy into the large room whose three windows looked on the garden, she still believed that they had been deceived. She did not, however, speak out her conviction to Brigit. Nothing could be done yet. They must wait and see what would happen.

The room was furnished in abominable taste, with cheap Trench furniture, upholstered with blue brocade that clashed hideously with the scarlet carpet. There were several sofas and chairs stiffly arranged round the walls; but no tables, save low maidahs of carved wood inlaid with pearl, such as they had seen in Cairo bazaars and hotels. The windows were closed, and the air heavy, as in a room seldom used. The two seated themselves close together, on one of the ugly sofas facing a door through which the beckoning negress had gone out. There was no sound except the harsh ticking of a huge, bulbous clock, all gilding and flowers, which stood in a corner. Monny's and Brigit's eyes met, with a question.

Who would open the door just closed? Would it be Mabel, or would Rechid Bey stride in, to reproach or insult them?

"*Are you sure it's loaded?*" Biddy whispered.

No need for Monny to ask what she meant.

"Sure," she answered.

The handle of the door turned.

CHAPTER XXII

THE DRIVER OF AN ARABEAH

"Thank God!" cried Biddy, as a slim figure in a loose white robe framed itself in the doorway.

With a sob, Mabel ran toward them, both hands held out, and in an instant she was being hugged and kissed and cooed over.

"You've found me—you've come!" she cried. "I never dared think you would, when *he* rushed me away from Asiut. He said he would keep me here all the rest of my life, to punish me for complaining to you."

"But how did he know?" Monny asked. "Did your sister-in-law tell him about the letter?"

"I don't think so, unless he has made her confess. It was like this: He was coming to his place here on business. I felt so thankful. It seemed providential he should be away then, just when you were starting up Nile. I was almost happy that morning, when suddenly he appeared again and I was ordered to put on a habberah and yashmak, and travel with him. Yeena, the woman who acts as my maid, had to get ready in a hurry, too. The chief eunuch, a hateful hypocritical wretch, followed. Some clothes have been sent to me since, but not many. At first I couldn't guess what had happened, and *he* was in such a fiendish temper I daren't ask questions. It wasn't till after we arrived that he explained. I'm sure he took pleasure in hurting me. He said that he left home early the morning he was going to Luxor, because he meant to stop and make a business call on the way to the depot, otherwise he wouldn't have been able to rush home and fetch me as he did, and still be in time to catch his train after the warning. It was some dragoman you employed in Cairo, he told me, who had seen us getting off the *Laconia*, and who ran after his carriage in the street, in Asiut. The wicked creature warned him that you were all there, and that he'd heard you say something which sounded as if there were a plot to get at me. Just at that minute, by the worst of luck, Mr. Sheridan passed. You know how foolish and cruel *he* was about Mr. Sheridan on the ship. Well, he hadn't forgotten. So he turned round and almost snatched me out of the house, rather than I should be left in Asiut with him away."

"This is exactly what we thought must have happened!" exclaimed Monny. "That beast, Bedr! And to think that Rachel and I wasted our time trying to convert him! How I wish I hadn't let Aunt Clara engage him at Alexandria! She thought he'd come from a man with her favourite name, Antony: but she wouldn't have insisted if I hadn't encouraged her. I feel as if this trouble were partly my fault. And if I hadn't been thoughtless enough at Asiut to blurt out your husband's name—."

"You're not to blame for anything, dearest," Biddy tried to comfort her. "It was your unfailing resolve to help, which has brought us here."

"You're both my good angels," said Mabel, "Oh, it's heavenly to see you. But I can't understand why I'm allowed to, after all the threats and punishments. I'm afraid I shall be made to pay somehow. He loves to torture me—and he knows how. I believe he hates me, now he's begun to realize that I'd give anything to leave him, that I don't consider myself his wife."

"If he hates you, why isn't he willing to let you go?" Monny questioned her.

"Partly because he's very vain, and it would humiliate him. Partly because he has no son yet, only that horrid little brown girl; and he's set his heart on a boy who's to possess all the qualities and strength of the West. No, he won't let me go!"

"Well, you'll do it in spite of him then," said Monny eagerly. "That's what we're here for. We shall take you with us. You must say to your servants that we've invited you to drive, and you've accepted. There's nothing in that to make them suspect. Lots of Turkish ladies go driving and motoring with European women, in Cairo. And you can have that fat black man sit on the box seat, with—with our coachman, if it would make things easier, taking him to guard you. He can be hustled or bribed or something, when the right time comes to get rid of him, never fear. Oh, it's going to be a glorious adventure, and at the end of it you'll be free! Nobody could blame you, as the man has another wife."

Mabella Hânem shook her head. "You're splendid to plan this. But it's too late. It was too late from the moment that dragoman warned—my husband. Why you've been allowed to come into the house and talk with me, I can't think, unless *he* is watching and listening through a hidden spyhole.

There's sure to be *some* secret reason in his head, anyhow—a reason that's for *his* good and not mine. And I shall not be able to get out, if you do."

"*If* we do!" echoed Biddy, a catch in her voice.

She glanced furtively at Monny. What had we all been dreaming of when we let this beautiful girl run into danger? I know Biddy well enough to be sure that her thought at that instant was for Monny Gilder, not Brigit O'Brien. But the fear in her heart was vague, until the next answer Mabel made—an answer that came almost with calmness; for Mabella Hânem's whole being was concentrated upon herself, and her own imbroglio. Everything else, everybody else—even these friends who were risking much to help her—were secondary considerations.

"I don't suppose real harm will come to you. I don't see how he'd *dare*. And yet—there may be something on foot. Three men had come to-day, one who might be a dragoman, and two Europeans. They came together. I saw them. And I haven't seen them go away. They're in the men's part of the house—the *selâmlik*. They must be with my husband. Perhaps there's only some business about the sugarcane. But—"

"Did you see the men distinctly?" Biddy asked, in a changed tone.

"Yes, quite distinctly, for they glanced up at the window where I was peeping out. Of course they couldn't see me, through the wooden lattice and the bougainvillia, but I had a good look at them. The dragoman seemed to have one blind eye. Oh! I hadn't thought of *that* before! Can it be the man who gave the warning?"

"What were the Europeans like?" Biddy questioned, without answering. "Were they wearing light tweed knickerbockers with big checks?"

"No, they were in dark clothes, not very noticeable."

"Had one a scar on his forehead?"

"Why, yes, I believe he had!"

The eyes of Brigit and Monny met: but there was none of that deadly fear in the girl's, which Biddy was trying to keep out of hers. Even now, it was hardly fear for herself. It was nearly all for Monny; but Monny must not know, lest she should lose her nerve when it was needed most. That idea of Brigit's, about Monny being mistaken for Esmé O'Brien by members of the Organization O'Brien betrayed, had seemed foolish and far fetched, although Esmé was hidden from her father's enemies near Monaco, and it was at Monaco that Miss Gilder and Rachel Guest and Mrs. East had joined

Brigit on the *Laconia*. I had laughed at the suggestion, and Biddy had been half-ashamed to make it. But now, in this lonely house where she and the girl had been unexpectedly welcomed, in this house where the master watched, entertaining three strange men, the thought did not appear quite so foolish, quite so far fetched. Indeed, Biddy marvelled why it had occurred to none of us that one of the dangers to be run in rescuing Mabel might come through Bedr, the same danger which had perhaps threatened in the House of the Crocodile.

Too late to think of this now! The fact remained that we had not thought of it when there was time. Not even Biddy had felt certain that there was a secret motive for taking the girls to the hasheesh den, or that Bedr had been guilty of anything worse than indiscretion. His warning to Rechid Bey we had put down to a petty desire for revenge, to "pay us out" for his discharge. Though Biddy had never felt sure of his new employers' German origin, and though she had had qualms at sight of the party, following or arriving before us on our pilgrimage through the desert and up the Nile, she had never associated their possible designs with Rechid Bey's grudge against us. Yet how obvious that Bedr should take advantage of it for his clients' sake, if those two men were what she sometimes feared! Brigit had never spoken out to Monny what was in her mind about Esmé O'Brien. She had known that Monny would laugh, and perhaps say "What fun!" For the girl had invited Biddy to Egypt "because she attracted adventures," and because Monny badly needed a few, her life having been, up to the date of starting, a "kind of fruit and flower piece in a neat frame." Now, perhaps Monny wouldn't laugh; but it was not the time to speak of new dangers.

"Well, if your husband thinks that creatures like Bedr and his Germans are going to help him stop us from getting out, or taking you out, he's wrong," said Monny, stoutly. "Bedr's the most sickening coward, as Rachel Guest and I have reason to remember. But I'm glad we know what we have to expect, aren't you, Biddy?"

It was hard to answer, because the girl was in reality so far from knowing what she might have to expect. Brigit tried to smile her reply, as Monny began to tell Mabel something of their plan: about the friends ready to rally round them, once they were in the carriage waiting outside the gate; and about the motor coat and veiled hood which had been brought for Mabel to put on, at a safe distance from the house. "You'll have to start in your own things," the girl was saying, "otherwise your servants would think it odd. Ring now, dear, for your woman, and have her give you your habberah and yashmak."

"There are no bells," said Mabella Hânem, with her soft air of obstinate hopelessness. "When I want Yeena, if she isn't in the room, I clap my hands as hard as I can. But I tell you, it is no use. It is too late." As she spoke, throwing up her arms and letting them fall with a gesture of helpless despair, both Brigit and Monny felt that Islam had already raised a barrier between them and this delicate creature it had taken into its keeping. In the white wool robe she wore—the kind of loose dressing gown affected by Turkish women—she looked more like a Circassian than an American girl. Always she had seemed to her would-be rescuers a charming doll, a feminine thing of exactly the type which would appeal to a Turk, weary of dark beauties: her hair was so very golden, her eyes so very big and blue, her lashes so very black, her mouth so very red and small: but now she had become an odalisque. Mabel's friends realized that she would do nothing to save herself. They must do all.

Hesitating no longer, Monny struck her hands loudly together. Yeena did not come. The girl clapped again, and yet again, till her palms smarted, but nothing happened.

"Yeena is in it—whatever they mean to do," said Mabel. "She's had her orders."

"Very well, then," Monny persisted, her eyes shining and her cheeks carnation, "you must go without your wraps. Come along. Don't be frightened. Isn't it better to risk something to get away than to stay here alone when we're gone?"

The pretty doll, with a little moan, gave herself up to her friends. Brigit as well as Monny realized that the moment had come. They must take her while she was in this mood.

"Let me go ahead," said Monny, in a low, firm voice. "You know why."

Brigit did know why. Monny had Anthony's Browning, and she alone understood the use of it. Yes, she must lead the way; yet Brigit longed to fling herself in front, to make of her body a shield for the tall white girl she had never so loved and admired. Biddy put Mabel in front of her, and behind Monny, keeping her between them with two cold but determined little hands on the shrinking shoulders, and so pushing her along, protected front and rear, in the piteous procession.

Of course, if the door leading toward the house entrance had been locked on the outside, there would have been the end of the endeavour, for the moment: but it opened to Monny's hand, and all three went on unchecked, until they came to the vestibule, where on the wall bench they had seen the koran of the fat negro, awaiting his return.

They had come tiptoeing, and had made no more sound than prowling kittens, yet he sat there facing the door, no longer heavy lidded, a black mountain of lazy flesh, but alert, beady eyed, as if he had been counting the minutes.

As they swept through the doorway, hoping to surprise him, the eunuch jumped to his feet as lightly as a man of half his weight, and smiling with pleasure in the excitement of an event to break monotony, he blocked with his great bulk the aperture between wall and projecting screen.

No wonder they had not needed to lock doors, with this giant for a jailer, and a big Sudanese knife conspicuously showing in a belt under his open galabeah! Rechid had perhaps wanted the white mouse in his trap to feel the thrill of hope, and then the shock of disappointment. He had counted completely on the guardian of his harem, but—though he had chosen an American wife, he had not counted on the courage of another type of American girl. The knife looked terrible; but it was sheathed and tucked into a belt. Anthony's Browning was in Monny's hand, and hidden only under her serge coat. Out it came, with a warning click of the trigger. And with an astonished, frightened gurgle in his throat the negro involuntarily fell back.

"Run!" Monny breathed, prisoning him where he stood, with the little bright eye of the Browning cocked up at his face. She had to be obeyed then, and they ran, the two of them, flashing past the black man, touching his clothes as they squeezed by, yet he dared not put out a detaining hand. When they were away—safe or not, she could not tell —Monny still kept the pistol in position, but began slowly to turn, that she too might pass the dragon, holding him at her mercy till the end. Not a word of Arabic could she recall, but the Browning spoke for her, a language understood without the trouble of learning, by all the sons of Adam.

When she had backed through the doorway, the girl still faced toward the inner vestibule, and it was well she did so, for scarcely was she out of his sight before the black giant was after her, taking the chance that she would have turned to run. But there was the resolute young face, with eyes defying his; and there was the weapon ready to blow out such brains as he had, if the hand on the knife moved. Again he fell back, and then Monny did run, making the best use she had ever made of those long limbs which gave her the air of a young Diana. She ran until she had caught up with the other two, flying toward the distant gate; for something told her that the negro would have hurried to tell his master of the trick the women had played—preferring the lash on his back perhaps, to a bullet through his head.

She was right, no doubt, to trust her instinct, for the eunuch did not pursue, though his tale of failure was not needed. Rechid Bey had been watching from a window of the selâmlik, as Mabel his wife had watched when he received visitors. He did not wait for the negro's warning, but dashed out of the house, followed and then passed by several long-robed men in Arab dress. The faces of these were almost hidden by the loose hoods which desert men pull over their heads in a high wind, but had they been uncovered the women would not have seen them. The thing was to escape, not to take note of the pursuers; and it was only Biddy, looking over her shoulder for Monny, who even saw that they were followed. She cried out to her friend to hurry, that some one was coming, that they must get to the gate or all would be ended; then feeling Mabel falter, she held her more tightly and ran the faster.

Rechid and his companions were shouting, not to the women, but to the gatekeeper; and as the master's furious voice rang out, just in front of the fugitive (all three together now), appeared the big form of the man at the gate.

Monny did not know what to do; for in whichever direction she faced with the Browning, she could be captured from the other. She might kill the negro, and then turn to keep the pursuers back: but the thought of killing a man sickened her. She had meant only to threaten, not to take life. Suddenly she felt afraid of the Browning. She hesitated, in a wild second of confusion, hating herself for failing her friends, yet unable to decide or act: but hardly had the gatekeeper sprung in sight than he went down, flat on his face, struck in the back of the neck by the shabby fellow who had driven their carriage. "Go on!" the dirty-faced Arab said in French. "There's some one else to drive you. I'll follow. I'm armed."

The three sped by him, as he stood aside to let them pass, showing to Monny a pistol which matched the one he had lent her. This consoled the girl in obeying; for as "Antoun" had trusted her courage in this adventure, so did she trust his, and his strength and wit against four men or four dozen men, if need were.

There was the waiting arabeah, and there on the box was a much cleaner, more self-respecting Arab to drive it than the soiled figure which had left the horses and strayed into the garden. Afterwards they learned that the new man was the "sister's cousin's uncle" of the Hadji's café acquaintance. He had been engaged to stroll past in the road, stop, speak, offer the gatekeeper a cigarette, drift into conversation, and be ready to jump onto the box seat the instant Antoun left it. His instructions included furious driving with the three ladies (once they had bundled into the arabeah), to the Temple of Mût.

Rechid Bey had every right, according to his own point of view, to resent the kidnapping of his wife, and to get her back in any way he could, even if blood had to be spilt. But his companions—they who were muffled in the cloaks and hoods to save their faces from the sharp wind—had perhaps not the same right or interest. In any case, when they saw that the women had a man, or men, to help them, and that so helped they had passed from the privacy of the garden to the publicity of the road, the three fell back. Publicity, it may be, did not please them: or else, thinking to have only women to deal with, they were not armed and did not like the look of the pistol. Rechid, evidently no coward, or past feeling fear in rage at the failure of his counterplot, ran on, wheezing slightly—he was fat for his age—toward the erect Arab and the prostrate negro.

"Beast! devil!" he panted breathlessly, and cried out other words of evil import in both Turkish and Arabic; threatening the silent man of the pistol with death and things even worse. But before he had gone far, the hooded men caught up with him, and surrounding, urged him back. What they said, Anthony could not hear, or what he said in return; but he thought they were proposing some plan which appealed to Rechid's reason, for he showed signs of yielding. There was now no longer anything to detain the protector of the ladies, for by this time, he hoped and believed that their arabeah must be far on its way toward the Temple of Mût, the meeting-place agreed upon. Accordingly, he stepped over the unconscious gatekeeper, who lay with his nose in the grass, and backed calmly out of the garden. Not far off, an arabeah was crawling along the road, so slowly that one might have thought the driver half asleep. But this supposition would have done him an injustice. Dusk had fallen now, the purple dusk which drops like a curtain just after the pageant of sunset is finished, yet the driver was wide enough awake to pierce the purple with a pair of sharp eyes, and recognize a figure expected. He whipped up his horse, and the dirty Arab running to meet it, in a few seconds the latter was on the box beside the coachman. Then the arabeah turned, and dashed wildly off according to the custom of arabeahs, back in the direction whence it had been crawling.

The two dark-faced men in the vehicle talked rapidly in low voices, speaking the language not only of the country but the *patois* of Luxor itself. "Your brother passed you in his arabeah?"

"Yes, Hadji, he passed with the three European ladies you told me had been in secret to visit their friend."

Then Anthony knew that Brigit and Monny had been able already to carry out their plan of wrapping Mabella Hânem in one of their own cloaks. This was well, and would save gossip, if the occupants of the arabeah were stared at by passers by. And at the temple also it would be well, for if possible the Set were to know nothing, now or later, of the adventure. But though Anthony was glad of the news he had got from this Arab ordered to meet him at the gate, he did not settle down comfortably and say to himself: "Thank goodness, the thing is over." Those men back there in the garden would not so easily have persuaded Rechid Bey to let his wife go unpursued, if they had not offered some alternative plan that could be carried out quickly.

Still, so far so good. Brigit and Monny had "won out," and secured the prize, as Anthony had prophesied that they would do. They were on their way to the temple, where I would be with the comfortable, commonplace crowd from the *Enchantress Isis*, and where the American Consul and his wife would just "happen" also to be wandering. Instead of driving straight there himself, Anthony went with a friend to an obscure, mud-built house in the village. When he came out of that house, his brown-stained face was no longer disfigured with dirt. It was as immaculate, as noble as the proudest Hadji's face should be, and above it was wound the green turban. Ahmed Antoun Effendi's own dignified, old-fashioned robes of the Egyptian gentleman flowed round his tall figure, when once more he took his place in the waiting arabeah—this time not on the box seat—and drove off at more furious speed than ever, toward the Temple of Mût.

CHAPTER XXIII

BENGAL FIRE

The Temple of Mût I think must always be mysterious even by day. That night it was more than mysterious. It was sinister.

Darkness shut us in among the pillars and the black, lion-faced statues. The least imaginative of my charges seemed to feel the influence of the place. Not an Arab, not even the superior boat dragoman, would come inside with us: because after the sun has set, dethroned Sekhet comes into her own again. Strange stories are whispered by Arabs, of the Temple of Mût, and of the ghostly, golden dahabeah that, once a year, sails slowly by to a faint sound of music, on the Sacred Lake. We had brought candles with us, protected by smoky glass from the wind that swept down the avenue of broken Sphinxes outside, and hissed like angry cats through the dark courts lined with granite statues of the Cat-goddess. Yet despite the mystery, or because of it, people seemed curiously happy. The spirit of the past, of Old Egypt, touched them in the shadowy spaces of this ruined temple, brushed them with its wings, and whispered half-heard words into their ears. They talked to each other in low tones, as if not to miss the whispers or the soft footfalls of unseen things; and they did not laugh and make jokes, or ask silly questions, according to their irritating custom.

I blessed this mood, for my nerves were jangled (more than ever after the Bronsons unobtrusively appeared) waiting for Brigit and Monny to come, wondering if they would come, or what we should do if they didn't; because suddenly in this place of gloom and eloquent silence all the clever little plans Anthony and I had made, in case of accident, seemed futile. How could we have let those two walk alone into a trap? I blamed myself, I blamed Anthony; and sometimes I gave the wrong answers to Mrs. East, who walked with me, trying to keep out of the way of the crowd.

She was anxious to talk of her niece, and to relate how she had been singing my praises to Monny. "You mustn't be discouraged," she said. "Never mind about the hieroglyphic letter. Oh, no, you needn't worry! I haven't told her it was yours. Better let her think what she thought at first. Did she *tell* you what she thought? *Please* answer me, Lord Ernest! I don't mind your knowing—*now*—that I believed it was from Antoun to me. Believing so, did no harm. Why should it, to me, or to him? I soon guessed that there was a mistake somewhere—when he didn't —didn't follow the letter up. I was not offended by the proposal as Monny would have been—oh, not if she'd known it was *yours*, but if she'd supposed Antoun was making love to her. Don't you see—you must have seen, you're so quick and observant—that she's been caught by the romance of him, just as she was afraid she might be by some thrilling prince, when she came to Egypt. She's miserable. She's hating herself. And you *won't* save her though I've prepared her mind!"

"So *that's* what you meant when you hinted that I could spare her humiliation!" I said, half in laughter, half in bitterness, suddenly able to concentrate my mind upon the talk. "Do you think a man would want a girl to take him for such a reason, when she's caring for some one else?"

"But, if it would be impossible for her to marry the some one else?"

"Why should it be impossible?"

"She would think it impossible."

"Would she, if—" I checked myself, but Mrs. East understood instantly. "If he has a secret," she said, "then none of us has a right to suggest it to her. Every man for himself, Lord Ernest, in *love*! Antoun Effendi has no reason too feel too kindly to Monny. You'll be robbing your friend of *nothing*, if you speak to her. If he's in *love* with any one, it isn't my niece."

"At least it's not *you*. Perhaps it's Biddy after all!" my thoughts interpolated.

"To care for Monny would be beneath his dignity, considering all that's passed. And you can make *her* happy, as well as yourself, by taking my advice," Mrs. East went on. "Aren't you going to be sensible?"

Just then came a murmur expressing surprise or some other new emotion, from one of the outer courts where the crowd wandered, Cleopatra having lured me—yes, "lured" *is* the word—into the sanctuary itself.

"Something has happened!" I said. "Let's go back, and see what it is."

"Perhaps Antoun has come!" Mrs. East caught me up eagerly. "He was coming, wasn't he, when he'd finished his business? Or maybe it's only Monny and Brigit."

"*Only* Monny and Brigit!"

In the hope of seeing Antoun, Cleopatra turned her back upon the dreary sanctuary not unwillingly, even though the burning question was left unanswered. I hurried her through the dark passages which lay between us and the courts, lighting our way with a glassed-in candle; and it was all I could do not to cry out aloud "Thank heaven!" or "Hurrah!" or something else that would have opened people's eyes, when I saw that indeed, Brigit and Monny had arrived. It was Rachel Guest and Willis Bailey who had hailed them from afar, as candlelights flashed across their faces; and suddenly to my eyes the gloomy temple seemed to be brilliantly illuminated. I don't know exactly how I contrived to leave Cleopatra, and get to the newcomers; but I did get to them in less than a minute. Perhaps I was a little rude to Mrs. East. I wasn't thinking of that at the time, however, nor of her.

I separated the two I wanted from the others. Their faces radiated excitement, but I was not sure if it meant success. I was sure only that they had been through an ordeal and were feeling the reaction.

"You're safe!" I said, and shook hands with them feverishly. Then I shook hands all over again.

"Safe, yes," Monny answered. "And Mabel—why don't you ask about her? Oh, Lord Ernest, we've done it—we've done it—thanks to Antoun Effendi! We should have failed at the last if it hadn't been for him. Just look over there, at the Bronsons, and see if you can guess who it is they're talking to?"

I looked and saw tall, thin Mr. Bronson, and short, plump Mrs. Bronson trying to form a hollow square around a little figure in a long gray coat of Biddy's, and a hood with a veil I remembered her wearing the day we motored to Heliopolis. It seemed about a hundred years ago. I had conducted so much and so violently since; but I was not too old to remember Biddy's hood. What if Neill Sheridan, poking about alone with a candle, could see through that veil?

"Triumph!" I exclaimed. "You're heroines!" (I didn't know then how true were my own words.) "Was it a great adventure?"

"*Was it*, Biddy?" the girl asked, half shyly of her friend.

"So great that I can't talk about it," Brigit answered, and her eyes implored mine not to ask questions. Also they said that she had things to tell me—not now but by and by. Things for me alone. Biddy's eyes could be wonderful.

"Where's Antoun Effendi?" Monny broke in, when I had taken Brigit's hint, and was beginning to say that we must go and speak to the Bronsons.

"He hasn't come yet," I answered; and then her eyes, too, began to implore.

"Not come yet? But—it's a long time. We found Mr. and Mrs. Bronson outside, hoping for us to arrive, and we talked to them and introduced Mabel, and explained things. They would have liked to go and take her away quickly, but Biddy and I begged them not to. We said it would be better to wait for the rest, and all the crowd to be together in case of—trouble. Oh, we discussed everything, for ages—minutes and minutes. I do think Antoun Effendi ought to be here, unless—"

I caught her up quickly. "Unless?"

"Well, you see, we left him inside Rechid's gate, where he'd just knocked down a big negro, and was keeping back Rechid and *lots* of other men—anyhow three—with a pistol—not the one he lent me. He told us to go, so we went."

He told them to go—so they went! A change, this, for the Gilded Rose. She spoke at the moment like an obedient little girl.

"If he told you to go—it was all right, you may be sure," I said encouragingly. But despite my faith in Anthony as a fighting man, I felt—well, somewhat dismayed at the picture called up. "Rechid and anyhow three men!" It was rather a large order. If with a wish I could have sent every member of the Set back to their peaceful homes in England and America, and thus rid myself of them in a second, they would all have found themselves walking in at their respective front doors.

I wished this wish, but having a mere smoking candle in my hand, and not Aladdin's lamp, it didn't work. There they inconveniently remained in the Temple of Mût, looking twice as large as life.

"What if I tell them they've seen everything?" I muttered. "They haven't, but that's a detail. If I could rush 'em all back to the boat —and you with them, of course, and get Mabella Hânem and the Bronsons off safely, I could go look for Anth—for Antoun. Of course we were to wait for him, but I don't like the picture you've painted—"

"Oh, *do* look for him!" broke in Monny. "Leave us to take care of ourselves. I'm sure we can. There are enough of us. And Mr. Bronson is a *Consul.* Go and get the police."

"I can't leave you," I said. "Antoun would be the last one to forgive me if I did that. But I'll start off the party, now. The arabeahs and donkeys are waiting. Listen to the stentorian voice of the Conductor, announcing—"

I tried to speak gayly; but the announcement, which I opened my mouth to roar through the temple, was never made. There came instead, at that instant, a rival roar from outside. Mine would have been the roar of a sucking dove. This other was a wild bull roar of rage. What it was for, who was making it, and whether it concerned us, we did not know; but it was the sound of many voices, and flowing to us on the wind, driving nearer out of distance, it was startling and caused the heart to miss a beat.

Suddenly the thought sprang into my mind that this was like something in a theatre. We were on the stage, in a play of Ancient Egypt, and a mob of supers was yelling for our lives in the wings. They would pour out upon the stage and attack us. Only the hero and heroine would be saved. All the villains and other unnecessary people would be polished off.

Everybody had stopped talking. Involuntarily groups drew together. We looked over our smoking candles, past the standing statues and the fallen statues, away toward the columns of the temple entrance.

Mr. and Mrs. Bronson, and the girl in Biddy's veiled hood and cloak, walked across the court and joined our party of three. Neill Sheridan was at a distance. His prophetic soul told him nothing. "I hope that fellow Rechid Bey hasn't worked up any trouble against us," the American Consul from Asiut said in a low, somewhat worried tone.

Instantly I was certain that what he hoped had not happened, was indeed the thing that had happened. I seemed to see Rechid stirring up a crowd of his fellow Mussulmans, telling them that dogs of Christians had robbed him of his foreign wife, who was on the point of accepting Islam. Nothing easier than for Rechid to find us. All Luxor knew we were in the Temple of Mût. These men of Luxor and other Nile towns of Upper Egypt, had not yet settled down after the outburst against Christian insults which had alarmed the authorities in Cairo. In three days Anthony Fenton had discovered the dregs at the bottom of the teapot and had doubtless done something toward calming the tempest in it, but the troubled water had not time to cool. It could easily be brought to the boil again; and the despoiling of a harem by Europeans —the harem of an important man—would be oil thrown onto the dying fire under the tempestuous teapot.

The furious voices grew louder. From the wave of sound words spattered out and up like spray. Perhaps in all that astonished crowd gathered in the Temple of Mût, Bronson and I were the only ones who knew enough Arabic to catch their meaning. His question was answered. And this was not a stage. Those shouting men were not supers in the wings. They were in earnest. Foolish and dreamlike and utterly unreal as it seemed, their hearts were hot with savage anger against men and women of an alien race: and though what they might do to us would be visited on their own heads to-morrow, they were not thinking of to-morrow now. As for us—it was just possible that owing to this silly dream we were having about a mob of common, uneducated Arabs, for some of us there might not be any to-morrow.

"Is there a back door where we can dash out and give them the slip?" asked Bronson.

I was thinking hard. Mine was the responsibility for my charges, these rich, comfortable tourists from London and New York, Birmingham and Manchester, Chicago and St Louis. None of them knew yet that they were in danger. They were thinking about their dinner, and their pleasant, lighted cabins on board the *Enchantress Isis*, waiting for them not far away. They realized that something was the matter out there, that a lot of Arabs were making a row; but it interested and amused them impersonally. If somebody had robbed or murdered somebody else, morally it was a pity, of course: but it added to the picturesqueness of the scene, and would be nice to tell about at home. I felt myself overflowing with a sudden, new tenderness for the Set, so often troublesome. This that was going to happen—unless we could stop it —was in truth the affair of Monny and Brigit, Mabella Hânem and the Bronsons, Anthony Fenton and me; but all would be involved, the innocent with the guilty, unless very quickly the duffer of the company could think of some way out.

"No," I heard myself say with decision, "we mustn't leave the temple. They're superstitious about it. Few, if any, will venture in. What they want is to lure us into the open. And there must be no panic. Certainly my friend, unless he's been hurt, is working for us—somewhere. It's only a question of minutes. He borrowed my Browning to-day. I wish—" I glanced toward Brigit and Monny. They stood at a little distance, with Mrs. Bronson and Mabel, but the faces of both were turned toward us. I saw that they guessed the meaning of the uproar outside. Biddy's great soft eyes spoke to mine, spoke, and told me all the truth about myself. How I loved her, Biddy O'Brien, and no one else on earth! How I would die for her, and let all the rest die, if need be, yes, even Monny Gilder, to whom I had been idiot enough to write that letter! If I could save Biddy, what did anything beside matter? But—yes, it did matter. I must save them all. And the light that had lit up my dim soul gave me inspiration. Because I loved Biddy, I knew what to do.

"I've got a little surprise for every one!" I yelled, to be heard over the noise outside, where Rechid Bey's mob was now probably trying to make our donkey-boys and arabeah-men join in the fight or the siege. "Mr. Neill Sheridan will kindly lead the whole party to the sanctuary, which his knowledge of architecture will enable him to find, on the axis of the temple. Down that passage, please! In fifteen minutes the surprise will be ready, and you will receive the signal to return, from Mr. Bronson, American Consul at Asiut—no time for introductions now."

Sheridan, amazed, but perhaps not displeased, emerged from the dark corner where, until the row began, he had been examining a half-erased wall-carving. "Come along, then, everybody!" he shouted good-naturedly; and as the procession formed—discussing the "surprise" and the noise, now mysteriously linked together in the minds of my charges—I saw the veiled and hooded Mabel shyly try to pull Mrs. Bronson into place with her, as near as possible to Sheridan. She must have suspected that there was trouble brewing, and guessed the cause. Her timid, self-centred little soul instinctively sought shelter in the neighbourhood of a friend, who would perhaps have been more than a friend, if he could. So she followed him, he not knowing what eyes the gray veil hid: but Mrs. Bronson broke away from the small hand and hurried back to her husband.

"What am I to do?" she asked.

"Go with the others," he said, quietly. "Take care of the girl. Lord Ernest has some plan."

She went reluctantly; but Brigit and Monny and Mrs. East lingered at the tail of the procession, returning to us as the others vanished down the passage that led toward the sanctuary. I motioned them away, but Monny ran forward, while Biddy kept Cleopatra from following. They talked together and argued, Biddy's arm round the taller woman's waist, as Monny came straight to me, and put into my hand Anthony Fenton's pistol.

"I didn't have to use it," she said. "It's all loaded and ready. And I'm going to stay here with you and Mr. Bronson, to help. What are you planning to do?"

"Please run away," I said, "and take Biddy and your aunt. You must. That's the only help we want—"

"Not till you tell me what you mean to do."

"Oh, only to try a trick to frighten those Arab sheep out there. They funk this temple at night anyhow. And I've just remembered that I brought some Bengal fire to light the place up and amuse the crowd. I thought if a red blaze suddenly burst out it would give those fellows a scare—and the police are on the way—"

"But the Arabs will see that you're only two!"

"They shan't see us at all. We'll hide behind those statues and pot at them if they do come in, which I doubt. Now, off with the three of you!" And I was getting my illumination ready.

To my surprise and relief, Monny obeyed without further argument. Dimly it passed through my mind that she had been profiting by her lessons lately. I threw one glance over my shoulder, more, I'm afraid, to see whether my dear Brigit were on her way to safety than through anxiety for Miss Gilder. The three figures had already disappeared in the darkness, and Bronson and I gave ourselves to the work of lighting up.

An ocean-roar of voices surged round the temple entrance now; but the red light flamed like the fires of hell, and I, peeping from behind a statue, revolver in hand, saw that the temple itself had not been invaded. The flare lit the foreground of the darkness outside, and the columns of the front court. I could see a moving throng of white and black clad figures, gesticulating, running to and fro, seeming to urge each other to some action, yet none coming forward. I sprinkled on more powder, and up blazed the Bengal fire again. Now somebody was taking the lead. A tall man was pushing through the crowd. Would they follow this brave one? My fingers closed round the Browning. He was between the columns at last, but the light was dying down. I threw on all I had of the powder, and stared through the red dazzle to make certain what was happening—since this might decide our fate. The tall man's back was turned to us. He seemed to be motioning the crowd away instead of urging them on. How to make sure, in the blood-coloured glare, whether a man's turban was white or green or crimson? But that gesture—that lift of the head! No mistaking that. The man was Antoun—Ahmed Antoun, the worshipful Hadji, haranguing the mob.

Hardly would they let him speak at first. Those on the outskirts tried to yell him down. I heard the word "traitor!" and before the light ebbed I thought I caught sight of Rechid's pale face under the red tarboosh, Rechid's broad shoulders in European coat, edging past jebbahs and galabeahs, toward the columns. Then, just as the light died, from behind us in the temple came a cry. Above the shouting of the Hadji, who was beginning to make himself heard by the crowd, it rang out shrill and clear—a woman's voice: Monny Gilder's. She called on the name of Antoun, and then was silent.

I lifted my candle-lantern—all that was left to illumine the darkness, and saw at the far end of the court shadowy figures struggling together. It seemed to me that there were not two, but four or five. I ran toward them, and Bronson ran, but some one bounded past us both—a tall man in a green turban. A shot was fired after him, and hit a statue. I heard subconsciously a miniature crash of chipped granite, but I don't think Anthony heard, or had heard anything since that call for "Antoun!"

He had dashed ahead, though we had had the start and were running fast. Rounding a group of statues, erect and fallen, I saw a candle-lantern on the floor, and knew that Monny—and perhaps Biddy—had not obediently followed the procession to the sanctuary, after all. They had waited to watch and listen, hiding behind the black statues of Sekhet, and men who had crept in by another way—doubtless by the small Ptolemaic gate opening on the lake—had taken them by surprise.

Anthony had got to the shadowy mass, which, moved like black, wind-blown clouds, vague and shapeless, before Bronson and I were near enough to distinguish one form from another. As for our eyes, his tall figure blended with the waving shadows; two revolver shots exploded with thunderous reverberations. We did not know if he, or another, had fired; but almost simultaneously with the second shot two black shapes separated themselves from the rest, fleeing into darkness. They took the way by which they must have come, the way leading toward the gate on the lake.

Three seconds later we were on the spot; and the only shadows left resolved themselves under my candle light into the forms of Brigit O'Neill, Monny Gilder, Anthony Fenton, and Mrs. East somewhat in the background.

Monny's hat was off, and Biddy's was apparently hanging by a hatpin. Their hair was in disorder, a rope of Biddy's falling over one shoulder, a shining braid of Monny's hanging down her back. Monny seemed to be more or less in the arms of Antoun, but only vaguely and by accident. Dimly I gathered that she had stumbled, and he had saved her from falling. Biddy was fastening up the front of her gray chiffon blouse, which was open, and torn. Her hands trembled and I could see that her breast rose and fell convulsively; for, though the light was dim, I was looking at her, while I merely glanced at the others. Mrs. East was crying. But Brigit and Monny had smiles for Bronson and me as we came blundering along, stumbling over unseen obstacles.

"Some one stole up behind with an electric torch, and tried to drag me away," said Monny, in a weak little voice, scarcely at all like her own. It sounded as if a ventriloquist were imitating her. "Some one called me Esmé O'Brien—whispered right in my ear. And I screamed, and fought, and Antoun came. I think then the man pushed me down as he ran away. Anyhow I fell, and Antoun picked me up. Oh, Biddy, are you safe? Why, your dress is torn!"

"Yes, but I'm safe," answered another small, weak voice. "I fought, too. I—I think they wanted to rob me. Thank goodness, I didn't have it on."

"The bag, dearest?"

"Yes, darling, the bag. I thought I wouldn't wear it to-day."

Out in the night the yells had subsided since the Hadji's harangue, if not wholly because of it.

"The police have come," said Anthony. "It occurred to me that Rechid and some friends of his were cooking up a plan, and while I was getting into my clothes in the village it jumped into my head what it might be. So on my way out to the temple I stopped and left a warning. We're all right now. And I don't think the Arab lot would have dared venture in anyhow. These chaps who sneaked in at the back and attacked the ladies were dressed like the rest, but I doubt they were Arabs."

He would have doubted still more, if he had known all that I knew. But the one secret I'd kept from him was Biddy's secret. The words "Esmé O'Brien" whispered to Monny, as yet meant nothing save bewilderment to Fenton.

"The fifteen minutes are up, and no signal yet for your famous surprise," called out Sir John Biddell's complaining voice, from the end of a dark passage. "Has anything gone wrong?"

"Oh, I was going to give you a Bengal fire illumination of the temple, for a climax," I explained, coming suavely forward to meet him with my candle. "But the beastly stuff—er—sort of went off by itself, and it's all used up. I was—er—just going to call you."

"Well, not much harm done," said Sir John. "We've seen the sanctuary, such as it is. A little disappointing, perhaps, especially as Mr. Sheridan found a friend with Mrs. Bronson, the Consul's wife, and preferred talking with her to giving out information to us, from his stores of knowledge. But luckily not more than twenty minutes wasted. By the way, what's become of the row outside? Seems to have fizzled down while we were away, like your red fire."

"Yes, a great man of some sort was addressing the crowd. But the police came along and made it move on. There's been a bit of native grumbling in these Nile towns lately—you may have read some paragraph about it in the Cairo papers? So the police are rather quick to break up meetings."

"Why should men meet near the Temple of Mût?" inquired Sir John. "*I* shouldn't think of doing it."

"Perhaps in the beginning they hoped to get something out of the Europeans," said I lightly. "But they've given that up, evidently."

"I hope they haven't seduced our donkey-boys and arabeah drivers!" exclaimed Sir John. "I'm hungry. And I'm in a hurry to get home."

"Not they. Donkey-boys and arabeah-men aren't easily seduced when there's a question of baksheesh. *They're* all right! I'm only sorry about the Bengal fire."

"Well, it was a good idea, anyhow," Sir John patronized me.

"*C'est vrai*," I heard murmur in his chosen language, the Hadji, who had saved the situation. "*C'etait une idée très bien pour un*—duffer."

CHAPTER XXIV

PLAYING HEAVY FATHER TO RACHEL

Never had the *Enchantress Isis* looked so enchanting to my eyes as she looked that night. I felt, as the Set trooped on board, like an anxious hen-mother who, contrary to her fears, has safely returned a brood of ducklings to the home chicken-coop after a swim out to sea. I valued each duckling, even the least downy, far more than I had dreamed it would be possible. But there was one duckling valued so much more than all the rest (how much more I had realized only when, cackling on the bank, I saw it on the wave)—that knowing it was safe made me hysterical with joy. I could have kissed its napkin when it slid off its lap and I picked it up—the napkin, not the duck—at dinner. The drawback was that I had not saved it, as Anthony had saved Monny. It had no reason to be grateful to me, or care more than it had always cared, for a friend. And still another drawback presented itself when the confusion of dressing in haste and dining, as the *Enchantress Isis* steamed out of Luxor, gave me time to think. The duckling was not my duckling: and considering that it had calmly laid plans for me to capture an heiress, considering also that it had not yet abandoned these plans, I saw little reason to hope that, now I had come to a few —just a few—of my senses—it would ever take the idea seriously, of becoming mine.

To abandon once and forever the duckling simile, the first thing I did on board the boat, after recovering from the excitement of seeing Mabel off by train with the Bronsons, was to wonder how I could make up for all this hideous waste of time when I might have been making love to Biddy. But there was no chance to say anything personal to her that night. I had to hear—and wanted to hear—the story of all that had happened from the moment she and Monny entered Rechid Bey's gate, to the moment they came out. Then there was Antoun's story to follow; and after that we had to compare notes: how everybody had felt, what everybody had thought, what everybody had done. This subject was inexhaustible, and kept cropping up in the midst of others; but that of Mabella Hânem, her escape from bondage and from "conversion" to Islam, and what revenge Rechid was likely to take, was almost as engrossing.

When at last, late that evening, I managed to get Biddy alone for a moment, she could no more be induced to talk of herself than if she had been a ghost without visible existence, a mere voice, to speak of others, Monny by preference. What a heroine Monny had been from first to last! And what did I think *now* about the foolishness of that theory—the theory that Bedr was a spy, and had led his employers to believe that "Mrs. Jones" was travelling with her stepdaughter concealed under an impeccably important *nom de guerre*?

What I thought was, that we must get hold of Miss Rachel Guest, and question her as to her whole acquaintance with the Armenian learning how, by all that was incredible, the double mystery of mixed names had originated. "Monny knows only that Rachel was supposed to be the heiress, testing her personal attractions by pretending to be the poor school teacher," said Brigit. "The child's been wildly enjoying the situation, for she was tired of young men. Rachel wasn't! And Rachel's been profiting by it—far more wickedly. As for Esmé, I'm sure no thought of her name coming into this business, ever entered Monny's head. We must try to find out what Bedr said to Rachel at the beginning, as you advise, Duffer—and all about it. After what I told you that I heard from Esmé about an exciting love romance, any mistake of *this* sort might be particularly dangerous. The Organization might think it had more right than ever to be bitter against us. And now, I don't mind your confiding in your friend Captain Fenton. I think I'd like him to know my story."

What Biddy had told me about Esmé was, that the girl had confessed, in a letter, having been made love to (during a summer holiday in the mountains with friends) by the son of a man her father had deeply injured. The accidental meeting had been a real romance: the girl and the young man thought that no one, save themselves, shared their secret. But who could tell, when Fate itself stood between them with a drawn sword? The love of Romeo for Juliet was a safe and simple affair compared with the merest flirtation between the daughter of Richard O'Brien and the son of John Halloran, whom O'Brien's testimony had sent to prison for life.

Sometimes I thought, as the days went on, that Biddy guessed—not my change of heart, but my new understanding of it: and that she wanted quietly and gently to show me, according to Bill Bailey's pet expression, there was "nothing doing." Her expressed wish that Fenton should hear her story, looked to my suddenly suspicious mind as if his strong personality and his extremely picturesque position had made an appeal to the romance in her, as it had in the case of Mrs. East and perhaps Monny Gilder. Always interested in "Mrs. Jones," from first sight, when he had laughingly said that the "little sprite of a woman" would be almost too alluring if surrounded by an atmosphere of mystery and intrigue, Anthony was now frankly preoccupied with her affairs. He was not even annoyed that, unaided by me, her quick mind had grasped the secret of his identity. "It was like her to spring on to it by instinct," he said, smiling that thoughtful smile of his, which was more than ever effective in his Arab get up. "And like her not to give anybody else a hint, except you, of course—though she must have been tempted sometimes. I suppose"—and he looked up quickly—"she *hasn't* given any one else a hint?"

"I'd swear she hasn't."

"Miss Gilder—you're sure she hasn't the slightest suspicion?"

"As sure as a man can be of anything about a woman."

"You aren't trying to evade the question, Duffer?"

"On my word, I'm not. I feel morally certain Miss Gilder labours under the impression that you're as brown as you're painted. That somehow or other you can't be Moslem because she's seen you without a turban, and you've got the hair of a Christian. Maybe she thinks you're a Copt. I heard her learnedly arguing the other day that the Copts are the only *real* Egyptians. She has the air of studying you, sometimes: but with all her study, she sees you only as an Egyptian of high birth and attainments, with a few drops of European blood in your veins, perhaps just enough to make things aggravating, and a vague right to a princely position if you chose to overlook something or other, and claim it. There you have her conception of you, in a nutshell."

There would still have been room in that nutshell for Cleopatra's ideas concerning her niece's feelings. But if she were right, it was Anthony's business to discover those feelings for himself, provided he cared to do so. And of this I was not sure. There was the doubt that it might be Biddy, even though he appeared to attach some unexplained importance to Miss Gilder's continued ignorance about himself.

The day after leaving Luxor, there was no time for the heart to heart talk I planned with Rachel Guest. Each hour, each minute almost, was taken up with my duties as Conductor, which I was obliged to regard seriously, whether I liked them or not. If I did not, the Set growled, snapped or clamoured; which gave me even more trouble than doing my duty.

For some reason best known to herself (but suspected by me) Mrs. East kept to her suite, nursing a grievance and the Siberian lap-dog from Asiut. This saved me a certain amount of brain strain, for among other places of interest we had to pass near was ancient Hermonthis, where in her Cleopatra incarnation she had built a temple with a portrait of herself adoring the patron Bull of the city. If she had known how easy it would be to visit the ruins, she would have been capable of desiring the boat to stop, or telegraphing complaints to Sir Marcus if it hadn't.

The two excitements of the day were passing through a huge lock (with sides like those of a canyon, and scarlet doors such as might adorn the house of an ogre) in which we nearly stuck, and were saved by Antoun seizing the pole from the inferior hands of a Nubian boatman; also a visit to Esneh, a very Coptic town, starred with convents built by the ever-present Saint Helena, sacred once to the Latos fish, now sacred to gorgeous baskets of every size and colour, also somewhat over-beaded, and over-scarabed. A ruined quay jutted into the wine-brown water, where Roman inscriptions could have been spied out, if any one had had eyes to spare from the basket sellers, the sellers of grape-fruit, and all the other shouting merchants who flocked to head us off on our way to the temple, despite a flurry of rain that freckled the deep sand of the landing hill. But nobody did have eyes for anything Roman, now that Cleopatra sulked in her throne-room, and our only archeologist was as absent-minded as if he had been his own astral body. He had seen the wisdom of "sticking to the trip," and not turning back by train with the Bronsons and Somebody Else, as he may have yearned to do (if Monny were right): but History had suddenly become as dry husks to Sheridan. His soul was no longer with us, journeying up the Nile; and I suspected his body of packing to join it, as soon as things had been arranged to un-Hânem Mabel, and send her, freed from a marriage which was not marriage, freed from this fear or forcible conversion, home to the United States.

It was just on the cards, Anthony and I thought, that there might be another "demonstration" at Esneh, that unruly town where Mohammed Ali banished the superfluous dancing girls of Cairo in the eighteen forties. If Rechid Bey had not discovered the truth about that hurried departure from Luxor for Asiut (as a matter of fact, Mabel and her guardians were almost thrown on board as the train began to move) he might have sent emissaries, or come himself to Esneh, where he must have known the *Enchantress Isis* would land. As for Bedr and his employers, Anthony (who now knew Biddy's suspicions) was inclined to think that, even if she were right, we had seen the last of them. After such a setback as that in the Temple of Mût, he thought they would not only be discouraged but frightened. They had run away from us, in the temple; and despite the proverb concerning those who fight and run, to fight another day, it was probable that men of their calibre would see the wisdom of abandoning the chase. They had shown themselves cowards, Anthony thought, whatever their object had been in attacking Miss O'Brien and Miss Gilder: and though we must be on the watch during the rest of the trip, his idea was that the men had retreated in fear of arrest.

In any case, we had no trouble at Esneh, and saw no sinister faces peering out of low doorways in the bazaars, or over the heads of the pretty (sometimes fair and blue-eyed) dancing girls' descendants.

Buried in the heart of the village we came upon the temple. Only the portico was visible under piled houses and a triumphant mosque; but once we were down in the entombed temple itself, it gave a sense of secrecy, and mystic rites, to look up from under the dark roof of heavy stone with its painted zodiac, out from hidden halls of carving and colour, to the clustered houses of dried brick built before the temple was uncovered. There was a sense of tragedy and failure, too, toiling up the steep slope to the town level, and passing, on the half-buried walls, gigantic carved figures making thwarted gestures, in commemoration of kingly triumphs forgotten hundreds upon hundreds of years ago.

At night there was *fantasia* on board, with our boatmen dancing each other down, like Highlanders, and the next day brought us to Edfu, which all the women were wild to see because Robert Hichens had called its green-blue the "true colour of love": an adorable temple sacred to Horus, as there he conquered and killed Set.

It was only after we had passed Sir Ernest Cassell's red house, with the smoky irrigation works where fourteen hundred Arabs have chased the desert into the background, and after we had visited the splendid twin temples of Light and Darkness at Kom Ombo, towering majestically above the Nile bank, that I found time to catechize and lecture Miss Guest. I contrived to separate her from her sculptor, and lure her to a part of the deck unfrequented because it was windy. Rachel was looking happy, young and prosperous, in one of Monny's most becoming (and expensive) dresses.

At first, I think she felt inclined to be flattered by my desire for her society, for I had never yet wished her joy, or formally congratulated Bailey. One look into my eyes, with those clever, slanting green orbs of hers, however, and instinct must have told her that my intention was different. She glanced round for an excuse to escape, but found none, for I hedged her in from all her friends. Then she quickly decided to shunt me off on an emergency track laid by herself.

"What a wonderful day it's been!" she remarked. And Kom Ombo is one of the best temples. The only thing I didn't like was those mummied crocodiles. Their smiles look so hypocritical, and to think they've been smiling them for thousands of years—"

"It must be unpleasant to smile the smile of a hypocrite, even for a few weeks," I seized the chance to work up to business.

"Yes, indeed," agreed Miss Guest a slight colour staining her cheeks. "And didn't you notice several new sorts of wall-inscriptions?"

"Yes," I admitted. "But if you don't mind, I'd like to skip sixteen or seventeen centuries and come down to you. I've been wanting a chat—"

"Why, I'm delighted!" she exclaimed, frightened, but all the more ingratiating. "Oh, isn't the Nile beautiful as we come toward Nubia? And aren't the sakkiyehs more interesting than the shadoofs, which they use mostly when the river is low? Willis said quite a lovely thing, about the sakkiyehs: that their chains of great water cups, going up and down, look like enormous strings of red and green prayer-beads, being 'told' by unseen hands. He ought to be a poet, he's so romantic."

"No doubt everything about you, Miss Guest, must make an appeal to his romantic side," I cut in, while she was forced to pause for breath.

"I hope I do appeal to him," she said, meekly, "I never thought to be so happy." This was a direct appeal to *me*; and it hit the mark. I didn't care a rap about Willis Bailey, or his sketches or the wooden statues with crystal eyes which he was going to make the fashion. If Miss Guest chose to hook her shining fish with a false fly it wasn't my business. It was hers and his, and perhaps Monny's, for Monny had backed Rachel up in creating a wrong impression, as if they two had been playing together, like children, to trick the grown-ups. But I had to find out what had started the ball rolling, because it looked as if that ball had come out of the pocket of Bedr.

"I'm glad you're happy," I said, "and my hope is that you'll remain so. I wish you so well, that perhaps you'll give me the right to ask a few questions. You see, I'm one of your oldest friends in Egypt, after Miss Gilder and her aunt—and Mrs. Jones. You met Miss Gilder and Mrs. East travelling in France, they've told me—"

"Yes, in a dining-car. We were put at the same table, and got talking. I just loved Monny at first sight, and she's been heavenly to me. What fun we've had! I never had *any* fun before. I hardly knew the meaning of the word."

"I suppose it must have amused you and Miss Gilder," I planted my arrow at last, though not remorselessly, "this quaint idea that's got round, about your having changed places."

Rachel's face crimsoned. "Oh, Lord Ernest!" she sighed in an explosive whisper, with a glance round to see if any one were near. But we were alone with the beginnings of a sunset, that flushed the dun hills as unripe peaches are flushed on a garden wall. "I've promised Monny not to say a word and spoil her fun, as long as the trip lasts. She's finding out, you see, which people are really attracted to her, for herself. She says it's a wonderful experience—and it's given her such a rest from men: the silly ones, you know. It isn't *my* fault. I'd tell in a *minute* if she'd let me."

"Was it she who began the game?" I dared to inquire. "Or was it Bedr? Now, this is a question I really *have* a right to ask. I'll tell you why afterward, if you don't know already from Monny."

"No, I don't think Monny's said anything to make me understand that," Rachel answered, stammering a little, and trying pathetically not to look anxious. "But I'll answer you, of course. There's nothing to hide from *you*—now—that I can see. It *was* Bedr who began. He was the most intelligent, extraordinary person! I don't believe any one fully realized it, except me. But from that first night at Alexandria, he seemed to feel that I saw something of value behind his poor face. He was *very* sensitive. And he attached himself to me in the most beautiful, faithful way. Really and truly, if there hadn't come that trouble about the hasheesh place (which *wasn't* his fault, because Monny wanted to go, and when she wants things she wants them very much) I believe I could have made a Christian of him. He would have been a wonderful convert! We talked more about religion than anything else, but he used to like to chat about America, because he'd been there, and hoped to go again. *That* was the way the joke about Monny and me started. He *did* ask me not to speak of it, but it can't matter now. He told me when he was in New York, with a family who took him from Egypt, one day the great Mr. Gilder's daughter was pointed out to him in the street. She was with her father, in an automobile, but there was a block in the traffic: a policeman was keeping it back, so he saw her distinctly for several minutes, and he was interested, because his employers told him how important the Gilders were, and how

Mr. Gilder used to have his daughter guarded every minute for fear she might be kidnapped for ransom, as several rich people's children had been. Monny couldn't have been more than fourteen then, as it's seven years ago; and Bedr said that the little girl he saw in the automobile was exactly like *me*—hardly at all like what Monny is now. He wanted me to tell him, for a reason which he vowed and swore was *very* important, whether I wasn't really Miss Gilder, and *she* Miss Guest."

"Well?"

"Well, I thought the idea so funny, so thoroughly *quaint*, you know, and like something in a book, that just for fun I answered that I couldn't tell him anything until I'd consulted my friend. Monny nearly went wild about it. She said she'd come to Egypt to have adventures and she was going to *have* them, no matter whether 'school kept or not'. That's just a little slang expression, people use at home, sometimes. I daresay you've heard her say much the same thing. She said this idea of Bedr's was too good to miss, and we'd get bushels of fun out of it. So we have—in different ways. And she's been lovely, about giving me dresses and things. When she and I talked the matter over, she understood why Bedr should have thought she was more like me, at the age of fourteen, than like her present self. She'd had typhoid fever just before the time she must have been pointed out to him, and it had left her thin as a rail, and as pale as a ghost. Her hair was short, too, and some of the colour had been burnt out of it by the fever. Now, you know, she has a brilliant complexion, and her face is much rounder than mine, as well as more pink and white. Compared to her, I am *sallow*, I'm afraid, and lanky: and when she and I stand together, her hair looks bright gold, and mine light brown in comparison.

"Monny wouldn't let me tell Bedr right out that he was mistaken about us. She said we wouldn't fib, but we'd act self-conscious, as if we had a secret, and he'd stumbled on it. He must have started the story—oh, if you could call it a story! I don't believe anything has ever been put into words. It was in the air. People got the idea. But Bedr must have put it into their heads. Neither Monny nor I did more than smile and look away, and change the subject if any one hinted. We said, 'You mustn't breathe such things to Mrs. East or Mrs. Jones, or they'll be angry.' Apparently nobody ever did dare to breathe it to them. And I think Monny mentioned you, too, Lord Ernest. She didn't want you to know. She was afraid you'd say that the whole thing was nonsense. I suppose it was Enid Biddell who came to you? She was afraid Mr. Snell —but it isn't worth talking about, now. Only she is a cat."

Miss Biddell had said exactly the same of Miss Guest. Naturally, however, I did not mention the coincidence.

"Now I've told you everything you wanted to know, haven't I?" Rachel went on. "Or were there any more questions you'd like to ask—I mean, about Bedr?"

"Only one more, I think. Did it ever strike you that he was curious about you—or rather, about Miss Gilder who, you both let him suppose, was really Miss Guest? Anything about your name?"

"Why, yes, he was curious. They say Arabs always are, if you let them be. Not that he is exactly an Arab. But I suppose Armenians are the same. He seemed to want to know things about me—what I'd done, where I'd lived, and—oh, lots of little questions he would ask. Monny and I made up our minds from the first, as I told you, that there mustn't be any fibs. I simply put him off. He never got anything out of me at all."

"I see," I said; and let myself drift away from her into thoughtfulness.

"Is that all, then?"

"Yes, that is all, thank you."

Her tone sounded as if she were relieved of a mental weight, and would like to go. I expected her to make some excuse: it would soon be time to dress for dinner: or she had a letter to write. But no, she lingered. She was trying to bring herself to say something. I waited, in silence, my eyes on the shining river, looking back at the golden trail of the sun that was like a rich mantle draping a gondola on a fête day in Venice.

"I suppose you think," she forced the words out at last, "that Willis Bailey wouldn't have—fallen in love—or proposed—if he hadn't thought like the rest, that I—I—" "I don't see why he shouldn't, Miss Guest."

"He—really does seem to care for me—as I *am*, you know. And I've never told him a single untruth. I've *nothing* to blame myself for."

"I'm sure of that."

"Yet you don't approve of me—one bit. You think I'm a—kind of adventuress. So does Mrs. Jones. *Me!* Why, what would the people at home in Salem say if any one suggested such a thing? You don't know the life I've led, Lord Ernest."

"I can imagine. You don't want to go back to it again, do you?"

"It does seem as if I *couldn't*, now. It's seemed so, even before Willis—oh, I'm sure you think I *never* meant to go back, once I'd broken free from the dull grind."

"No harm in that!"

"I'm glad you say so. I took all my legacy to see the world a little —well, nearly all, not quite, perhaps, to tell the truth. And being brave has brought me this reward: the love of a man who can give me everything worth having. I shan't be *outside* life any more. And Willis won't have any reason to blame me when he—when he—"

"No reason, of course," I fitted into her long pause. "But men as well as women are unreasonable, sometimes, you know. And if he should be so —er—wrong-headed as to think you'd deceived him about yourself—"

"Then he ought to blame Monny, not me!"

"He ought, perhaps. But the question is, what he will do. And you can't like having a sword hanging over your head? Supposing he should be unjust, and refuse to carry out—"

"Oh, Lord Ernest, you don't think he will, after he's sworn that I'm the only woman in the world he could ever have loved? He thinks me *much* better looking than Monny. He says she hasn't got a *soul*, yet. He doubts if she ever will have one."

I didn't doubt it. I thought I had heard it stirring in the throes of birth, a soul such as would blind the eyes of a Rachel Guest, with its white shining. Monny had said that she would "find her soul in Egypt." But the mention of this was not indicated just then.

"I haven't the courage to tell him, even if there were really anything definite enough to tell," Rachel went on. "It would be insulting a man like Willis to suggest that he'd been influenced—you know what I mean. But—now we're talking of it—oh, do advise me! We're planning to be married in Egypt, at the end of this trip, and then settle down in Cairo, for Mr. Bailey's studies at the museum. He came up the Nile only for me, you see! And he says I shall be his first model for the new style—my eyes are *just* right, as if they'd been made on purpose to help him. I lie awake nights wondering what if, before the wedding, when he finds out for certain that my name is really only Rachel Guest, and that I'm I—oh, I daren't *think* of it!"

"Then, if you want me to advise, why don't you in some tactful, perhaps joking way, speak of the story Bedr started, and—"

"I can't—I simply can't."

"Yet you feel it would be better?"

"Yes—sometimes I feel it. *You* help me, Lord Ernest. *You* tell him. And then, if you see any signs—you'll make him understand how dreadful it would be to throw me over because I'm poor and have been a nobody till now?"

"I'll do my best," I heard myself weakly promising.

No wonder I have earned the nickname of Duffer!

CHAPTER XXV

MAROONED

Had any human fly ever buzzed himself so fatally into the spider-webs of other people's love affairs? I asked myself sternly. As soon as Providence plucked me out of one web, back I would bumble into another, though I had no time for a love affair of my own.

When the *Enchantress Isis* had slipped past many miles of desert shore, black-striped and tawny as a leopard's skin, and other desert shores so fiercely yellow as to create an effect of sunshine under gray skies, we arrived at Assuan. I had not yet kept my promise to Rachel, though whether from lack of opportunity or courage I was not sure.

Here we were at historic Assuan; and nothing had happened, nothing which could be written down in black and white, since the excitements at Luxor. Nevertheless, some of us were different within, and the differences were due, directly or indirectly, to those excitements.

Now we were nearing Ethiopia, alias the Land of Cush, though Monny said she could not bear to have it called by that name, except, of course, in the Bible, where it couldn't be helped. How would any of us like to "register" at an hotel as Mr. or Miss So-and-So, of Cush? Oshkosh sounded more romantic.

No land, however, could look more romantic than Assuan, City of the Cataracts, Greek Syene, that granite quarry whose red syenite made obelisks and sarcophagi for kings of countless dynasties. "Suan," as the Copts renamed it (a frontier town of Egypt since the days of Ezekiel the prophet), now appeared a gay place, made for pleasure-pilgrims.

Sky and river were dazzling blue, and the sea of sand was a sea of gold, the dark rocks lying like tamed monsters at the feet of Khnum, god of the Cataract, glittered bright as jet, over which a libation of red wine had gushed. The river-front of the town, with its hotels and shops, was brightly coloured as a row of shining shells from a southern sea; tints of pink and blue and amber, translucently clear in contrast with the dark green of lebbek trees and palms, in whose shadow flowers burned, like rainbow-tinted flames of driftwood. Between our eyes and the brilliant picture, a network of thin dark lines was tangled, as if an artist had defaced his canvas with scratches of a drying brush. These scratches were in reality the masts of moored feluccas, bristling close to the shore like a high hedge of flower stems, stripped of blossoms and bent by driving wind.

On the opposite side of the river, the desert crouched like a lion who flings back his head with a shake of yellow mane, before he stoops to drink. And in the midst of the stream rose Elephantine Island, with its crown of feathery palms, its breastwork of Roman ruins (a medal of fame for the kings it gave to Egypt) and its undying lullaby sung by the cataract, among surrounding rocks.

Very strange rocks they were, black as wet onyx, though for thousands of years they had been painted rose by sunrise and sunset; shapes of animal gods, shapes of negro slaves, shapes of broken obelisks and fallen temples; shapes of elephants like those seen first by Egyptians on this island; shapes which one felt could never have taken form except in Egypt.

Over our heads armies of migrating birds made a network like a great floating scarf of beads, each bead a bird: and the blue water round the slow-gliding *Enchantress* was crowded with boats of so many hitherto unknown sorts, that they might have been visiting craft from another world: feluccas with sails red or white, or painted in strange patterns, or awninged; some with rails like open trellis work of many colours, over which dark faces shone like copper in the sunshine; rowing boats, "galleys" with fluttering flags, and old soap-boxes roughly lined with tin, in which naked imps of boys perilously paddled. Out from the boats rushed music in clouds like incense; wild, African music of chanting voices, beating tom-toms, or clapping hands that clacked together like castanets. Very old men and very young youths thumped furiously on earthen drums shaped like the jars of Elephantine, once so famous that they travelled the length of Egypt filled with wine. The breeze that fanned to us from beyond the palms and lebbeks, the roses and azaleas, was soft and flower-laden. There was a scent in it, too, as of ripe grapes, as if a fragrance lingered from vanished days when wine for the gods was made from Elephantine vineyards, and fig-trees never lost their leaves. We ourselves, and our big three-decked boat were alone in our modernity, if one forgot the line of gay buildings on the shore. Everything else might have been of the time when the world supposed Elephantine to be placed directly on the Tropic of Cancer, and believed in the magic lamp which lit the unfathomable well; the time when quarries of red and yellow clay gave riches to the island, and all Egypt thanked its gods when Elephantine's Nilemeter showed that the Two Lands would be plentifully watered.

Most of us were going to live on board the *Enchantress* for our three days at Assuan; but, hearing that lords and ladies of high degrees swarmed at the Cataract Hotel with its wild, watery view of tumbled rocks, and at the Savoy in its flowery gardens, some went where they might hope to cross the path of dukes and duchesses.

The Monny-ites were not "wild" about the aristocracy, nor would royalty (of later date than the Ptolemies) have lured Cleopatra from her suite on the boat. But the whole party was eager for shore, and no sooner had the *Enchantress* put her foot on the yellow sands than she was deserted by her passengers. The bazaars were the first attractions, for "everybody said" that they were as fine in their way as the bazaars of Cairo; so very soon we were all buying silver, ivory, stuffed crocodiles and ostrich feathers from the Sudan, which now opened its gates not far ahead: the Sudan, mysterious, unknown, and vast.

Cleopatra clung to me, with a certain wistfulness, as if in this incarnation she were not so intimately at home in Upper Egypt as she had hoped to be. Perhaps this loneliness of her soul was due to the fact that instead of seeking her society, "Anthony with an H" seldom came near her now. Something had warned him off. He would never tell me or any one on earth: but, unused to the ways of women as he was, I felt sure that he had been uncomfortably enlightened as to Cleopatra's feelings. The cure, according to his prescription, was evidently to be "absent treatment." But there was another which I fancied might be efficacious; the sudden arrival on the scene of Marcus Antonius Lark.

I happened to know that he proposed a dash from Cairo to Assuan by train, for I had received two telegrams at the moment of walking off the boat. The first message announced his almost immediate advent; the second regretted unavoidable delay, but expressed an intention not to let us steam away for Wady Halfa without seeing him. The excuse alleged was business, but I thought I saw through it, and sympathized; for he whom I had once cursed as a brutal tyrant of money-bags now loomed large as a pathetic figure.

Despite the lesson of the lotuses, I believed that his motive was to try his chance with Mrs. East; that life had become intolerable, unless "Lark's Luck" might hold again; and that he could not wait till the cruel lady returned to

Cairo. It was a toss-up, as we walked side by side to the incense-laden bazaar, whether I told her the news or left her to be surprised by the unexpected visitor. Eventually I decided that silence would help the cause; and in thus making up my mind I was far from guessing that my own fate and Monny's and Anthony's and Brigit's hung also on that insignificant decision. I was thankful that Mrs. East said no more of bringing her niece and me together, and that, on the contrary, she dropped dark hints about "everything in life which she had wanted" being now "too late, and useless to hope for" in this incarnation. Why she had changed her plans for Monny I could not be sure; enough for me that she apparently had changed them.

Sir Marcus did not appear the next day or the next, and I heard no more. Indeed, between dread of breaking the truth to Bill Bailey, and self-reproach at letting time pass without breaking it, I almost forgot Lark's love affair. I salved my conscience by working unnecessarily hard, and even helping Kruger with his accounts, when Anthony too generously relieved me of other duties.

How I envied Fenton at this time, because no girls asked him what men they ought to marry; or implored him to prevent men from jilting them; or urged him to enlighten handsome sculptors with wavy, soft hair, and hard eyes resembling the crystal orbs which were to become fashionable in Society! Anthony loved Assuan, and apparently enjoyed displaying its beauties. Not knowing that I hid a fox under my mantle, he meant to be kind in "taking people off my hands," giving them tea on the Cataract Hotel veranda; escorting them to the ruined Saracen Castle which, with Elephantine opposite, barred the river and made a noble gateway; leading them at sunset to the Arab cemetery in the desert, and to the Bisharin village where wild, dark creatures (whose hair was pinned with arrows and whose ancestors were mentioned in the Bible) sold baskets and bracelets and what not. There were really, as Sir John Biddell remarked, a "plethora of sights," not counting the magnificent Rock Tombs, since the Set had definitely "struck" against tombs of all descriptions. But even with an excursion to the ancient quarries, for a look at half-finished obelisks, for once I had not enough to do. And Fenton had snatched Biddy from me as well as Monny. Mercilessly he had them sightseeing every moment. And I could no longer scold Rachel for "letting things slide." To blame her would be for the pot to call the kettle black.

It was on the day of the Great Dam that I screwed my courage to the sticking-place, and made Bailey understand that his fiancée was nobody but Rachel Guest; that she would be Rachel Guest all her life until she became

Mrs. Some One-or-Other: preferably Mrs. Willis Bailey. Somehow it seemed appropriate to do the deed at the Dam. And always in future, when people ask what impression the eighth wonder of the world made upon me, I shall doubt for an instant whether they refer to the American sculptor, or to the Barrage.

The way in which we went was so impressive that it was comparatively easy to be keyed up to anything.

Most travellers make the trip on donkey back; or else, as far as Shellal, in a white, blue-eyed desert train, where violet window-glass soothes their eyes and prepares their minds for a future journey to Khartum. After Shellal they go on in small boats to the wide, still lake which the Great Dam has stored up for the supply of Egypt. But we of the *Enchantress Isis* were super-travellers. Our boat being of less bulk than her new rivals, she was able to reach the Barrage by passing up through its many locks and proceed calmly along the Upper Nile, between the golden shores of Nubia, to Wady Haifa. We remained on board for the experience; and though I had the task of telling Bailey, still before me, I would not have changed places with a king, as standing on deck, with Biddy by my side, I felt myself ascending the once impassable Cataracts of the god Khnum.

If Biddy had been the only person by my side, I should have risked telling her the secret she ought always to have known. But there were as many others as could crowd along the rail. For once they were reflective, not inclined to chatter. Perhaps the same thought took different forms, according as it fitted itself into different heads; the thought of that marvellous campaign of the boats which fought their way past these cataracts to relieve Gordon. The ascent was a pageant for us. For them it had meant strife and disaster and death. We admired the glimpses of yellow desert: we exclaimed joyously at the mad turmoil of green water, the blood-red and jet-black rocks, below the Dam. For us it was a scene of unforgettable majesty. For those others, the waste of stone-choked river must have yawned like a wicked mouth, full of water and jagged black teeth, which opened to gulp down boats and men.

It was on the brink of the Barrage itself that I spoke to Bailey. And there, looking down over the immense granite parapet, upon line after line of tamed cataracts breathing rainbows, we were so small, so insignificant, that surely it could not matter to a man whether the girl of his heart were an heiress or a beggar maid! There was room in the world only for the mighty organ-music of these waters, and the ever underlying song of love.

I saw by the look in Bailey's eyes, however, as he gazed away from me to the long-necked dragon form of a huge derrick, that it *did* matter. I had been tactful. I had mentioned the mistake in identity as if it were a silly game played by children, a game which neither he nor I nor any one could ever have regarded seriously. He controlled himself, and took it well, so far as outward appearance went: but soon he made an excuse to escape: and presently I saw him strolling off alone, head down, hands in pockets. Luncheon was being prepared on the veranda of a house belonging to the chief engineer of the Dam. Its owner was a friend of Sir Marcus Lark, and, being away, had agreed to lend his place to our party, Kruger having done no end of writing and telegraphing to secure it. Many of our people had got off the *Enchantress Isis* in one of the locks, and had walked up the steps to the summit-level of the Barrage, Brigit and I among others. And as we assembled for lunch it was an odd sight to see our white, floating home rising higher and higher, until at last she rode out on the surface of the broad sea of Nile which is held up by the granite wall of the Barrage. She was to be moored by the Dam, and to wait for us there until evening, when we should have exhausted the Barrage and ourselves; and have visited Philae.

By and by luncheon was ready, served by our white-robed, red-sashed waiters from the *Isis*, but Bailey did not return. Rachel begged that our table might wait for a few minutes. Perhaps he had gone the length of the Dam in one of those handcars, on which some of our people had dashed up and down the famous granite mile, their little vehicles pushed by Arabs. He might be back in a few minutes. But the minutes passed and he did not come. The dragon-derrick stretched its neck from far away, as if to peer curiously at Rachel. The black and red and purple monsters disguised as rocks for this wild, masquerade ball of the Nile, foamed at the mouth with watery mirth at the trouble these silly things called girls had always been bringing on themselves, since Earth and Egypt were young together. The look of the forsaken, the jilted, was already stamped upon Rachel's face. She tried to eat. when the picnic meal could be put off no longer, but could scarcely swallow. Monny glanced at her anxiously from time to time, perhaps suspecting something of the truth. And the eyes of both, girls turned to me now and then with an appeal which made unpalatable my well-earned hard-boiled eggs, and drumsticks. Bother the whole blamed business! thought I. Hadn't I done all I could? Wasn't I practically running the lives of these tiresome tourists, as well as their tour? What did that adventuress out of a New England schoolroom want of me now, when I'd washed my hands of her and her affairs?

But all through, there was no real use in asking myself these questions. I knew what Rachel wanted, and that I should have to do it, if only to please Biddy, who would be broken-hearted if Monny's indiscretions should wreck the happiness of even the most undeserving young female. Darling Monny must be saved from remorse at all costs!

One of the costs to me was luncheon as well as peace of mind. I excused myself from the table. I pretended to have forgotten some business of importance. I whispered to the *Enchantress* dining-room steward, who had come to look after the waiters, that the meal must be served as slowly as possible. "Drag out the courses," said I. "Make 'em eat salad by itself, and everything separate, except bread and butter." Having given these last instructions, I was off like an arrow shot from the bow, a reluctant arrow sulking at its own impetus. Instinct was the hand that aimed me; the *Enchantress Isis* was the target; and deck cabin No. 36 was the bull's-eye. As I expected, Bailey was in his stateroom. I had not far to go; only to hurry from the engineer's house, along the riverbank to the landing place, where a number of native boats were lying; jump into one, and row out a few yards. But the heat of noon, after the cool shade of the veranda, was terrific. I arrived out of breath, my brow richly embroidered with crystal beads, just in time to find Bailey squeezing his bath sponge preparatory to packing it, in a yawning kitbag already full. At such a moment he could squeeze a sponge! I hated him for this, as though the sponge had been Rachel's heart.

On his berth lay a letter addressed to her, and another to me. No doubt he told us both that he had received an urgent telegram. He was so taken aback at sight of the task master that he let me withdraw the sponge from his pulseless fingers. I laid it reverently on the washhand-stand, as a heart should be laid on an altar.

"My dear fellow," I began. (Yes, to my credit be it spoken, I said "dear fellow!") "You don't know what you are doing. I speak for your own sake. Think what people will say! Everyone will see why you left her. And you don't *want* to leave her, you know! Of course you don't! You love Miss Guest. She loves you. Not all the crystal eyes in the world can make you the fashion, if the eyes of your fiancée are red with tears because you jilted her, when you found out she was—only herself! People don't like such things. They won't have their artists cold and calculating. It isn't done. You can't afford to squeeze a sp—I mean, break a heart in this fashion. It will ruin your reputation."

So I argued with a certain eloquence, forcing conviction until with a fierce gesture Bailey snatched six collars from his bag and flung them on the bed. Seeing thus clearly what I thought showed him what others were sure to think: and the world's opinion was life itself to Bailey. He was cowed, then conquered. At last I dared to say: "May I?"

He nodded.

Instantly I tore the letters into as many pieces as there were collars. Afterward, when we walked off the boat, arm in arm, I dropped them into the water.

We got back to the engineer's before the picnickers had finished their belated Turkish coffee. Bailey took the vacant chair between Rachel Guest and Monny Gilder. Biddy said that she had asked to have some coffee kept hot for me. I needed it!

That is what delayed our start for Philae and is, I suppose, why everything that took place there afterward happened exactly as it did. If we had left the Dam an hour earlier, there would have been no excuse to stop for sunset at the temple which those who love it call the "Pearl of Egypt." As it was—but that comes afterward.

When Strabo went from Syene to Philae, he drove in a chariot with the prefect of that place, "through a very flat plain," and on both sides of their road (I fear, for their bones, it was a rough one!) rose "blocks of dark, hard rock resembling Hermes-towers." Nearly two thousand years later we were rowed to the same temple, across an immensely deep, vast sheet of shining crystal. We lolled (I am fond of that word, though aware that it's reserved for villainesses) in "galleys" painted in colours so violent that they looked like tropical birds. They were awninged, and convulsively propelled by Nubians whose veins swelled in their full black throats, and whose ebony faces were plastered with a grayish froth of sweat. Each pressed a great toe, like a dark-skinned potato, on the seat in front of him for support in the fierce effort of rowing. Turbans were torn off shaved, perspiring heads, and even skull-caps went in the last extreme. Wild appeals were chanted to all the handiest saints to grant aid in the terrible undertaking. An eagle-eyed child at the steering wheel gazed pityingly at his agonized elders. And then, just as you expected the whole crew to fall dead from heart failure, they chuckled with glee at some joke of their own. There was always breath and energy enough to spare when they wanted it. But what would you? The labourer must be worthy of his hire, and a little something over. When Strabo saw Philae, she was a distant neighbour of the mighty Cataracts. Now, the waters which once rushed down are prisoned by the Great Dam, and stand enslaved, to wall the temple round like a great pearl in a crystal case. She is the true Bride of the Nile; for, as long ago the fairest of maidens gave herself to the water as a sacrifice, so Philae gives herself for the life of the people. She drowns, but in death she is more beautiful than when the eyes of the old historian beheld her, glowing with the colours of her youth, yet already old, deserted by gods and priests and worshippers. Now she has worshippers from the four ends of the earth, and the greatest singers of the world chant her funeral hymn. For in all Egypt, with its many temples of supreme magnificence, there is nothing like Philae. None can forget her. None can confuse her identity for a moment with that of any other monument of a dead religion. And if she were the only temple in Egypt, Egypt would be worth crossing the ocean to see, because of this dying pearl in its crystal case.

Venus rose from the sea. Philae, the Marriage Temple of Osiris and Isis—Venus of Egypt—sinks into the sea of waters poured over her by Khnum, god of the Cataracts. Thus the great enchantress sings her swan-song to touch the heart of the world, her fair head afloat like a sacred lotus on the gleaming water. I think there were few among us who did not fancy they heard that song, as our Nubian men rowed across the sea stored up by the great Barrage. From far away we saw a strange apparition, as of a temple rising from the waters. It seemed unreal at first, a mere mirage of a temple. Then it took solid outline; darkly cut in silver; a low, column-supported roof; a pylon towering high; and to the south, separated from both these, a thing that might have been a huge wreath of purple flowers. We knew, however, from too many photographs and postcards, that this was "Pharaoh's Bed," the unfinished temple of Augustus and Trajan, standing on a flooded island.

Our boat glided close to the flower-like stems of the columns supporting the low roof. Far down in the clear depths we could see the roots of the pillars, or their phantom reflections. And in the light of afternoon, the water was so vivid a green that the colour of it seemed to have washed off from the painted stones. Onto this roof we scrambled, up a flight of steps, and found that we were not to have Philae to ourselves. There were other boats, other tourists; but we pretended that they were invisible, and they played the same game with us. Ignoring one another, the rival bands wandered about, wondered what the place would be like with the water "down," quoted poetry and guide-books, and climbed the pylon. From that height the kiosk called "Pharaoh's Bed" showed a mirrored double, like an old ivory casket with jewelled sides, piled full of a queen's emeralds. We loitered; we explored; and having descended sat down to rest, dangling irreverent feet over beryl depths, splashed with gold. Thus we whiled away an hour, perhaps. Then the Set, impressed at first, had had enough of the mermaid temple's tragic beauty. Sir John Biddell reminded me that it had been a long day for the ladies, and very hot. Hadn't we better get back to the *Enchantress* before sunset? But that was exactly what some of us did not want to do.

The matter was finally settled by retaining our one small boat, with two rowers, and sending off the two larger "galleys" with their full complement of passengers, excepting only "Mrs. Jones," Miss Gilder, Antoun Effendi, the melancholy Cleopatra, and the guilty shepherd of the flock, who knew he had no business to desert his sheep. He did nevertheless feel, poor brute, that after such a day he had earned a little pleasure, and, accordingly proceeded to snatch it from Fate, despite disapproving glances. Punishment, however, fell as soon as it was due. I had stayed behind with the intention of amusing Brigit. But Monny took her from me, as if she had bought the right to use my childhood's friend whenever it suddenly occurred to her to want a chaperon. Instead of Biddy, I got Cleopatra. And by this time, so far as we knew, all tourists save ourselves had gone.

I knew in my heart that, in accusing Monny Gilder of claiming Brigit O'Neill because she was paying her expenses, I did the girl an injustice. Monny was afraid of herself with Anthony. I saw that plainly, since the fact had been laid under my nose by Mrs. East. She feared the glamour of this magical place, perhaps, and felt the need of Biddy's companionship to keep her strong, not realizing that any one else was yearning for the lady. This was the whole front of her offending; yet I was so disappointed that I wanted to be brutal. Without Biddy, I should wish but to howl at the sunset, as a dog bays the moon. And feeling thus I may not have made myself too agreeable to Cleopatra. In any case, after we had sat in silence for a while, waiting for a sunset not yet ready to arrive, she turned reproachful eyes upon me. "Lord Ernest," she said, "I think you had better go and join Monny."

"Why?" I surlily inquired. "I thought *you* thought that idea of yours was too late to be of any use now?"

"I do think so," she replied. "*Everything* interesting is too late now. Still, you'd better go."

"Are you tired of me?" I stupidly catechised her.

"Well, I feel as if I should like to be alone in this wonderful place. *I want to think back.*"

"I see," said I, scrambling up from my seat on the edge of the temple roof, and trying not to show by my expression that I was pleased, or that both my feet had gone to sleep. "In that case, I'll leave you to the spooks. May none but the right ones come!"

"Thank you," she returned dryly; and I limped off, walking on air, tempered with pins and needles. Joy! my luck had turned! At the top of the worn stone stairway, cut in the pylon, I met Biddy. She was dim as one of Cleopatra's Ptolemaic ghosts, in the darkness of the passage; but to me that darkness was brighter than the best thing in sunsets.

"Salutation to Caesar from one about to die!" I ejaculated.

"What *do* you mean?" she asked.

"I mean that both my feet are fast asleep, and I shall certainly fall and kill myself if I try to go one step further, up or down."

"You, the climber of impossible cliffs after sea-birds' nests!" she laughed. But she stood still.

"I'm after something better than sea-birds' nests now," said I. "The question is, whether it's not still more inaccessible?"

"Are you talking about—Monny?" she wanted to know, in a whisper.

"Sit down and I'll tell you," was my answer.

"Oh, not here at the top of the steps, if it's anything as private as *that*," Biddy objected, all excitement in an instant. "Let's come into a tiny room off the stairway, which the guardian showed me a few minutes ago. There's a bench in it. You see, he's up there on the pylon roof now with Monny and Captain Fenton (I *can't* call him Antoun when I talk to you; its *too* silly!) and he'll probably be coming down in a minute. Then, if we stop where we are, we'll have to jump up and get out of the way, to let him pass. And he's sure to linger and work off his English on us. I don't think we'll want to be interrupted that way, do you?"

"No, nor any other way," I agreed.

"Oh, but what about the sunset? We may miss it."

"Hang the sunset! Let it slide—down behind the Dam if it likes!"

"I don't wonder you feel so, you poor dear," Biddy sympathized, "when it's a question of Monny, and all our hopes going to pieces the way they are doing, every minute. There isn't a second to lose."

So we went into the little room in the tower, which was lit only by a small square opening over our heads. We sat down on the bench. It was beautifully dark. I began to talk to Biddy. We had forgotten my feet; and I forgot Mrs. East. But I must tell what was happening to her at the time (as I learned afterward, through the confession of an impenitent), before I begin to tell what happened to us. Otherwise the situation which developed can't be made clear.

I left Cleopatra calling spirits from the vasty deep, or rather one spirit; the spirit of Antony. I am morally sure that any other would have been *de trop*. And sailing to her across the wide water from Shellal came Marcus Antonius Lark.

I can't say whether she considered him an answer to her prayer, or a denial of it. Anyhow, there he was; better, perhaps, than nobody, until she learned from his own lips—tactless though ardent lips—that he had come from Cairo to Assuan, from Assuan to Philae, to see her. Then she took alarm, and remarked in the old, conventional way of women, that they'd "better go look for the others." But Sir Marcus hadn't spent his money, time, and gray matter in hurrying to Philae from Shellal, for nothing. Finding himself too late to catch us at Assuan, he had paid for a special train in order to follow his "Enchantress" (the lady and the boat).

Taking a felucca with a fine spread of canvas and many rowers, which (characteristically) he bargained for at the Shellal landing-place, he sailed across to the moored steamer, only to learn from Kruger that we had gone on our expedition to Philae. That meant a long sail and row for the impatient lover. For us, the longer it was, the better: one of the chief charms of our best day. But for him it must have been tedious, despite a good breeze that filled the sails and helped the rowers.

On his way to the temple, he met the galleys going "home" to the *Enchantress Isis*. An instant's shock of disappointment, and then the glad relief of realizing that the one he sought was still at the place where he wished to find her. There were only four Obstacles which might prevent an ideal meeting. The names of these Obstacles, in his mind were: Jones, Gilder, Fenton, and Borrow; and being an expert in abolishing Obstacles, the great Sir Marcus began to map out a plan of action.

Luckily for him, our small boat had moved out of Cleopatra's sight, as she sat and dreamed on the low temple-roof, while we four Obstacles disported ourselves on different parts of the high pylon. The two Nubians wished to play a betting game with a kind of Egyptian Jack-stones, and it was not desirable that the pensive lady should behold them doing it. Observing the graceful figure of Mrs. East silhouetted against the sky's eternal flame of blue, and at the same time noticing that she could not see the waiting boat, Sir Marcus got his inspiration. He knew that the four Obstacles were somewhere about the temple. Now was his great chance, while they were out of the way! And if he resolved to play them a trick, perhaps he salved his conscience by telling it that the Obstacles, male and female, ought to thank him.

Cleopatra probably thought, if she glanced up to see his boat: "Oh dear, another load of tourists!" and promptly looked down to avoid the horrid vision. By the time Sir Marcus came within "How do you do?" distance, he had bribed our waiting boatmen to row away. This in order not to be caught in a lie.

With our Nubians and their craft out of his watery way, he was free to fib when the time came. "Go look for the others?" he echoed Mrs. East's proposal. "Why, they've gone. I met them."

"Gone! And left me behind when they knew I was here?" she exclaimed. "They can't have done such a thing."

"I'm afraid there's been a mistake," replied Sir Marcus presently. "They certainly *have* gone. I met the boat. Borrow was expecting me to-day, you know—or maybe you don't know. And when he saw me in my felucca, he stopped his to explain that evidently there'd been a *contretemps*." (I'm sure Lark mispronounced that word!) "The temple guardian said a gentleman had arrived and taken the lady who was waiting, off in a boat. Of course Borrow thought I had come along, and persuaded you to go with me, after telling the guardian to let him know. I expect the guardian's got mighty little English: and they say white ladies all look alike to blacks. He must have mixed you up with some other lady. I suppose my folks haven't been the only people at Philae since you came?"

Mrs. East admitted that a number of "creatures" had come and gone. But she thought all had vanished before the departure of the galleys.

"You see you thought wrong. That's all there is to it," Sir Marcus assured her. And having taken these elaborate measures to secure the lady's society for himself alone (Nubian rowers don't count) he proceeded to lure her hastily into his own boat, lest any or all of the Obstacles should arrive to spoil his *coup*.

That was the manner of our marooning.

At the time, we were ignorant of what was happening behind our backs; the sunset for instance, and the only available boat calmly rowing away from the drowned Temple of Philae.

We were thinking of something else; and so was Sir Marcus, or he would not have forgotten the repentant promise he made himself, soon to send back a boat and take us off. We were, therefore, in the position of unrehearsed actors in a play who don't know what awaits them in the next act: while those who may read this can see the whole situation from above, below, and on both sides. Four of us, marooned at Philae, not knowing it, and night coming on.

CHAPTER XXVI

WHAT WE SAID: WHAT WE HEARD

"Biddy, you were never wiser in your life," I exploded as I got her on the bench. "You warned me there wasn't a second to lose. I've lost years already, and I can't stand it the sixtieth part of a minute longer, without telling you how I love you!"

"My goodness!" gasped Biddy. "Do be serious for once, Duffer. This is no time for jokes. Don't you know you've delayed and delayed in spite of my advice, till you've practically lost that girl? And if there's any chance left—"

"The only chance I want is with you," I said. "Darling, I want you with my heart and soul, and all there is of me. *Have* I any chance?"

"And how long since were you taken this way?" demanded Biddy, at her most Irish, staring at me through the darkness of the little dim room in the pylon.

"Ever since you were an adorable darling of four years," I assured her. "Only I was interrupted by going to Eton and Oxford, and your being married. But the love has always been there, in a deep undertone. The music's never stopped once. It never could. And when I saw you on the *Laconia*—"

"You fell in love with Monny!" breathlessly she cut me short.

"Nothing of the kind," I contradicted her fiercely. "You *ordered* me to fall in love with Miss Gilder. I objected politely. You overruled my objections, or tried to. I let you think you had. And for a while after that, you know perfectly well, Biddy, the Set gave me no time to think any thoughts *at all*, connected with myself."

"You poor fellow, you have been a slave!" The soft-hearted angel was caught in the trap set for her pity.

"And a martyr. A double-dyed martyr. I deserve a reward. Give it to me, Biddy. Promise, here in this beautiful Marriage Temple, to marry me. Let me take care of you all the rest of your life."

"My patience, a nice reward for you!" she snapped. "Let you be hoist by the same petard that's always lying around to hoist me! What do you *think* of me, Duffer—and after all the proofs we've just had of the dangerous creature I am? Why, the whole trouble at Luxor was on my account. Even you must see that. Monny and I wouldn't have been let into Rechid's house if those secret men hadn't persuaded him to play into their hands, and revenge himself on you men as well as on us, for interfering with Mabel. It was *their* plot, not Rechid's, we escaped from! And it was theirs at the Temple of Mût, too. Rechid was only their cat's-paw, thinking he played his own hand. *Just* what they wanted to do I can't tell, but I can tell from what one of them said to Monny in the temple, that they took her for Richard O'Brien's daughter. Poor child, her love for me and all her affectionate treatment of me, must have made it seem likely enough to them that she was Esmé, safely disguised as an important young personage, to travel with her stepmother. Bedr must have assured his employers that he was certain the pale girl was really Miss Gilder; so they thought the other one with me must be Esmé. You can't laugh at my fears any more! And I ask you again, what *do* you think of me, to believe I'd mix you up in my future scrapes?"

"I think you're the darling of the world," said I. "And my one talent, as you must have noticed, is getting people out of scrapes. It'll be wasted if I can't have you. Besides, under the wing of an Embassy no one will dare to try and steal you, or blow you up. We'll be diplomats together, Biddy. Come! You say I've 'duffed' all my life, to get what I wanted. Certainly I've done a lot of genuine duffing in love; but do bear out your own expressed opinion of the work by saving it from failure. Couldn't you try and like me a little, if only for that? You were always so unselfish."

"Hush!" said Biddy, suddenly, "Hush!"

"Do you hate me, then? Is it by any chance, Anthony, you love?"

"No—no! Hold your tongue, Duffer."

"'No' to *both* questions? I shan't stop till you answer."

"No, to both, then! *Now* will you be silent?"

"Not unless you say you do care for me."

"Yes—yes, I do care. But, Sh! Don't you hear, they're talking just outside that window in the wall? If you can't keep a still tongue in your head, then for all the saints whisper!"

Her brogue was exquisite, and so was she. I worshipped her. When I slipped my arm round her waist, she dared not cry out. The same when I clasped her hand. Things were coming my way at last. And if I put my lips close against her ear I could whisper as low as she liked. I liked it too. And I *loved* the ear.

She was right. They were indeed talking just outside the window, Monny Gilder and Anthony Fenton. The prologue was evidently over, and the first act was on. It began well, with a touch of human interest certain to please an audience. But unfortunately for every one concerned, this was a private rehearsal for actors only, not a public performance. Biddy and I had no business in the dark auditorium. We were deadheads. We had sneaked in without paying. The situation was one for a nightmare.

"For heaven's sake, let me cough, or knock something over!" I implored Biddy's ear, which (it struck me at the moment) was more like a flower than an unsympathetic shell, best similes to the contrary. Who could have imagined that it would be so heavenly a sensation to have your nose tickled by a woman's hair?

"There's nothing you can knock over, but me," Biddy retorted, as fiercely as she could in a voice no louder than a mosquito's. "And if you cough, I'll know you're a dog-in-the-manger."

"Why?" curiosity forced me to pursue.

"Because, you donkey, ye say ye don't want her yourself, yet ye won't give yer best friend a chance!"

"Can't be a dog and a donkey at the same time," I murmured. "Choose which, and stick to it, if ye want me to know what ye mean."

"Why, you—you Man, don't ye see, if we interrupt at such a minute, and such a conversation, they can *never* begin again where they left off? If *you'd* wanted her, I'd have tried to save her for ye, at any cost. But as ye don't, for goodness' sake give the two their chance to come to an understanding. Now be still, I tell ye, or they may hear us."

"We can't just sit and eavesdrop."

"Stop yer ears then. It'll take both hands."

It would; which is the reason I didn't do it. That would have been asking too much, of the most honourable man, in the circumstances.

Meanwhile, the two outside went on talking. Believing themselves to be alone with the sunset, there was no reason to lower their voices. They spoke in ordinary tones, though what they said was not ordinary; and we on the other side of the little unglazed window could not help hearing every word.

"I've been wanting to say it for a long time," in a voice like that of a penitent child Monny was following up something we had (fortunately) lost. "Only how could I begin it? I don't see even now how I did begin, exactly. It's almost easy though, since I have begun. I was horrid —horrid. I can't forgive myself, yet I want you to forgive me for doing your whole race a shameful injustice, for not understanding it, or you, or—or anything. You've shown me what a modern Egyptian man can be, in spite of things I've read and heard, and been silly enough to believe. Oh, it isn't just that you come from some great family, and that you could call yourself a prince if you liked, as Lord Ernest says. He's told me how you could have a fortune, and a great place in your country if you'd reconcile yourself with your grandfather in Constantinople; but that you won't, because it would mean going against England. It isn't your position, but what you *are*, that has made me see how small and ridiculous I've been, Antoun Effendi. Can you possibly forgive me for the way I treated you at first, now I've confessed and told you I'm very, very sorry and ashamed?"

"I would forgive you, if there were anything to forgive," Anthony answered. And it must have taken pretty well all his immense self-control to go on speaking to the girl in French—an alien language —just then.

"Perhaps there would be something to forgive, if I weren't on my side a great deal more to blame than you. Will you let *me* confess?"

"If you wish. Otherwise, you needn't. For I've deserved—"

"I do wish. But first, will you answer me a question?"

"I'm sure you wouldn't ask me a question I oughtn't to answer."

"It's only this: Did Ernest Borrow tell you anything else about me?"

"Nothing, except his opinion of you. And you must know that, by this time."

"I think I do. Or Mrs. Jones—or Mrs. East? Neither have for any reason—*advised* you to apologize to me for what you very nobly felt was wrong in your conduct?"

"No. Not a soul has advised me. If they *had*—"

She didn't finish, but Biddy and I both knew the Monny-habit of conscientiously going against advice.

"Thank you. You've changed your opinion of me, then, without urging from outside."

"It has all come from *inside*. From recognition of—of what you are, and what you've done for—for us all. You've been a hero. And you've been kind as well as brave. Antoun Effendi, I think you are a very great gentleman, and I respect Egyptians for your sake."

"Wait!" said Anthony. "You haven't heard my confession. When I first saw you on the terrace at Shepheard's, I willed you to look at me, and you did look."

"How strange! Yes, I felt it. Something made me look. Why did you will me, Antoun Effendi?" Monny's voice was soft. But it was not like a child's now. It was a woman's voice.

Listening with tingling ears, I knew what she wanted him to answer. Perhaps he also knew, but he boldly told the truth. "It was a kind of wager I made with myself. There was some troublesome business I had to carry out in Cairo. A good deal hung upon it. I saw your profile. You didn't turn my way, and I said to myself: 'If by willing I can make that girl look at me, I'll take it for a sign that I shall succeed in my work.'"

"Oh! It was nothing to do with *me*?"

"Not then. Afterward I knew that, while I thought my own free will suggested my influencing you, it was destiny that influenced me. Kismet! It had to happen so. But you punished me for my presumption. You treated me as if I were a slave, a Thing that hardly had a place in your world."

"I know! That's what I've asked you to forgive me for."

"And because you've asked me to forgive, I'm telling you this. I was furious; and I said, 'She shall be sorry. I will make her sorry.' My whole wish was to humble you. I wanted to conquer, and though you classed me with servants, to be your master."

"I don't blame you, Antoun Effendi! And you *have* conquered, in a better way than you meant when you were angry and hating me. You've conquered by showing your true self. You are my friend. That's what you want, isn't it?—Not to be my master, when you don't hate me any longer."

"No, that is not what I want. I still want to be your master."

"Then you *do* hate me, even now?"

"No, I don't hate you, Mademoiselle Gilder, although you've punished me over and over again for being the brute I was at first. You have conquered me, not I you. But I don't want to be your friend. If you didn't look at me as being a man beyond the pale, you would understand very well what I want."

"Don't say that!" cried Monny, quickly. "Don't say that you're a man beyond the pale. I can't stand it. Oh! I *do* know what you want. I do understand. I think I should have died if you hadn't wanted it. And yet—I could almost die because you do."

"You could die because I love you?"

"Yes, of joy—and—"

"You *care* for me?"

"Wait! I could die of joy, and sorrow too. Joy, because I do care, and my heart longs for you to care. Sorrow, because—oh, it's the saddest thing in the world, but we can never be any more to each other than we are now." "You say that so firmly, because you think of me in your heart as a man of Egypt. Dearest and most beautiful, you are great enough if you choose, to mount to your happiness over your prejudice. If you can love me in spite of what I am—"

"I love you in spite of it, and because of it, too; and for every reason, and for no reason."

"Thank God for that! You've said this to me against your convictions. I have won."

"No, for it's all I can ever say. There can be no more between us."

"You couldn't love me enough to be my wife, though I tell you now that you're the star of my soul? Never till I saw you, have I loved a woman or spoken a word of love to one, except my beautiful mother. I've kept all for you, more than I dreamed I had to give. And it's yours for ever and ever. But just because you've said to yourself that we're of stranger races, who mustn't meet in love, you raise a barrier between us. Are our souls of stranger races?"

"No. Sometimes it almost seems as if our souls were one. You have waked mine with a spark from your own. I think I was fast asleep. I didn't know I had a soul—scarcely even a heart. But now I know! Learning to know you has taught me to know myself. And if I'm kinder to everybody, all the rest of my life—even silly rich people I used to think didn't need kindness—it will be through loving you. I'm not afraid to tell you that, and though I *used* to be afraid I might love you, I'm glad I do, now—glad! I shall never regret anything, even when I suffer. And I shall suffer, when we're parted."

"You're sure we must part?"

"Sure, because there's no other way, being what we are, and life being what it is. Always I've thought since my father died, that he was near me, watching to see what I did with my life. For he loved me dearly, and I loved him. We were everything to each other. Even if that were the only reason, I couldn't do a thing that would have broken his heart. It would be treacherous, now that he's helpless to forbid me. Don't you see?"

"I see. And if it were not for that reason?"

"If it were not for that—oh, I don't know, I don't know! But yes, I do know. The truth comes to me. It speaks out of my heart. If it were only for myself if I felt free from a vow, nothing could make me say to you, 'Go out of my life!'"

"That's what I wanted to be sure of. I could thank you on my knees for those words. For I, too, have made a vow which I won't break. And if I were free of it, I might tell you a thing now which would beat down the barrier. Well! We will keep our vows, both of us, my Queen."

"Yes, we must keep them. But oh, how are we to bear it? Fate has brought us together, and it's going to part us. We love each other, and we must go out of one another's lives. What shall we do when we can't see each other any more—ever any more?"

"That time shall not come."

"But it must—soon."

"Will you trust me, till Khartum?"

"I'll trust you always."

"I mean for a special thing—just till Khartum. In the foolish days when I wished to conquer you, and make you humble yourself to me, I vowed by my mother's love that I'd not tell you, or let Borrow tell, a fact about myself which might win your favour. It was a bad vow to make: a stupid vow. But a vow by my mother's love I could not break, any more than you can break one to your father's memory. I'll abide by it: but trust me till Khartum, and there you shall know what I can't tell you now. I always hoped you would find out there—if we went as far as Khartum together. Then I hoped, because I was a conceited fool. Now I hope this thing—and all it means—because I am your lover."

"Ah, dear Antoun, don't hope. Because it seems to me that nothing nearer than Heaven can bring us the kind of happiness you want."

"If you hadn't told me you cared, nothing that may come at Khartum could have brought any happiness to me at all. For it would have been too late after that, for you to say you cared—and for the word to have the value it has now. You've said it—in spite of yourself. Trust me for the rest. Will you?"

"If you ask me like that—yes. I trust you. Though I don't understand."

"That's what I want. Say this. 'I believe that we shall be happy; and I trust without understanding, that it will be proved at Khartum.'"

Monny repeated the words after him. And although I was that vile worm, an eavesdropper, I was so happy that I could have picked Biddy up in my arms, and waved her like a flag. Anthony was going to be happy, and that ought to be a good omen that I should be happy too.

"I am almost happy now," Monny went on. "Happier than I thought I could be, with things as they are. I used to be miserable, partly about myself, partly because I thought you were in love with Biddy (you were so much nicer to her than me!), and partly because I believed, till I knew you well, that you wanted to marry Aunt Clara for money, though you cared for someone else. I even told Lord Ernest that about you. I had to tell somebody! And besides, I felt it would be good for him to think you cared for Biddy. Being jealous might wake him up to see that he was in love with her himself. He really is rather a duffer, at times! And oh, talking of him and Biddy reminds me of them! Where can they be, all this time?"

"Heaven alone knows—or cares," replied Anthony. And I realized the truth of the proverb about listeners, even where their best friends are concerned. I was obliged to kiss Biddy to keep from laughing out loud. And she couldn't scream or box my ears, or all our dreadful precautions would have been vain.

"We must find them," said Monny.

"Why?"

"Oh, if we don't, they might find us."

Anthony laughed—a give-away, English-sounding laugh. But Monny did not recognize its birthplace. Her own laugh interrupted it too soon, ringing out so happily, it probably surprised herself.

"*If* they find us here!" quavered Biddy, clinging to me.

"They can't, if only you'll let me hold you tight enough," I whispered. "If they look in, they'll just take us for a black spot in the dark!"

But they didn't look in. They went downstairs. And then was the time to get in the rest of my deadly work with Biddy. We *must* wait a few minutes, or they couldn't help knowing we'd been near them: and I made the best use of those few minutes. Biddy wouldn't promise anything, but said that she would think it over, and let me know the result of her thinking in a day or two.

To our great surprise, on arriving in open air at the level of the roof below, we saw that the sun was gone, and a slim young moon was sliding down the rose-red trail. It is indeed wonderful, say prophets of the obvious, how quickly time passes when your attention is engaged! And one comfort of being obvious is, that you are generally right.

We tried to flit forth from the dark recess of the pylon stairway without being seen or heard; but as luck would have it, Monny and Fenton had had just time to discover that our boat was gone. The girl was hunting for us, to see if we were "anywhere," or if in some mad freak we could have gone off and left them to their fate. As we sneaked guiltily out, she caught us.

"Biddy! Lord Ernest!" she exclaimed. "Why—why—you have been *upstairs*!"

A good rule for diplomats, duffers, and others, is never to tell a falsehood when there is no hope that any one will believe it.

"We—er—yes," we both mumbled.

"But—there isn't any upstairs except—where we were."

"Yes there is," Biddy assured her hastily—too hastily. "You were on the roof. We were in the little room of the guardian."

"He showed it to us. There's a window. Oh, we were *under* it! You must both have heard."

"Murder will out," I said, with the calmness of despair. But then it occurred to me that there was a way of using the weapon which threatened, as a boomerang.

"Dearest," Biddy adjured her beloved, humbly, "you wouldn't have had us spoil everything by moving, would you? I said to the Duffer when he wanted to do something desperate, 'If we interrupt them, nothing will ever come right—'"

"Besides, we were too busy getting engaged ourselves," said I, "to bother for long about what anybody else was saying or doing."

"You *were*! Oh, Biddy, that's what I've prayed for."

"Nothing of the sort!" began Mrs. O'Brien, ferociously. But the boomerang had come to my hand, and I'd caught it on the fly. Before she could go on contradicting me, Anthony, followed by the guardian of the temple, had mounted the steps from the lower ledge of the roof, where we had landed in the afternoon.

"It wasn't you who took the boat, then, for a joke!" said Fenton, at sight of us. And the mystery of our felucca's disappearance had to be discussed. Biddy saw to it that Monny couldn't edge in a word on the forbidden subject. How those two would talk later, in Miss Gilder's stateroom!

Nobody could explain what had happened, not even the guardian. He, it seemed, spent his night at the siren temple in the water, sleeping in the cell where I had blackmailed Biddy, and not even appearing to know that the custom scintillated with romance. By and by his companion who joined him for night work, would arrive in a small boat, bringing food; but this man rowed himself, and neither could leave the temple again that night.

"You will lend the boat to us," said Anthony. "We'll row, and send it back to you here by some one who is trustworthy."

"We have no right to lend the boat," returned the Nubian.

"Then I will steal it," replied the Hadji.

But none of us cared how long a time might pass before deliverance came. The *Enchantress Isis* couldn't steam away and leave her Conductor behind. As Mrs. East had disappeared, I vaguely associated the puzzle of our missing craft with Sir Marcus; and anyhow, curiosity wasn't the strongest emotion in my being just then. I thought that perhaps never in my life again would love and romance and beauty all blend together in one, as here at Philae in the moonlight. The sharp sickle of the young moon cut a silver edge on each tiny wave, that murmured against the submerged pillars like a chanting of priests under the sea. The temple commemorating love triumphant was carved in silver, and drowned in a silver flood. The flowering capitals of the columns as they showed above the water, blossomed white as lilies bound together in sheaves with silver cords, and placed before an altar.

Yes, Egypt was giving us what we asked. But would she give us all we asked? Just as there might have been a renewed chance of getting an answer to this question, black men in a black boat hailed us. Sir Marcus had deigned at last to remember our plight.

CHAPTER XXVII

THE INNER SANCTUARY

We made a sensation when we returned to the fold. Everybody wondered so much that they gave us no time to answer their questions, even if we would. But somehow it seemed to be taken for granted that the whole thing was my fault. Perhaps Mrs. East or Sir Marcus had spread the report. I let it pass.

As for Sir Marcus, he stayed only long enough for a talk with me. It began with trumped-up business, and ended in a confession. She had snubbed him, it seemed. Snubs being new to Sir Marcus, he had been dazed, and had forgotten for a while to send us a boat. I assured him that we bore no grudge, really none whatever. It had been quite an adventure. And I tried to cheer him up. Better luck next time! Why wouldn't he go on with us? Fenton and I could chum together, to give him cabin-room. And Neill Sheridan, the American Egyptologist, had let me know that he was obliged to leave us at Wady Haifa. There would be an empty cabin, going down again. But no, the "Boss" refused his Conductor's hospitality. "I think the less she sees of me, the better she likes me," he said dismally. "She was civil enough until I—but no matter. I suppose a man can't expect his luck to always hold."

"Don't split your infinitives till things get desperate," I begged. "It hasn't come to that yet. If you must go back, I'll take it on my shoulders to watch your private interests a bit, as well as the rest. Look out for a telegram one of these fine days, saying 'Come at once.' You'll know what it means."

"I will, bless you, my boy," he said heartily. "Though I am hanged if I know what you mean by a split infinitive. I hope if its improper, I've never inadvertently done it before a lady."

There seemed to be an atmosphere of suspense for everybody who mattered, as we steamed on between strange black mountainettes, and tiger-golden sands toward Wady Halfa. Anthony was in suspense about the way his fate might arrange itself at Khartum. I was in suspense as to Biddy's decision, which nothing I was able to say could wheedle or browbeat out of her. He and I were both in suspense together, about the Mountain of the Golden Pyramid. It would be ours now, we knew that. But what would be in it? Would it be full of treasure, or full of nothing but mountain, just as a crusty baked pudding is full of pudding? The doubt was harder to bear, now that Anthony was in love with a very rich girl, and desired something from the mountain more substantial than the adventure which would once have contented him. Harder to bear for me, too, wanting Biddy and wanting to give her luxury as well as peace, such as she had never known in her life of tragedy and brave laughter.

Monny was in suspense quite equal to Anthony's about Khartum, and what could possibly happen there to give her happiness. Brigit was in suspense about the two men who had so strangely and secretly worked with their spy, Bedr, and whom she expected to meet again later. Rachel was in suspense about Bailey, although I had told her it was "going to be all right," and he had said not a word of the business to her. What she wanted, was to make sure of him, and there was the difficulty at present, since we had failed to arrange for a registry-office or a clergyman on board. Other hearts were no doubt throbbing with the same emotions, but they were of comparatively small importance to me.

Our feelings were all so different and so much more intense than they had been, that the extraordinary difference in the scenery gave us a vague sense of satisfaction. We were in another world, now that we had heard the first cataract's roar, and left it behind; a world utterly unlike any conceptions we had formed of Egypt. But we did not for a long time leave the influence of the Barrage. Black rocks ringed in a blue basin so lake-like that it was hard to realize it as the Nile. Now and then a yellow river of sand poured down to the sapphire sea, and where its bright waves were reflected, the water became liquid gold under a surface of blue glass. The sky was overcast, and through a thick silver veil, the sun shone with a mystic light as of a lamp burning in an alabaster globe; yet the flaming gold of the sand created an illusion as of sunshine. It was as if the treasure of all the lost mines of Nub had been flung out on the black rocks, and lay in a glittering carpet there.

We passed small, submerged temples, with their foreheads just above water; drowning palm groves whose plumes trailed sadly on the blue expanse, and deserted mud-villages where the high Nile looked in at open doors to say, "This is for Egypt's good!"

Then there was the little Temple of Dendur, whose patron goddess was prayed to spit if rain were needed; and so many other ruined temples that we lost count (though one was the largest in Nubia) until we came to Wadi-es-Sabuá, "the Valley of the Lions." This we remembered, not because it was imposing, or because it had a dromos of noble-faced sphinxes—the only hawk-faced ones in Egypt—or because of its prehistoric writings, on dark boulders; or because it had been used as a Christian Church: but owing to the fact that the ladies bought rag dolls from little Nubian girls, who wore their hair in a million greased braids. Here the influence of the Dam faded out of sight. Forlorn trees and houses no longer crawled half out of water. Mountains crowded down to the shore, wild and dark and stately as Nubian warriors of ancient days. Then came Korosko, point of departure for the old caravan route, where kings of forgotten Egyptian dynasties sent for acacia wood, and Englishmen in the Campaign of the Cataracts fought and died; deserted now, with houses dead and decayed, their windows staring like the eye-sockets of skulls; and the black, tortured mountain-shapes behind, lurking in the background as hyenas lurk to prey. More temples, and many sakkeyehs (no shadoofs here, on the Upper Nile) but few boats. The spacious times were past, when loads of pink granite, honey-coloured sandstone, fragrant woods, and spices from the Land of Punt, went floating down the stream!

There were tombs as well as temples which we might have seen, savage gorges and mild green hills. There was the great grim fort of Kasr Ibrim; and at last—there was Abu Simbel.

Somehow I knew that things were bound to happen at Abu Simbel. I didn't know what they would be, but they hovered invisible at my berth-side in the night, and whispered to warn me that I might expect them.

A few people rose stealthily before dawn to prepare for Abu Simbel, because it had been hammered into their intellects by me that this Rock-Temple was the Great Thing of the Upper Nile. Also that every he, she, or it, who did not behold the place at sunrise would be as mean a worm as one who had not read the "Arabian Nights."

Not everybody heeded the advice, though at bedtime most had resolved to do so. We had anchored for the night not far off, in order to have the mysterious light before sun-up, to go on again, and see the grand approach to the grandest temple of the Old World. But after all, most of the cabin eyelids were still down when we arrived before dawn at our journey's end, and only a few intrepid ghosts flitted out on deck; elderly male ghosts in thick dressing-gowns: youthful ghosts of the same sex, fully clothed and decently groomed because of cloaked girl-ghosts, with floating hair (if there were enough to float effectively: others made a virtue of having it put up): and middle-aged female ghosts, with transformations apparently hind-side in front.

No ghost's looks mattered much, however, for good or ill, once the slowly moving *Enchantress* had swept aside a purple curtain of distance and shown us such a stagesetting as only Nature's stupendous theatre can give.

It was a stage still dimly, but most effectively revealed: lights down: pale blue, lilac and cold green; a thrilling, almost sinister combination: no gold or rose switched on yet. Turned obliquely toward the river, facing slightly northward, four figures sat on thrones, super-giants, immobile, incredible, against a background of rock whence they had been released by forgotten sculptors—released to live while the world lasted. These seated kings gave the first shock of awed admiration; then lesser marvels detached themselves in detail from the shadows of the vast façade; the frieze, the cornice, the sun-god in his niche over the door of the Great Temple: the smaller Temple of Hathor, divided from her huge brother by a cataract of sand, whose piled gold-dust already called the sun, as a magnet calls iron.

The stage-lights were still down when the *Enchantress* moored by the river bank, within a comparatively short walk of the mountain which Rameses II had turned into a temple, as usual glorifying himself. But though the walk was comparatively short, on second thoughts elderly ghosts already chilled to the bone, funked it on empty stomachs. They made various excuses for putting off the excursion (the boat was to remain till late afternoon), until finally the sun-worshippers were reduced to a party of ten.

Since Philae, Biddy had kept out of my way when she could do so without being actually rude; but as our small, shivering procession formed, she suddenly appeared at my side. Thus we two headed the band, save for a sleepy dragoman who knew the rather intricate paths through scaly dried mud, sand, and vegetation.

"I want to say something to you, Duffer," she murmured; and the roughness of the way excused me for slipping her arm through mine.

"Not as much as I want to say something to you," I retorted fervently.

"But this is *serious*," she reproached me.

"So is—"

"Please listen. There isn't much time. I heard this only last night, or I'd have spoken before, and asked you what you thought. Do you happen to know whether Captain Fenton wrote a note to Monny, asking her to wait for him in the inner sanctuary of the temple till after the people had gone, as he wanted to see her alone about something of great importance?"

"I don't know," I said. "Anthony hasn't mentioned Miss Gilder's name to me since Philae. As a matter of fact he's been particularly taciturn."

"You haven't quarrelled, surely?"

"Anthony and I! Thank goodness, no. But I'm afraid he misunderstands, and is a bit annoyed. Miss Gilder of course told him we'd overheard a certain conversation, and he's never given me a chance to explain. After Khartum it will be all right, if not before, but meanwhile—"

"I see. Then let me tell you quickly what's happened. When we came back on board the boat, after climbing about the fort of Kasr Ibrim, Monny found on the table in her cabin a note in French, typewritten on *Enchantress Isis* paper. It had no beginning or signature, only an urgent request to grant the writer five minutes just after sunrise, in the sanctuary at Abu Simbel, *as soon as every one was out of the way.* There's only one typewriter on board, isn't there?"

"Yes, Kruger's."

"And nobody but you and he and Captain Fenton ever use it, I suppose?"

"Nobody else, so far as I know."

"Captain Fenton didn't land with us to see the fort, but came up later, just as we were ready to go down. Well, for all these reasons and the note being in French Monny thinks it was written by Antoun Effendi. It was only in chatting last night about the sunrise expedition that she mentioned finding the letter. I begged her to make certain it *was* from him, before doing what it asked; because, you see, I'm still afraid of anything that seems queer or mysterious. But she laughed and said, 'What nonsense! Who else could have written it except Lord Ernest, unless you think Mr. Kruger's in a plot.' And she refused to question Antoun, because if he'd wanted the thing to be talked over, he'd have spoken instead of writing. As for doing what he asked, she pretended not to have made up her mind. She said she'd 'see what mood she was in,' after the others had finished with the sanctuary. Well, what I want, is for you and me to stay in the place ourselves when the others have gone."

"With the greatest of pleasure on earth!" said I.

"Don't be foolish. You aren't to torment me there."

"That depends on what you call 'tormenting.' If I'm to be made a spoilsport for Fenton and Miss Gilder, a kind of live scarecrow, I mean to get something out of it for myself."

There was no time for more. We had arrived at the foot of the long flight of stone steps which lead up to the rocky plateau of the Great Temple. In the east, a golden fire below the horizon was sending up premonitory flames, and the procession must bestir itself, or be too late. The whole object of arriving at this unearthly hour would be defeated, if, before the sun's forefinger touched the faces of the altar statues, we were not in the sanctuary. No time to study the features of the Colossi, or to search for the grave of Major Tidwell. These things must wait. The dark-faced guardian examined our tickets, and let us file through the rock-hewn doorway, whose iron *grille* he had just opened. As we passed into the cavernous hall of roughly carved Osiride columns, the huge figures attached to them loomed vaguely out of purple gloom. There was an impression of sculptured rock walls, with splashes of colour here and there; of columns in a chamber beyond, and still a third chamber, whence three rooms opened off, the side doorways mere blocks of ebony in the dimness. But already the sun's first ray groped for its goal, like the wandering finger of a blind man. We had only time to hurry through the faintly lit middle doorway, and plaster ourselves round the rock walls of the sanctuary, when the golden digit touched the altar and found the four sculptured forms above: Harmachis, Rameses, Amen and Ptah. Night lingered in the temple, a black, brooding vulture. But suddenly the bird's dark breast was struck by a golden bullet and from the wound a magic radiance grew. The effect, carefully calculated by priests and builders thousands of years ago, was as thrilling to-day as on the morning when the sun first poured gold upon the altar. The sightless faces of the statues were given eyes of an unearthly brilliance to stare into ours, and search our souls. But with most of the party, to be thrilled for a minute was enough. As the sun's finger began to move, they found it time to move also. There was the whole temple to be seen, and then the walk back to the boat before dressing for breakfast.

Soon Biddy and I had—or seemed to have—the sanctuary to ourselves. Even the sun's ray had left us, mounting higher and passing above the doorway of the inner shrine. The momentarily disturbed shadows folded round us again, with only a faint glimmer on the wall over the altar to show that day was born.

"Did you notice that Monny wasn't with the others?" asked Brigit, in a low voice. "She lingered behind, I think, and never came near us. I wasn't sure till I watched the rest filing out of this room. Then I saw she wasn't among them. Neither was Captain Fenton."

"If they're together, it's all right," I assured her.

"Yes, but are they? That affair of the typewritten note has worried me."

"You're very nervous, darling. But no wonder!"

"You mustn't call me 'darling.'"

"Why not? It's no worse than Duffer. I like your calling me that."

"I wonder if we ought to go, as she never came—or stay and wait?"

"If we go, we shall be playing into Miss Gilder's hands. If we stay, we shall be playing into mine. Which do you prefer?"

"Oh, I suppose we'd better stay—for fear of something. But you must be good."

Then abruptly I attacked her with a change of weapons. I had fenced lightly, knowing that Biddy liked a man who could laugh. But now I threw away my rapier and snatched a club. I told her I would stand no more of this. Did she want to spoil my life and break my heart? She was the one thing I needed. Now she would have to say whether she'd put me off because she didn't love me and never could, or because of that trash about not wanting to involve me in her troubles. No use prevaricating! I should know whether she lied or told the truth by the sound of her voice. But I might as well confess before she began, that I'd rather be loved by her and refused, than *not* loved and refused. Women seemed to think the unselfish thing was to pretend not to care, if a man had to be sent away; because in the end that made it easier for him. But in real life, with a real man, it was the other way round.

"I think you're right, Duffer," Biddy said softly. "That's why I wouldn't answer you for good and all, that night at Philae. I felt then it might be kinder to tell you I could never care. But I've thought of nothing else since—except a little about Monny—and I decided that if it were *me*, I'd rather be loved, whatever happened. Men can't be so very different where their hearts are concerned. So I'm going to tell you I *do* love you. It was hard to give you to Monny. But I thought it would be for your happiness. I nearly died of love for you when I was a little girl. I kept every tiniest thing you ever gave me. I was in love with your memory when you went up to Oxford. And it was then Richard O'Brien came. He swept me off my feet, and made me think my heart was caught in the rebound. When it was too late, I realised that it hadn't been caught at all. Only hypnotized for a while. I've loved you always, Duffer dear. The thought of you was my one comfort, often, although I hardly expected to see you again: or maybe, for that very reason. No, don't touch me! please let me go on now, or I'll not tell you any more. I wonder if you never guessed what I had in that chamois-skin bag you're so worried about?"

"Why, yes, I did guess, Biddy, right or wrong."

"And I'll *bet* you it was wrong! What did you think, when I wouldn't understand any of your hints to tell what I wore over my heart?"

"I thought then," I answered after a moment's deliberation, "that you kept—compromising documents which might be of interest to the organization you and I have talked about. Now I think differently. I think you kept a lock of my childish hair, or my first tooth."

"You conceited Duffer!—not so bad as that, because I had never a chance of getting either. Once I *did* keep in that bag just what you said: compromising documents, that the organization would have given thousands of dollars to get. And my life wouldn't have stood in their way for a minute, I'm sure. But that was before Richard died. He was afraid—I mean, I thought it would be better and less suspicious if *I* had charge of the papers. And if the Society had ever got hold of him, he believed the letters and lists of names I had, might have bought back his safety, if I played my hand well. He'd told me just what to do. But when he was ill, he had a nurse whom I began to suspect as a spy. Once when I was called into Richard's room suddenly, half dressed, the chamois-skin bag showed, as my wrapper fell open at the breast. I caught her looking at it with an eager look; and that very night I had it locked up in a bank. It was only a few days later that Richard died; and with him gone, I felt there was no more need to keep papers which might cost the lives or liberty of men. Richard had wronged his friends, and I wanted none of them to come to harm through me, though they'd made me suffer with him. I burned every scrap of paper I had, every single one! And it wasn't till there was an attempt to kidnap Esmé that I asked myself if I'd been right. Still, even now, I am not sorry. I wouldn't hurt a hair of their heads. For a while the bag was empty; but coming away from America and feeling a bit lonesome, I thought it would do me good to look now and then at the only love-letter you ever wrote me. It was on my ninth birthday—but I don't believe you could write a better one now. There was a photograph, too, of my lord when he was seventeen. I stole that, but it was all the dearer. At this very minute, the letter and the picture are lying on my heart. So now you know whether I care for you or not; and you can understand why I wouldn't put the bag into a bank."

"Oh, Biddy darling," I said, "you've made me the happiest man in the world."

"Well, I'm glad," she snapped, twisting away from me, "that it takes so little to make you happy."

"So little, when I'm going to have you for my wife?"

"But you're not. You said you'd rather be loved and refused—"

"I would, if I had to choose between the two. That's not the case with me, for I shall marry you, now I know the truth, in spite of fifty, or fifty thousand, refusals, or any other little obstacles like that."

"Never, Duffer! Not for all the world would I be your wife, loving you as I do, unless the organization would forget or forgive Esmé and me. And that I can't fancy they'll ever do, till the millenium. I shall be past the marrying age then! Oh, Duffer, I *almost* wish you had fallen in love with Monny as I wanted you to do—'

"Honest Injun, you really wanted that to happen?"

"Well, I tried to want it, for your sake; and in a way for my own, too. If I'd seen you caring for Monny, I should have found some medicine to cure my heartache. Oh, it would have been a very good thing all around, except for your friend, Anthony Fenton."

"And I was half afraid he was in love with you! I can tell you I've had my trials, Biddy. It's my turn to be happy now, and yours, too. Just think, nearly everybody in the world is engaged, but us—or next door to being engaged. Miss Gilder and Anthony—who's the only man on earth to keep her in order: and Rachel Guest and Bailey; and Enid Biddell and Harry Snell; and even your stepdaughter, Esmé O'Brien—"

"Duffer, she's *married*!"

"What, to young Halloran? How did they manage it?"

"I don't know yet. I've had only a telegram. It came to Assuan too late, and Sir Marcus Lark brought it to the boat. I found it that night when we got back from Philae. But I haven't told, because I dared not be with you alone long enough to speak of private affairs, till I could decide whether to let you know I loved you, or make believe I didn't care a scrap."

"As if I could have believed your tongue, unless you had shut your eyes! So Esmé is married, and off your hands?"

"Not off my hands, I'm afraid. This may be visited on me. They must have known of her meeting Tom Halloran at St. Martin Vesubie, last summer. They find out everything, sooner or later. Probably they thought I'd whisked her off to Egypt with me (helped by my rich friend Miss Gilder, for whom they took Rachel Guest) in order to let her meet Tom Halloran again, and marry him secretly. Well, she has *married* him secretly. When they discover what's happened, they're sure to put the blame on poor me. And indeed, it is a shocking thing for the son of that man in prison, and the daughter of the man who sent him there, to be husband and wife."

"I don't see that at all," I argued. "Why shouldn't their love end the feud?"

"It can't, for strong as it may be, it won't release prisoners, or bring back to life those who are dead."

"Anyhow, don't borrow trouble," said I. "If Esmé's married the more reason for us to follow her example. After Khartum, when Miss Gilder—"

"Who's taking my name in vain?" inquired the owner of it, at the sanctuary door.

"Oh, then you *have* come, Monny!" Brigit exclaimed. "I—I'd given you up."

"I haven't come for the reason you thought," returned the girl promptly. "I was sure you meant to head me off. And I've learned without asking, that Antoun Effendi didn't write that note."

"I told you so! Who did?"

"He's trying to find out. Probably it was a silly practical joke some one wanted to play on me. There are *lots* quite capable of it, on board! Antoun Effendi said the sunrise was much finer really, from on top of the great sandhill, so we climbed up. And it came out that he hadn't asked me to meet him here. If any one not on the boat wrote the letter, some steward must have been bribed to sell a bit of writing-paper, and allow a stranger to come on board, while we were away at Kasr Ibrim. There was a steam dahabeah moored not far off, if you remember, with Oriental decorations; so we fancied it must belong to an Egyptian or a Turk."

"It could easily have been hired at Assuan," Biddy exclaimed. "And it could have beaten us. We've stopped at such heaps of temples where other boats only touch coming back."

"If there were a plot, as you are always imagining, the dahabeah would have to be near here, too," Monny laughed incredulously.

"And so it may be. We haven't seen round the corner of the Great Temple yet."

"One would think to hear you talk, that you'd expected this poor little sanctuary to be stuffed with murderers, or at the least, kidnappers."

"Ugh, don't speak of it!" Biddy shuddered, "Let's go out into the sunlight again, as quick as ever we can!"

CHAPTER XXVIII

WORTH PAYING FOR

When Anthony says that he will find out things he seldom fails. Perhaps nobody but a green-turbaned Hadji could so speedily have screwed information out of secretive Arabs, paid to be silent. And he had to fit deductions into spaces of the puzzle left empty by fibs and glib self-excusings. What he did learn was this: a dragoman had come, in a small boat, from a steam dahabeah to the *Enchantress Isis* while we were away at Kasr Ibrim. He presented credentials written out for him in Cairo by Miss Rachel Guest, and dated a few weeks ago. Inquiring for her, he seemed sorry to hear that she had gone on the excursion. The dragoman refused to disturb Antoun Effendi, on hearing that the Hadji was writing in his cabin. His errand was not of enough importance to trouble so illustrious a man. All he wanted was permission to type one or two letters for his employers on the neighbouring dahabeah, which possessed no machine. In the absence of Mr. Kruger, who had gone on shore for exercise, the dragoman was given this privilege. Possibly he had taken some of the boat's letter-paper. Who could be certain of these trifles? Possibly, also, he had walked about with one of the cabin stewards, to see the luxurious appointments of the *Enchantress Isis*. As for paying money for these small favours, who could tell? And nobody knew if the steam dahabeah had hurried on before us, to anchor out of sight round the oblique façade of Abu Simbel. In any case, when we went to look for the suspicious craft seen near Kasr Ibrim, she was not among the two or three small private dahabeahs of artists and others, moored within a mile of the Great Temple. Notwithstanding her absence, however, Anthony and I (suddenly confidential friends again) thought it likely that the shadows in the Sanctuary had not been its only tenants when we entered there. The invaluable Bedr knew enough of the Nile Temples to know that the sun's first light strikes only the altar and the statues over it, in Abu Simbel's inner shrine: that the four corners of the small cavern-room remain pitch black, unless the place is artificially illuminated: and that this is never done at sunrise. The dragoman and one or both of his employers would have had no difficulty in getting into the temple before the first streak of dawn, if they had warned its guardian the night before. So far, our deductions were simple, after learning how the trick of the typewritten note had been managed: but it was not so easy to guess the object of the plot. Was Monny Gilder to have been murdered in the dark Sanctuary, or was she to have been kidnapped? Either seemed an impossible undertaking, unless the plotters were willing to face certain detection and arrest.

As it was, we had no more tangible proof against the man than we had before, at the House of the Crocodile, in the desert near Medinet, at Asiut, and at Luxor. With a sly cleverness which did Bedr, or those employing him, much credit, they had screened themselves behind others. Even if we had the names of the "tourists" Bedr had served as dragoman, and if we could lay our hands on their shoulders, we had not enough evidence of what they had done to obtain a warrant of arrest: and this of course they knew. Our best chance, Anthony thought, lay in springing a surprise on them, as they had vainly (so far) tried to do with us; and when we got them somehow at our mercy, force out the truth.

It was almost certain that a steam dahabeah could not unseen have passed the *Enchantress Isis* at Abu Simbel in broad daylight, going back toward Assuan. Therefore, since it was not moored near the temple, if it had been in the neighbourhood at all it must have dashed on ahead of us in the direction of Wady Haifa. With pleasure would we have given immediate chase, had not the *Enchantress* been pledged to remain at Abu Simbel till afternoon. Even as it was, I expected to catch up with a boat so much smaller than our own; but Anthony damped my hopes, explaining the difficulties of navigation between Abu Simbel and Wady Haifa. There were, he said, great shifting sandbanks in the water which looked so transparently green, so treacherously clear. Without the most prudent piloting the river was actually dangerous, as new sandbanks had a habit of forming the minute you shut your eyes or turned your back. The *Enchantress* would have to pick her way slowly through the silver sands of the Nile, which mingled with the spilt gold-dust of the desert shore. All the same, these impudent rascals would find it hard to hide from us at Wady Haifa, especially if we stopped the boat and wired from the next telegraph station to have them watched on the arrival of their dahabeah.

"Perhaps, as they're so clever they'll be clever enough not to arrive at all," was my suggestion. And Anthony could only shrug his shoulders. "Wait and see" had to be our policy.

Happily the Set wandered in and out of the two temples, big and little, all the morning, ignorant of our worries which, even to us, seemed small under the benign gaze of the great Colossi. The three stone Rameses who had faces, wore expressions no one could ever forget; and there was a sense of loss in turning away from them.

A crocodile swam past the *Enchantress* as she steamed up river; a long, dark, prehistoric shape. He seemed an anachronism, but so did Bedr, with his plottings; yet both were real, real as this Nile-dream of dark rocks, of conical black mountains shaped like ruined pyramids, and yellow sandhills whose dazzling reflections turned the blue-green river to gold.

The next day at noon, we came to Wady Halfa; and the *Enchantress Isis* who had brought us eight hundred miles from Cairo, was now to be deserted by those with Khartum in view. All save three of the party were going on through this gate of the Sudan, where the river way ended and the desert-way began. Neill Sheridan was turning back immediately, in a government steamer; and a bride and groom who cared not where they were, if with each other, would wait on board the *Enchantress* until the band of passengers should return from Khartum.

These things had to be thought of. But I meant to let Kruger do most of the thinking, when we landed at the neat, colourful town of Halfa, which lies (as Assuan lies) all pink and blue and green along the river bank, sentinelled with trees. From a distance Anthony and I caught sight of the steam dahabeah seen near Kasr Ibrim, and we could hardly wait to get on shore. The camp was but a mile and a half away, and I had wired in Lark's name, to an officer whom he was sure to know, asking as a great favour to have the passengers on board a boat of that description watched; and requesting him if possible to meet the *Enchantress* on her arrival. "There he is!" said Fenton, standing at the rail. "I mustn't seem to recognise him, of course. Can't give myself away! But you—" "Good Lord, there's Bedr!" I broke in, hardly believing my eyes. And there Bedr was, looking as if butter would by no means melt in his mouth: Bedr, smiling from the pier, evidently there for the special purpose of meeting us. His ugly squat figure, and the tall, khaki-clad form of the officer, were conspicuous among squatting blacks, male and female, in gay turbans, veils, and mantles, muffled babies in arms, and children dressed in exceedingly brief fringes.

"I'll attend to him, while you powwow with Ireton," said Anthony, ready for the unexpected situation. And while the indispensable if humble Kruger showed the passengers how to get to the desert train, superintended the landing of the luggage, and made himself perspiringly useful, I thanked Major Ireton in Sir Marcus Lark's and my own name.

His news was astonishing. There were no passengers on board the steam dahabeah *Mamoudieh*. She had arrived with none save her crew, and the dragoman now talking with that good-looking Hadji there. As I murmured "Yes," and "No," and "Indeed—Really!" to the officer, who had kindly worked on our behalf, I was saying to myself, "My *dear* Duffer, what an ass you were not to think of that!" For of course the men had remained at Abu Simbel, hiding till we should be out of the way, and sending their boat on to put us off the track. A Cook steamer and a Hamburgh-American boat were due to stop at the temple. We had passed both on the river. By this time the two men were doubtless on their way north, making for Cairo and safety.

Still, here was Bedr, looking like a fat fly who had deliberately come to pay a call on the lean and hungry spider. I was impatient for the moment when the need for genuine gratitude and "faked" explanations was over, and Major Ireton had gone about other business.

Then I could follow the Hadji and the Armenian, who had mounted the steps leading up from river-level to the town. Not far off I could see the blue-windowed, white-painted desert train, round which, on the station platform, buzzed and scolded the Set, demanding their hand-luggage and their compartments. But Anthony and his victim (or was it by chance vice versa?) were keeping out of eyeshot and earshot of the late passengers of the *Enchantress*. Brigit and Monny, who must have seen Bedr, were too tactful to hover near: also they knew "Antoun Effendi" too well to think it necessary.

Bedr gave me no time to speak. He rushed forward to greet me with effusion, as if I were a long-lost and well-loved patron. "I bin so glad see you again after these days, milord. Sure!" he began. "Antoun Effendi, he tell you I come here on purpose to do you good. I find out those genlemens very wicked men, so I leave them quick. They want to pay me for go back with them, but no money big enough now I know they try to do harm to my nice young lady. She wasn't so good to me as the other nice young lady, but that makes no matter. I not stand for any hurt to her, sure I will not, milord."

"The meaning of this rigmarole," Anthony cut him short, speaking in German (which he knew I understood and trusted Bedr didn't) "is, that the fellow wants us to buy information from him. He pretends to have broken with his employers on our account (though his explanation of getting here to

Halfa on their dahabeah is ridiculous) and that, having come for our benefit against their wishes, he's without pay, penniless, and stranded."

"A lie of course," I took for granted, also in German.

"The part about being broke—certainly. But it's certain, too, that he must know some things we'd like to know."

"Could we trust a word he says?"

"No, as far as his moral sense is concerned. But my idea is to bargain with him. We to pay according to value received. That might be bait for a fish worth hooking."

"Yes, that's our line. We haven't much time to hear and digest his story, though. The train will start in less than an hour."

"We shan't waste a minute. Without waiting for you, I began to bargain on the line I've just suggested."

"How far did you get?"

"A good way, for I was able to scare him a bit. You see, he earns his living in Cairo, and I've persuaded him that I have some influence there, in quarters that can make or break him. He hasn't much more time to spare than we have, if it's true that he wants to start back on the government boat. You know they take natives, third class. My suggestion, subject to your approval, is this: in any case we give a thousand piasters, ten pounds. But if what he can tell us is of real use or even interest, we rise to the extent of ten times that sum."

"It's a good deal for a beastly baboon like him."

"Remember, he has been doing services lately for which he probably got high pay."

"All right, whatever you say, goes," I agreed.

"I trust to your honours, my genlemens," remarked the beastly baboon in question, in a manner so apropos that I guessed him not entirely ignorant of German, after all.

"Thanks for the compliment," I responded gratefully.

"We shall have to talk here. There's no time to find a more convenient place," said Fenton, returning to Arabic as a medium of communication. "Fire away, Bedr. But don't start your story in the middle. Begin where you took service with these Irish-American gentlemen."

"Was the genlemens Irish? I never know that," purred the guileless Bedr; but Fenton brought him to his bearings. All questions were to be from us to him. So Bedr "fired away": and there, within a stone's throw of the train getting up steam for Khartum, we listened to a strange tale—as strange, and as great an anachronism as that dark crocodile-shape we had seen—except in the Nile country, where live crocodiles and many other dark things can easily happen any day.

Blount's name, according to Bedr, was not Blount, but something else, well-known in America. It was a name already associated with that of O'Brien, which inclined us to hope for some grains of truth in the chaff of lies we expected. Bedr said that in New York, years ago, he had known the man "Blount." He was related to the American family who took Bedr from Cairo. Later, when the Armenians had returned to Egypt, "Blount" had come with him, for a "rest cure." He had engaged Bedr as dragoman, and on leaving had asked for Bedr's card. That was years ago, and nothing had been heard from him since: but before the *Laconia* was due to arrive, Bedr had received a telegram from Blount instructing him to meet the ship, and wire to Paris whether Miss Gilder of New York and a "Mrs. Jones" were on board, with a party. "Blount" knew that Bedr had seen Miss Gilder as a child, and might now be able to recognize her. On the day in New York when a block in traffic had given a glimpse of the little girl in a motor-car with her father, Bedr and "Blount" had been together.

As soon as possible after Bedr's reply, "Blount" and another man, who called himself Hanna, had arrived in Cairo. Bedr knew that they had a fixed theory in regard to the young lady who passed as Miss Gilder. Who they supposed her to be, he could not tell; but once he had "happened" to be near, when they were not aware of his presence, and had heard one of them mention a woman's name, which sounded like "Esny." They accepted his word that he had been able to identify the so-called Miss Guest as Rosamond Gilder, and in her they appeared to take no further interest. Their attention was concentrated on Mrs. Jones and on the lady who, according to their belief, was but posing as Miss Gilder. Apparently they imagined her to be quite another person, one whom they had taken a great deal of trouble to reach. Also they had an idea that Mrs. Jones possessed something of which they were anxious to get hold. It was a thing which ought to be theirs, and they had been after it for years; but she had contrived to hide herself and it, until lately.

Why he had been told to guide the two younger ladies to the House of the Crocodile, Bedr pretended not to know. Perhaps—only perhaps —Blount and his companion, Hanna, wished to kidnap the one we called Miss Gilder, and they called "Esney." But good, kind Bedr had never dreamed that they meant any real harm. There had been a plan of some sort for that night. Blount and Hanna were to arrive at the House of the Crocodile for a close look at the young ladies, when the latter had gone to sleep under the influence of the hasheesh they intended to smoke. But the two gentlemen had not kept the appointment. At first, Bedr had not understood why, and had not known what to do. Afterward, of course, when he had heard of the row in the street, which had caused the closing of the house for many tedious hours, he had guessed. And later when he learned that poor Mr. Blount lay wounded in a hospital, it had all become clear. Mr. Hanna, who seemed to work under Mr. Blount's orders, had not been able to act alone.

Then, as to all the travelling up the Nile, Bedr had never been told why "his genlemen" made the journey. Every one who came to Egypt went up the Nile. Only, he had been instructed to find out, always, where we were, and told to arrange their arrival at about the same time. At Medinet they had not camped, or gone to an hotel, but had stayed in the house of a friend of Bedr's. It was convenient, though not as comfortable as he could wish for his clients. The advantage was, that from the roof it was possible to see into our camp. Bedr had made friends with one of the camel-boys who went to market to buy the black lamb: and while we were away, had found out which was the tent where Mrs. Jones and Miss Gilder (or "Esney") slept. What happened in the night he could not say. He had stayed at his friend's house, while the two gentlemen went out. He had done nothing at all for them in Medinet, except to discover the ladies' tent, and also to buy a bottle of olive oil. When the gentlemen came home in the middle of the night, they were angry with him because they said he had shown them the wrong tent. But that was unjust. It was the only time they had been unkind. Except for that, they had been good, and had given him plenty of money for a while. At Asiut and Luxor they had been pleased with him. All they wanted at Rechid Bey's house, was to get the thing Mrs. Jones had, which ought to be theirs. They had not told him this, but he heard them talk sometimes. He knew more languages than they thought. If they wanted to steal the young lady, they had never said so. When the plan failed, they did not blame Bedr. It was not his fault. They saw that.

The *Mamoudieh* had been engaged as long ago as just after Medinet, when the thing the gentlemen wanted to do there could not be done. But Bedr thought that, if the Luxor plan had been a success, the steam dahabeah would have gone north from there instead of south. It was because of that failure the boat had followed us up the Nile. At Abu Simbel Bedr had quarrelled with the gentlemen, because he began to suspect they meant harm to the ladies, or to one of them. He had been clever, and got on board the *Enchantress* as they told him to do. He had obtained writing-paper, and typed a copy of a letter. In America, he had learned to do typing. Often he could make better money in an engagement now, because he knew how to use a machine. And when the steward showed him over the boat, he left the letter in the stateroom which the Arab boy said was Miss Gilder's. In spite of all these good services, which no other dragoman in Egypt could have given, those gentlemen would not listen to a word of advice. Bedr heard them speak with the guardian of the temple, about going in before any one else came to see the sunrise: and afterward they talked of hiding in the Sanctuary. First, they had asked him if it were always dark there, as the guide-books said. After hearing this he had put two and two together: and when he remembered what was in the note he typed for Miss Gilder, Bedr feared for her and Mrs. Jones. He begged the gentlemen not to do anything rash, and they were so angry at his interference that they sent him off with no more pay—nothing at all since Luxor.

Oh, no, they were not afraid of him, and what he could tell, because they said nobody would believe a dragoman's word, against rich white gentlemen. People would say he lied, for spite. But Bedr thought maybe we should believe, because we knew already that something strange had been going on. The gentlemen paid off the men on the *Mamoudieh* and ordered her to go on to Wady Halfa. They did not know that Bedr had slipped on board, and hidden there, on purpose to find us, and tell his story.

A part of this tale carried truth on its face. But Anthony and I agreed that there was a queer discrepancy at the end. If Bedr spoke the truth, Blount and his comrade must have had a reason for wishing to get rid of the fellow, or for not caring what became of him, a reason unconnected with a quarrel. And it was certain that, if there had been a quarrel, it was not because of virtuous plain-speaking from Bedr. It seemed impossible that he could have got on board their hired boat to follow us, without his employers' knowledge. Was his appearance at Wady Halfa, and his apparent betrayal of his clients, all a part of their plan?

We could not decide this question in our minds, or by cross-questioning Bedr, while the train waited, for only time could prove. But what we had heard was interesting enough to be worth the promised thousand piasters, and the fare north on the government boat just starting. To make sure that Bedr did start, we called Kruger, put the whole sum into his hands, asking him to help the dragoman by buying his ticket and getting the notes changed into gold and silver. This little manoeuvre left the Armenian so calm, however, that we fancied his wish must really be to depart on the government boat. Such inquiries as we had time to make concerning the *Mamoudieh* seemed to show that she must remain at Halfa for slight repairs to her engine, and instructions from her owner, who was staying at Assuan. It was just at the last minute of grace, with the station-master adjuring, and the Set reproaching us, that Anthony and I jumped on board the train.

Strange that two rows of blue glass windows should have power to turn the whole world topsy-turvy, or to create a new one, of an entirely original colour-scheme! But so it was. Those people seated in their grand, travelling "bed-sitting rooms," had only a superficial resemblance to the passengers of the *Enchantress Isis*. Monny, for instance, had pale green hair, with immense purple eyes; and showed every sign of rapid transformation into a mermaid. Cleopatra's auburn waves had turned to a vivid magenta: Biddy's black tresses had a blue, grapey bloom on them: and Anthony's dark eyes were a sinister green, with red lights. Ghostly, mother o' pearl faces with opal shadows, peered through the violet glass at an unreal landscape, which would instantly cease to exist if the windows were opened. But the windows could not be opened, or a rain of sand would pour in; so we gazed out on an impossible fairy land consisting of golden sea, with mountainous shores carved from amethyst, through which shone the glow of pulsing fires. Always we carried with us an immense shadow, like a trailing purple banner, unfurling as we moved. Men and women and animals seen at the numbered white stations in the sand, were but fantastic figures in a camera obscura. The shadow of the train was torn with fiery streaks: and when the sun had burned to death on a red funeral-pyre, the moon stole out to mourn for him. Her coming was sudden. She seemed abruptly to draw aside a hyacinth curtain, and hold up a lamp over the desert, when the sun's fire had died. And the lamp gave forth an unearthly light, which poured over the endless sands a sheet of primrose-yellow flame. The warm sun-shadow was chilled from purple to gray, and flowed over the magic primrose fields like a river of molten silver.

At Number Six Station, where we stopped for water after dinner, a hyena came galumping over the sand like a humpbacked dog, to stare at us, as we strolled in couples away from the train into the desert. Next morning, every one was up early to see the gray hornets' nest huts which were Sudanese villages, and the villagers themselves, who urged us to buy straw rugs, baskets, fans, oranges, dried beans, live birds, and milk in wooden bowls, whenever the train stopped: respectable old ladies, dressed in short fringes, and small, full-stomached boys dressed in nothing at all.

I had not told Biddy about our bargain with Sir Marcus: Anthony's and my services in exchange for the Mountain of the Golden Pyramid. Why should she be forced to share our suspense? For she would share it, if she knew, even though she didn't yet yield to me, in the matter of a united future. I wanted to wait before telling her the story, until Fenton and I had made sure if there were anything golden about the mountain, except its name. If we were doomed to disappointment I could then give the tale a humorous turn, easier to do in retrospect than anticipation. Now, when in blinding light of noon we pointed out, in an impersonal manner, to all who cared to see, the pyramid-field of Meröe, it seemed strange to think that no heart but Anthony's and mine beat the faster. The sun was so hot that most people, blinking dazedly, retired behind their screens of blue glass almost as soon as the train stopped, close to Garstang's camp. I had informed the Set, casually, that wonderful things were being found here in the rocky desert: that the few neat white tents sheltered men who were going to make of Meröe a world's wonder: that not only had the army of stunted black pyramids visible from the train, yielded up treasures, but three tiers of palaces were being unearthed, or rather, unsanded. I said nothing, however, of the more distant dark shapes, like the pyramids yet unlike them. Among those low, conical mountains which perhaps gave inspiration to the pyramid builders, was our mountain. And I was not sorry when the burning sun smote curiosity from eyes and brains, and sent nearly all my flock back to their places, while the train had still some minutes at the station.

Cleopatra had not come out. She had frankly lost interest in scenic history, and did not want to be intelligent: but as Anthony and I stepped off the train, we saw that Brigit and Monny stood arm in arm in the doorway.

"Would you like to jump down?" I asked, reluctantly. For the first time I did not wish Biddy O'Brien to give me her society. I hoped she would say "No, thank you," for I wanted Fenton to point out our mountain (which he had told me could be seen): and it would be inconvenient to answer questions.

"Yes, we should like it," they both replied together: so Anthony and I had to look delighted. It really was a pleasure to help them down: but even that we could have waited for till our arrival at Khartum. And the first remark that

Biddy made was too intelligent. "What are those weird things off there in the distance, that look exactly like ruined pyramids—sort of mudpie pyramids?"

"Mountains," said Fenton.

"What, didn't anybody *make* them?"

"The legend is, that Djinns, or evil spirits, created them to use as tombs for themselves."

"But they're almost precisely like the made pyramids, only a little more tumbledown. Have they names?"

"Some have, I believe," Anthony returned, with his well-put-on air of indifference. "That blackest and most ruined looking one of all, for instance, between two which are taller—there, away to the left, I mean—that is called the 'Mountain of the Golden Pyramid.'"

Our eyes met over the girls' veiled hats. After all, he had found an opportunity of telling me what I wanted to know.

"What a fascinating name!" said Monny. "It sounds as if there were some special story connected with it. Is there?"

"Ye—es," Anthony was obliged to admit. "There is a legend that it was used as a tomb by the first Queen Candace, who lived about two hundred years B.C. after Ptolemy Philadelphus. She used to reign over what they called the "Island of Meröe." It was this once fertile kingdom, between the Atbara River over there, and the Blue Nile. They say she wished to be buried with all her jewels and treasure, and was afraid of her tomb being robbed, so she wouldn't trust to a man-made pyramid. She ordered a secret place to be hollowed out in the heart of a mountain; and that's the one they pretend it is."

"What a lovely legend! But I suppose there's nothing in it, really, or clever people like those who're digging here now would have found the tomb and the treasure long ago," said Monny.

"I don't know," I left Anthony to answer; wondering what he would say. "Only a very few have ever put enough faith in the story to search, and they have never been able to discover traces of an entrance into that mountain or any other. Of course, in trying to enter the great pyramid of Ghizeh, they looked a long time before they succeeded. But that was different. There was never any doubt of there being something worth seeing, inside, whereas this black lump may be solid rock, and nothing more. It's many years since anybody has tried to get at the secret."

"I beg your pardon," politely said (in French) an elderly man, in a pith helmet, blue spectacles, and khaki clothes, who stood near. "I couldn't help hearing your conversation; and it may interest you and these ladies to learn that at this very moment work is going on at the so-called Mountain of the Golden Pyramid."

I envied Anthony the brown stain on his face, for I felt the blood rushing to mine.

"Indeed!" I ejaculated in English. "We are very much interested. Work—actually going on!"

"Yes, it was begun about four or five weeks ago, by an agent of Sir Marcus Lark, the well-known financier, who got the concession which some other party was said to be trying for. I am here," went on the helmeted man, gazing benevolently through his blue spectacles at the two pretty women, "I am here with my son, who is one of Garstang's men. We have nothing to do with the Mountain of the Golden Pyramid. Luckily for Sir Marcus, it was adjudged to be off our 'pitch.' Still, we are interested. They are keeping their work very secret, but—these things are in the air. The talk here is that they're on the point of making, if they haven't made already, some very startling discovery."

"All aboard, *if* you please!" shouted the Greek guard.

CHAPTER XXIX

EXIT ANTOUN

If there had been no Brigit and no Monny in the world we should have let that train go on without us, and—hang the Set and its feelings! But there was a Brigit; there was a Monny; and they were more to us than all the treasure Sir Marcus was apparently stealing while we slaved.

What fools we had been to trust in such a man! And I had actually wasted pity on the fellow. Now, as we were borne away from Meröe, we saw our hopes, which had begun to seem certainties, dissolving into air. They were like the mirage of the desert which lured us with siren enchantment and mystery in this Never-Never-land which thousands of brave men had died to win: shimmering blue lakes, that mirrored green trees and low purple mountains, and the gold of sand-dunes, so real, so near, it seemed we might walk to them in a few moments: only mocking dreams, like our belief in a famous financier's loyalty; like our hopes of fortune. For if Sir Marcus Lark had secretly begun work at the Mountain of the Golden Pyramid, it meant that he intended to steal everything best worth having, for himself.

It was maddening to realize that we might be too late to thwart him, but we had to risk this, or risk losing something dearer than the jewels of a Queen Candace. Anthony was staking the happiness of his future on the events of the following night. Now that the small cloud of misunderstanding had passed from the clear sky of our friendship, we were one again in confidence, as we had been before the Philae eavesdropping: and I knew the plan he meant to carry out at the Sirdar's ball. It was rather a melodramatic plan, perhaps, but somehow it fitted into the circumstances of his queer courtship, and I could see why Anthony preferred it to any other more conventional. As for me, I too counted on Khartum to give me a present of happiness. Bedr's story, largely false as it might be, must have a basis of truth. I'd ceased to argue with Biddy. "We'll leave the subject of the future alone till we get to Khartum," I had said. She thought, maybe, that she had half convinced me of her worldly wisdom.

But this was far from being the case. I was only waiting to see whether my theory were right or wrong. I couldn't know until Khartum: and nothing on earth, or hidden under earth, would have induced me to put off the moment of finding out.

North Khartum was standing in a mirage as we approached. And Fenton and I were superstitious enough to wonder if it were a bad omen, that lovely lake which was not there, reflecting clearly each white and ochre-coloured house of the city in the sand. Only the blue glitter of the Nile was real, as the train crossed the river on a high bridge, and landed us in the surprising garden of beauty which is Khartum itself. Wide streets, bordered with flowering trees, rose-pink acacias and coral pendants of pepper-berries; lawns green as velvet; big, verandaed houses of silver-gray or ruddy stone; roses climbing over hedge and wall; scent of lilies and magnolias floating in an air clear as crystal; droning sakkeyehs spraying pearls over the warm bodies of slow-moving oxen; white sails like butterflies' wings dotting the Blue Nile: this was the new city created as if by magic, in sixteen years, upon the sad ruins of Gordon's stronghold.

On the wide veranda of the Grand Hotel, where pretty girls were giving tea to young officers in khaki, Fenton came up to Brigit and Monny, who were questioning me about letters. The look on his face struck the girl into silence.

"What is it?" she asked, almost sharply.

"Don't let me interrupt you," he said. "I can wait a few minutes."

"No," Monny insisted. "Please speak. I know it's something important."

"Important only to myself, perhaps," he answered, with a smile that was rather wistful. "I have to say good-bye now."

"Good-bye?" echoed Monny, surprised and even frightened, more by his look and tone than the words themselves.

"My engagement with Sir Marcus Lark ended when our train stopped at Khartum. I have other business to attend to here. I've just made my adieux with everybody else. I saved you till the last."

Monny was pale. Even the fresh young rose that was her mouth had blanched. Otherwise she controlled herself perfectly. Was this part of Anthony's plan? I wondered. He had told me what he intended to do at the Palace ball to-morrow night; but he had said nothing about this preliminary scene. I understood, however, why he had not manoeuvred to get Monny to himself, in a deserted corner of this big ground-floor balcony of the hotel.

Even when with the Set it was a question of getting their tea, or looking at their rooms, eyes were always ready to observe Miss Gilder, especially since it was "in the air" that she really *was* Miss Gilder—"*the* Miss Gilder." He did not want Miss Hassett-Bean and Mrs. Harlow to be saying: "Look, my dear, at the tragic, private farewell Antoun Effendi and our American Beauty are having!" Since Philae, there would have been no use in trying to conceal his feelings for Monny from Brigit or me. Therefore we made useful chaperons, and could be regarded as dummies.

"You never told me you were leaving us at Khartum," the girl stammered. "I thought—" But, though we knew what she thought, she could go no further before an audience.

"My business prevents me from staying at the hotel," Anthony explained. "And—though I shall see you, never again will you see poor Ahmed Antoun."

"I don't understand," Monny said.

"I know. But that was what we agreed upon. You promised to trust me without understanding. To-morrow night, at the Sirdar's ball, you will understand. I've arranged with Lord Ernest that you and Mrs. Jones and Mrs. East and he shall write your names in the book at the Palace. Then you will all receive invitations for the ball; you four only, of the party."

"And you will be there?"

"I've just told you," Anthony repeated, "that Antoun is saying good-bye to you forever."

"Yet you told me, too, that after Khartum I should be hap—" She cut herself short, and shut her lips closely. I was angry with Fenton for what seemed cruelty to one who had very nobly confessed her love for him. Biddy's eyes protested, too; but the man and the girl cared no more for us or our criticism, at that moment, than if we had been harmless, necessary chairs for them to sit upon.

"There are many paths to happiness," Fenton answered. "I shall see you to-morrow night, and I shall know whether you are happy. Meanwhile I say again—trust me. And good-bye."

He held out his strong, nervous hand, so browned by the sun that it needed little staining for the part he had played—and was to play no more. As if mechanically, Monny Gilder laid her hand in it. They looked into each other's eyes, which were almost on a level, so tall was she. Then Antoun Effendi turned abruptly away, forgetting apparently that he had not taken leave of Brigit or me.

"Let's go upstairs at once, dear, and see our rooms," Biddy said quickly.

An instant later, I stood alone on the veranda. But I knew well enough where to find Captain Anthony Fenton when I wanted him, although the death knell of Antoun was sounding. I was not in the least melancholy, and despite the tense emotion of that short scene, I had never felt less sentimental in my life. My whole being concentrated itself in a desire to visit the post-office, and to bash Sir Marcus Lark's head.

When Anthony came up for his farewell I had been asking Brigit and Monny if they expected letters at the Poste Restante. Both said no, but advised by me, they gave me their cards, armed with which I could ask for letters and obtain them if there were any. "It's very unlikely any one will address me there," Biddy had assured me. "The only letter I'm hoping for will come to the hotel."

I was not jealous: because I was sure the said letter was from Esmé O'Brien, now for weal or woe Mrs. Halloran. The letter I hoped for would be from a very different person, though if it materialized it would certainly mention the runaway bride. And if such a letter came to Khartum, the place to look for it, I thought, would be the Poste Restante. The writer not being a personal friend of Mrs. O'Brien, and presumably not knowing Khartum, could not be certain at which hotel she would stop.

I was hurrying away, a few minutes later, to prove once and for all whether I were a budding Sherlock Holmes or merely an imaginative fool, when a servant came out from the hotel and handed me a telegram.

"*Lark!*" I read the signature at the end with a snort of rage. "I wonder he has the cheek to—" But by that time I was getting at the meat of the message. "What the dev—by Jove! Here's a complication!" I heard myself mutter a running accompaniment to Marcus Lark's words—

This is what he had to say on two sheets of paper:

LORD ERNEST BORROW, Grand Hotel, Khartum:

In train leaving Assuan met man from Meröe told me work begun at our place strange news don't understand but sure you two haven't gone ahead of bargain must be foul play or else mistake but thought matter too serious go on north left train returned Assuan caught government steamer for Halfa just arrived too late for train de luxe but will proceed by ordinary train to camp better meet me there soon as possible leaving boat people take care of themselves. Wire Kabushîa Lark.

His loyalty to us shamed me. We had not given him the benefit of the doubt, but had at once believed the worst. He, though "not a gentleman" in the opinion of Colonel Corkran and some others, was chivalrously sure that we had "not gone ahead of the bargain!" A revulsion of feeling gave me a spasm of something like affection for the big fellow whom his adored Cleopatra sneered at as "common."

I longed to show the telegram to Anthony; but he would now be at the Palace, reporting to the Sirdar. Later he would be at his own quarters, transforming himself from a pale brown Hadji in a green turban into a sunburned young British officer in uniform. Meantime I would go to the Poste Restante, and then (whatever the result of the visit) I would return, collect Brigit and Monny, and take them to the Palace to write their names in the book.

I dare not think what my blood pressure must have been as I waited for a post-office official to look through a bundle of letters.

"Mrs. B. Jones," he murmured. "No, nothing for B. Jones—unless it's O'Brien Jones. Here's a letter addressed to Mrs. O'Brien Jones."

"That's it," said I, swallowing heavily, "Mrs. O'Brien Jones. I think the letter must be postmarked Assuan."

Without further hesitation the post-office man handed me the envelope, on the strength of Mrs. B. Jones' visiting card.

Going out of the office, I walked on air. "Sherlock Holmes it is!" I congratulated myself. And I ventured to be wildly happy, because it seemed to me that a letter sent to Mrs. O'Brien Jones, from Assuan, could mean only one thing; a justification of my theory.

I went straight to Biddy's door and knocked. There was no answer, and I stood fuming with impatience on the upstairs balcony, upon which each bedroom opens. It seemed impossible to live another minute without putting that letter into Biddy's hand. And not for the world would I have let it come to her from any one else. I was tempted to tear open the envelope, but before I had time to test my character, Biddy appeared on the balcony, coming round the corner from Monny's room.

"Why, Duffer! You look as if the sky had fallen!" she exclaimed.

"It has," I returned. "It's lying all over the place. There's a bit of it in this letter. A bit of heaven, maybe."

"A letter for me?"

"Yes. And if you aren't quick about opening it I'll commit hari kari."

She was quick about opening it.

As she read, almost literally my eyes were glued to her face. It went white, then pink. "Thank heaven!" I said within myself. If she had been pink first and white afterward, I should have been alarmed. For a woman's colour to blossom warmly from a snowfield, means good news.

"Duffer!" she breathed. "Do you—know—what's in this?"

"I—thought it would come." My voice sounded rather queer. I'd fancied I had more self-control. "That's why I—wanted your card—for the Poste Restante."

"Read this," she said, and gave me the open letter.

It was written on paper of a hotel at Assuan, near the railway station, and was as follows:

MADAM: Let me explain frankly before I go further, that my name is Thomas Macmahan. You may remember it. If you do, you will not think it strange that I—as a private person, as well as a member of a Society—whose name it is not necessary to mention—wanted certain papers you were supposed to possess. For a long time I, and others almost equally interested, tried to trace you, after learning that you had the documents, or in any case knew where they were. Naturally we were prepared to go far in order to make you give them up. We believed that your step-daughter was with you. As the need was pressing, and we had failed more than once, we would, if necessary, have worked upon your feelings through her. Had we questioned you, and you had replied that we were mistaken concerning the young lady and the papers, we should have been incredulous. But accident enabled us to hear from your own lips, details which we could not disbelieve. As a woman we wish you no harm, therefore we rejoice in this turn of events, for your sake. Your step-daughter must now be one of us, through her husband. She has nothing further to fear, much as we regret her marriage into a family so deeply injured by her father. As for you, Madam, you may be at rest where we are concerned. You said to Lord Ernest Borrow in the Temple of Abu Simbel, that you could never be happy, until the Organization Richard O'Brien betrayed, "forgot and forgave his daughter and yourself." Through me, the Organisation now formally both forgets and forgives.

Wishing you well in future, Yours truly,

T. MACMAHAN (alias Blount).

P. S. Kindly acknowledge receipt of this letter in care of Bedr el Gemály whose address you have at Cairo. Not hearing from you, we shall try to communicate this news in some other way. The present method has occurred to us, as you may find it useful to know the state of affairs without delay.

"Oh, Biddy, *do* you find it useful?" I asked.

She held out her hands to me. There was no one on the veranda just then and I kissed her.

"Mine!" I said. "What a gorgeous place Khartum would be, to be married in!"

Monny was very brave next day. She went to Omdurman with the rest of us. And it was the chance of a lifetime, because (through Anthony) Slatin Pasha himself took us to the place of his captivity: Slatin Pasha, slim, soldierly, young, vital and brilliant. It was scarcely possible to believe that this man, who looked no more than thirty-five, and radiated energy, could have passed eleven years in slavery terrible beyond description. He spoke of those experiences almost lightly, as if telling the story of some one else, and it was "all in the day's work" that he should have triumphed over his persecutors in a way more complete, more dramatic than any author of romance would dare invent for his hero.

He took us, from the river-steps in front of his own big, verandaed house, down the Blue Nile in a fast steam launch. It was a Nile as blue as turquoise; and after the low island of Tuli had been left behind it was strange to see the junction of the Blue and the White Niles, in a quarrelsome swirl of sharply divided colours. Landing on the shore at Omdurman, we met carts loaded with elephant-tusks, and wagons piled with hides. Giant men, like ebony statues, walked beside pacing camels white as milk. The vegetable market was a town of little booths: the grain markets had gathered riches of green and orange-gold. Farther on, in the brown shadows of the roughly roofed labyrinth of bazaars, were stores of sandalwood, and spices smelling like Araby the blest; open-fronted shops showing splendid leopard skins, crocodile heads bristling with knives, carved tusks of elephants, shields, armour said to have been captured from crusaders; Abyssinian spears, swords and strange headgear used by the Mahdi's and Khalifa's men. The bazaars of Cairo and even Assuan seemed tame and sophisticated compared to this wild market of the Sudan, where half the men, and all the bread-selling women who were old enough, had been the Khalifa's slaves.

With Slatin Pasha we went to the Khalifa's "palace" to gaze at the "saint's" carriage, the skeleton of Gordon's piano, and scores of ancient guns which had cut short the lives of Christian men. Slatin's house we saw, too, and the gate whence he had escaped: the Mahdi's shattered tomb, and the famous open-air Mosque.

Then we had a run up the Blue Nile, as far as "Gordon's Tree," and lunched on board the launch. In the afternoon, back at Khartum again, there was still time to group round the statue of Gordon on his camel, holding the short stick that was his only weapon, and gazing over the desert. The Set were allowed to walk through the Palace gardens, to behold the spot at the head of the grand staircase, where Gordon fell, and to have a glimpse, in the Sirdar's library, of the Khalifa's photograph, taken after death. This was a special favour, and as they knew nothing about the four invitations to the ball, they were satisfied with their day.

Dinner was in the illuminated garden of the hotel: and when it was over, I smuggled Brigit and Monny and Cleopatra inconspicuously away. No one suspected; and if the lovely dresses worn by Mrs. East and Miss Gilder were commented upon, doubtless aunt and niece were merely supposed to be "showing off."

Never, I think, had Monny come so near to being a great beauty. In her dress of softly folding silver cloth she was a tall white lily. She wore no jewels except a string of pearls, and there was no colour about her anywhere, except the deep violet her hazel eyes took on at night, and the brown-gold of her hair. Even her lips were pale as they had been when Antoun bade her good-bye. Hers was no gay, dancing mood. She was going to the ball because Antoun Effendi had ordered, rather than asked, her to go. But she was like some fair, tragic creature on trial for her life, waiting to hear what the verdict of the jury might be.

CHAPTER XXX

THE SIRDAR'S BALL

Biddy, radiating joy, walked beside me with wide-open, eager eyes, taking in every detail of the historic house. She admired the immense hall, whose archways opened into dim, fragrant gardens. She was entranced with the Sudanese band, ink-black giants uniformed in white, playing wild native music in the moonlight. She wanted to stop and make friends with the Shoebill, a super-stork, apparently carved in shining metal, with a bill like an enormous slipper, eyes like the hundredth- part-of-a-second stop in a Kodak, and feet that tested each new tuft of grass on the lawn, as if it were a specimen of some hitherto undiscovered thing.

No question but she was happy! I was proud of her, and proud of myself because my love had power to give her happiness. What matter now if I were being robbed at the Mountain of the Golden Pyramid, by some unknown thief? Neither he nor any one could steal Biddy.

Even Cleopatra seemed pleased to be coming to the Sirdar's ball, though gloom lay heavy upon her. She wanted to look her best. She wanted to be admired by the officers she was to meet, and to have as many partners as she could split dances for. To be admired by some one was essential to her just now, a soothing medicine to heal the smart of hurt vanity. Monny, I felt, had made herself look beautiful only because she thought that Antoun, unseen, would see her. As we entered the ballroom, her eyes were wistful, searching, yet not expecting to find. He had said that she would never see Antoun again.

I found friends in the ballroom: men I knew at home, and a few pretty women I had met in England or abroad: but there was no more than time to be received by the Aide-de-Camp, and to introduce a few officers to my three ladies, when the moment came for the formal entry of our host and hostess, the soldier-Sirdar and his graceful wife, the Royalties of the Sudan. We were presented: and I guessed at once that the Sirdar had been prepared in advance to take a special interest in Rosamond Gilder.

"Anthony has told him the whole thing, and asked his help," was my thought. From the instant of his kindly greeting for the girl, I found myself suddenly, excitedly assuming the attitude of a spectator in a theatre, on the night of a new play. I knew the plot of the play, but not how it would be presented, nor how it would work out. I saw that the Sirdar had made up his mind to a certain line of action where Monny was concerned. And by and by, when he had time to spare from his general duties as host, I heard him ask if she would like to go on the roof, where Gordon used to stand watching for the English soldiers to come.

"I will take you," he said. "And if you like to stay longer than I can stop away from our guests, I'll give you another guide."

He turned to Biddy and me. (Cleopatra was dancing with Baron Rudolph von Slatin Pasha, gorgeous in medals and stars: Brigit and I had just stopped.)

"Would you like to come, too?" the Sirdar asked.

I answered for Biddy, knowing what she would want me to say. And still the sense of being a spectator in a wonderful theatre was dreamily upon me. Stronger and stronger the impression grew, as the Sirdar led us out onto a wide loggia white with moonlight, and up a flight of stairs to a flat roof. Overhead a sky of milk was spangled with flashing stars. Beneath our eyes lay the palace gardens, where the torches of the Sudanese band glowed like transfixed fireflies, in the pale moon-rays. Palms and acacias and jewelled flower-beds, were cut out sharply in vivid colour by the lights which streamed from open windows. Beyond —past the zone of violet shadow so like a stage background—was the sheen of the river, bright as spilt mercury under the moon. And beyond again, on the other side of the Nile, the tawny flame of that desert across which came the Khalifa's fierce army. "This is where Gordon used to stand," the Sirdar stopped us near the parapet. "Only the roof was one story lower then. He climbed up here every day, till the last, to look out across the desert, saying: 'The English *will* come!' There's a black gardener I have, who thinks he meets him now, on moonlight nights like this, walking in the garden. It wasn't much of a garden in his day; only palms and orange trees: but a rose-bush he planted and loved is alive still. I've just asked one of my officers —one whom I particularly want you to meet, Miss Gilder—to pluck a rose from Gordon's bush and bring it to you here. He knows where to find us; and when he comes, I must go back to the ballroom and leave you—all three—to his guidance. Lord Ernest and he used to be friends as boys, I believe. Perhaps you've heard him speak of Captain Anthony Fenton?"

"Perhaps. I don't remember," Monny answered, apologetically. She, so self-confident and self-possessed, was charmingly shy with this great soldier who had made history in the Sudan.

"If you don't remember, Lord Ernest can't have done justice to the subject. Fenton's one of the finest young officers in Egypt, or indeed, in the service. We're rather proud of him. Lately he's been employed on a special mission, which he has carried out extremely well. Few others could have done it, for a man of great audacity and self-restraint was needed: a combination hard to find. He has been in the Balkans. And since, has had a particularly delicate task intrusted to him, to be conducted with absolute secrecy. No 'kudos' to be got out of it in case of success. And failure would almost certainly have cost his life. It was a question of disguise, and getting at the native heart."

"It sounds like something in a story book," said Monny, while Brigit and I kept mum, drinking in gulps of moonlight.

"Yes," the Sirdar agreed, "or the autobiography of Sir Richard Burton. Fenton has the same extraordinary gift of language and dialect that Burton had: the art of 'make-up,' too; and he's been to Mecca; a great adventure I believe he had. Perhaps you can get him to talk of it: though he's not fond of talking about himself. Altogether he's what I sometimes hear the ladies call 'a romantic figure.' His father was a famous soldier. If you were English you would have heard of him. He broke off a brilliant career in Egypt by running away with a beautiful princess. She was practically all Greek and Italian, though her father called himself a Turk: no Egyptian blood whatever. But there was a great row, of course, and Charles Fenton left the Army. Now Anthony Fenton's grandfather, who lives in Constantinople, would like to adopt his grandson: but the young man is in every sense of the word an Englishman, devoted to his career, and doesn't want a fortune or a Turkish title."

"Why, that sounds—" Monny faltered.

"Like a man of character, and a born soldier, doesn't it? Here he comes now."

There was a sound of quick, light footsteps on the stairs. In silence we turned to see a tall young officer in uniform walk out upon the flat roof. The moon shone straight into a face grave, yet eager, so deeply sunburned as to be brown even in that pale light: long eyebrows sketched sharply as if in ink—the black lines running down toward the temples; large, sad eyes; a slight upward hitch of the mouth on one side; clear cut Roman nose; aggressive chin.

"Miss Gilder, let me introduce Captain Anthony Fenton," the Sirdar said.

"I've brought you a rose," said Anthony.

They stood looking at one another for a long moment, the sun-browned British officer, and the pale girl. We, Biddy and I, stared at them both from our distance; and when the spell of the instant had broken, we saw that the Sirdar had gone.

We, too, would have gone, though the man and the girl were between us and the stairway, and we should have had to push past them. But Anthony, seeing our hesitation, spoke quietly. "Don't go," he said. "I may want you."

Never until to-night had Monny Gilder heard him speak English.

"You see," he said to her, "why I told you yesterday you would never see Antoun again. I had to tell you that, to make sure you would trust me—fully, through everything. You *have* trusted me, and so you've made it possible for me to keep my vow—a wrong and stupid vow, but it had to be kept. When I was angry because you treated me like a servant, I swore that never, no matter how I might be tempted, would I tell you with my own lips who I was—or let Borrow tell. I was going to make myself of importance in your life as Ahmed Antoun, if I could, not as Anthony Fenton. But long before that night at Philae I was ashamed. I —but you said then, you would forgive me. Now, when you understand what you didn't understand then, can you still say the same?"

"I—hardly know what to say," she answered. "I don't know how I feel —about anything."

"Well, I know, you goose!" exclaimed Biddy, rushing to the rescue, where angels who haven't learned to think with their hearts might have feared to tread. "You feel so happy you're afraid you're going to howl. Why, it's all perfectly wonderful! And only the silliest, earliest Victorian girls would sulk because they'd been 'deceived.' If anybody deceived you, you deceived *yourself. I* knew who he was from the first! So did your Aunt Clara. We'd kept our ears open, and heard the Duffer talk about his friend Anthony Fenton who was coming to meet us. *You* were mooning I suppose, and didn't listen. We didn't give him away partly because it wasn't our business, and partly because each of us was up to another game, never mind what. Captain Fenton never tried to play you a trick. You threw yourself at his head, you know you did, from Shepheard's terrace. He had his *mission* to think of, and you'd be *very* conceited if you thought he ought to have let you interfere with it. As it happened, you worked in quite well with the mission at first. Then

Fate stepped in, and made the band play a different dance tune; no military march, but a love-waltz. That wasn't his fault. And I have to remind you of all this, because you're glaring at Captain Fenton now as if he'd done something wrong instead of fine, and he can't praise himself."

As she finished, out of breath, having dashed on without a single comma, the giant black musicians in the garden began to sing a strange African love song, in deep rich voices, their instruments, which had played with precision European airs, suddenly pouring out their primitive, passionate souls.

"Biddy dear," said the girl in a small, meek voice, "thank you very much, and you're just sweet. But I *didn't* need even you to defend him to me. I was only just stopping to breathe, for fear my heart would burst, because I was *dizzy* with too much joy. I *worship* him! And —and you can both go away now, please. We don't want you."

We went. Biddy would have fallen downstairs, if I hadn't caught her round the waist. Needless to say, I didn't look back; but Biddy did, and should by rights have been turned into a pillar of salt.

"My gracious, but they're beautiful!" she gasped. "For goodness' sake, let's dash as fast as we can, down into the garden, and do the same thing!"

"What?" I floundered.

"Why, you *duffer*, kiss each other like mad!"

Boiling with excitement, when I met Cleopatra later in the ballroom, I told her what was going on above, in the moonlight, on the roof.

"At last your niece knows what I think you have guessed all along, but so wisely kept to yourself," I said. "About Fenton, I mean. It's all right between those two now. They will come downstairs engaged."

"Everybody is engaged!" Cleopatra stormily retorted.

"That's exactly what I remarked to Brigit, before I could persuade her to follow the general example. 'Everybody in the world is engaged except ourselves,' are the words I used."

"And except me," added Mrs. East. "You forgot me, didn't you?"

"Never!" I insisted. "You could be engaged to a dozen men any moment, if you wanted to."

"I think you're exaggerating a little, Lord Ernest," Cleopatra replied modestly and unsmilingly. But her countenance brightened faintly. "Of course there are a few men—there were some in New York—"

"You don't need to tell me that," I assured her.

"I feel as if I'd like to tell you something else," she went on, "if you can spare a few minutes."

"Will you sit out the next dance?" I asked. "It isn't a Bunny Hug or Tango, or anything distracting for lookers-on."

"Aren't you dancing with Brigit?"

"No such luck—I mean, fortunately not. She has grabbed Slatin Pasha, and forgotten that I exist. By jove, there come Miss Gilder and Fenton. What a couple! They're rather gorgeous, waltzing together—what?"

"Very nice," said Cleopatra, trying with all her over-amuleted heart, not to be acid. "But oh, Lord Ernest, that *settles* it! I *must* be engaged myself, *before* Monny brings him to show me, like a cat with a mouse it's caught. Otherwise I couldn't *stand* it; and afterward would be too late."

Hastily I rushed her out into the garden, where the Shoebill regarded her with one eye of prehistoric wisdom. If she really were a reincarnation, I'm sure he knew it: and had probably belonged to her in Alexandria, when she was Queen.

"There's a Mr. Talmadge in New York," she went on, wildly. "He said he would come to me from across the world, at a moment's notice, if I wired. Only it would be awkward if I announced our engagement to-night, and then found he'd changed his mind. Besides, he'd be a *last* resort: and Sayda Sabri said I ought—"

"Why not wire *Sir Marcus*?" I ventured. (If his telegram had not come yesterday, I would as soon have advised Cleopatra to adopt an asp.)

"Oh! well—I *was* thinking of it. That's one thing I wanted to ask your advice about. I believe he does love me."

"Idolizes is the word."

"And now and then in the night I've had a feeling, it was almost like wasting something *Providential*, to refuse a Marcus Antonius. Sayda Sabri warned me to wait for a man named Antony, whom I should meet in Egypt. That's why I—but no matter now. The 'Lark' is a dreadful obstacle, though. How could I live with a lark?"

"Lady Lark has quite a musical lilt."

"Do you think so? There's one thing, even if you're the wife of a marquis or an earl, you can only be called 'Lady' This or That. You might be *anything*. He's taller than Antoun—I mean, Captain Fenton. And his eyes are just as nice—in their way. They quite haunt me, since Philae. But Lord Ernest, he has some horrid, common little tricks! He scratches his hair when he's worried. If you look up his coat sleeves you catch glimpses of gray Jaeger, a thing I always felt I could *never* marry. And worst of all, when he finishes a meal and goes away from the table, he walks off *eating!*"

"I don't suppose," said I, "that your first Marcus Antonius ever went away from a table at all—on his feet; anyhow, while you were doing him so well in Egypt. He had to be carried. *I* call Sir Marcus (and I stole the Sirdar's epithet for the other Anthony) a Romantic Figure! His adoration for you is a—a sonnet. There's no 'h' in his name to bother you. And he fell in love at first sight, like a real sport—I mean, like the hero of a book. If he has ways you don't approve, you can cure them; redecorate and remodel him with the latest American improvements. Why, I believe he'd go so far as to give his Lark a tail if you asked him to spell it with an 'e'."

"Well—I suppose you're right about what I'd better do," she sighed. "A bird in the hand—oh, I'm not making a silly pun about a lark—is worth two in New York! Please tell *every one* you see I'm engaged to Sir Marcus, for he is my bird in the hand: and I'll send off a telegram the first thing to-morrow morning, for fear he hears the news that he's engaged to me, prematurely. Where is he—do you know?"

"By to-morrow he'll be at Meröe Camp," I said: But I did not add: "So shall we!"

CHAPTER XXXI

THE MOUNTAIN OF THE GOLDEN PYRAMID

There was not much room in our hearts for mountains or gold just then: yet somehow, before we left the Palace, Anthony and I had told Brigit and Monny the secret which had been the romance of our lives, until they came into it to paint dead gold with the living rose of love.

Victorian women would have been grieved or angry with men who could leave them at such a time; but these two, instead of reproaching us, urged us on. Naturally, they wanted to go with us. They said, if there were danger, they wished to share it. And if there were to be a "find," they wished to be among the first to see what no eyes had seen for two thousand years. But when Anthony explained that there wasn't time to get tents together and make a decent camp for ladies, even if we were sure not to tumble into trouble, they said no more. This was surprising in Monny, if not in Brigit. I supposed, however, that she was being on her best behaviour, as a kind of thank-offering to Providence for its unexpected gift of legitimate happiness.

Our secret was to be kept. Only the Sirdar knew—and gave Fenton leave of absence for a few days. The Set did not suspect the existence of a mountain at Meröe more important than its neighbours. They did not even know what had become of Antoun Effendi after he bade them farewell, and "good luck." From the first, he had given it out that he must leave the party at Khartum. The object of returning to Meröe was to "meet Sir Marcus;" and I promised to be back in plenty of time to organize the return trip to Cairo. My departure, therefore, was all in the day's work: and the great sensation was Mrs. East's engagement. Even though, for obvious reasons, Monny's love affair was kept dark, Cleopatra could not resist parading hers, the minute her wire to Sir Marcus had been safely sent. I got an invitation for all the members of the Set to a tennis party in the Palace gardens, at which the Sultan of Dafur and a bodyguard armed with battle axes would be the chief attraction. Also I induced the landlord of our hotel to promise special illuminations, music, and an impromptu dance for the evening. This was to make sure that none of our friends should find time to see me off at the train. Anthony was to join me there, in mufti, and might be recognised by sharp eyes on the lookout for mysteries. Once we got away, that danger would be past: unless Cleopatra told. But I was certain that she would not to any one ever again mention the name of Antoun.

It was a full train that night, but no one in it who knew Antoun. Many people who had been visiting friends or staying at an hotel for weeks, were saying good-bye. The narrow corridors of the sleeping-cars had African spears piled up on the floor against the wall, very long and inconvenient. Ladies struggled in, with rainbow-coloured baskets almost too big for their compartments. Seats were littered with snake-skins like immense, decayed apple parings; fearsome, crescent-shaped knives; leopard rugs in embryo; and strange headgear in many varieties. Stuffed crocodiles fell down from racks and got underfoot: men walked about with elephant tusks under their arms; dragomans solicited a last tip; a six-foot seven Dinka, black as ink and splendid as a Greek statue, brought flowers from the Palace for some departing acquaintance of the Sirdar and his wife. Officers in evening dress dashed up through the sand, on donkey-back, to see the last of friends, their mess jackets making vivid spots of colour in the electric light. All the fragrant blossoms of Khartum seemed to be sending farewell messages of perfume on the cool evening air. No more fantastic scene at a railway-station could be imagined. If the world and its doings is but a moving picture for the gods on Olympus they must enjoy the film of "a train departing from Khartum."

Anthony did not join me until just as the train was crawling out of the station, for we had asked Brigit and Monny not to see us off, and they had been startlingly acquiescent. We had a two-berthed compartment together, and talked most of the night, in low voices; of the mountain; of the legends concerning it, and the papers of the dead Egyptologist Ferlini, which indirectly had brought Fenton into Monny Gilder's life, and given Brigit back to me. There was the out-of-doors breakfast party, too, on the terrace at Shepheard's. Had it not been for this incident Antoun, the green-turbaned Hadji, would never have been selected by Miss Gilder, in words she might now like to forget. "I'll have *that*!" But, had not a distressed artist called on me one morning in Rome, months ago, with an old notebook to sell, I should not have come to Egypt for my sick-leave; and none of us would have met. I had visited the artist's studio to please a friend, and bought a picture to please him (not myself); therefore he regarded me as a charitable dilettante, likely to buy anything if properly approached. Bad luck had come to him; he wanted to try pastures new, and needed money at short notice: therefore he wished to dispose of a secret which might be the key to fortune. Why didn't he use the key himself? was the obvious question; which he answered by saying that a poor man would not be able to find the lock to fit it.

The notebook he had to sell had been the property of a distinguished distant relative, long since dead; the Italian, Ferlini, who about 1834 ransacked the ruins of Meröe in the kingdom of Candace. Ferlini had given treasure in gold, scarabs, and jewels to Berlin, all of which he had discovered in a secret *cache* in the masonry of a pyramid, in the so-called "pyramid field" of Meröe. But he had been blamed for unscientific work, and in some quarters it was not believed that he had found the hoard at Meröe. This jealousy and injustice had prevented Ferlini's obtaining a grant for further explorations he wished to make. He claimed to have proof that in a certain mountain not far from the Meröe pyramids, and much resembling them in shape, was hidden the tomb of a Candace who lived two hundred years earlier than the queen of that name mentioned in the New Testament, mistress of the eunuch baptized by St. Philip. In the notebook which had come down with other belongings of Ferlini the Egyptologist, to Ferlini the artist, was a copy of certain Demotic writing, of a peculiar and little known form. The original had existed, according to the dead Ferlini's notes, on the wall of an antechapel in one of the most ruinous pyramids at Meröe, decorated in a peculiarly barbaric Ethiopian style. The wall-writing described the making of the mountain tomb, ordered by Candace in fear that her body might be disturbed, according to a prophecy which predicted the destruction of the kingdom if the jewels of the dead were found.

Ferlini, a student of the Demotic writings which had superseded hieroglyphics, doubted not that he had translated the revelation aright, though he admitted supplying many missing words in accordance with his own deductions. He was in disfavour at the time he tried to organize an expedition in search of the queen's hoard, and though legends of the mountain confirmed the writings which Ferlini was the first to translate, the Italian could induce no one to finance his scheme. The one person he succeeded in interesting had a relative, already excavating in Egypt: but eventually addressed on the subject, this young man replied that the antechapel in question had fallen completely into ruin. It would be impossible, therefore, to find the wall-writing, "if indeed it ever existed."

This verdict had put an end to Ferlini's hopes, and nothing remained of them save the translated copy of the writing in his notebook (the missing words inserted) and the legends of the negroes who, generation after generation since forgotten times, had told the story of the "Mountain of the Golden Pyramid." Nobody, within the memory of man, had ever searched for the problematical tomb: and as tales of more or less the same character are common in Egypt, I did not place much faith in the enthusiastic jottings of Ferlini. However, my love of the unknown, the mysterious and romantic, made me feel that the possession of the notebook was worth the price asked: two thousand lire. When I had brooded over it myself, I posted it to Fenton at Khartum; and his opinion had brought me to Egypt. Thinking of the matter in this way, it seemed that we owed our love stories to the impecunious artist, who had probably spent his eighty pounds and forgotten me by this time. In a few hours, or a few days, we might owe him even more.

Anthony, acquainted with Meröe, its pyramids and pyramidal mountains, since his first coming to the Sudan, had been able to plan out our campaign almost at an hour's notice. He knew where to wire for camels [to take us to our destination, eighteen miles from Kabushîa], also for trained excavators. And he knew one who, if the white men were in ignorance, could tell us all the most hidden happenings of the desert for fifty miles around. This was the great character of the neighbourhood, among the blacks, the Wise Man of the Meröitic desert, who claimed to be over a hundred years old, had a tribe of sons and grandsons, and practically ruled the village of Bakarawiya. For countless generations his forbears had lived under the shadow of the ruined pyramids. Family tradition made them the descendants of those Egyptian warriors who revolted in the time of King Psammetichus, migrating from Elephantine Island to Ethiopia. There they were well received by the sovereign, given lands in Upper Nubia, and the title of Autolomi, or Asmack, meaning "Those who stand on the left side of the King." Anthony's friend and instructor in the lore of legends rejoiced in the name of "Asmack," which, he proudly said, had been bestowed on the eldest son in his family, since time immemorial.

Asmack the old and wise was to meet us at Kabushîa Station, with camels, one for each, and one for Sir Marcus, in case he had arrived and wished to ride to the Mountain of the Golden Pyramid.

It was orange-red afternoon when our white train slowed down, to pause for a moment at Kabushîa Station, and the first face we saw was that of Sir Marcus Antonius—a radiant face whose beaming smile was, I knew, not so much a welcome for us as a sign that he had received the telegram from Cleopatra. He hurried along the platform to the steps of our sleeping car; and Anthony, ready to swing himself down before the train stopped, pointed out Asmack not far off,—a thin old black man who must once have been a stately giant, but bent forward now as if searching the earth for his own grave. He had got to his feet, from a squatting position in the coal-stained, alluvial clay of this strange desert, and was gazing toward us, his few rags fluttering in the warm wind. Beside him stood a mere youth of fifty or so, and two or three young men, with several sulky camels.

Sir Marcus began to shake hands almost before we were on the platform; and so did he engross himself in us and absorb our attention that none of us quite knew when the train went out.

"My dear boys!" he addressed us, nearly breaking our finger bones. "Lord, Fenton, you're even better looking as a true Britisher than a false Arab! But never mind that now. Borrow, you're a trump. I believe I owe everything to you. I mean, in the matter of Mrs. East—*Clara*. It always was my favourite name. Fenton knows? Thanks for the congratulations. Thanks to you both. You must be my best men. What? Can't have but one? Well, it must be Borrow, then, I suppose. Oh, about the mountain? Why, of course you're anxious. Don't think I have not been busy. I have. Got here by special train. Cost me a lot of money. But who cares? It's worth it. I want to hurry things up, and get to Khartum. What your blessed mountain is to you, that is a certain lady to me."

"What have you found out?" I managed at last to cut short his rhapsodies.

"Why, not much, I'm bound to confess. But I've had only a few hours. Some one—heaven knows who—came here, it seems, with Arabs he'd engaged heaven knows where, and pretended to be my agent, empowered by me to work at the Mountain of the Golden Pyramid, where it was well known I'd got the right to excavate. Well, the chap was armed with credentials, and had a contract signed by me, so the authorities thought he was all right of course, and let him go on. This was more than a month ago. He pitched his camp out by the mountain, and nobody disturbed him. Fact is, from what I hear, I don't believe the excavating men from the Liverpool School of Archeology or whatever you call it, thought much of his chances of success. A case of looking for Captain Kidd's treasure! He and his men were excavating round the mountain, and he'd engaged some more fellows from the neighbourhood to make the work go faster. But a few days ago—not yet a week—he discharged the lot, paid them up and sent them off saying he'd abandoned hope of finding any entrance to an alleged tomb. The Arabs departed by train; but the fellows from hereabouts gossiped a bit, it seemed, and the story was started that they'd been got rid of because the Boss had hit on something, and wanted to be left to himself.

"You haven't told us yet the name of the man," Anthony reminded him.

"By Jove, no more I haven't! I'm so excited about everything. You won't know it, but Borrow will. Colonel Corkran."

Anthony gave me a look. "I do know the name," he said. "It's the man of my dream."

"The man of your dream? Corkran a *dream*?"

"A dream which has kept repeating itself until I grew superstitious about it. A red-faced man with a purplish sort of moustache, I saw coming between you and us, or looking at me out of a dark recess, something like a deep doorway. Borrow said when I told him, I was describing your man, Corkran, whose place he took on your yacht *Candace*."

"Well, I'm hanged! If that's not the rummiest go! I only hope he's not in that recess or deep doorway now, if it leads into your mountain. You remember, Borrow, my telling you he'd been alone for a while in the sitting-room I use as an office at the Semiramis Hotel, and had had a good chance if he wanted to browse among my papers? Well, I didn't mention this to you at the time, but an unsigned contract with you for your services, in return for all my rights in the Mountain of the Golden Pyramid, was lying on the desk. (As for the contract he's been showing here, it could only have been for the trip; but it showed him to be my agent right enough.) And there were two confidential letters on my desk: one from a man I'd written to, an Egyptologist chap, saying in his opinion there *might* be a tomb in the mountain; the other, an answer, not finished, telling him I meant to run the risk, and had secured the rights. You know how queer I thought it, Corkran should throw up his job, which was paying him pretty well? But it wasn't my business, and I was jolly glad to be rid of him as it happened. Well, here we have the mystery explained."

"Not quite yet! I wish we had," I said, thinking of the sly old poacher on our preserves, who had perhaps by this time skimmed the cream off the secret. It was easy to guess why he had sent away his workers if, indeed, he had imagined himself on the eve of a discovery. Rights to dig are given on the understanding that the Egyptian government shall have half of anything found, worth the taking. Corkran's scheming to be alone must mean that he intended annexing what treasure he could carry off, and then getting out of the bad business. Already six days had passed since the Arabs and Nubians had left him alone in his camp; and though it was lucky that we had learned what was going on, it might be too late to profit by the information. Even if we caught Corkran red-handed, he might have hidden his spoil where none but he, or some messenger, could ever find it.

"You'll go out with us to the mountain, Sir Marcus?" I went on. "We'll be ready to start—"

But Sir Marcus had suddenly become deaf. He had turned as if to gaze after the long ago departed train. Instead of answering me, he was stalking off toward a group of people at the far end of the platform: three ladies and two men in khaki. For a second I felt an impulse of indignation. Cheek of him to march away like that, not caring much that we had been robbed, largely through his carelessness, and by one of his own men!

But the indignation turned to surprise, sheer incredulous amazement. I glanced at Anthony to learn whether he had seen; but he was beckoning the old wise man of the desert. "Fenton," said I, "it seems we weren't the only passengers to get off here. There are three people we know, talking to two we don't."

Anthony looked. "Great Scott!" said he. And in another instant we were following Sir Marcus hastily along the platform to greet—or scold (we weren't sure which it ought to be) the big hatted, green-veiled, khaki-dressed but easily recognised figures of Brigit O'Brien, Monny Gilder, and Mrs. East.

"We couldn't help it," Monny cried in self-defence to Anthony, before he had time to reach the group. "We knew you wouldn't let us come, so we came—because we *had* to be in this with you. Even Biddy wanted to —and she's so *wise*. As, for Aunt Clara, I believe she'd have started without us, if we hadn't been wild for the journey. So you *see* how it was!"

We did see. And we couldn't help rejoicing in their pluck, as well as in the sight of them, though it was all against our common sense.

"We've ordered our own camels, and a tent, and things to eat and drink, so we shan't be any bother to you," Monny went on, as Anthony rather gravely shook hands, his eager brows lifted, his eyes smiling in spite of himself. "We couldn't have done it, if it hadn't been for Slatin Pasha. We first went and confided *everything* to him, because we knew he loved adventures and would be sure to sympathize. These gentlemen from the camp are his friends, and they've organized our little expedition at his request. More than one person can use the telegraph, you know! And oh, won't it be lovely going with you out into the desert!"

It was not yet evening when we set forth; but it was the birth of another day when we arrived within sight of Corkran's camp. The tents glimmered pale in the light which comes up out of the desert before dawn, as light rises from the sea; and so deep was the stillness that it might have been a ghost camp. There was not even the howling of a dog; and this silence was more eerie than the silence of sleep in a lonely place; because of the tale a grandson of Asmack's had brought to the village. He was one of the Nubian men Corkran had engaged to help his Arab workmen from the north; and when the whole gang had been discharged he, suspecting that some secret thing was on foot, hid in the desert-scrub that he might return by night to spy. He had wished his brothers to stay with him, but they, fearing the djinns who haunt the mountain and have power at night, refused, and begged him to come away lest he be struck by a terrible death. The legend was that Queen Candace, the queen who ordered the making of the tomb—had been a witch. When she died, by her magic arts learned from the lost Book of Thoth, she had turned all those aware of the tomb's existence, into djinns, to guard the secret dwelling of her soul. Even the great men of the court who by her wish hid in the mountain her body and jewels and treasure, became djinns the moment they had closed and concealed the entrance to the tomb. They could never impart the secret to mortals; and because of the knowledge which burned within their hearts, and the anguish of being parted forever from those they loved, the tortured spirits in prison grew malevolent. While the sun (still worshipped by them as Rā) was above the horizon they had no power over men, but the moment that Rā "died his red death" the djinns could destroy those who ventured within such distance of the mountain as its shadow might reach: and if any man ventured nearer in the darkness of night, he heard the wailing of the spirits. Camp had been pitched beyond the shadow's furthest reach; but the night after the workmen were discharged, Asmack's one brave grandson had been led by curiosity to approach the haunted mountain. When he had crept within the trench most lately dug, he had heard the wicked voice of the djinns raging and quarrelling together. There had been a threatening cry when they knew how a man had defied their power, and the Nubian had escaped a fate too horrible to put in words, only by running, running, until his breath gave out, and the sun rose.

This story gave the silent desert power even over European minds, as we came where the small camp glimmered, just outside the Shadow's wicked circle.

Not one of Asmack's men would go with us to the tent, which was evidently that of the leader. He might be lying there dead, struck by the djinns, they said, and all those who looked upon the body would be accursed. The three women would not have gone to Corkran's tent, even had we allowed them to do so; and Sir Marcus, already a slave, though a willing one, stayed with his adored lady and her friends, inside the ring which the Nubians proceeded to make with the camels. Carrying a lighted lantern Anthony and I walked alone to the tent.

The flap was down, but not fastened, and the canvas moved slightly as if trembling fingers tried to hold it taut.

"Colonel Corkran!" I called out, sharply. But there was no answer.

CHAPTER XXXII

THE SECRET

Anthony lifted the flap, holding up the lantern, and we both looked in.

No one was there—but the tent had the look of recent occupation. It was neatly arranged, as the tent of an old soldier should be: but on the table stood a half-used candle stuck in a bottle; and beside it a book lay open, face downward. Entering the tent the first thing I did was to glance at the title of this book. It was a learned archeological treatise. Here and there a paragraph was marked, and leaves dog's-eared. Three other volumes of the same sort were piled one upon the other. Anthony and I had read all four during the last few months, since our minds had concentrated on the subject of pyramids and rock tombs.

"What do you think has become of Corkran?" I said to Anthony.

"I think the djinns have got him," he answered, gravely.

"You mean—"

"I don't quite know what I mean. But—he must have hit upon something, and then—have been prevented from coming back."

"Why should he have had such luck, after a few weeks' work, an unscientific fellow like him, if the secret of the mountain has been inviolate for over two thousand years?"

"Wait and see what's happened to him before you call it 'luck,' Duffer. But you must remember that nobody except Ferlini and a few superstitious blacks ever believed that the mountain had a secret. Incredulity has protected it. And Corkran had to work like a thousand devils if he hoped to get hold of anything before he was found out. I believe he has got hold of something, and—that it then got hold of him. But we shall see."

"Yes, we shall see," I repeated. "And before long if we too have luck."

"I hope it won't be the same kind as his. But come along out of this. We must get to work before sunrise, and try for a result of some sort before the worst of the heat. If *he's* found anything, we ought pretty quickly to profit by his weeks of frantic labour. That, maybe, will be our revenge."

We had to tell the party what we had found in the tent, and what we meant to do next. Sir Marcus was now excused by Mrs. East; but until summoned by us the ladies were to remain where they were, under shelter of the tent which the camel-boys were getting into shape. When exhorted to be patient, they received the advice in sweet silence; but we did not until later attach much importance to this unusual mood. Perhaps at the moment we were too preoccupied to notice expressions, even in the eyes we loved best.

We took with us two men whom Asmack had provided as diggers, and in five minutes we were at the base of the little dark, conical mountain which for weeks had been the object of our dreams. Now, standing face to face with it, the glamour faded. The Mountain of the Golden Pyramid was exactly like a dozen other tumbled shapes of black rock, grouped or scattered over the dull clay desert which many centuries ago had been the fertile realm of Candace. Why should a queen have selected it from among its lumpish fellows, to do it secret honour? But Corkran had had faith. Here were traces of what Fenton called his "frantic labours."

A parallel trench had been dug with the evident object of unearthing a buried entrance into the mountain. Down it went through hardened sand and clay, to a depth of eight or ten feet; and descending, we found as we expected to do, several low tunnels driven at right angles toward the mountain itself. One after another we entered, crawling on hands and knees, only to come up against a solid wall of rock at the end. Each of these burrows represented just so much toil and disappointment. But Corkran, whose undertaking could be justified even to his own mind only by success, had not been discouraged. The trench went round three sides of the mountain, as we soon discovered; and the corner of the fourth façade not having yet been turned, it seemed a sign that Corkran had, as Anthony said, "hit upon something," or thought that he had done so. Otherwise he would not have discharged his men before the fourth gallery was begun. We had started from the south because our camp faced the long trench on that side, and it was quicker to jump into it than to walk round and examine the excavations from ground-level. On the east, the plan of the work was the same as on the south, except that the tunnels leading mountainward were driven at different distances, relatively to each other; and each of these also ended in a *cul de sac*. Now remained the trench on the north side of the mountain, which was the most promising direction for a "find": and as we turned the corner which brought us into this third trench the sun rose, making the sky blossom like the primrose fields of heaven.

On this side, sand driven by the northerly wind which never rests had banked itself high against the mountain, and the excavation had been a more serious task. There were only two tunnels, and into both sand had fallen. One was nearly blocked up, and impossible to enter without reopening; but we took it for granted hopefully that the second had been made later. This ran toward the mountain with a northeasterly slant; and though it was partly choked by sand, it was possible to crawl in. Anthony insisted on going first. I followed, at the pace of my early ancestor the worm, and Sir Marcus comfortably waited outside. He wanted to be a pioneer only in financial paths; and after all, this was *our* mountain now. It wasn't worth his while to be killed in it. Besides, as he pointed out, if anything happened to us there must be some one to organize a rescue, and break the news to the ladies.

Anthony had a small electric torch, and I a lantern, but going on hands and knees, we could use the lights only now and then. When we had crept ahead (descending always) for twelve or fifteen feet, Anthony stopped. "Hullo!" I heard him call, in a muffled, reverberating voice. "Here's the reason why Corkran sent his Arabs away!"

"What is it?" I yelled, my heart jumping.

"The rock's been cut back, by the hands of men."

"His men, perhaps."

"No, it isn't done like that nowadays. The tunnel turns here, dips down, and goes on along this flat wall. I bet Corkran always kept ahead of the men. When he saw this, he discharged his workers—And yet, it may be nothing of importance after all. Only a flat surface for some old wall-inscription such as Romans and even Egyptian soldiers made constantly, on the march."

The rumbling voice ceased, as Anthony crawled round the turn of the passage. I followed, literally close on his heels, the burrow descending like a rabbit-hole. Suddenly Anthony stopped again. "I've come into a sort of chamber Corkran's scooped out," I heard him say. "It's high enough to sit up in—no, to stand up in. This is the end of the passage, I think. By Jove, look out!" He had disappeared in the darkness behind a higher arch in the roof of the gallery. As he cried out, I slipped through after him, slid down a steep, abrupt slope, and by the light of my agitated lantern saw Anthony standing waist-deep in a well-like hole, into which he had evidently stumbled.

"Let me give you a hand up," I said.

"No thank you," he answered, in a tense, excited voice. "This is where I want to be. Look!"

I looked and saw, at the bottom of the scooped-out hole, a crevice in the flat wall of rock which we had been following down the passage, after its turn from the right angle way to creep along the mountainside. Out of this crevice protruded a large iron crowbar, apparently jammed into place, the first tool we had seen anywhere.

The chamber in which I stood, was littered and piled up with hard masses of earth which had been thrown out of the hole; and on the rough floor of the latter I stepped on the spade which had done the work. It nearly turned my ankle as I jumped on to it, but I hardly felt the pain. Torch and lantern showed clearly that the crevice in the wall was not a natural crack, but a man-made opening. It was as if a slab of rock fitted roughly into grooves had first been lifted, and had then fallen heavily on to the crowbar.

I set the lantern on the earthy floor and its yellow light streamed through the crack, whence the crowbar protruded like a black pipe in a negro's mouth. It was all darkness on the other side; from behind the screen of rock, set in its deep grooves, came the strangest sound I ever heard, or shall ever hear. It was a voice, groaning, yet it was not like a human voice. The horrid idea jumped into my head that it was the howl of an evil spirit sitting in a dead man's skull.

"He's alive then," exclaimed Anthony, pale in the sickly light. "Is that you, Corkran?" he called. The only answer was another groan.

"I see the whole business now, don't you?" Fenton said. "This passage is very steep. Already it was far under ground-level, before we got to the cutting on the mountain wall, and it must have been under ground-level for many centuries. They dug deep down, to make the tomb, and then covered up the entrance with earth. When Corkran got to his portcullis, he thought he'd reached the reward of his labours. Well—so he had—the punishment. Here's the heap of stone he used as a fulcrum for his lever. The heap tumbled when he was on the other side, and the slab of rock came down to trap him. We'll have to build up his fulcrum again, before we can do anything ourselves."

Together we forced the flat end of the crowbar into the crevice, pressed a piece of rock under it, and exerted all our strength. The slab moved upward an inch or two, grating in its rough grooves. The crack, no higher than the diameter of the crowbar plus a stone or two, when we saw it first, was now twice its original height. In went another stone, and so on. We worked like demons in hell, and in an atmosphere almost as hot and breathless. Yet we could breathe. Whether all the air we got came through the long twisting passage Corkran had made, or whether there were ventilation from the other side of the rock-curtain—some opening in an unseen cave—we could not tell. All we knew was that the mountain had a secret, and that the man who had tried to rob us of our rights to it, was caught in the trap of the djinns.

Our "rights!" How fragile as spider-webs, how almost laughable they seemed down here! Rights we had bargained for with men, which they, not owning them, had gravely given! I suddenly realized, and I think Anthony realized, as sweating and silent we piled up the fulcrum of stones thrown down by the djinns, that they alone, or the sleeping queen they guarded, had "rights" in this hidden place.

When we had raised the slab to a height of about two feet in its grooves, and had made sure that the stones held it firmly in place, we told each other that it was time to cross the threshold. The rock-door was scarcely more than a yard in width, and we crawled through in single file, Anthony going ahead as before, with his torch. I passed my lantern in after him, and then followed. As I crept through the narrow aperture I was conscious, among other emotions, of vague disappointment. "If this is the way to a tomb, and the only way, there can't be anything very fine to discover," I said to myself. "Why, the entrance isn't big enough to let in a decent-sized sarcophagus."

"It's the man of my dreams all right, and he's lying close to a deep-set doorway, like the one where I've seen him often. I told you so!" Anthony was saying in quite a commonplace voice, as I picked myself up, on the other side of the rock-screen.

We were in a small chamber more roughly hewn, and not so large as the inner sanctuary of Abu Simbel, which I had such good cause to remember. Exactly opposite the entrance by which we had come in was—as Anthony had said—a door, deeply set in the rock—a door of the same type as that through which we had passed; and in the shadow of the overhanging arch lay the heavy figure of Colonel Corkran, dressed in khaki.

His eyes were open, but he did not stir as we bent over him. Only his lips moved slightly, as if he were making a grimace.

"He's trying to ask for something to eat or drink," said Fenton. "What a confounded fool I am!—I've nothing, not even a flask. Have you?"

"No. I'll go back at once and get something," I answered. Strange, but I was not in the least angry with Corkran, whom I had been execrating.

Perhaps this was partly because the impression that the djinns had sole rights here was growing stronger every moment. We were all interlopers, usurpers.

Without stopping for more words, I turned my back to the secret still unsolved. To my surprise, however, I saw a light stronger than our own shining outside the partly raised screen of rock. Getting on my knees to crawl out, my face almost met the face of Monny Gilder, about to crawl in. Involuntarily I gave way, and in she crept like a big baby, Biddy coming after. Then we laughed, though I had seldom felt less like laughing. And the echo of our laughter was as if the spirits laughed, behind our backs.

"We never *promised* we wouldn't come," Monny hastily began, before Anthony could speak. "We just kept still. And Sir Marcus thought you wouldn't much mind, because the two nicest Nubians brought us quite safely. Oh, isn't it wonderful? And to be here when you open that door! But—why, it *isn't* one of our men with you. It's—it's the *thief!*"

"Don't call him names now, dearest," Brigit begged. "Poor wretch! He looks nearly dead. What a good thing we brought the biscuits and brandy."

"I was going for some," I said. Not only had I got to my feet again, but had helped Biddy to hers, and Anthony had snatched his tall Monny up, as if she had been a bundle of thistle-down. The Angels! It would never have done to tell them how glad we were that they had disobeyed us. It was Providence, apparently, not Marcus Lark, who had sent them to the rescue.

"We thought perhaps if you found anything interesting you'd want to stay with it a long time," explained Monny. "That's why we brought you food and drink. It is a good thing we came, isn't it?"

Fenton and I did not answer. Instead, we occupied ourselves with ministering to the enemy: a few bits of crumbled biscuit, a few drops of brandy to moisten them. He mumbled and swallowed and choked; and slowly the veinous red came back to the flabby gray cheeks, with their prickles of sprouting beard.

"It's fresh air he needs now," said Anthony. "He won't die from two or three days' fasting, not he! And it can't be more, for it would have taken him days and nights of hard work to get here, after his men were sent off. Jove, I believe it's more funk than anything else, that's laid him low. Thought he was done for, and all that. Look, there's his candle-lantern upset on the floor. It couldn't have been very gay for him when the light went out. Lend a hand, Duffer, and we'll give him to the Nubians the girls have brought. They'll carry

IT HAPPENED IN EGYPT | 323

him to his own tent. He never got as far in as the second door here, so we needn't search him. Otherwise I would, like a shot."

Yes, it was Something higher than a mere financier who sent the girls to us in the antechamber of the secret. We could not, for their own sakes, have risked bringing them. But here they were, and we should always have this memory together, we told ourselves, though we did not tell the disobedient ones. That would have been a bad precedent. What there was to see, they would see with us. And even the djinns could not work harm to Angels.

We went out and collected more stones with which to prop up the second screen of rock, which was not so thick as the first, and used Corkran's spade to hold it up at last. Beyond, was another roughly hewn chamber, and at the far end, set in a curiously fitted frame of wood, a wooden door, looking almost as new as though it had been made yesterday. Anthony flashed his electric torch over it, and we saw the grain of deal. There was a bronze lock, and a latch of strange, crude workmanship which Monny touched deprecatingly. "May I?" she half whispered. For to her also the place was haunted. She seemed to ask permission of spirits rather than of her lover. But the latch did not move.

"It would be sacrilege to break the lock," she said. "What shall you do?"

"Take the door off its supports: they're not hinges," Fenton answered, in the queer low tone which somehow we all instinctively adopted. "We've got one or two implements may help to do the trick."

He worked cautiously, even tenderly: for this queen's secret was our secret in the finding, even if the right to it was in the keeping of the djinns. Monny held my lantern, and it was a good half hour before Anthony and I together could carefully lift the deal door, unbroken, from its place.

Still Monny held the lantern, and at the threshold of a dimly seen room beyond, we all drew back: for on the sanded floor were footprints. To them the girl pointed, her eyes turning to Anthony's face, as if to ask; "How can it be that any one came in, when the door was locked, and there was that screen of rock to raise?"

But as we looked, over one another's shoulders, we realised that the prints were not made by modern boots. They were the marks of sandals; and they went across the floor to a thing that glittered in the middle of the room—a vague shape like a draped coffin, with something high and pointed on top: crossed to a glittering table on which a ray from the lantern revealed offerings to the dead: a loaf; a roasted duck, its wings neatly tied with string: cakes and fruit, all dried and blackened, but perfect in form: and a saucer of incense, from which a little ash had fallen from a ghostly pastille onto the table. There the sandalled feet had paused, while the incense caught a spark, and moving on, had walked straight to the door.

A faint fragrance from perfume jars came to our nostrils: a strange, subtle fragrance still, though most of its sweetness had gone, leaving more marked the smell of fat which had held the perfume all these years, while civilizations grew up and perished. The man who had lit the incense and locked the door seemed to have hurried back from—who knew where?—to stand behind us, saying "I forbid you entrance, in the name of the ancient gods!" We could not see him, nor hear his voice; but we could feel that he was there, and something in us revolted against the ruthlessness of disobeying, of forcing our way into the room in spite of him, to crush his footprints with ours.

"Why does the sand glitter so?" Monny asked. "Everything glitters! Everything looks as if it were made of gold."

"The Mountain of the Golden Pyramid," Biddy murmured.

"Go in first, you two, and bless the place," I said, my heart wildly beating.

They obeyed for once, moving delicately as if to music which ears of men were not fine enough to hear. They went hand in hand: and as Monny in her straight, pale-tinted dress, held up the lantern, I thought of the Wise Virgin. When this room had last been lighted, the parable of the Virgins of the Lamps was yet unspoken.

"It is not sand," said Monny, gasping a little in the heavy air. "It is sprinkled gold dust. Now it is on the soles of our feet. It shines—it shines!"

Anthony and I followed, still with that curious sense of hesitation, as if we ought to apologize to some one. The room of the dead was very close, and we drew our breath with difficulty for a moment. But the discomfort passed. Mechanically we avoided the footmarks printed in gold—avoided them as if they had been covered by invisible feet.

Monny was right. Everything was gold—and it shone—it shone. Dust from the terrible mines of Nub, whence the convict-miners never returned, lay thickly scattered over the rock-floor. The walls of rock were plastered with gold leaf, as high as the low ceiling: and upon the ceiling itself, on a background of deep blue colour, was traced in gold the form of Nut, goddess of Night, her long arms outspread across an azure sky of golden stars.

The table of offerings was decorated with gold in barbaric patterns, and the saucer which held the burnt pastille of incense was of gold, crudely designed, but beautiful. Cloth of gold, soft as old linen, draped a coffin in the centre of the room, and hid the conical object on the coffin's lid. On a sudden half savage impulse I lifted the covering, with a pang of fear lest the fabric should drop to pieces. But it did not. Its limp, yet heavy folds fell across my feet, as I stood looking at the wonderful thing it had concealed.

There was no sarcophagus of stone. The doors leading to the rock-tomb were not large enough to have admitted one. Instead, there was an extraordinarily high, narrow coffin or mummy-case, richly gilded, and decorated with intricate designs different from any I had seen in the museum at Cairo. The top of the case represented the figure of a woman, with a smiling golden face, painted lips and hair. But the strangeness and wonder were under the long eyelids, and in the woman's hands. The slanting eyes had each an immense cabuchon emerald for its iris, set round with brilliant stones like diamonds, curiously cut. And the carved, gilded hands of wood, with realistic fingers wearing rings, were clasped round a pyramid of gold. This it was which had betrayed its conical shape through the drapery of gold cloth.

The opening in the miniature pyramid was not concealed. There was a little door, guarded by a tiny golden sphinx; and on the neck of the sphinx, suspended by a delicate chain, was a bell.

"It is to call the spirit of the queen, if a profane touch should violate her tomb," Fenton said, dreamily. He was beginning to look like a man hypnotized. Perhaps it was the close air, with its lingering perfume of two thousand years ago. Perhaps it was something else, more subtle; something else that we could all feel, as one feels the touch of a living hand that moves under a cloak.

No one spoke for an instant. I think we half expected the bell to ring. Then Fenton said: "Monny, you and Mrs. O'Brien must choose which is to have the privilege of finding out the secret of the golden pyramid. The Duffer and I want it to be one of you."

"Oh no, not I!" cried Monny, almost angrily.

"Nor I," Biddy firmly echoed.

"Duffer, the papers were yours. Will you—" Anthony began.

"No—I—It was *your* faith in the mountain that brought us to it," I reminded him. "It ought to be you—"

"If—if it ought to be *any one of us*," Monny broke in, with a little breathless catch in her voice.

"If—But what do you mean?" Anthony turned an odd, startled look upon the girl.

"I—hardly know what I mean. Only—I couldn't touch anything here. They are—*hers*. They've been hers for two thousand and two hundred years. I never thought I should feel like this. I'd rather drop dead, this minute, than try to take that little pyramid out of those golden hands. They've clasped it so long! She wanted so much to keep the secret. Anthony—this is the strongest feeling that ever came into my heart —except love for you, this feeling that— we have no right—that it would be monstrous to rob—this queen."

"It wouldn't be robbing," Anthony said, heavily, "we have the right—"

"Oh, I *wonder*?" Biddy whispered.

"What would become of museums if everybody felt as you suddenly feel —or think you feel?" Fenton went on. "If it were wrong to open tombs, the best men in Egypt—"

"Not wrong, perhaps," Monny explained, "but—oh, I'm sure you understand. I'm sure in your hearts you both—you men—feel just as we do now we're in this wonderful secret place. That something forbids—I don't know whether it's something in ourselves or outside, but it's *here*. It says "No; whatever others do, *you* cannot do this thing." If you didn't feel it, you would have taken the pyramid out of those poor hands, and tried to tear off the rings, and open the coffin itself, to get at the mummy. But you haven't— either of you. You don't want to do it. You can't! I dare one of you to tell me it's only for Biddy and me that you've kept your hands off."

"We've come a long way, and have done a good deal to find this secret that we expected Egypt to give us," I said, dully, instead of answering her challenge.

Monny had no argument for me. She turned to Anthony.

"The secret you expected Egypt to give!" she echoed. "And hasn't Egypt given you a secret?"

"Yes," said Anthony, "Egypt has given us a secret: the greatest secret of all. But—"

"Is there a 'but'? I wonder if that isn't the only secret which one *can* open and learn by heart, without breaking the charm?" Biddy seemed to be speaking to herself, but we heard. "The secret of love goes on forever being a secret, doesn't it, the more you find out about it, just as the world and its beauty grows greater and more wonderful the higher you climb up a mountain?

But other secrets!—You find them out, and they're gone, like a bright soap bubble. Nothing can mend broken romance!"

"If we didn't touch anything here, what a memory this would be to carry away!" Monny said. "Don't you remember, Anthony, my saying once how I loved to dream of all the beautiful lost things, hidden beneath the sea and earth, never to be found while the world lasts, and stuck miserably under glass cases? You said you felt the same, in some moods. I love those moods!"

"I felt—I feel—so about things in general," Anthony admitted. "It was my romantic side you appealed to—"

"Have you a better side?"

"No better, but more practical. *This* isn't 'things in general.' It's a thing particular, personal, and definite. If we should be quixotic enough not to take what we've earned the right to take, we should be called fools. Instead of claiming our half, the Egyptian government would get all—"

"Let it!" Monny cried. "A government is a big, cold, soulless — impersonality! It never could know the thrill that's in our blood this wonderful minute—or miss the thrill if it were destroyed. Do you mind being called a fool, Anthony—and you, Lord Ernest?"

Anthony was silent; but something made me speak. "I don't mind. You know, I've always been a Duffer."

"Our future largely depends on this," Fenton persisted, with a conscientious wish to persuade us—and himself.

"I believe it does!" Monny strangely agreed with him.

"What do you mean?" Anthony's voice was suddenly sharp with some emotion; which sounded more like anxiety than anger. "Do you mean, that if Ernest Borrow and I insist on our rights to whatever treasure is hidden here, you and Mrs. O'Brien will think less of us?"

"Not less. Nothing you could do would make us think less, after all that has happened to us, together. But—could it ever be as it has been—as beautiful, as sweet, with all the dearest kind of romance in our thoughts of you? You see, you *have* the glory of finding the secret. Queen Candace saved it for you. She wouldn't give it to such a man as Colonel Corkran. She knew he wouldn't respect her. Maybe she hoped *you* would. I seem to hear her saying so. All this gold, and the treasure we haven't seen, is hers. It's been hers for more than two thousand years. Why should we steal it? *We* aren't a horrid, cold Government. It won't be our fault, whatever a Government may choose to do. She'll know that, and so shall we. Besides, we can beg to have the tomb kept like this for the great shrine of Meröe. Our memory of this place can't have the glamour torn away whatever happens. Nothing sordid will come between it and us, as it would if—why, after all, where's the great difference between opening the coffin of a woman dead thousands of years ago, or a few months? Supposing people wanted to dig up Queen Elizabeth, to see what had been buried with her? Or Napoleon? What an outcry there'd be all over the world. This poor queen is defenceless, because her civilization is dead, too. Could *you* force open the lid of her coffin, Lord Ernest, and take the jewels off her neck?"

"Just now, I feel as if I couldn't," I confessed humbly.

"And you, Anthony? What if *I* died, and asked to have the jewels I loved because you'd given them, put on my body to lie there till eternity, and—"

"Don't," Anthony cut her short. "There are some things I can't listen to from you."

"And some things you can't *do*. You may think you could, but—Go and take the golden pyramid out of those golden hands if you can!"

"I shall not take it," said Anthony, "I shall never take it now. You must know that."

"I'm not saying I shan't go on loving you if you go against me. I shall love you always. I can't help that. But—"

"That's it: the 'but'. Let it all go! At least, we've had the adventure. And we've got Love. I don't want the treasure, now. Or the secret. I give up my part in them forever."

"For me?"

"Yes, for you. But there's something more."

"Another reason?"

"I think so. Frankly, it isn't all for you. Only, you've made me feel it. Without you, I might have felt it—but too late. If there's a drop of Egyptian blood in my veins—why, yes, it must be that, telling me the same thing that you have told. This Egyptian queen may lose her treasure, and must lose her secret; but it won't be through me."

"And because you wouldn't steal them, she has given you the secret and the treasure, the best of both, with her royal blessing," Biddy said. "*This* is what Ferlini's papers, and the legends, really meant for you and Ernest. Everything that's happened, not only in Egypt, but in our whole lives, has been leading up to the discovery of the Treasure and the Secret that we can take without stealing. Do you know what I'm talking about? And if you do, was it worth coming so far to find—this treasure that I mean, and this secret?"

"We know very well," Anthony said, "and *you* know that we realize it was worth journeying to the end of the world for—or into the next."

"Or into the next!" Monny echoed. "Here we're on the threshold of the next. That's why the Queen's blessing feels so near."

THE END